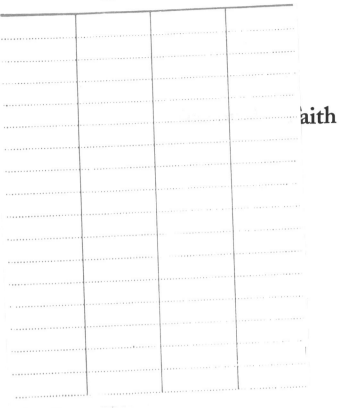

aith

W9-BPQ-035

Reasonable Faith

CHRISTIAN TRUTH AND APOLOGETICS

William Lane Craig

CROSSWAY BOOKS • WHEATON, ILLINOIS
A DIVISION OF GOOD NEWS PUBLISHERS

Reasonable Faith

Originally published by Moody Press,
copyright © 1984 by the Moody Bible Institute of Chicago

Revised edition copyright © 1994 by William Lane Craig

Published by Crossway Books
    a division of Good News Publishers
    1300 Crescent Street
    Wheaton, Illinois 60187

Edited by John S. Feinberg and Leonard G. Goss

First printing, revised edition, 1994

Printed in the United States of America

Library of Congress Cataloging-in-Publication Data
Craig, William Lane.
 Reasonable faith : Christian truth and apologetics / William Lane
Craig.—Rev. ed.
   p. cm.
 Rev. ed. of: Apologetics. 1984.
 Includes bibliographical references and index.
 1. Apologetics. I. Craig, William Lane. Apologetics. II. Title.
BT1102.C665 1994   239—dc20   94-21577
ISBN 0-89107-764-2

02   01

15 14 13 12 11 10 9 8 7

*For my sister
by birth and by new birth*

CONTENTS

Preface   IX

Introduction   XI

FAITH
1 FAITH AND REASON: HOW DO I KNOW CHRISTIANITY IS TRUE?   17

MAN
2 THE ABSURDITY OF LIFE WITHOUT GOD   51

GOD
3 THE EXISTENCE OF GOD   77

CREATION
4 THE PROBLEM OF MIRACLES   127
5 THE PROBLEM OF HISTORICAL KNOWLEDGE   157

SACRED SCRIPTURE
6 THE HISTORICAL RELIABILITY OF THE NEW TESTAMENT   193
   by Craig L. Blomberg

CHRIST
7 THE SELF-UNDERSTANDING OF JESUS   233
8 THE RESURRECTION OF JESUS   255
   CONCLUSION: THE ULTIMATE APOLOGETIC   299
   Literature Cited or Recommended   303
   Notes   325
   Index   345

A S A CHRISTIAN PHILOSOPHER OF RELIGION, I have been privileged to teach the subject of apologetics over several years to graduate students in seminary. This book is the product of those classes. The course it offers represents my personal approach to apologetics. I cover neither the history of apologetics nor options in evangelical apologetic systems, but assign reading to the students to cover these two areas.

For the history of apologetics, I recommend Avery Dulles, *History of Apologetics* (Philadelphia: Westminster, 1971), a scholarly masterpiece and an invaluable reference work. As for evangelical systems, I assign Gordon Lewis, *Testing Christianity's Truth Claims* (Chicago: Moody, 1976), which surveys the systems of the most prominent evangelical apologists of our day. In order to gain maximum profit from my book, the reader, like the students in my class, ought to avail himself of this adjunct reading.

This book is structured according to the *loci communes* of systematic theology. Let me explain. I often used to hear it said that modern theology had become so irrational and fideistic that apologetics no longer found a place in the course offerings of neo-liberal theological schools. But during a summer of study at the University of Erlangen, West Germany, I discovered that that was not exactly correct. It is true that no courses in apologetics *per se* are offered, but it is also true that German theology itself is very apologetically oriented. Hence, in classes in, say, Christology or soteriology, one will discuss as a matter of course various issues and challenges raised by non-Christian philosophy, science, history, and so forth. (Unfortunately, the result of this interaction is inevitably capitulation on the part of theology and its retreat into non-empirical doctrinal sanctuaries, where it achieves security only at the expense of becoming irrelevant and untestable.) It bothered me that in evangelical seminaries our theology courses spend so little time on such issues. How much time is spent, for example, in an evangelical course on the doctrine of God on arguments for God's existence? Then it occurred to me: maybe the theology professors are expecting *you* to handle those issues in the apologetics class, since at my institution apologetics *is* offered as a separate course. The more I thought about that, the more sense it made. Therefore, I have structured the lectures around various apologetic issues in the *loci communes theologiae*.

The *loci communes* were the so-called "common places" or chief themes or topics of post-Reformation Protestant theology. It was Luther's colleague Melanchthon who first employed these "common places" as the framework for writing his systematic theology. Some of the most frequently discussed *loci* included *de Scriptura sacra* (doctrine of Scripture), *de creatione* (doctrine of creation), *de peccato* (doctrine of sin), *de Christo* (Christology), *de gratia* (soteriology), *de ecclesia* (ecclesiology), and *de novissimus* (eschatology). In almost all of these *loci* apologetical issues confront us. In our limited space, I have chosen to discuss several important issues in the *loci de fide* (faith), *de homine* (man), *de Deo* (God), *de creatione* (creation), and *de Christo* (Christ). I have invited Dr. Craig Blomberg, a fine New Testament scholar, to contribute a chapter under *de Scriptura sacra*. I have taken the liberty to rearrange these *loci* from their normal order in a systematic theology into an order following the logic of apologetics. That is to say, our goal is to build a case for Christianity, and that determines the order in which we shall consider the issues. I am painfully aware of other issues that are also interesting and important, but that I have omitted. Nevertheless, we shall be considering the most crucial issues involved in building a positive case for the Christian faith.

Though the Latin terms have been omitted in the Table of Contents, the topics do fit within the classic *loci*. Under *faith,* I shall consider the relation between faith and reason; under *man,* the absurdity of life without God; under *God,* the existence of God; under *creation,* the problem of miracles and the problem of historical knowledge; under *sacred Scripture,* the historical reliability of the gospels; and finally, under *Christ,* the personal claims of Christ and the historicity of the resurrection of Jesus. Our consideration of each question will fall into three sections. First, we shall take a look at the historical background of the issue in question to see how past thinkers have dealt with it. Second, I shall present and defend my personal views on the topic at hand, seeking to develop a Christian apologetic on the point. Third, I shall share some thoughts and personal experiences on applying this material in evangelism. In the back of the book, I provide bibliographical information on the literature cited or recommended for your future reading.

I am grateful to Crossway for the invitation to produce a second edition of this book, which is considerably updated and revised. Special thanks are due to John Feinberg for his editorial work in the preparation of this second edition.

A POLOGETICS (from the Greek *apologia*: a defense) is that branch of Christian theology which seeks to provide a rational justification for the truth claims of the Christian faith. Apologetics is thus primarily a theoretical discipline, though it has a practical application. In addition to serving, like the rest of theology in general, as an expression of our loving God with all our minds, apologetics specifically serves to show to unbelievers the truth of the Christian faith, to confirm that faith to believers, and to reveal and explore the connections between Christian doctrine and other truths. As a theoretical discipline, then, apologetics is not training in the art of answering questions, or debating, or evangelism, though all of these draw upon the science of apologetics and apply it practically. This means that a course in apologetics is not for the purpose of teaching you "If he says so-and-so, then you say such-and-such back." Apologetics, to repeat, is a theoretical discipline that tries to answer the question, What rational defense can be given for the Christian faith? Therefore, most of our time must be spent in trying to answer this question.

Now, this is bound to be disappointing to some. They're just not interested in the rational justification of Christianity. They want to know, "If someone says, 'Look at all the hypocrites in the church!' what do I say?" There's nothing wrong with that question; but the fact remains that such practical matters are logically secondary to the theoretical issues and cannot in our limited framework occupy the center of our attention. The use of apologetics in practice ought rather to be an integral part of courses and books on evangelism.

Indeed, we dare not ignore the theoretical issues! Christians need to grasp a wider picture of Western thought and culture, rather than concentrating exclusively on their immediate evangelistic contacts. As Francis Schaeffer reminded us, we are living in a post-Christian era, when the thought-forms of society are fundamentally anti-Christian. His warnings are now more applicable than ever. If the situation is not to degenerate further, it is imperative that we turn the whole intellectual climate of our culture back to a Christian world view. If we do not, then what lies ahead for us in the United States is already evident in Europe: utter secularism. Throughout Europe, evangelism is immeasurably more difficult because the intellectual climate and culture there are determined by the conviction that the Christian world view is false and therefore irrelevant. Therefore, Christian missionaries often must labor years to get a handful of converts. If we lose the theoretical issues, then in the end our practical application will be fruitless.

Charles Malik, former Lebanese ambassador to the U.S., in his inaugural address at the dedication of the Billy Graham Center in Wheaton, Illinois, emphasized that as Christians we face two tasks in our evangelism: saving the soul and saving the mind, that is to say, not only converting people spiritually, but intellectually as well. And the Church is lagging dangerously behind with regard to this second task. Mark his words well:

> I must be frank with you: the greatest danger confronting American evangelical Christianity is the danger of anti-intellectualism. The mind in its greatest and deepest reaches is not cared for enough. But intellectual nurture cannot take place apart from profound immersion for a period of years in the history of thought and the spirit. People who are in a hurry to get out of the university and start earning money or serving the church or preaching the gospel have no idea of the infinite value of spending years of leisure conversing with the greatest minds and souls of the past, ripening and sharpening and enlarging their powers of thinking. The result is that the arena of creative thinking is vacated and abdicated to the enemy. Who among evangelicals can stand up to the great secular or naturalistic or atheistic scholars on their own terms of scholarship? Who among evangelical scholars is quoted as a normative source by the greatest secular authorities on history or philosophy or psychology or sociology or politics? Does the evangelical mode of thinking have the slightest chance of becoming the dominant mode in the great universities of Europe and America that stamp our entire civilization with their spirit and ideas?[1]

Malik goes on to say:

> It will take a different spirit altogether to overcome this great danger of anti-intellectualism. For example, I say this different spirit, so far as philosophy alone—the most important domain for thought

and intellect—is concerned, must see the tremendous value of spending an entire year doing nothing but poring intensely over the *Republic* or the *Sophist* of Plato, or two years over the *Metaphysics* or the *Ethics* of Aristotle, or three years over the *City of God* of Augustine. But if a start is made now on a crash program in this and other domains, it will take at least a century to catch up with the Harvards and Tübingens and the Sorbonnes—and by then where will *these* universities be? For the sake of greater effectiveness in witnessing to Jesus Christ himself, as well as for their own sakes, evangelicals cannot afford to keep on living on the periphery of responsible intellectual existence.[2]

These words hit like a hammer. Evangelicals really have been living on the periphery of responsible intellectual existence. The average Christian does not realize that there is an intellectual war going on in the universities and in the professional journals and scholarly societies. Christianity is being attacked from all sides as irrational or outmoded, and millions of students, our future generation of leaders, have absorbed this viewpoint.

This is a war which we cannot afford to lose. As J. Gresham Machen warned in 1913, on the eve of the Fundamentalist Controversy, if we lose this intellectual war, then our evangelism will be immeasurably more difficult in the next generation. He wrote,

> False ideas are the greatest obstacles to the reception of the gospel. We may preach with all the fervor of a reformer and yet succeed only in winning a straggler here and there, if we permit the whole collective thought of the nation or of the world to be controlled by ideas which, by the resistless force of logic, prevent Christianity from being regarded as anything more than a harmless delusion. Under such circumstances, what God desires us to do is to destroy the obstacle at its root.[3]

Unfortunately, Machen's warning went unheeded, and biblical Christianity retreated into the intellectual closets of Fundamentalism, from which we have only recently begun to re-emerge. The war is not yet lost, and it is one which we dare not lose.

Already in his day, Machen observed that "many would have the seminaries combat error by attacking it as it is taught by its popular exponents" instead of confusing students "with a lot of German names unknown outside the walls of the university." But to the contrary, Machen insisted, it is crucial that Christians be alert to the power of an idea before it reaches its popular expression. The scholarly method of proceeding, he said,

. . . is based simply upon a profound belief in the pervasiveness of
ideas. What is to-day a matter of academic speculation begins to-
morrow to move armies and pull down empires. In that second
stage, it has gone too far to be combatted; the time to stop it was
when it was still a matter of impassionate debate. So as Christians
we should try to mold the thought of the world in such a way as to
make the acceptance of Christianity something more than a logical
absurdity.[4]

The mentality which says that our seminaries should aim at producing
pastors rather than scholars is ironic because it is precisely our future pastors, not simply our scholars, who will have need of this scholarly training.
Take the realm of science, for example: John La Shell, himself pastor of a
Baptist church, warns that "pastors can no longer afford to ignore the
results and the speculations of modern physics. These ideas are percolat-
ing down into the common consciousness through magazines, popularized
treatises, and even novels. If we do not familiarize ourselves with them we
may find ourselves in an intellectual backwater, unable to deal with the
well-read man across the street."[5] The same goes for philosophy and biblical criticism: what good does it do to preach on, say, Christian values
when a large percentage of people, even Christians, say that they don't
believe in absolute truth, or what good will it do to simply quote the Bible
in your evangelistic Bible study when somebody in the group says that the
Jesus Seminar has disproved the reliability of the gospels? If we fail to do
our homework in these areas, then there will remain a substantial portion
of the population—unfortunately, the most intelligent and therefore most
influential people in society, such as doctors, educators, journalists, lawyers,
business executives, and so forth—who will remain untouched by our
ministry.

Moreover, it's not just Christian scholars and pastors who need to be
intellectually engaged with the issues. Christian laymen, too, need to
become intellectually engaged. Our churches are filled with Christians who
are idling in intellectual neutral. As Christians, their minds are going to
waste. One result of this is an immature, superficial faith. People who simply ride the roller coaster of emotional experience are cheating themselves
out of a deeper and richer Christian faith by neglecting the intellectual side
of that faith. They know little of the riches of deep understanding of
Christian truth, of the confidence inspired by the discovery that one's faith
is logical and fits the facts of experience, of the stability brought to one's
life by the conviction that one's faith is objectively true. Intellectual impov-
erishment with respect to one's faith can thus lead to spiritual impover-

ishment as well. But the results of being in intellectual neutral extend far beyond oneself. If Christian laymen don't become intellectually engaged, then we are in serious danger of losing our children. In high school and college Christian teenagers are intellectually assaulted on every hand by a barrage of anti-Christian philosophies and attitudes. As I speak in churches around the country, I continually meet parents whose children have left the faith because there was no one in the church to answer their questions. For the sake of our youth, we desperately need informed parents who are equipped to wrestle with the issues at an intellectual level.

Machen, like Malik, believed that "The chief obstacle to the Christian religion to-day lies in the sphere of the intellect," and that it is in that sphere that the issues must be addressed. "The Church is perishing to-day through the lack of thinking, not through an excess of it."[6]

I share this conviction, and therefore our focus in this book will be on the theoretical issues. At the same time, I recognize that there remains the problem of how to apply the theoretical material learned in this course. I've always thought that this problem was best left to each individual to work out according to the type of ministry to which he feels called. After all, I'm interested not only in training pastors but also systematic theologians, philosophers of religion, and church historians. But it has become clear to me that some people simply don't know how to translate theory into practice. Therefore, I've included a sub-section on practical application after each major section of the course. I *know* the theoretical material is practical because I employ it in evangelism often and see God use it.

Now the field of apologetics may be broadly divided into two sorts: offensive (or positive) apologetics and defensive (or negative) apologetics. Offensive apologetics seeks to present a positive case for Christian truth claims. Defensive apologetics seeks to nullify objections to those claims. Offensive apologetics tends to sub-divide into two categories: natural theology and Christian evidences. The burden of natural theology is to provide arguments and evidence in support of theism, or the existence of God. The ontological, cosmological, teleological, and moral arguments for the existence of God are classical examples of the project of natural theology. The goal of Christian evidences is to show why a specifically Christian theism is true. Typical Christian evidences include fulfilled prophecy, the radical personal claims of Christ, the historical reliability of the gospels, and so forth. A similar sub-division exists within defensive apologetics. In the area corresponding to natural theology, defensive apologetics will address objections to theism. The alleged incoherence of the concept of God and the problem of evil would be the paramount issues here. Corresponding to Christian evidences will be a defense against objections to biblical theism.

The objections posed by modern biblical criticism and by contemporary science to the biblical record dominate this field.

In actual practice, these two basic approaches—offensive and defensive—can blend together. For example, one way to offer a defense against the problem of evil would be to offer a positive moral argument for the existence of God precisely on the basis of moral evil in the world. Or again, in offering a positive case for the resurrection of Jesus, one may have to answer objections raised by biblical criticism to the historical credibility of the NT. Nonetheless, the overall thrust of these two approaches remains quite distinct: the goal of offensive apologetics is to show that there is some good reason to think that Christianity is true, while the goal of defensive apologetics is to show that no good reason has been given to think that Christianity is false.

Now it is evident from a glance at the Table of Contents that this book constitutes a course in offensive, rather than defensive, apologetics. Although I hope someday to write a book offering a course in defensive apologetics, I think that a first course in this discipline ought to be positive in nature. There are two related reasons undergirding this conviction. First, a purely negative apologetic only tells you what you ought *not* to believe, not what you should believe. Even if one could succeed in refuting all known objections to Christianity, one would still be left without any reason to think that it is true. In the pluralistic age in which we live, the need for a positive apologetic is especially urgent. Second, by having in hand a positive justification of the Christian faith, one automatically overwhelms all competing world views lacking an equally strong case. Thus, if you have a sound and persuasive case for Christianity, you don't have to become an expert in comparative religions and Christian cults so as to offer a refutation of every one of these counter-Christian views. If your positive apologetic is better than theirs, then you have done your job in showing Christianity to be true. Even if you're confronted with an objection which you can't answer, you can still commend your faith as more plausible than its competitors if the arguments and evidence in support of Christian truth claims are stronger than those supporting the unanswered objection. For these reasons, I have sought in this book to lay out a positive case for the Christian faith which, I hope, will be helpful to the student in confirming and commending his faith.

For many of you much of this course material will be new and difficult. Nevertheless, *all* of it is important, and if you apply yourself diligently to mastering and interacting personally and critically with this material, you will, I am sure, find it as exciting as it is important.

CHAPTER ONE

Faith and Reason: How Do I Know Christianity Is True?

BEFORE PRESENTING A CASE FOR CHRISTIANITY, we must come to grips with some very fundamental questions about the nature and relationship of faith and reason. Exactly how do we know Christianity to be true? Is it simply by a leap of faith or on the authority of the Word of God, both unrelated to reason? Does religious experience assure us of the truth of the Christian faith, so that no further justification is needed? Or is a rational foundation for faith necessary, without which faith would be unjustified and irrational? We can better answer these questions if we briefly survey some of the most important representative thinkers of the past.

HISTORICAL BACKGROUND

MEDIEVAL

In our historical survey, let's look first at Augustine (354-430) and Thomas Aquinas (1224-74). Their approaches were determinative for the Middle Ages.

Augustine

Augustine's attitude toward faith and reason is very difficult to interpret, especially because his views apparently evolved over the years. Sometimes he gives the impression of being a strict authoritarian; that is to say, he held that the ground for faith was sheer, unquestionable, divine authority. This authority might be expressed in either the Scriptures or in the Church. Thus, Augustine confessed, "I should not believe the gospel except as moved by the authority of the Catholic Church."¹ The authority of Scripture he held in even higher esteem than that of the Church. Because the Scriptures are inspired by God, they are completely free from error and are therefore to be believed absolutely.² Such a view of authority would seem to imply that reason has no role to play in the justification of belief, and sometimes Augustine gives that impression. He asserts that one must first believe before he can know.³ He was fond of quoting Isaiah 7:9 in the Septuagint version: "Unless you believe you shall not understand." The fundamental principle of the Augustinian tradition throughout the Middle Ages was *fides quaerens intellectum*: faith seeking understanding.

But certain statements of Augustine make it clear that he was not an unqualified authoritarian. He maintained that authority and reason cooperate in bringing a person to faith. Authority demands belief and prepares man for reason, and reason in turn leads to understanding and knowledge. But at the same time, reason is not entirely absent from authority, for one has to consider whom to believe, and the highest authority belongs to clearly known truth; that is to say, the truth, when it is clearly known, has the highest claim to authority because it demands our assent. According to Augustine, it is our duty to consider what men or what books we ought to believe in order to worship God rightly. Gerhard Strauss in his book on Augustine's doctrine of Scripture explains that although for Augustine Scripture is absolutely authoritative and inerrant in itself, it does not carry credibility in itself—that is, people will not automatically accept its authority upon hearing it. Therefore, there must be certain signs (*indicia*) of credibility that make its authority evident. On the basis of these signs, we can believe that the Scripture is the authoritative Word of God, and submit to its authority. The principal signs adduced by Augustine on behalf of the authority of Scripture are miracle and prophecy. Though many religions boast of revelations showing the way of salvation, only the Scriptures have the support of miracle and prophecy, which prove it to be the true authority.

Thus, Augustine's authoritarianism would seem to be drastically qualified. Perhaps Augustine's apparent inconsistency is best explained by the medieval understanding of authority. In the early church, authority (*auctoritas*) included not just theological truths, but the whole tradition of past knowledge. The relationship between authority and reason was not the same as that between faith and reason. Rather it was the relationship between all past knowledge and present-day understanding. Knowledge of the past was simply accepted on the basis of authority. This seems to have been Augustine's attitude. He distinguishes between what is *seen* to be true and what is *believed* to be true. We *see* that something is true by either physical perception or rational demonstration. We *believe* that something is true on the basis of the testimony of others. Hence, with regard to miracle and prophecy, Augustine says that the trustworthiness of reports of either past or future events must be believed, not known by the intelligence. Elsewhere he declares that one should believe in God because belief in him is taught in the books of men who have left their testimony in writing that they lived with the Son of God and saw things that could not have happened if there were no God. Then he concludes that one must believe before he can know. Since for Augustine the historical evidence for miracle and prophecy lay in the past, it was in the realm of authority, not reason. Today, on the other hand, we would say that such a procedure would be an attempt to provide a rational foundation for authority via historical apologetics.

Now the obvious question at this point is, Why accept the authority of the writers of the past, whether they be the classical writers or the authors of Scripture? Clearly, if Augustine is to avoid circular reasoning, he cannot say that we should accept the authority of the evangelists because of the authority of Scripture, for it is the evangelists' testimony to miracle and prophecy that is supposed to make evident the authority of Scripture. So Augustine must either come up with some reason to accept the evangelists' testimony as reliable, or abandon this historically oriented approach. Since he lacked the historical method, the first alternative was not open to him. Therefore, he chose the second. He frankly admits that the books containing the story of Christ belong to an ancient history that anyone may refuse to believe. Therefore, he turns to the present miracle of the Church as the basis for accepting the authority of Scripture. He saw the very existence of the mighty and universal Church as an overwhelming sign that the Scriptures are true and divine.

Now notice that Augustine is not basing the authority of Scripture on the authority of the Church, for he held the Scripture's authority to exceed even that of the Church. Rather, his appeal is still to the sign of miracle, not indeed the gospel miracles, which are irretrievably removed in the past, but the present and evident miracle of the Church. In *The City of God* he states that even if the unbeliever rejects all biblical miracles, he is still left with one stupendous miracle, which is all one needs, namely, the fact of the whole world believing in Christianity without the benefit of the gospel miracles.[4] It's interesting that, by appealing to a present miracle as the sign of the authority of Scripture, Augustine seems to have implicitly denied

authoritarianism, since this sign was not in the past, in the realm of authority where it could only be believed, but in the present, where it could be
seen and known. Be that as it may, Augustine's emphases on biblical
authority and signs of credibility were to set the tone for subsequent
medieval theology.

Thomas Aquinas

Aquinas's *Summa contra gentiles*, written to combat Greco-Arabic philosophy, is the greatest apologetic work of the Middle Ages and so merits our
attention. Thomas develops a framework for the relationship of faith and
reason that includes the Augustinian signs of credibility. He begins by
making a distinction within truths about God. On the one hand, there are
truths that completely surpass the capability of human reason, for example, the doctrine of the Trinity. On the other hand, many truths lie within
the grasp of human reason, such as the existence of God. In the first three
volumes of the *Summa contra gentiles*, Thomas attempts to prove these
truths of reason, including the existence and nature of God, the orders of
creation, the nature and end of man, and so forth. But when he comes to
the fourth volume, in which he handles subjects like the Trinity, the incarnation, the sacraments, and the last things, he suddenly changes his
method of approach. He states that these things are to be proved by the
authority of Holy Scripture, not by natural reason. Because these doctrines
surpass reason, they are properly objects of faith.

Now at first blush this seems to suggest that for Aquinas these truths of
faith are mysteries, somehow "above logic." But here we must be very careful. For as I read Aquinas, that's not how he defines his terms. Rather he
seems to mean that truths of faith surpass reason in the sense that they are
neither empirically evident nor demonstrable with absolute certainty. He
makes no suggestion that truths of faith transcend Aristotelian logic.
Rather there are just no empirical facts which make these truths evident
or from which these truths may be inferred. For example, although the
existence of God can be proved from his effects, there are no empirical facts
from which the Trinity may be inferred. Or again, the eschatological resurrection of the dead cannot be proved, because there is no empirical evidence for this future event. Elsewhere Thomas makes it clear that truths
of faith cannot be demonstrated by reason alone, either. He maintains that
we Christians must use only arguments that prove their conclusions with
absolute certainty; for if we use mere probability arguments, the insuffi-
ciency of those arguments will only serve to confirm the non-Christian in
his unbelief.[5]

Thus, the distinction Thomas makes between truths of reason and truths of faith is rather like Augustine's distinction between seeing and believing. Truths of reason may be "seen"—that is, either proved with rational certainty or accepted as empirically evident—whereas truths of faith must be believed, since they are neither empirically evident nor rationally provable. This does not mean that truths of faith are incomprehensible or "above logic."

Now because truths of faith can only be believed, does this imply that Thomas is in the end a fideist or an authoritarian? The answer seems clearly no. For like Augustine he proceeds to argue that God provides the signs of miracle and prophecy, which serve to confirm the truths of faith, though not demonstrating them directly. Because of these signs, Aquinas held that a man can see the truths of faith: "Then they are indeed seen by the one who believes; he would not believe unless he saw that they are worthy of belief on the basis of evident signs or something of this sort."[6] Thomas calls these signs "confirmations," "arguments," and "proofs" for the truths of faith.[7] This seems to make it clear that Aquinas believed there are good grounds for accepting the truths of faith as a whole. The proofs of miracle and prophecy are compelling, although they are indirect. Thus, for example, the doctrine of the Trinity is a truth of faith because it cannot be directly proved by any argument; nevertheless, it is indirectly proved insofar as the truths of faith taken together as a whole are shown to be credible by the divine signs.

Thomas's procedure, then, may be summarized in three steps: (1) Fulfilled prophecies and miracles make it credible that the Scriptures taken together as a whole are a revelation from God. (2) As a revelation from God, Scripture is absolutely authoritative. (3) Therefore, those doctrines taught by Scripture that are neither demonstratively provable nor empirically evident may be accepted by faith on the authority of Scripture. Thus, Aquinas can say that an opponent may be convinced of the truths of faith on the basis of the authority of Scripture as confirmed by God with miracles.[8]

Again the question arises: How do we know that the purported miracles or fulfilled prophecies ever took place? The medieval thinkers, lacking the historical method, could not answer this question. They developed a philosophical framework in which the signs of credibility confirmed the truths of faith, but they had no way of proving the signs themselves. About the only argument was Augustine's indirect proof from the miracle of the Church. Thus, Thomas declares,

> Now such a wondrous conversion of the world to the Christian faith
> is a most indubitable proof that such signs did take place. . . . For it

would be the most wondrous sign of all if without any wondrous signs the world were persuaded by simple and lowly men to believe things so arduous, to accomplish things so difficult, and to hope for things so sublime.[9]

A final word might be added. With Aquinas we see the reduction of faith to an epistemological category; that is to say, faith was no longer trust or commitment of the heart, but became a way of knowing, complementary to reason. Faith was essentially intellectual assent to doctrines not provable by reason—hence, Aquinas's view that a doctrine cannot be both known and believed: if you know it (by reason), then you cannot believe it (by faith). Thus, Aquinas lost the view of faith as trust or commitment. This same intellectualist understanding of faith characterized the documents of the Council of Trent and of Vatican I but was adjusted in the documents of Vatican II.

THE ENLIGHTENMENT

The fact that the Enlightenment is also known as the Age of Reason no doubt gives us a good clue as to how thinkers of that period regarded the relationship between faith and reason. Nevertheless, there was not complete agreement on this issue, and the two figures we shall survey represent two fundamentally opposed viewpoints.

John Locke

The thought of John Locke (1632-1704) was determinative for the eighteenth century. His *Essay Concerning Human Understanding* (1689) laid down the epistemological principles that were to shape religious thought during that age. Though he rejected the philosophical rationalism of Descartes, Locke was nevertheless an ardent theological rationalist. That is to say, he maintained that religious belief must have a rational foundation and that where such a foundation is absent, religious belief is unwarranted. Locke himself attempted to provide such a rational foundation.

Locke argued for the existence of God by means of a cosmological argument—indeed, he maintained that the existence of God is "the most obvious truth that reason discovers," having an evidence "equal to mathematical certainty."[10] When one moves beyond such matters of demonstrative reason into matters of faith, Locke insisted that revealed truths cannot contradict reason. God can reveal to us both truths attainable by reason (though reason gives greater certainty of these than does revelation) as well as truths unattainable by reason. The revealed truths unattainable by reason cannot contradict reason, because we will always be more certain of the truth of reason than we will be of a purported revelation that contradicts reason. Therefore, no proposition contrary to reason can be accepted as divine revelation. Thus, although we know that a revelation from God must be true, it still lies within the scope of reason to determine if a supposed revelation really is from God and to determine its meaning.[11]

More than that, revelation must not only be in harmony with reason, but must itself be guaranteed by appropriate rational proofs that it is indeed divine. Otherwise, one degenerates into irresponsible enthusiasm:

> Revelation is natural reason enlarged by a new set of discoveries communicated by God immediately, which reason vouches the truth of by the testimony and proofs it gives that they come from God. So that he that takes away reason to make way for revelation, puts out the light of both; and does much the same as if he would persuade a man to put out his eyes, the better to receive the remote light of an invisible star by a telescope.[12]

Religious enthusiasm was the form of religious expression most scorned by the intellectualist believers of the Age of Reason, and Locke would have nothing to do with it. Only if reason makes plausible that a purported revelation is genuine can that revelation be believed.

Hence, in his subsequent works *The Reasonableness of Christianity* (1695) and *Discourse on Miracles* (1690), Locke argued that fulfilled prophecy and palpable miracles furnish proof of Christ's divine mission. He set forth three criteria for discerning a genuine revelation: First, it must not be dishonoring to God or inconsistent with natural religion and the natural moral law. Second, it must not inform man of things indifferent, insignificant, or easily discovered by natural ability. Third, it must be confirmed by supernatural signs. For Locke, the chief of these signs was miracle. On the basis of Jesus' miracles, we are justified in regarding him as the Messiah and his revelation from God as true.

As the fountainhead for both Deist works and orthodox apologetics, Locke's outlook shaped the religious thought of the eighteenth century. Be they Deist or orthodox, most thinkers of the century after Locke agreed that reason was to be given priority even in matters of faith, that revelation could not contradict reason, and that reason provided the essential foundation to religious belief.

Henry Dodwell

That is not to say that dissenting voices could not be heard. Henry Dodwell (1700-1784) in his *Christianity Not Founded on Argument* (1742) attacked the prevailing theological rationalism as antithetical to true

Christianity. Dodwell was so out of step with his times that he has even been suspected of being an unbeliever who appealed to an arational, subjective basis for religious faith as a subterfuge for undermining the rationality of Christianity. It seems to me, however, that Dodwell is to be taken straightforwardly as a spokesman for the anti-rationalistic religious tradition, which was not altogether absent even during the Enlightenment.

Dodwell argues that matters of religious faith lie outside the determination of reason. God could not possibly have intended that reason should be the faculty to lead us to faith, for faith cannot hang indefinitely in suspense while reason cautiously weighs and re-weighs arguments. The Scriptures teach, on the contrary, that the way to God is by means of the heart, not by means of the intellect. Faith is simply a gift of the Holy Spirit. What then is the basis of faith? Dodwell answers, authority—not indeed the arbitrary authority of the Church but rather the inner light of a constant and particular revelation imparted separately and supernaturally to every individual. Dodwell's appeal is thus to the inner, faith-producing work of the Holy Spirit in each individual's heart. His subjectively based apologetic appears to have generated no following among the scholars of his day, but later a similar emphasis on the witness of the Spirit by the Wesleys and Whitefield was to be an earmark of the great revivals that opened fresh springs for the dry souls of the English laity.

CONTEMPORARY

During the present century, theological discussion of the relationship between faith and reason has replayed many of these same themes.

Karl Barth and Rudolph Bultmann

Both the dialectical theology championed by Karl Barth (1886-1968) and the existential theology propounded by Rudolf Bultmann (1884-1976) were characterized by a religious epistemology of authoritarianism.

According to Barth, there can be no approach to God whatsoever via human reason. Apart from God's revelation in Christ, human reason comprehends absolutely nothing about God. The fundamental reason for this agnosticism concerning human knowledge of God seems to be Barth's firm commitment to the thesis that God is "wholly other" and therefore transcends all categories of human thought and logic. This belief led Barth to deny the Roman Catholic doctrine of an analogy of being between God and man. According to that doctrine, creation as the product of its Creator shares in an analogous way certain properties possessed most perfectly by God such as being, goodness, truth, and so forth. According to Barth, God is so transcendent that no analogy exists between him and the creature.

Hence, it follows that there can be no natural knowledge about God at all. But God has revealed himself to man in Jesus Christ; indeed, Christ is the revelation or Word of God. In him alone there is found an analogy of faith that affords some knowledge of God. But even this seems to be experiential rather than cognitive: it is a personal encounter with the Word of God, who confronts us now and again through different forms, such as the Bible or preaching. Even in his self-disclosure God remains hidden: "He meets us as the One who is hidden, the One about whom we must admit that we do not know what we are saying when we try to say who He is."[13] God remains incomprehensible and the propositions we assert about him are true in an incomprehensible way.

This might lead one to think that for Barth fideism is the only route by which someone might come to the knowledge of God. This does not, however, seem to be precisely correct. For Barth emphasizes that the personal encounter with the Word of God results entirely from the sovereign, divine initiative. Lost in sin, man cannot even begin to *move* in the direction of faith, so that even a leap of faith is impossible for him. No, it must be God who breaks into man's indolent sinfulness to confront him with the Word of God. As Barth writes, "Knowledge of God is a knowledge completely effected and determined from the side of its object, from the side of God."[14] Or again, "*the fact that* he did come to this decision, *that* he really believed, and that he actually had freedom to enter this new life of obedience and hope—all this was not the work of *his* spirit, but the work of the *Holy* Spirit."[15] Barth believed that the Reformation doctrine of justification by grace through faith is incompatible with any human initiative—even fideism. If knowing God depends wholly on God's grace, then even the act of faith would be a sinful work were it not wholly wrought by God. If it be asked how one knows that it is indeed the Word of God that confronts him and not a delusion, Barth would simply respond that such a question is meaningless. When the Word of God confronts a man, he is not free to analyze, weigh, and consider as a disinterested judge or observer—he can only obey. The authority of the Word of God is the foundation for religious belief.

Like Barth, Bultmann also rejects any human apprehension of the Word of God (which he seems to identify primarily with the call to authentic existence embodied in the gospel) apart from faith. Bultmann construes faith in epistemological categories, opposing it to knowledge based on proof. In the existentialist tradition, he considers it essential to faith that it involve risk and uncertainty. Therefore, rational evidence is not only irrelevant, but actually contrary to faith. Faith, in order to be faith, must exist in an evidential vacuum. For this reason Bultmann denies any significance for the Christian message to the historical Jesus, apart from his bare existence. Bultmann recognizes that Paul in 1 Corinthians 15 does "think that he can guarantee the resurrection of Christ as an objective fact by listing the witnesses who had seen him risen."[16] But he characterizes such historical argumentation as "fatal" because it tries to produce proof for the Christian proclamation.[17] Should an attempt at proof succeed, this would mean the destruction of faith. Only a decision to believe wholly apart from evidence will bring one into contact with the existential significance of the gospel. Bultmann emphasizes that this does not mean such a step is made arbitrarily or light-heartedly. No, the existential issues of life and death weigh so heavily that this decision to believe is the most important and awesome step a person can take. But it must be taken in the absence of any rational criteria for choice.

This might lead one to think that Bultmann is a pure fideist; but again this does not seem quite correct. For he insists that the very authority of the Word of God strips away all demands for criteria: "As though God had to justify himself to man! As though every demand for justification (including the one concealed in the demand for criteria) did not have to be dropped as soon as the face of God appears!"[18] As Pannenberg explains, the "basic presupposition underlying German Protestant theology as expressed by Barth or Bultmann is that the basis of theology is the self-authenticating Word of God which demands obedience."[19] Thus, it would seem that in both dialectical and existential theology the final appeal is authoritarian.

Wolfhart Pannenberg

Pannenberg's rigorously evidential approach to theological questions has been widely acclaimed as ushering in a new phase in European Protestant theology. In 1961 a circle of young theologians for whom Pannenberg served as the principal spokesman asserted in their manifesto *Offenbarung als Geschichte* (*Revelation as History*) that revelation ought to be understood exclusively in terms of God's acts in history, not as some self-authenticating Word.

Because this "Word," which was understood as God's self-disclosure in a divine-human encounter, needs no external authentication, theology, according to Pannenberg, has depreciated the relevance of history to faith and walled itself off against secular knowledge. On the one hand, Bultmann's existentialist theology has neglected objective historical facticity in favor of finding the conditions for authentic human existence in the apostolic proclamation, to which historical facts are thought to be strictly irrelevant. On the other hand, Barth's understanding of peculiarly

Christian events as belonging, not to the course of ordinary, investigable history, but rather to redemptive history, which is closed to historical research, equally devalues real history. Both schools share a common motive in their depreciation of the importance of history for faith, namely, the desire to secure for faith an impregnable stronghold against the assaults of modern historical-critical studies. Dialectical theology fled into the harbor of supra-history, supposedly safe from the historical-critical floodtide, while existential theology withdrew from the course of objective history to the subjective experience of human authenticity. Theology's attempt at self-isolationism backfired, however, because the secular sciences turned upon it to criticize and contradict it. "For much too long a time faith has been misunderstood to be subjectivity's fortress into which Christianity could retreat from the attacks of scientific knowledge. Such a retreat into pious subjectivity can only lead to destroying any consciousness of the truth of the Christian faith."[20]

Therefore, if Christianity is to make any meaningful claim to truth, it must, according to Pannenberg, submit to the same procedures of testing and verification that are employed in the secular sciences. This method of verification will be indirect, for example, by means of historical research. A theological interpretation of history will be tested positively by "its ability to take into account all known historical details," and negatively by "the proof that without its specific assertions the accessible information would not be at all or would be only incompletely explicable."[21] Since the Christian faith is based on a real past event, and since there is no way to know the past other than by historical-critical research, it follows that the object of Christian faith cannot remain untouched by the results of such research. On the one hand, a kerygmatic Christ utterly unrelated to the real, historical Jesus would be "pure myth"; and on the other hand, a Christ known only through dialectical encounter would be impossible to distinguish from "self-delusion."[22] Therefore, the unavoidable conclusion is that the burden of proving that God has revealed himself in Jesus of Nazareth must fall upon the historian.

Pannenberg acknowledges that if the historical foundation for faith were removed, then Christianity should be abandoned. He is, however, confident that given the historical facts that we now have, this eventuality will not occur. Pannenberg realizes that the results of historical investigation always retain a degree of uncertainty, but nevertheless, through this "precarious and provisional" way a knowledge of the truth of Christianity is possible. Without this factual foundation logically prior to faith, faith would be reduced to gullibility, credulity, or superstition. Only this evidential approach, in contrast to the subjectivism of modern theology, can establish Christianity's truth claim. The historical facts at the foundation of Christianity are reliable, and therefore we can base our faith, our lives, and our future on them.

Alvin Plantinga

Appealing to what he (erroneously, I think) calls the Reformed objection to natural theology, Alvin Plantinga has recently attacked theological rationalism with regard to belief in God. Plantinga wants to maintain that belief in God is rational wholly apart from any evidentiary foundations for the belief.

This brings him into conflict with what he calls the evidentialist objection to theistic belief. According to the evidentialist, one is rationally justified in believing a proposition to be true only if that proposition is either foundational to knowledge or is established by evidence that is ultimately based on such a foundation. According to this viewpoint, since the proposition "God exists" is not foundational, it would be irrational to believe this proposition apart from rational evidence for its truth.

But, Plantinga asks, why can't the proposition "God exists" be itself part of the foundation, so that no rational evidence is necessary? The evidentialist replies that only propositions that are properly basic can be part of the foundation of knowledge. What, then, are the criteria that determine whether or not a proposition is properly basic? Typically, the evidentialist asserts that only propositions that are self-evident or incorrigible are properly basic. For example, the proposition "The sum of the squares of the two sides of a right triangle is equal to the square of the hypotenuse" is self-evidently true. Similarly, the proposition "I feel pain" is incorrigibly true, since even if I am only imagining my injury, it is still true that I *feel* pain. Since the proposition "God exists" is neither self-evident nor incorrigible, it is not properly basic and therefore requires evidence if it is to be believed. To believe this proposition without evidence is therefore irrational.

Now Plantinga does not deny that self-evident and incorrigible propositions are properly basic, but he does ask how we know that these are the *only* properly basic propositions or beliefs. If they are, then we are all irrational, since we commonly accept numerous beliefs that are not based on evidence and that are neither self-evident nor incorrigible. For example, take the belief that the world was not created five minutes ago with built-in memory traces, food in our stomachs from the breakfasts we never really ate, and other appearances of age. Surely it is rational to believe that the world has existed longer than five minutes, even though there is no evidence for this. The evidentialist's criteria for proper basicality must be flawed. In fact, what about the status of those criteria? Is the proposition

"Only propositions that are self-evident or incorrigible are properly basic" *itself* properly basic? Apparently not, for it is certainly not self-evident nor incorrigible. Therefore, if we are to believe this proposition, we must have evidence that it is true. But there is no such evidence. The proposition appears to be just an arbitrary definition—and not a very plausible one at that! Hence, the evidentialist cannot exclude the possibility that belief in God is a properly basic belief.

And in fact, Plantinga maintains, following John Calvin, belief in God is properly basic. Man has an innate, natural capacity to apprehend God's existence even as he has a natural capacity to accept truths of perception (like "I see a tree"). Given the appropriate circumstances—such as moments of guilt, gratitude, or a sense of God's handiwork in nature—man naturally apprehends God's existence. In the same way that certain perceptual beliefs, like "I see a tree," are properly basic given the appropriate circumstances, so belief in God is properly basic in appropriate circumstances. Neither the existence of the tree nor of God is *inferred* from one's experience of the circumstances. But being in the appropriate circumstances is what renders one's belief *properly* basic; the belief would be irrational were it to be held under inappropriate circumstances. Thus, the basic belief that God exists is not arbitrary, since it is properly held only by a person placed in appropriate circumstances. Similarly, taking belief in God as properly basic does not commit one to the relativistic view that virtually any belief can be properly basic for a normal adult. In the absence of appropriate circumstances, various beliefs taken as basic by certain persons will be arbitrarily and irrationally held. Even in the absence of an adequate criterion of proper basicality to replace the flawed evidentialist criterion, the fact is that we can know that some beliefs are just not *properly* basic. Thus, the Christian who takes belief in God as properly basic can legitimately reject the proper basicality of other beliefs. Plantinga thus insists that his epistemology is not fideistic; the deliverances of reason include not only inferred propositions, but also properly basic propositions. God has so constructed us that we naturally form the belief in his existence under appropriate circumstances, just as we do the belief in perceptual objects, the reality of the past, and so forth. Hence, belief in God is among the deliverances of reason, not faith.

Plantinga emphasizes that the proper basicality of the belief that God exists does not imply its indubitability. This belief is defeasible; that is to say, it can be defeated by other incompatible beliefs which come to be accepted by the theist. In such a case, the individual in question must give up some of his beliefs if he is to remain rational, and perhaps it will be his belief in God that is jettisoned. Thus, for example, a Christian who encounters the problem of evil is faced with a potential defeater of his belief in God. If he is to remain rational in his Christian belief, he must have an answer for the defeater. This is where Christian apologetics comes in; it can help to formulate answers to potential defeaters, such as the Free Will Defense in response to the problem of evil. But Plantinga also argues that in some cases, the original belief itself may so exceed its alleged defeater in rational warrant that it becomes an intrinsic defeater of its ostensible defeater. He gives the example of someone accused of a crime and against whom all the evidence stands, even though that person knows he is innocent. In such a case, that person is not rationally obligated to abandon belief in his own innocence and to accept instead the evidence that he is guilty. The belief that he did not commit the crime intrinsically defeats the defeaters brought against it by the evidence. Plantinga makes the theological application by suggesting that belief in God may similarly intrinsically defeat all the defeaters that might be brought against it. Intriguingly, Plantinga intimates that the circumstances which could produce so powerful a warrant for belief in God are the implanted, natural sense of the divine (Calvin's *sensus divinitatis*), deepened and accentuated by the testimony of the Holy Spirit.[23]

Plantinga argues that belief in God is not merely *rational* for the person who takes it as properly basic, but that this belief is so warranted that such a person can be said to *know* that God exists. A belief that is merely rational could in fact be false. When we say that a belief is rational, we mean that the person holding it is within his epistemological rights in so doing or that he exhibits no defect in his noetic structure in so believing. But in order that some belief constitute knowledge, it must be true and in some sense justified or warranted for the person holding it.

The notion of warrant, which is necessary in order for a true belief to be knowledge, is philosophically controversial, and it is to the analysis of this notion that Plantinga's most recent, creative work has been dedicated. He first exposits and then criticizes all major theories of warrant which are offered by epistemologists today, such as deontologism, reliablism, coherentism, and so forth. Fundamentally, Plantinga's method of exposing the inadequacy of such theories is to construct thought experiments or scenarios in which all the conditions for warrant stipulated by a theory are met and yet in which it is obvious that the person in question does not have knowledge of the proposition which he believes because his cognitive faculties are malfunctioning in forming the belief. This common failing suggests that rational warrant inherently involves the notion of the proper functioning of one's cognitive faculties. But this raises the troublesome question, what does it mean for one's cognitive faculties to be "functioning properly"? Here Plantinga drops a bomb into mainstream epistemology by proposing a peculiarly theistic account of rational warrant and proper functioning, namely, that one's cognitive faculties are functioning properly only if they are functioning as God designed them to.

Although he adds various subtle philosophical qualifications, the basic idea of Plantinga's account is that a belief is warranted for a person just in the case his cognitive faculties are, in forming that belief, functioning in an appropriate environment as God designed them to. The more firmly such a person holds the belief in question, the more warrant it has for him, and if he believes it firmly enough, it has sufficient warrant to constitute knowledge. With respect to the belief that God exists, Plantinga would hold that God has so constituted us that we naturally form this belief under certain circumstances; since the belief is thus formed by properly functioning cognitive faculties in an appropriate environment, it is warranted for us, and, insofar as our faculties are not disrupted by the noetic effects of sin, we will believe this proposition deeply and firmly, so that we can be said, in virtue of the great warrant accruing to this belief for us, to know that God exists.

ASSESSMENT

"How do I know Christianity is true?" Probably every Christian has asked himself that question. "I believe God exists, I believe Jesus rose from the dead, and I've experienced his life-changing power in my life, but how do I *know* it's really true?" The problem becomes especially acute when we're faced with someone who either does not believe in God or Jesus or who adheres to some other world religion. They may demand of us how we know Christianity is true and to prove it to them. What are we supposed to say? How *do* I know that Christianity is true?

In answering this question, I think we need to distinguish between *knowing* Christianity to be true and *showing* Christianity to be true.

KNOWING CHRISTIANITY TO BE TRUE

Here I want to examine two points: first, the role of the Holy Spirit, and second, the role of argument and evidence.

Role of the Holy Spirit: Self-Authenticating Witness

May I suggest that, fundamentally, the way we know Christianity to be true is by the self-authenticating witness of God's Holy Spirit? Now what do I mean by that? I mean that the experience of the Holy Spirit is veridical and unmistakable (though not necessarily irresistible or

indubitable) for him who has it; that such a person does not need sup-
plementary arguments or evidence in order to know and to know with
confidence that he is in fact experiencing the Spirit of God; that such
experience does not function in this case as a premiss in any argument
from religious experience to God, but rather is the immediate experiencing of God himself; that in certain contexts the experience of the
Holy Spirit will imply the apprehension of certain truths of the
Christian religion, such as "God exists," "I am condemned by God," "I
am reconciled to God," "Christ lives in me," and so forth; that such an
experience provides one not only with a subjective assurance of
Christianity's truth, but with objective knowledge of that truth; and that
arguments and evidence incompatible with that truth are overwhelmed
by the experience of the Holy Spirit for him who attends fully to it. It
seems to me that the NT teaches such a view with respect to both the
believer and unbeliever alike.

The Believer

First, let's look at the role of the Holy Spirit in the life of the believer.
When a person becomes a Christian, he automatically becomes an adopted
son of God and is indwelt with the Holy Spirit: "for in Christ Jesus you
are all sons of God, through faith. . . . And because you are sons, God has
sent the Spirit of his Son into our hearts, crying, 'Abba! Father!'" (Gal 3:26;
4:6). Paul emphasizes the point in Romans 8. Here he explains that it is
the witness of the Holy Spirit with our spirit that allows us to know that
we are God's children: "for you did not receive the spirit of slavery to fall
back into fear, but you have received the spirit of sonship. When we cry,
'Abba! Father!' it is the Spirit himself bearing witness with our spirit that
we are children of God" (Rom 8:15-16). Paul uses the term *plerophoria*
(complete confidence, full assurance) to indicate that the believer has
knowledge of the truth as a result of the Spirit's work (Col 2:2; 1 Thess
1:5; cf. Rom 4:21; 14:5; Col 4:12). Sometimes this is called "assurance of
salvation" by Christians today; now assurance of salvation entails certain
truths of Christianity, such as "God forgives my sin," "Christ has reconciled me to God," and so on, so that in having assurance of salvation one
has assurance of these truths.

The apostle John also makes quite clear that it is the Holy Spirit within
us that gives believers conviction of the truth of Christianity. "But you have
been anointed by the Holy One, and you all know . . . the anointing which
you received from him abides in you, and you have no need that any one
should teach you; as his anointing teaches you about everything, and is
true, and is no lie, just as it has taught you, abide in him" (1 John 2:20, 27).

Here John explains that it is the Holy Spirit himself who teaches the believer the truth of divine things. John is clearly echoing the teaching of Jesus himself, when he says, "But the Counselor, the Holy Spirit, whom the Father will send in my name, he will teach you all things, and bring to your remembrance all that I have said to you" (John 14:26). Now the truth that the Holy Spirit teaches us is not, I'm convinced, the subtleties of Christian doctrine. There are too many Spirit-filled Christians who differ doctrinally for that to be the case. What John is talking about is the inner assurance the Holy Spirit gives of the basic truths of the Christian faith. This assurance does not come from human arguments but directly from the Holy Spirit himself.

Now someone might point to 1 John 4:1-3 as evidence that the testimony of the Holy Spirit is not self-authenticating, but needs to be tested:

> Beloved, do not believe every spirit, but test the spirits to see whether they are of God; for many false prophets have gone out into the world. By this you know the Spirit of God: every spirit which confesses that Jesus Christ has come in the flesh is of God, and every spirit which does not confess Jesus is not of God. This is the spirit of antichrist . . .

But such an understanding would be a misinterpretation of the passage. John is not talking about testing the witness of the Spirit in our own hearts; rather he's talking about testing people who come to you claiming to be speaking by the Holy Spirit. He referred to the same people earlier: "Children, it is the last hour; and as you have heard that antichrist is coming, so now many antichrists have come, therefore we know that it is the last hour. They went out from us, but they were not of us . . ." (1 John 2:18-19). John never encourages the believer to doubt the witness of the Spirit in his own heart; rather he says that if someone else comes claiming to speak by the Holy Spirit, then, since the situation is external to oneself and involves additional truth claims not immediately apprehended, we must test that person in order to determine if his claim is true. But in our own lives, the inner witness of God's Spirit is sufficient to assure us of the truths to which he testifies.

John also underlines other teachings of Jesus on the work of the Holy Spirit. For example, according to Jesus it is the indwelling Holy Spirit that gives the believer certainty of knowing that Jesus lives in him and that he is in Jesus, in the sense of being united with him.

> And I will pray the Father, and he will give you another Counselor, to be with you for ever, even the Spirit of truth, whom the world

cannot receive, because it neither sees him nor knows him; you know him, for he dwells with you, and will be in you. . . . In that day you will know that I am in my Father, and you in me, and I in you (John 14:16-17, 20).

John teaches the same thing: "And by this we know that he abides in us, by the Spirit which he has given us. . . . By this we know that we abide in him and he in us, because he has given us of his own Spirit" (1 John 3:24; 4:13). John uses his characteristic phrase "by this we know" to emphasize that as Christians we have a confident knowledge that our faith is true, that we really do abide in God, and God really does live in us. In fact John goes so far as to contrast the confidence which the Spirit's testimony brings to that brought by human evidence:

> This is he who came by water and blood, Jesus Christ, not with the water only but with the water and the blood. And the Spirit is the witness, because the Spirit is the truth. There are three witnesses, the Spirit, the water, and the blood; and these three agree. If we receive the testimony of men, the testimony of God is greater; for this is the testimony of God that he has borne witness to his Son. He who believes in the Son of God has the testimony in himself. He who does not believe God has made him a liar, because he has not believed in the testimony that God has borne to his Son (1 John 5:6-10).

The "water" here probably refers to Jesus' baptism, and the "blood" to His crucifixion, those being the two events which marked the beginning and end of his earthly ministry. "The testimony of men" is therefore nothing less than the apostolic testimony to the events of Jesus' life and ministry. Though John had laid such great weight on precisely that apostolic testimony in his gospel (John 20:31; 21:24), here he declares that even though we quite rightly receive this testimony, still the inner testimony of the Holy Spirit is even greater! As Christians we have the testimony of God living within us, the Holy Spirit who bears witness with our spirit that we are children of God.

Thus, although arguments and evidence may be used to support the believer's faith, they are never properly the basis of that faith. For the believer, God is not the conclusion of a syllogism; he is the living God of Abraham, Isaac, and Jacob dwelling within us. How then does the believer know that Christianity is true? He knows because of the self-authenticating witness of God's Spirit who lives within him.

The Unbeliever

But what about the role of the Holy Spirit in the life of an unbeliever? Since the Holy Spirit does not indwell him, does this mean that he must rely only upon arguments and evidence to convince him that Christianity is true? No, not at all. According to the Scripture, God has a different ministry of the Holy Spirit especially geared to the needs of the unbeliever. Jesus describes this ministry in John 16:7-11:

> It is to your advantage that I go away, for if I do not go away, the Counselor will not come to you; but if I go, I will send him to you. And when he comes, he will convince the world concerning sin and righteousness and judgment: concerning sin, because they do not believe in me; concerning righteousness, because I go to the Father, and you will see me no more; concerning judgment, because the ruler of this world is judged.

Here the Holy Spirit's ministry is three-fold: he convicts the unbeliever of his own sin, of God's righteousness, and of his condemnation before God. The unbeliever so convicted can therefore be said to know such truths as "God exists," "I am guilty before God," and so forth.

This is the way it has to be. For if it weren't for the work of the Holy Spirit, no one would *ever* become a Christian. According to Paul, natural man left to himself does not even seek God: "None is righteous, no, not one; no one understands, no one seeks for God" (Rom 3:10-11). Man in himself cannot understand spiritual things: "The unspiritual man does not receive the gifts of the Spirit of God, for they are folly to him, and he is not able to understand them because they are spiritually discerned" (1 Cor 2:14). And he is hostile to God: " For the mind that is set on the flesh is hostile to God; it does not submit to God's law, indeed it cannot" (Rom 8:7). As Jesus said, men love darkness rather than light. Left to himself, natural man would never come to God.

The fact that we do find people who are seeking God and are ready to receive Christ is evidence that the Holy Spirit has already been at work, convicting them and drawing them to him. As Jesus said, "No one can come to me unless the Father who sent him draws him" (John 6:44).

Therefore, when a person refuses to come to Christ it is never just because of lack of evidence or because of intellectual difficulties: at root, he refuses to come because he willingly ignores and rejects the drawing of God's Spirit on his heart. No one in the final analysis really fails to become a Christian because of lack of arguments; he fails to become a Christian because he loves darkness rather than light and wants nothing to do with

God. But anyone who responds to the drawing of God's Spirit with an open mind and an open heart can know with assurance that Christianity is true, because God's Spirit will convict him that it is. Jesus said, "My teaching is not mine, but his who sent me; if any man's will is to do his will, he shall know whether the teaching is from God or whether I am speaking on my own authority" (John 7:16-17). Jesus affirms that if anyone is truly seeking God, then he will know that Jesus' teaching is truly from God.

So then for the unbeliever as well as for the believer, it is the testimony of God's Spirit that ultimately assures him of the truth of Christianity. The unbeliever who is truly seeking God will be convinced of the truth of the Christian message.

Therefore, we find that for believer and unbeliever alike it is the self-authenticating work of the Holy Spirit that supplies knowledge of Christianity's truth. Thus, I would agree that belief in the God of the Bible is a properly basic belief, and emphasize that it is the ministry of the Holy Spirit that supplies the circumstances for its proper basicality. And because this belief is formed in response to the self-disclosure of God himself, who needs no external authentication, it is not merely rational for us, but constitutes knowledge. We can be confident of Christianity's truth.

Role of Argument and Evidence

But what about the second point: the role of argument and evidence in knowing Christianity to be true? We've already said that it's the Holy Spirit who gives us the ultimate assurance of Christianity's truth. Therefore, the only role left for argument and evidence to play is a subsidiary role. I think Martin Luther correctly distinguished between what he called the magisterial and ministerial uses of reason. The *magisterial use* of reason occurs when reason stands over and above the gospel like a magistrate and judges it on the basis of argument and evidence. The *ministerial use* of reason occurs when reason submits to and serves the gospel. Only the ministerial use of reason can be allowed. Philosophy is rightly the handmaid of theology. Reason is a tool to help us better understand and defend our faith; as Anselm put it, ours is a faith that seeks understanding. A person who knows Christianity is true on the basis of the witness of the Spirit may also have a sound apologetic which reinforces or confirms for him the Spirit's witness, but it does not serve as the basis of his belief. Should a conflict arise between the witness of the Holy Spirit to the fundamental truth of the Christian faith and beliefs based on argument and evidence, then it is the former which must take precedence over the latter, not vice versa.

A Danger

Now there is a danger in all this so far. Some persons might say that we should never seek to defend the faith. Just preach the gospel and let the Holy Spirit work! But this attitude is unbalanced and unscriptural, as we shall see in a moment. For now, let us just note in passing that as long as reason is a minister of the Christian faith, Christians should employ it.

An Objection

Some people disagree with what I've said about the role of argument and evidence. They would say that reason can be used in a magisterial role, at least by the unbeliever. They ask how else we could determine which is true, the Bible, the Koran, or the Baghavad-Gita, unless we use argument and evidence to judge them? Now I've already answered that question: The Holy Spirit teaches us directly which teaching is really from God. But let me suggest two other reasons I think those who support the magisterial role of reason are wrong.

First, such a role would consign most believers to irrationality. The vast majority of the human race have neither the time, training, nor resources to develop a full-blown Christian apologetic as the basis of their faith. Even the proponents of the magisterial use of reason at one time in the course of their education presumably lacked such an apologetic. According to the magisterial role of reason, these persons should not have believed in Christ until they finished their apologetic. Otherwise, they would be believing for insufficient reasons. I once asked a fellow seminary student, "How do you know Christianity is true?" He replied, "I really don't know." Does that mean he should give up Christianity until he finds rational arguments to ground his faith? Of course not! He knew Christianity was true because he knew Jesus, regardless of rational arguments. The fact is that we can know the truth whether we have rational arguments or not.

Second, if the magisterial role of reason were valid, then a person who had been given poor arguments for Christianity would have a just excuse before God for not believing in him. Suppose someone had been told to believe in God because of an invalid argument. Could he stand before God on the judgment day and say, "God, those Christians only gave me a lousy argument for believing in you. That's why I didn't believe"? Of course not! The Bible says all men are without excuse. Even those who are given no good reason to believe and many persuasive reasons to disbelieve have no excuse, because the ultimate reason they do not believe is that they have deliberately rejected God's Holy Spirit.

Therefore, the role of rational argumentation in knowing Christianity to be true is the role of a servant. A person knows Christianity is true because the Holy Spirit tells him it is true, and while argument and evidence can be used to support this conclusion, they cannot legitimately overrule it.

SHOWING CHRISTIANITY TO BE TRUE

Such are the roles of the Holy Spirit and of argument in *knowing* Christianity is true. But what about their roles in *showing* Christianity is true? Here things are somewhat reversed.

Role of Reason: Systematic Consistency

Let's look first at the role of argument and evidence in showing Christianity is true. Here we're concerned about how to prove to another person that our faith is true. Even if I myself know personally on the basis of the Spirit's witness in my heart that Christianity is true, how can I demonstrate to somebody else that what I believe is true?

The task of showing that Christianity is true involves the presentation of sound and persuasive arguments for Christian truth claims. Accordingly, we need to ask ourselves first how it is that one proves something to be true. A statement or proposition is true if and only if it corresponds to reality—that is to say, reality is just as the statement says that it is. Thus, the statement "The Cubs won the 1993 World Series" is true if and only if the Cubs won the 1993 World Series. In order to prove a proposition to be true, we present argument and evidence which have that proposition as the conclusion. Such reasoning can be either deductive or inductive.

In a sound deductive argument, the conclusion follows inevitably from the premises. The two prerequisites of a sound deductive argument are that the premises be true and the logic be valid. If the premises are true, but the logic is fallacious, then the argument is invalid. An example of an invalid argument would be:

1. If God exists, objective moral values exist.
2. Objective moral values exist.
3. Therefore, God exists.

Although both the premises are true, the conclusion does not follow logically from them, because the argument commits the fallacy known as "affirming the consequent." On the other hand, an argument can be logically valid but still unsound, because it has false premises. An example of such an unsound argument would be:

1. If Jesus were not Lord, he would be a liar or a lunatic.
2. Jesus was neither a liar nor a lunatic.
3. Therefore, Jesus is Lord.

This is a valid argument, inferring the negation of the first premiss' antecedent based on the negation of its consequent. But the argument is still unsound, because the first premiss is false: there are other unmentioned alternatives, for example, that Jesus as described in the gospels is a legend. Hence, in presenting a deductive argument for some Christian truth we need to be careful to construct arguments which are logically valid and have true premisses.

An inductive argument is one for which it is possible that the premisses be true and the logical inferences valid, but the conclusion still be false. In such reasoning the evidence and rules of inference are said to "underdetermine" the conclusion; that is to say, they render the conclusion plausible or likely, but do not guarantee its truth. For example, a sound inductive argument would be:

1. Groups A, B, C were composed of similar persons suffering from the same disease.
2. Group A was administered a certain new drug, group B was administered a placebo, and group C was not given any treatment.
3. The rate of death from the disease was subsequently lower in group A by 75% in comparison with both groups B and C.
4. Therefore, the new drug is effective in reducing the death rate from said disease.

The conclusion is quite likely true based on the evidence and rules of inductive reasoning, but it is not inevitably true; maybe the people in group A were just lucky or some unknown variable caused their improvement. Although inductive reasoning is part and parcel of everyday life, the description of such reasoning is a matter of controversy among philosophers. Some suggest that we utilize a hypothetico-deductive model of inductive reasoning: we frame a hypothesis to account for the facts and then deduce from the hypothesis predictions which, if true, would prove the hypothesis false; we then test those predictions and if they do not come true, our hypothesis is corroborated. Other philosophers advocate what they call inference to the best explanation: confronted with certain evidence, we infer what explanation would, if it were true, provide the best explanation of that evidence. What qualities go toward making an explanation best is a disputed issue (simplicity, explanatory power, and so on), but minimally such an explanation must fit all the facts of experience and be logically consistent. These minimal conditions will apply on either model to a sound inductive inference.

In both deductive and inductive reasoning, then, logic and facts are the keys to showing soundly that a conclusion is true. Since a proposition that is logically contradictory is necessarily false and so cannot be the conclusion of a sound argument, and since a proposition validly inferred from factually true premisses ought to be regarded as factually true, one may generalize these notions to say that a world view ought to be regarded as true just in case it is logically consistent and fits all the facts known in our experience. Such a test for truth has been called *systematic consistency*: "consistency" meaning obedience to the laws of logic and "systematic" meaning fitting all the facts known by experience.[24] Notice that such a test does not guarantee the truth of a world view. For more than one view could be consistent and fit all the facts yet known by experience; or again, a view which is systematically consistent with all that we now know could turn out to be falsified by future discoveries. Systematic consistency thus underdetermines world views, and so, as in the case of inductive reasoning, we must be content with plausibility or likelihood, rather than rational certainty.

Now some Christian believers might be troubled by the notion that one's apologetic case for Christianity yields only probability rather than certainty. But the fact that Christianity can only be shown to be probably true need not be troubling when two things are kept in mind: first, that we attain no more than probability with respect to almost everything we infer (for example, that smoking contributes to lung cancer or that it is safe to cross the street) without detriment to the depth of our conviction and that even our non-inferred, basic beliefs may not be held with any sort of absolute certainty (for example, my memory belief that I had waffles for breakfast on Monday); and second, that even if we can only *show* Christianity to be probably true, nevertheless we can on the basis of the Spirit's witness *know* Christianity to be true with a deep assurance that far outstrips what the evidence in our particular situation might support (think analogously of the person convinced of his innocence even though all the evidence stands against him). To demand logically demonstrative proofs as a pre-condition for making a religious commitment is therefore just being unreasonable.

We should, then, test world views by their logical consistency and by how well they fit the facts known by experience. In our day and age, however, certain people, under the influence of Eastern mysticism or its Western step-child, the New Age Movement, deny that consistency is a test for truth. They affirm that reality is ultimately illogical or that logical contradictions correspond to reality. They assert that in Eastern thought the Absolute or God or the Real transcends the logical categories of human thought. They are apt to interpret the demand for logical consistency as a piece of Western imperialism. Trying to reason with such people can be very frustrating, because they will cheerfully concede that their view is logically incoherent and yet insist that it is true.

What such people seem to be saying is that the classical law of thought known as the Law of Excluded Middle is not necessarily true; that is to say, they deny that of a proposition and its negation, necessarily, one is true and the other is false. Such a denial could take two different forms. It could be interpreted on the one hand to mean that a proposition and its negation *both* can be true (or both false). Thus, it is true both that God is love and, in the same sense, that God is not love. Since both are true, the Law of Contradiction, that a proposition and its negation cannot both be true (or both false) at the same time, is also denied. On the other hand, the original denial could be interpreted to mean that of a proposition and its negation *neither* may be true (or neither false). Thus, it is not true that God is good and it is not true that God is not good; there is just no truth value at all for such propositions. In this case, it is the classical Principle of Bivalence, that for any proposition, necessarily that proposition is either true or false, that is denied along with the Law of Excluded Middle.

Now I am inclined to say that such claims are frankly crazy and unintelligible.[25] To say that God is both good and not good in the same sense or that God neither exists nor does not exist is just incomprehensible to me.

In our politically correct age, there is a tendency to vilify all that is Western and to exalt Eastern modes of thinking as at least equally valid if not superior to Western modes of thought. To assert that Eastern thought is seriously deficient in making such claims is to be a sort of epistemological bigot, blinkered by the constraints of the logic-chopping Western mind. But this attitude is far too simplistic. In the first place, there are thinkers within the tradition of Western thought alone who have held the mystical views under discussion (Plotinus would be a good example), so that there is no need to play off East against West in this matter. Secondly, the extent to which such thinking represents "the Eastern mind" has been greatly exaggerated. In the East the common man—and the philosopher, too—lives by the Laws of Contradiction and Excluded Middle in his everyday life; he affirms them every time he walks through a doorway rather than into the wall. It is only at an extremely theoretical level of philosophical speculation that such laws are denied. And even at that level, the situation is not monochromatic: Confucianism, Hinayana Buddhism, pluralistic Hinduism as exemplified in Sankhya-Yoga, Vaishesika-Nyaya, and Mimasa schools of thought, and even Jainism do not deny the application of the classical laws of thought to ultimate reality.[26] Thus, a critique of Eastern thought from within Eastern thought can be—and has been—made. We in the West should not therefore be embarrassed or apologetic about our heritage; on the contrary, it is one of the glories of ancient Greece that her thinkers came to enunciate clearly the principles of logical reasoning, and the triumph of logical reasoning over competing modes of thought in the West has been one of the West's greatest strengths and proudest achievements.

Why think then that such self-evident truths as the principles of logic are in fact invalid for ultimate reality? Such a claim seems to be both self-refuting and arbitrary. For consider a claim like "God cannot be described by propositions governed by the Principle of Bivalence." If such a claim is true, then it is not true, since it itself is a proposition describing God and so has no truth value. Thus, such a claim refutes itself. Of course, if it is not true, then it is not true, as the Eastern mystic alleged, that God cannot be described by propositions governed by the Principle of Bivalence. Thus, if the claim is not true, it is not true and if it is true, it is not true, so that in either case the claim turns out to be not true. Or consider the claim that "God cannot be described by propositions governed by the Law of Contradiction." If this proposition is true, then, since it describes God, it is not itself governed by the Law of Contradiction. Therefore, it is equally true that "God can be described by propositions governed by the Law of Contradiction." But then which propositions are these that are so governed? There must be some, for the Eastern mystic is committed to the truth of this claim. But if he produces any, then they immediately refute his original claim that there are no such propositions. His claim thus commits him to the existence of counter-examples which serve to refute that very claim.

One might try to escape the above self-refuting situation by maintaining that when one denies the validity of such logical principles for propositions about God, one is talking in a meta-language (or higher level language) about propositions in another, lower level language, much as one could talk in English, for example, about the rules for German grammar, and that since the principles of the lower level language don't apply to the meta-language, no self-refuting situations arise. For example, when I say, "If you have a subordinate clause, the verb goes at the end of the clause," that statement is true for the German language, and I do not refute myself in asserting it because it is a statement in another language (English) and so doesn't need to have the verb go at the end of the subordinate clause which it itself contains. In the same way someone could say that when we deny the validity of logical principles for propositions about God, we are speaking in a meta-language, which is governed by those principles, about ordinary language, which is not. But the futility of this response with respect to propositions about God is evident in the fact that one could then use the meta-language to describe God, since you *can* talk about God in it in a logical way and the restrictions only apply to the *lower* language.

Furthermore, apart from the issue of self-refutation, the mystic's claim is wholly arbitrary. Indeed, no reason can ever be given to justify denying the validity of logical principles for propositions about God. For the very statement of such reasons, such as "God is too great to be captured by categories of human thought" or "God is wholly other," involves the affirmation of certain propositions about God which are governed by the principles in question. In short, the denial of such principles for propositions about ultimate reality is completely and essentially arbitrary.

Some Eastern thinkers realize that their position, as a position, is ultimately self-refuting and arbitrary, and so they are driven to deny that their position really is a position! They claim rather that their position is just a technique pointing to the transcendent Real beyond all positions. But if this claim is not flatly self-contradictory, as it would appear, if such thinkers literally *have no position*, then there just is nothing here to assess and they have nothing to say. This silence is perhaps the most poignant illustration of the bankruptcy of the denial of the principles of logical reasoning.

This same debate between certain Eastern/New Age modes of thought and classical logical thinking is being played out on another stage of the contemporary scene: the debate between modernism and radical post-modernism. Modernism is that mode of thought which is more or less synonymous with Enlightenment rationalism, whereas post-modernism is a much heralded new mode of thought that rejects Enlightenment epistemology and tends to denigrate rational metaphysics, deny moral absolutes, and exalt pluralism. Post-modernism is frequently accompanied by deconstructionism, which seeks to dismantle traditional, rational, objective notions found in modernism. Now in rejecting Enlightenment theological rationalism in favor of the self-authenticating witness of the Holy Spirit as the ground of our knowledge of the Christian faith, I have already, in one sense, opted for a "post-modern" epistemology; similarly, the provisional character of systematic consistency accords with the intellectual humility advocated by post-modernism. But really radical post-modernists would scorn these sops. They reject altogether Western rationality and metaphysics, claiming that there is no objective truth about reality. "The truth," as John Caputo says, "is that there is no truth."[27] But such a claim falls prey to precisely the same objections as above—indeed, the post-modernist claim is not really distinguishable from certain Buddhist philosophies. To assert that "The truth is that there is no truth" is self-refuting and arbitrary.[28] For if this statement is true, it is not true, since there is no truth. So-called deconstructionism thus cannot be halted from deconstructing itself. Moreover, there is just no reason that can be given for adopting the post-modern perspective rather than, say, the outlooks of Western capitalism, male chauvinism, white racism, and so forth, since post-modernism has no more truth to it than these perspectives. Caught in this self-defeating trap, some post-modernists have been forced to the same recourse as Buddhist mystics: denying that post-modernism is really a view or position at all. But then, once again, why do they continue to write books and talk about it? They are obviously making some cognitive claims—and if not, then they literally have *nothing* to say and no objection to our employment of the classical canons of logic.

Some of the same mystical traditions that reject classical logic would also appear to reject the requirement that a true world view must fit the facts known by experience as well as be logically consistent. For they subscribe to a sort of phenomenal illusionism according to which the world apprehended by the five senses is ultimately unreal. Again such illusionism is not unrepresented in Western thought (Parmenides, for example), nor universal among Eastern philosophical traditions and is, in any case, operative only at extremely speculative metaphysical levels in those traditions that do affirm it. The contemporary Western equivalent of such views seems to be the hypothesis that you are just a brain in a vat being stimulated by electrodes to have sensations of the external world as you apprehend it. The veridicality of your senses cannot be justified by your senses themselves, since they are the very mechanisms being questioned. Rather a deeper epistemological theory, such as those discussed by Plantinga, is needed to explain why our senses are to be trusted in their deliverances. Perhaps a simpler route is also open to us. For phenomenal illusionism does not in a sense deny that an adequate world view must explain the facts known through experience. It denies that we know, for example, that the external world exists, but it does provide some account of our experience of the world as it appears to us. It makes some attempt to explain the data of experience; it does not simply deny that we have an experience of the external world and the things in it. The question, then, is what is the best explanation of our experience of the world, that it is illusory or that we have some apprehension of the world as it is? The arguments for illusionism have been generally recognized as failures, so that there is no reason to abandon our common sense belief in the general veridicality of our senses.

So in showing a proposition to be true, we must present either deductively or inductively sound arguments for the proposed conclusion. In general we shall try to show that the Christian world view is systematically consistent, that is to say, that it is logical and fits the facts known through experience.

But there is more to showing Christianity to be true than just the provision of sound arguments in its favor. A successful apologetic must also be persuasive. If this second condition is unmet, the task of providing sound arguments for Christianity can become utterly trivial. For example, consider the following argument on behalf of the Christian faith:

1. Either Christianity is true or I'm a monkey's uncle.
2. I am not a monkey's uncle.
3. Therefore, Christianity is true.

This is a logically valid argument, and, since Christianity is in fact true and I am not a monkey's uncle, its premises are true. Accordingly, it is a sound argument for the Christian faith. But nobody would regard this as much of an apologetic! The argument has no power to persuade, since nobody who is not already convinced of the truth of Christianity will be prepared to accept the first premise. In showing Christianity to be true, therefore, we must use arguments that are not only sound, but also convincing. This raises a difficulty, since persuasiveness is to some degree person-relative. Some people are easy to convince, while others simply refuse to be convinced. Plantinga has observed that you can actually reduce someone from knowledge to ignorance by presenting him with a valid argument containing premisses he knows to be true for a conclusion which he simply refuses to accept, so that he has to deny one of the premisses he knew to be true. No better illustration of this can be given than the natural man's refusing to believe in God or Christ at the expense of adopting some outlandish hypothesis which he ought to know is false (for example, that the universe came into being uncaused out of nothing or that Jesus was a man from outer space). Since we cannot hope to persuade everybody, our aim should be to make our cumulative apologetic case as persuasive as possible. This can best be done by appealing to facts which are widely accepted or to intuitions that are commonly shared (common sense). When we appeal to expert testimony, our authorities should not be partisan, but neutral or even anti-Christian. And of course, the persuasiveness of an argument as it is presented on any particular occasion may depend on a host of arational considerations, such as courteousness, openness, genuine concern for the listener, and so forth.

In showing Christianity to be true, therefore, we try to prove that the

Christian world view is systematically consistent by appealing to common sense and widely accepted facts about the world.

Role of the Holy Spirit

Now we come to the second point: the role of the Holy Spirit in showing Christianity to be true. The role of the Holy Spirit is to use our arguments to convince the unbeliever of the truth of Christianity. When one presents reasons for his faith, one is not working apart from or against the Holy Spirit. To return to a point mentioned earlier: it is unbalanced and unscriptural to simply preach the gospel *if* the unbeliever has questions or objections.

First, it's unbalanced because it assumes the Holy Spirit works only through preaching. But he can work through rational argumentation, too. We should appeal to the head as well as to the heart. If an unbeliever objects that the Bible is unreliable because it is a translation of a translation of a translation, the answer is not to tell him to get right with God. The answer is to explain that we have excellent manuscripts of the Bible in the original Greek and Hebrew languages—and *then* tell him to get right with God!

But second, it's unscriptural to refuse to reason with an unbeliever. Look at Paul. It was Paul's standard procedure to present reasons for the truth of the gospel and so defend the faith:

> And Paul went in, as was his custom, and for three weeks he argued with them from the scriptures, explaining and proving that it was necessary for the Christ to suffer and to rise from the dead. . . . So he argued in the synagogue with the Jews and the devout persons, and in the market place every day with those who chanced to be there. . . .
>
> And he entered the synagogue and for three months spoke boldly, arguing and pleading about the kingdom of God. . . .
>
> And he expounded the matter to them from morning till evening, testifying to the kingdom of God and trying to convince them about Jesus both from the law of Moses and from the prophets. And some were convinced by what he said, while others disbelieved (Acts 17:2-3, 17; 19:8; 28:23-4).

Indeed, Scripture actually *commands* us to be prepared to give such a defense to an unbeliever: ". . . always being ready to make a defense to every one who asks you to give an account for the hope that is in you" (1 Pet 3:15b). So as Christians, we are to have an apologetic case ready to show that Christianity is true. To ignore the unbeliever's questions or objections is therefore both unbalanced and unscriptural. Of course, it is true that we can never argue anyone into the kingdom of God. Conversion is exclusively the role of the Holy Spirit. But the Holy Spirit may use our arguments to draw people to himself.

A Danger

Now there is also a danger in all this. There is the danger that we may focus our attention on the argument instead of on the sinner. We must never let apologetics distract us from our primary aim of communicating the gospel. Indeed, I would say that with most people there is no need to use apologetics at all. Only use rational argumentation after sharing the gospel and when the unbeliever still has questions. If you tell him, "God loves you and has a wonderful plan for your life," and he says he doesn't believe in God, don't get bogged down at that point in trying to prove the existence of God to him. Tell him, "Well, at this point I'm not trying to convince you what the Bible says is *true*; I'm just trying to share with you what the Bible *says*. After I've done that, then perhaps we can come back to whether there are good reasons to believe what it says is true." Remember our primary aim is to present Christ.

An Objection

Some would disagree with what I've said about the role of the Holy Spirit in showing Christianity to be true. They would contend that the believer and the unbeliever have no common ground on which to argue; therefore it is futile to try to convince an unbeliever that Christianity is true. I think I've already indicated what our common ground with unbelievers is: the laws of logic and the facts of experience. Starting from these, we build our case for Christianity.

But in addition, I think that the example of Jesus and the apostles confirms the validity of such an approach. Jesus appealed to miracles and to fulfilled prophecy to prove that his claims were true (Luke 24:25-27; John 14:11). What about the apostles? In dealing with Jews, they appealed to fulfilled prophecy, Jesus' miracles, and especially Jesus' resurrection. A model apologetic for Jews is Peter's sermon on the Day of Pentecost in Acts 2. In verse 22 he appeals to Jesus' miracles. In verses 25-31 he appeals to fulfilled prophecy. In verse 32 he appeals to Christ's resurrection. By means of these arguments the apostles sought to show Jews that Christianity is true.

In dealing with non-Jews, the apostles sought to show the existence of God through his handiwork in nature (Acts 14:17). In Romans 1, Paul says that from nature alone all men can know that God exists (Rom 1:20).

According to Michael Green in his book *Evangelism in the Early Church*, the standard procedure of the apostles in dealing with Gentiles was to point to nature to show God's existence. Paul also appealed to eyewitness testimony of the resurrection of Jesus to show further that Christianity is true (1 Cor 15:3-8). So it is quite apparent, I think, that both Jesus and the apostles were not afraid to argue for the truth of Christianity. This doesn't mean they didn't trust the Holy Spirit to bring people to God. Rather they trusted the Holy Spirit to use their arguments to bring people to God.

Therefore, in showing Christianity to be true, it is the role of argument and evidence to show that the Christian *Weltanschauung* is the most systematically consistent position one can hold. And it is the role of the Holy Spirit to use these arguments, as we lovingly present them, to bring people to him.

CONCLUSION

In summary, we've seen that in answering the question "How do I know Christianity is true?" we must make a distinction between *knowing* it is true and *showing* it is true. We *know* Christianity is true primarily by the self-authenticating witness of God's Spirit. We *show* Christianity is true by demonstrating that it is systematically consistent.

What, then, should be our approach in apologetics? It should be something like this: "My friend, I know Christianity is true because God's Spirit lives in me and assures me that it is true. And you can know it is true, too, because God is knocking at the door of your heart, telling you the same thing. If you are sincerely seeking God, then God will give you assurance that the gospel is true. Now to try to show you it's true, I'll share with you some arguments and evidence that I really find convincing. But should my arguments seem weak and unconvincing to you, that's my fault, not God's. It only shows that I'm a poor apologist, not that the gospel is untrue. Whatever you think of my arguments, God still loves you and holds you accountable. I'll do my best to present good arguments to you. But ultimately you have to deal, not with arguments, but with God himself."

PRACTICAL APPLICATION

The foregoing discussion has profound practical application both in our Christian walk and in our evangelism. With regard to our Christian walk, it helps us to have a proper assurance of the truth of our faith. A student once remarked to me after class, "I find this view so liberating!" He had struggled for some time to sort out the relation between faith and reason, but without success. Christians often fall into the extremes of fideism or theological rationalism. But the view just expounded enables us to hold to a rational faith which is supported by argument and evidence without our making that argument and evidence the foundation of our faith. It is tremendously liberating to be able to know that our faith is true and to commend it as such to an unbeliever without being dependent upon the vagaries of argument and evidence for the assurance that our faith is true; at the same time we know confidently and without embarrassment that our faith is true and that the unbeliever can know this, too, without our falling into relativistic subjectivism.

This view also underlines the vital importance of cultivating the ministry of the Holy Spirit in our lives. For though all Christians are indwelt by the Spirit, not all are filled with the Spirit. The New Testament teaches that we can grieve the Holy Spirit of God by sin (Eph 4:30) and quench the Spirit by repressing his working in our lives (1 Thess 5:19). The Christian who is not filled with the Spirit may often be wracked with doubts concerning his faith. I can testify personally that my intellectual doubts seem most poignant when I am in a carnal condition. But when a Christian is walking in the Spirit, then, although his intellectual questions may remain, he can *live* with those questions, without their robbing his faith of its vitality. As the source of the assurance that our faith is true, the Holy Spirit's ministry in our lives needs to be cultivated by spiritual activities that help us to walk close to God, such as Bible study, prayer, devotional reading, inspirational music, evangelism, and Spirit-filled worship.

In evangelism, too, this view enables us to give the unbeliever rational arguments and evidence for the truth of the Gospel, instead of challenging him to "just have faith." I have met many non-Christians who came from conservative Christian backgrounds and who were turned off to the gospel by having their honest questions squelched and being told to just believe. By contrast, let me tell you about the experience of one university student I shared the gospel with. After I finished, he asked, "But how do you know this is all true?" I replied, "Well, we need to have some test for truth. What is your test for truth?" When he confessed he did not have one, I continued, "What about systematic consistency?" I explained that notion to him, and to my surprise that was enough—he did not even ask me to show him that Christianity was systematically consistent! All he needed was just to hear a test for truth that could be applied to Christianity. With tears in his eyes, he then prayed with me to receive Christ.

At the same time, however, this view reminds us that unbelief is at root a spiritual, not an intellectual, problem. Sometimes an unbeliever will throw up an intellectual smoke screen so that he can avoid personal, existential involvement with the gospel. In such a case, further argumentation may be futile and counterproductive, and we need to be sensitive to moments when apologetics is and is not appropriate. If we sense the unbeliever's arguments and questions are not sincere, we may do better to simply break off the discussion and ask him, "If I answered that objection, would you then really be ready to become a Christian?" Tell him lovingly and forthrightly that you think he's throwing up an intellectual smoke screen to keep from confronting the real issue: his sin before God. Apologetics is thus most appropriate and effective when the unbeliever is spiritually open and sincerely seeking to know the truth.

That leads to a final point. Many times a person will say, "That argument wasn't effective because the unbeliever I shared it with was not convinced." Here we have to be very careful. In the first place, don't expect an unbeliever to just roll over and play dead the minute he hears your apologetic argument. Of course, he's going to disagree! Think of what's at stake for him! You need to be prepared to listen carefully to his objections and questions, to engage him in dialogue, and to continue the conversation as long as is profitable. Effectiveness in using apologetics in evangelism requires study, practice, and revision in light of experience, not just pat answers. Second, remember that being "convincing" is person-relative. Some people will simply refuse to be convinced. Hence, an argument cannot be said to be ineffective because some people remain unconvinced by it. When one reflects on the fact that "the gate is small, and the way is narrow that leads to life, and few are those who find it" (Matt 7:14), it should not surprise us if most people find our apologetic unconvincing. But that does not mean that our apologetic is ineffective; it may only mean that many people are close-minded. Of course, if *nobody* finds our arguments convincing, then they can be said to be ineffective, even if they are cogent.

What we need to develop is an apologetic that is both cogent and persuasive to as many people as possible. But we must not be discouraged and think our apologetic is ineffective if many or even most people find our arguments unconvincing. Success in witnessing is simply communicating Christ in the power of the Holy Spirit and leaving the results to God. Similarly, effectiveness in apologetics is presenting cogent and persuasive arguments for the Gospel in the power of the Holy Spirit, and leaving the results to God.

CHAPTER TWO

The Absurdity of Life Without God

O NE OF THE APOLOGETIC QUESTIONS that contemporary Christian theology must treat in its doctrine of man is what has been called "the human predicament," that is to say, the significance of human life in a post-theistic universe. Logically, this question ought, it seems to me, to be raised prior to and as a prelude to the question of God's existence.

HISTORICAL BACKGROUND

The apologetic for Christianity based on the human predicament is an extremely recent phenomenon, associated primarily with Francis Schaeffer. Often it is referred to as "cultural apologetics" because of its analysis of post-Christian culture. This approach constitutes an entirely different sort of apologetics than the traditional models, since it is not concerned with epistemological issues. Indeed, in a sense it does not even attempt to show in any positive sense that Christianity is true; it simply explores the disastrous consequences for human existence, society, and culture if Christianity should be false. In this respect, this approach is somewhat akin to existentialism: the precursors of this approach were also precursors of existentialism, and much of its analysis of the human predicament is drawn from the insights of twentieth-century atheistic existentialism.

BLAISE PASCAL

One of the earliest examples of a Christian apology appealing to the human predicament is the *Pensées* of the French mathematician and physicist Blaise Pascal (1623-62). Having come to a personal faith in Christ in 1654, Pascal had planned to write a defense of the Christian faith entitled *L'Apologie de la religion chrétienne*, but he died of a debilitating disease at the age of only 39 years, leaving behind hundreds of notes for the work, which were then published posthumously as the *Pensées*.[1]

Pascal's approach is thoroughly Christocentric. The Christian religion, he claims, teaches two truths: that there is a God whom men are capable of knowing, and that there is an element of corruption in men that renders them unworthy of God. Knowledge of God without knowledge of man's wretchedness begets pride, and knowledge of man's wretchedness without knowledge of God begets despair, but knowledge of Jesus Christ furnishes man knowledge of both simultaneously. Pascal invites us to look at the world from the Christian point of view and see if these truths are not confirmed. His *Apology* was evidently to comprise two divisions: in the first part he would display the misery of man without God (that man's nature is corrupt) and in the second part the happiness of man with God (that there is a Redeemer).[2] With regard to the latter, Pascal appeals to the evidences of miracle and especially fulfilled prophecy. In confirming the truth of man's wretchedness Pascal seeks to unfold the human predicament.

For Pascal the human condition is an enigma. For man is at the same time miserable and yet great. On the one hand, his misery is due principally to his uncertainty and insignificance. Writing in the tradition of the French skeptic Montaigne, Pascal repeatedly emphasizes the uncertainty of conclusions reached via reason and the senses. Apart from intuitive first principles, nothing seems capable of being known with certainty. In particular, reason and nature do not seem to furnish decisive evidence as to whether God exists or not. As man looks out around him, all he sees is darkness and obscurity. Moreover, insofar as his scientific knowledge is correct, man learns that he is an infinitesimal speck lost in the immensity of time and space. His brief life is bounded on either side by eternity, his place in the universe is lost in the immeasurable infinity of space, and he finds himself suspended, as it were, between the infinite microcosm within and the infinite macrocosm without. Uncertain and untethered, man flounders in his efforts to lead a meaningful and happy life. His condition is characterized by inconstancy, boredom, and anxiety. His relations with his fellow men are warped by self-love; society is founded on mutual deceit. Man's justice is fickle and relative, and no fixed standard of value may be found.

Despite their predicament, however, most people, incredibly, refuse to seek an answer or even to think about their dilemma. Instead, they lose themselves in escape. Listen to Pascal's description of the reasoning of such a person:

> I know not who sent me into the world, nor what the world is, nor what I myself am. I am terribly ignorant of everything. I know not what my body is, nor my senses, nor my soul and that part of me which thinks what I say, which reflects upon itself as well as upon all external things, and has no more knowledge of itself than of them.
>
> I see the terrifying immensity of the universe which surrounds me, and find myself limited to one corner of this vast expanse, without knowing why I am set down here rather than elsewhere, nor why the brief period appointed for my life is assigned to me at this moment rather than another in all the eternity that has gone before and will come after me. On all sides I behold nothing but infinity, in which I am a mere atom, a mere passing shadow that returns no more. All I know is that I must soon die, but what I understand least of all is this very death which I cannot escape.
>
> As I know not whence I come, so I know not whither I go. I only know that on leaving this world I fall for ever into nothingness or into the hands of a wrathful God, without knowing to which of these two states I shall be everlastingly consigned. Such is my condition, full of weakness and uncertainty. From all this I conclude that I ought to spend every day of my life without seeking to know my fate. I might perhaps be able to find a solution to my doubts; but I cannot be bothered to do so, I will not take one step towards its discovery.[3]

Pascal can only regard such indifference as insane. Man's condition ought to impel him to seek to discover whether there is a God and a solution to his predicament. But people occupy their time and their thoughts with trivialities and distractions, so as to avoid the despair, boredom, and anxiety that would inevitably result if those diversions were removed.

Such is the misery of man. But mention must also be made of the greatness of man. For although man is miserable, he is at least capable of *knowing* that he is miserable. The greatness of man consists in thought. Man is a mere reed, yes, but he is a *thinking* reed. The universe might crush him like a gnat; but even so, man is nobler than the universe because he *knows* that it crushes him, and the universe has no such knowledge. Man's whole dignity consists, therefore, in thought. "By space the universe encompasses and swallows me up like a mere speck; by thought I comprehend the universe." Man's greatness, then, lies not in his having the solution to his predicament, but in the fact that he alone in all the universe is aware of his wretched condition.

> What a chimaera then is man, what a novelty, what a monster, what chaos, what a subject of contradiction, what a prodigy! Judge of all things, yet an imbecile earthworm; depositary of truth, yet a sewer of uncertainty and error; pride and refuse of the universe. Who shall resolve this tangle?[4]

Pascal hopes that by explaining man's greatness as well as his misery, he might shake people out of their lethargy to think about their condition and to seek a solution.

Pascal's analysis of the human predicament leads up to his famous Wager argument, by means of which he hopes to tip the scales in favor of theism.[5] The founder of probability theory, Pascal argues that when the odds that God exists are even, then the prudent man will gamble that God exists. This is a wager that all men must make—the game is in progress and a bet must be laid. There is no option: you have already joined the game. Which then will you choose—that God exists or that he does not? Pascal argues that since the odds are even, reason is not violated in making either choice; therefore, reasons cannot determine which bet to make. Therefore, the choice should be made pragmatically in terms of maximizing one's happiness. If one wagers that God exists and he does, one has gained eternal life and infinite happiness. If he does not exist, one has lost nothing. On the other hand, if one wagers that God does not exist and he does, then one has suffered infinite loss. If he does not in fact exist, then one has gained nothing. Hence, the only prudent choice is to believe that God exists.

Now Pascal does believe that there is a way of "getting a look behind the scenes" to rationally determine how one should bet, namely, the proofs of Scripture of miracle and prophecy, which he discusses in the second half of his work. But for now, he wants to emphasize that even in the absence of such evidence, one still ought to believe in God. For given the human predicament of being cast into existence and facing either eternal annihilation or eternal wrath, the only reasonable course of action is to believe in God: "for if you win, you win all; if you lose, you lose nothing."[6]

FYODOR DOSTOYEVSKY

Another apologetic based on the human predicament may be found in the magnificent novels of the great Russian writer of the last century Fyodor Dostoyevsky (1821-81). (May I add that I think the obsession of contemporary evangelicals with the writings of authors like C. S. Lewis to the neglect of writers like Dostoyevsky is a great shame? Dostoyevsky is a far, far grander writer.) The problem that tortured Dostoyevsky was the problem of evil: How can a good and loving God exist when the world is filled with so much suffering and evil? Dostoyevsky presented this problem in his works so persuasively, so poignantly, that certain passages of his, notably "The Grand Inquisitor" section from his *Brothers Karamazov*, are often reprinted in anthologies as classic statements of the problem of evil. As a result, some people are under the impression that Dostoyevsky was himself an atheist and that the viewpoint of the Grand Inquisitor is his own.

Actually, he sought to carry through a two-pronged defense of theism in the face of the problem of evil. Positively, he argued that innocent suffering may perfect character and bring one into a closer relation with God. Negatively, he tried to show that if the existence of God is denied, then one is landed in complete moral relativism, so that no act, regardless of how dreadful or heinous, can be condemned by the atheist. To live consistently with such a view of life is unthinkable and impossible. Hence, atheism is destructive of life and ends logically in suicide.

Dostoyevsky recognizes that this constitutes no positive proof of Christianity. Indeed, he rejects that there could be such. Men demand of Christ that he furnish them "bread and circuses," but he refuses to do so. The decision to follow Christ must be made in loneliness and anxiety. Each person must face for himself the anguish of a world without God and in the solitude of his own heart give himself to God in faith.

SØREN KIERKEGAARD

The Danish existentialist of the late nineteenth century, Søren Kierkegaard (1813-55), also presents a sort of negative apologetic for the Christian faith. He thinks of life as being lived on three different planes or stages: the aesthetic stage, the ethical stage, and the religious stage. Man in the aesthetic stage lives life only on the sensual level, a life that is self- and pleasure-centered. This need not be a gross hedonism. Man on this level could be very cultivated and even circumspect; but nevertheless his life revolves around himself and those material things—whether sex, art, music, or whatever—that bring him pleasure. The paradox of life on this level is that it leads ultimately to unhappiness. The self-centered, aesthetic man finds no ultimate meaning in life and no true satisfaction. Thus, the aesthetic life leads finally to despair, a sort of sickness with life.

But this is not the end, for only at this point is a person ready to live on the second plane of existence, the ethical plane. The transition to the ethical stage of life is a sort of leap motivated by despair to a higher level, where one affirms trans-personal moral values and guides life by those objective standards. No longer is life lived only for self and for pleasure; rather one is constrained to seek the ethical good and to change one's conduct to bring it into conformity with that good. Thus, man in the ethical stage is the moral man. But life on this level, too, ends in unhappiness. For the more one tries sincerely to bring one's life into conformity with the objective standards of the good, the more painfully aware one is that one cannot do it. Thus, the ethical life, when earnestly pursued, leads ultimately to guilt and despair.

But there is one more stage along life's way: the religious stage. Here one finds forgiveness of sins and a personal relationship with God. Only here, in intimate communion with one's Creator, does man find authentic existence and true fulfillment. Again, Kierkegaard represents the transition to this stage from the ethical as a leap. The decision to believe is a criterionless choice, a leap of faith into the dark. Although man can be given no rational grounds to leap, unless he does so he will remain in despair and inauthentic existence.

FRANCIS SCHAEFFER

As I remarked earlier, Francis Schaeffer (1912-84) is the thinker responsible for drafting a Christian apologetic based on the so-called modern predicament. According to Schaeffer, there can be traced in recent Western culture a "line of despair," which penetrates philosophy, literature, and the arts in succession. He believes the root of the problem lies in Hegelian philosophy, specifically in its denial of absolute truths. Hegel developed the famous triad of thesis-antithesis-synthesis, in which contradictions are seen not as absolute opposites, but as partial truths, which are synthesized in the whole. Ultimately all is One, which is absolute and non-contradictory. In Schaeffer's view, Hegel's system undermined the notion of particular absolute truths (such as "That act is morally wrong" or "This painting is aesthetically ugly") by synthesizing them into the whole. This denial of absolutes has gradually made its way through Western culture. In each case, it results in despair, because without absolutes man's endeavors degenerate into absurdity. Schaeffer believes that the Theater of the Absurd, abstract modern art, and modern music such as is composed by John Cage are all indications of what happens below the line of despair. Only by reaffirming belief in the absolute God of Christianity can man and his culture avoid inevitable degeneracy, meaninglessness, and despair.

Schaeffer's efforts against abortion may be seen as a logical extension of this apologetic. Once God is denied, human life becomes worthless, and we see the fruit of such a philosophy in the abortion and infanticide now taking place. Schaeffer warns that unless Western man returns to the Christian world and life view, nothing will stop the trend from degenerating into population control and human breeding. Only a theistic world view can save the human race from itself.

ASSESSMENT

THE NECESSITY OF GOD AND IMMORTALITY

Man, writes Loren Eiseley, is the Cosmic Orphan. He is the only creature in the universe who asks, "Why?" Other animals have instincts to guide them, but man has learned to ask questions.

"Who am I?" man asks. "Why am I here? Where am I going?" Since the Enlightenment, when he threw off the shackles of religion, man has tried to answer these questions without reference to God. But the answers that came back were not exhilarating, but dark and terrible. "You are the accidental by-product of nature, a result of matter plus time plus chance. There is no reason for your existence. All you face is death."

Modern man thought that when he had gotten rid of God, he had freed himself from all that repressed and stifled him. Instead, he discovered that in killing God, he had also killed himself.

For if there is no God, then man's life becomes absurd.

If God does not exist, then both man and the universe are inevitably doomed to death. Man, like all biological organisms, must die. With no hope of immortality, man's life leads only to the grave. His life is but a spark in the infinite blackness, a spark that appears, flickers, and dies forever. Compared to the infinite stretch of time, the span of man's life is but an infinitesimal moment; and yet this is all the life he will ever know. Therefore, everyone must come face to face with what theologian Paul Tillich has called "the threat of non-being." For though I know now that I exist, that I am alive, I also know that someday I will no longer exist, that I will no longer be, that I will die. This thought is staggering and threatening: to think that the person I call "myself" will cease to exist, that I will be no more!

I remember vividly the first time my father told me that someday I would die. Somehow as a child the thought had just never occurred to me. When he told me, I was filled with fear and unbearable sadness. And though he tried repeatedly to reassure me that this was a long way off, that did not seem to matter. Whether sooner or later, the undeniable fact was that I would die and be no more, and the thought overwhelmed me. Eventually, like all of us, I grew to simply accept the fact. We all learn to live with the inevitable. But the child's insight remains true. As the French existentialist Jean-Paul Sartre observed, several hours or several years make no difference once you have lost eternity.

Whether it comes sooner or later, the prospect of death and the threat of non-being is a terrible horror. But I met a student once who did not feel this threat. He said he had been raised on the farm and was used to seeing the animals being born and dying. Death was for him simply natural—a part of life, so to speak. I was puzzled by how different our two perspectives on death were and found it difficult to understand why he did not feel the threat of non-being. Years later, I think I found my answer in reading Sartre. Sartre observed that death is not threatening so long as we view it as the death of the other, from a third-person standpoint, so to speak. It is only when we internalize it and look at it from the first-person perspective—"*my* death: *I* am going to die"—that the threat of non-being becomes real. As Sartre points out, many people never assume this first-person perspective in the midst of life; one can even look at one's own death from the third-person standpoint, as if it were the death of another or even of an animal, as did my friend. But the true existential significance of *my death* can only be appreciated from the first-person perspective, as I realize that I am going to die and forever cease to exist. My life is just a momentary transition out of oblivion into oblivion.

And the universe, too, faces death. Scientists tell us that the universe is expanding, and everything in it is growing farther and farther apart. As it does so, it grows colder and colder, and its energy is used up. Eventually all the stars will burn out and all matter will collapse into dead stars and black holes. There will be no light at all; there will be no heat; there will be no life; only the corpses of dead stars and galaxies, ever expanding into the endless darkness and the cold recesses of space—a universe in ruins. The entire universe marches irreversibly toward its grave. So not only is the life of each individual person doomed; the entire human race is doomed. The universe is plunging toward inevitable extinction—death is written throughout its structure. There is no escape. There is no hope.

THE ABSURDITY OF LIFE
WITHOUT GOD AND IMMORTALITY

If there is no God, then man and the universe are doomed. Like prisoners condemned to death, we await our unavoidable execution. There is no God, and there is no immortality. And what is the consequence of this? It means that life itself is absurd. It means that the life we have is without ultimate significance, value, or purpose. Let's look at each of these.

No Ultimate Meaning Without Immortality and God

If each individual person passes out of existence when he dies, then what ultimate meaning can be given to his life? Does it really matter whether he ever existed at all? It might be said that his life was important because it influenced others or affected the course of history. But this only shows a relative significance to his life, not an ultimate significance. His life may be important relative to certain other events, but what is the ultimate significance of any of those events? If all the events are meaningless, then what can be the ultimate meaning of influencing any of them? Ultimately it makes no difference.

Look at it from another perspective: Scientists say that the universe originated in an explosion called the "Big Bang" about 15 billion years ago. Suppose the Big Bang had never occurred. Suppose the universe had never existed. What ultimate difference would it make? The universe is doomed to die anyway. In the end it makes no difference whether the universe ever existed or not. Therefore, it is without ultimate significance.

The same is true of the human race. Mankind is a doomed race in a dying universe. Because the human race will eventually cease to exist, it makes no ultimate difference whether it ever did exist. Mankind is thus no more significant than a swarm of mosquitos or a barnyard of pigs, for their end is all the same. The same blind cosmic process that coughed them up in the first place will eventually swallow them all again.

And the same is true of each individual person. The contributions of the scientist to the advance of human knowledge, the researches of the doctor to alleviate pain and suffering, the efforts of the diplomat to secure peace in the world, the sacrifices of good men everywhere to better the lot of the human race—all these come to nothing. In the end they don't make one bit of difference, not one bit. Each person's life is therefore without ultimate significance. And because our lives are ultimately meaningless, the activities we fill our lives with are also meaningless. The long hours spent in study at the university, our jobs, our interests, our friendships—all these are, in the final analysis, utterly meaningless. This is the horror of modern man: because he ends in nothing, he is nothing.

But it is important to see that it is not just immortality that man needs if life is to be meaningful. Mere duration of existence does not make that existence meaningful. If man and the universe could exist forever, but if there were no God, their existence would still have no ultimate significance. To illustrate: I once read a science-fiction story in which an astronaut was marooned on a barren chunk of rock lost in outer space. He had with him two vials: one containing poison and the other a potion that would make him live forever. Realizing his predicament, he gulped down the poison. But then to his horror, he discovered he had swallowed the wrong vial—he had drunk the potion for immortality. And that meant that he was cursed to exist forever—a meaningless, unending life. Now if God does not exist, our lives are just like that. They could go on and on and still be utterly without meaning. We could still ask of life, "So what?" So it is not just immortality man needs if life is to be ultimately significant; he needs God and immortality. And if God does not exist, then he has neither.

Twentieth-century man came to understand this. Read *Waiting for Godot* by Samuel Beckett. During this entire play two men carry on trivial conversation while waiting for a third man to arrive, who never does. Our lives are like that, Beckett is saying; we just kill time waiting—for what, we don't know. In a tragic portrayal of man, Beckett wrote another play in which the curtain opens revealing a stage littered with junk. For thirty long seconds, the audience sits and stares in silence at that junk. Then the curtain closes. That's all.

One of the most devastating novels I've ever read was *Steppenwolf*, by Hermann Hesse. At the novel's end, Harry Haller stands looking at himself in a mirror. During the course of his life he had experienced all the world offers. And now he stands looking at himself, and he mutters, "Ah, the bitter taste of life!" He spits at himself in the looking-glass, and then he kicks it to pieces. His life has been futile and meaningless.

French existentialists Jean-Paul Sartre and Albert Camus understood this, too. Sartre portrayed life in his play *No Exit* as hell—the final line of the play are the words of resignation, "Well, let's get on with it." Hence, Sartre writes elsewhere of the "nausea" of existence. Camus, too, saw life as absurd. At the end of his brief novel *The Stranger*, Camus's hero discovers in a flash of insight that the universe has no meaning and there is no God to give it one. The French biochemist Jacques Monod seemed to echo those sentiments when he wrote in his work *Chance and Necessity*, "Man finally knows he is alone in the indifferent immensity of the universe."

Thus, if there is no God, then life itself becomes meaningless. Man and the universe are without ultimate significance.

No Ultimate Value Without Immortality and God

If life ends at the grave, then it makes no difference whether one has lived as a Stalin or as a saint. Since one's destiny is ultimately unrelated to one's behavior, you may as well just live as you please. As Dostoyevsky put it: "If there is no immortality then all things are permitted." On this basis, a writer like Ayn Rand is absolutely correct to praise the virtues of selfishness. Live totally for self; no one holds you accountable! Indeed, it would be foolish to do anything else, for life is too short to jeopardize it by acting out of anything but pure self-interest. Sacrifice for another person would be stupid. Kai Nielsen, an atheist philosopher who attempts to defend the viability of ethics without God, in the end admits,

> We have not been able to show that reason requires the moral point of view, or that all really rational persons, unhoodwinked by myth or ideology, need not be individual egoists or classical amoralists. Reason doesn't decide here. The picture I have painted for you is not a pleasant one. Reflection on it depresses me. . . . Pure practical reason, even with a good knowledge of the facts, will not take you to morality.[7]

But the problem becomes even worse. For, regardless of immortality, if there is no God, then there can be no objective standards of right and wrong. All we are confronted with is, in Jean-Paul Sartre's words, the bare, valueless fact of existence. Moral values are either just expressions of personal taste or the by-products of socio-biological evolution and conditioning. In the words of one humanist philosopher, "The moral principles that govern our behavior are rooted in habit and custom, feeling and fashion."[8] In a world without God, who is to say which values are right and which are wrong? Who is to judge that the values of Adolf Hitler are inferior to those of a saint? The concept of morality loses all meaning in a universe without God. As one contemporary atheistic ethicist points out, "to say that something is wrong because . . . it is forbidden by God, is . . . perfectly understandable to anyone who believes in a law-giving God. But to say that something is wrong . . . even though no God exists to forbid it, is *not* understandable. . . ." "The concept of moral obligation [is] unintelligible apart from the idea of God. The words remain but their meaning is gone."[9] In a world without God, there can be no objective right and wrong, only our culturally and personally relative, subjective judgments. This means that it is impossible to condemn war, oppression, or crime as evil. Nor can one praise brotherhood, equality, and love as good. For in a universe without God, good and evil do not exist—there is only the bare valueless fact of existence, and there is no one to say you are right and I am wrong.

No Ultimate Purpose Without Immortality and God

If death stands with open arms at the end of life's trail, then what is the goal of life? To what end has life been lived? Is it all for nothing? Is there no reason for life? And what of the universe? Is it utterly pointless? If its destiny is a cold grave in the recesses of outer space, the answer must be yes—it is pointless. There is no goal, no purpose, for the universe. The litter of a dead universe will just go on expanding and expanding—forever.

And what of man? Is there no purpose at all for the human race? Or will it simply peter out someday lost in the oblivion of an indifferent universe? The English writer H. G. Wells foresaw such a prospect. In his novel *The Time Machine* Wells's time traveler journeys far into the future to discover the destiny of man. All he finds is a dead earth, save for a few lichens and moss, orbiting a gigantic red sun. The only sounds are the rush of the wind and the gentle ripple of the sea. "Beyond these lifeless sounds," writes Wells, "the world was silent. Silent? It would be hard to convey the stillness of it. All the sounds of man, the bleating of sheep, the cries of birds, the hum of insects, the stir that makes the background of our lives—all that was over."[10] And so Wells's time traveler returned. But to what?—to merely an earlier point on the purposeless rush toward oblivion. When as a non-Christian I first read Wells's book, I thought, "No, no! It can't end that way!" But if there is no God, it will end that way, like it or not. This is reality in a universe without God: there is no hope; there is no purpose. It reminds me of T.S. Eliot's haunting lines:

> This is the way the world ends
> This is the way the world ends
> This is the way the world ends
> Not with a bang but a whimper.[11]

What is true of mankind as a whole is true of each of us individually: we are here to no purpose. If there is no God, then our life is not qualitatively different from that of a dog. I know that's harsh, but it's true. As the ancient writer of Ecclesiastes put it: "The fate of the sons of men and the fate of beasts is the same. As one dies so dies the other; indeed, they all have the same breath and there is no advantage for man over beast, for all is vanity. All go to the same place. All come from the dust and all return to the dust" (Eccles 3:19-20). In this book, which reads more like a piece of modern existentialist literature than a book of the Bible, the writer shows the futility of pleasure, wealth, education, political fame, and honor in a life doomed to end in death. His verdict? "Vanity of vanities! All is vanity" (1:2). If life ends at the grave, then we have no ultimate purpose for living.

But more than that: even if it did not end in death, without God life would still be without purpose. For man and the universe would then be simple accidents of chance, thrust into existence for no reason. Without God the universe is the result of a cosmic accident, a chance explosion. There is no reason for which it exists. As for man, he is a freak of nature— a blind product of matter plus time plus chance. Man is just a lump of slime that evolved into rationality. There is no more purpose in life for the human race than for a species of insect; for both are the result of the blind interaction of chance and necessity. As one philosopher has put it: "Human life is mounted upon a subhuman pedestal and must shift for itself alone in the heart of a silent and mindless universe."[12]

What is true of the universe and of the human race is also true of us as individuals. Insofar as we are individual human beings, we are the results of certain combinations of heredity and environment. We are victims of a kind of genetic and environmental roulette. Psychologists following Sigmund Freud tell us our actions are the result of various repressed sexual tendencies. Sociologists following B. F. Skinner argue that all our choices are determined by conditioning, so that freedom is an illusion. Biologists like Francis Crick regard man as an electro-chemical machine that can be controlled by altering its genetic code. If God does not exist, then you are just a miscarriage of nature, thrust into a purposeless universe to live a purposeless life.

So if God does not exist, that means that man and the universe exist to no purpose—since the end of everything is death—and that they came to be for no purpose, since they are only blind products of chance. In short, life is utterly without reason.

Do you understand the gravity of the alternatives before us? For if God exists, then there is hope for man. But if God does not exist, then all we are left with is despair. Do you understand why the question of God's existence is so vital to man? As one writer has aptly put it, "If God is dead, then man is dead, too."

Unfortunately, the mass of mankind do not realize this fact. They continue on as though nothing has changed. I'm reminded of Nietzsche's story of the madman who in the early morning hours burst into the marketplace, lantern in hand, crying, "I seek God! I seek God!" Since many of those standing about did not believe in God, he provoked much laughter. "Did God get lost?" they taunted him. "Or is he hiding? Or maybe he has gone on a voyage or emigrated!" Thus they yelled and laughed. Then, writes

Nietzsche, the madman turned in their midst and pierced them with his eyes.

> 'Whither is God?' he cried, 'I shall tell you. *We have killed him*—you and I. All of us are his murderers. But how have we done this? How were we able to drink up the sea? Who gave us the sponge to wipe away the entire horizon? What did we do when we unchained this earth from its sun? Whither is it moving now? Away from all suns? Are we not plunging continually? Backward, sideward, forward, in all directions? Is there any up or down left? Are we not straying as through an infinite nothing? Do we not feel the breath of empty space? Has it not become colder? Is not night and more night coming on all the while? Must not lanterns be lit in the morning? Do we not hear anything yet of the noise of the gravediggers who are burying God? . . . God is dead. . . . And we have killed him. How shall we, the murderers of all murderers, comfort ourselves?'[13]

The crowd stared at the madman in silence and astonishment. At last he dashed his lantern to the ground. "I have come too early," he said. "This tremendous event is still on its way—it has not yet reached the ears of man." Men did not yet truly comprehend the consequences of what they had done in killing God. But Nietzsche predicted that someday people would realize the implications of their atheism; and this realization would usher in an age of nihilism—the destruction of all meaning and value in life. The end of Christianity, wrote Nietzsche, means the advent of nihilism. This most gruesome of guests is standing already at the door. "Our whole European culture is moving for some time now," wrote Nietzsche, "with a tortured tension that is growing from decade to decade, as toward a catastrophe: restlessly, violently, headlong, like a river that wants to reach the end, that no longer reflects, that is afraid to reflect."[14]

Most people still do not reflect on the consequences of atheism and so, like the crowd in the marketplace, go unknowingly on their way. But when we realize, as did Nietzsche, what atheism implies, then his question presses hard upon us: how *shall* we, the murderers of all murderers, comfort ourselves?

THE PRACTICAL IMPOSSIBILITY OF ATHEISM

About the only solution the atheist can offer is that we face the absurdity of life and live bravely. Bertrand Russell, for example, wrote that we must build our lives upon "the firm foundation of unyielding despair."[15] Only by recognizing that the world really is a terrible place can we successfully come to terms with life. Camus said that we should honestly recognize life's absurdity and then live in love for one another.

The fundamental problem with this solution, however, is that it is impossible to live consistently and happily within such a world view. If one lives consistently, he will not be happy; if one lives happily, it is only because he is not consistent. Francis Schaeffer has explained this point well. Modern man, says Schaeffer, resides in a two-story universe. In the lower story is the finite world without God; here life is absurd, as we have seen. In the upper story are meaning, value, and purpose. Now modern man lives in the lower story because he believes there is no God. But he cannot live happily in such an absurd world; therefore, he continually makes leaps of faith into the upper story to affirm meaning, value, and purpose, even though he has no right to, since he does not believe in God. Modern man is totally inconsistent when he makes this leap, because these values cannot exist without God, and man in his lower story does not have God.

Let's look again, then, at each of the three areas in which we saw life was absurd without God, to show how man cannot live consistently and happily with his atheism.

Meaning of Life

First, the area of meaning. We saw that without God, life has no meaning. Yet philosophers continue to live as though life does have meaning. For example, Sartre argued that one may create meaning for his life by freely choosing to follow a certain course of action. Sartre himself chose Marxism.

Now this is utterly inconsistent. It is inconsistent to say life is objectively absurd and then to say one may create meaning for his life. If life is really absurd, then man is trapped in the lower story. To try to create meaning in life represents a leap to the upper story. But Sartre has no basis for this leap. Without God, there can be no objective meaning in life. Sartre's program is actually an exercise in self-delusion. For the universe does not really acquire meaning just because *I* give it one. This is easy to see: for suppose I give the universe one meaning, and you give it another. Who is right? The answer, of course, is neither one. For the universe without God remains objectively meaningless, no matter how *we* regard it. Sartre is really saying, "Let's *pretend* the universe has meaning." And this is just fooling ourselves.

The point is this: if God does not exist, then life is objectively meaningless; but man cannot live consistently and happily knowing that life is meaningless; so in order to be happy he pretends life has meaning. But this is, of course, entirely inconsistent—for without God, man and the universe are without any real significance.

Value of Life

Turn now to the problem of value. Here is where the most blatant inconsistencies occur. First of all, atheistic humanists are totally inconsistent in affirming the traditional values of love and brotherhood. Camus has been rightly criticized for inconsistently holding both to the absurdity of life and the ethics of human love and brotherhood. The two are logically incompatible. Bertrand Russell, too, was inconsistent. For though he was an atheist, he was an outspoken social critic, denouncing war and restrictions on sexual freedom. Russell admitted that he could not live as though ethical values were simply a matter of personal taste, and that he therefore found his own views "incredible." "I do not know the solution," he confessed.[16] The point is that if there is no God, then objective right and wrong cannot exist. As Dostoyevsky said, "All things are permitted."

But Dostoyevsky also showed that man cannot live this way. He cannot live as though it is perfectly all right for soldiers to slaughter innocent children. He cannot live as though it is all right for dictatorial regimes to follow a systematic program of physical torture of political prisoners. He cannot live as though it is all right for dictators like Pol Pot to exterminate millions of their own countrymen. Everything in him cries out to say these acts are wrong—really wrong. But if there is no God, he cannot. So he makes a leap of faith and affirms values anyway. And when he does so, he reveals the inadequacy of a world without God.

The horror of a world devoid of value was brought home to me with new intensity a few years ago as I viewed a BBC television documentary called "The Gathering." It concerned the reunion of survivors of the Holocaust in Jerusalem, where they rediscovered lost friendships and shared their experiences. Now, I had heard stories of the Holocaust before and had even visited Dachau and Buchenwald, and I thought I was beyond shocking by further tales of horror. But I found that I was not. Perhaps I had been made more sensitive by the recent birth of our beautiful baby girl, so that I applied the situations to her as they were related on the television. In any case, one woman prisoner, a nurse, told of how she was made the gynecologist at Auschwitz. She observed that pregnant women were grouped together by the soldiers under the direction of Dr. Mengele and housed in the same barracks. Some time passed, and she noted that she no longer saw any of these women. She made inquiries. "Where are the pregnant women who were housed in that barracks?" "Haven't you heard?" came the reply. "*Dr. Mengele used them for vivisection.*"

Another woman told of how Mengele had bound up her breasts so that she could not suckle her infant. The doctor wanted to learn how long an infant could survive without nourishment. Desperately this poor woman tried to keep her baby alive by giving it pieces of bread soaked in coffee, but to no avail. Each day the baby lost weight, a fact that was eagerly monitored by Dr. Mengele. A nurse then came secretly to this woman and told her, "I have arranged a way for you to get out of here, but you cannot take your baby with you. I have brought a morphine injection that you can give to your child to end its life." When the woman protested, the nurse was insistent: "Look, your baby is going to die anyway. At least save yourself." And so *this mother took the life of her own baby*. Dr. Mengele was furious when he learned of it because he had lost his experimental specimen, and he searched among the dead to find the baby's discarded corpse so that he could have one last weighing.

My heart was torn by these stories. One rabbi who survived the camp summed it up well when he said that at Auschwitz it was as though there existed a world in which all the Ten Commandments were reversed. Mankind had never seen such a hell.

And yet, if God does not exist, then in a sense, our world *is* Auschwitz: there is no absolute right and wrong; *all things* are permitted. But no atheist, no agnostic, can live consistently with such a view. Nietzsche himself, who proclaimed the necessity of living "beyond good and evil," broke with his mentor Richard Wagner precisely over the issue of the composer's anti-Semitism and strident German nationalism. Similarly Sartre, writing in the aftermath of the Second World War, condemned anti-Semitism, declaring that a doctrine that leads to extermination is not merely an opinion or matter of personal taste, of equal value with its opposite.[17] In his important essay "Existentialism Is a Humanism," Sartre struggles vainly to elude the contradiction between his denial of divinely pre-established values and his urgent desire to affirm the value of human persons. Like Russell, he could not live with the implications of his own denial of ethical absolutes.

A second problem is that if God does not exist and there is no immortality, then all the evil acts of men go unpunished and all the sacrifices of good men go unrewarded. But who can live with such a view? Richard Wurmbrand, who has been tortured for his faith in communist prisons, says,

> The cruelty of atheism is hard to believe when man has no faith in the reward of good or the punishment of evil. There is no reason to be human. There is no restraint from the depths of evil which is in

man. The communist torturers often said, 'There is no God, no Hereafter, no punishment for evil. We can do what we wish.' I have heard one torturer even say, 'I thank God, in whom I don't believe, that I have lived to this hour when I can express all the evil in my heart.' He expressed it in unbelievable brutality and torture inflicted on prisoners.[18]

The English theologian Cardinal Newman once said that if he believed that all evils and injustices of life throughout history were not to be made right by God in the afterlife, "Why I think I should go mad." Rightly so.

And the same applies to acts of self-sacrifice. A number of years ago, a terrible mid-winter air disaster occurred in which a plane leaving the Washington, D.C. airport smashed into a bridge spanning the Potomac River, plunging its passengers into the icy waters. As the rescue helicopters came, attention was focused on one man who again and again pushed the dangling rope ladder to other passengers rather than be pulled to safety himself. Six times he passed the ladder by. When they came again, he was gone. He had freely given his life that others might live. The whole nation turned its eyes to this man in respect and admiration for the selfless and good act he had performed. And yet, if the atheist is right, that man was not noble—he did the stupidest thing possible. He should have gone for the ladder first, pushed others away if necessary in order to survive. But to die for others he did not even know, to give up all the brief existence he would ever have—what for? For the atheist there can be no reason. And yet the atheist, like the rest of us, instinctively reacts with praise for this man's selfless action. Indeed, one will probably never find an atheist who lives consistently with his system. For a universe without moral account-ability and devoid of value is unimaginably terrible.

Purpose of Life

Finally, let's look at the problem of purpose in life. The only way most people who deny purpose in life live happily is either by making up some purpose, which amounts to self-delusion as we saw with Sartre, or by not carrying their view to its logical conclusions. Take the problem of death, for example. According to Ernst Bloch, the only way modern man lives in the face of death is by subconsciously borrowing the belief in immortality that his forefathers held to, even though he himself has no basis for this belief, since he does not believe in God. Bloch states that the belief that life ends in nothing is hardly, in his words, "sufficient to keep the head high and to work as if there were no end." By borrowing the remnants of a belief in immortality, writes Bloch, "modern man does not feel the chasm that unceasingly surrounds him and that will certainly engulf him at last. Through these remnants, he saves his sense of self-identity. Through them the impression arises that man is not perishing, but only that one day the world has the whim no longer to appear to him." Bloch concludes, "This quite shallow courage feasts on a borrowed credit card. It lives from earlier hopes and the support that they once had provided."[19] Modern man no longer has any right to that support, since he rejects God. But in order to live purposefully, he makes a leap of faith to affirm a reason for living.

We often find the same inconsistency among those who say that man and the universe came to exist for no reason or purpose, but just by chance. Unable to live in an impersonal universe in which everything is the product of blind chance, these persons begin to ascribe personality and motives to the physical processes themselves. It is a bizarre way of speaking and represents a leap from the lower to the upper story. For example, the brilliant Russian physicists Zeldovich and Novikov, in contemplating the properties of the universe, ask, Why did "Nature" choose to create this sort of universe instead of another? "Nature" has obviously become a sort of God-substitute, filling the role and function of God. Francis Crick halfway through his book *The Origin of the Genetic Code* begins to spell nature with a capital "N" and elsewhere speaks of natural selection as being "clever" and as "thinking" of what it will do. Fred Hoyle, the English astronomer, attributes to the universe itself the qualities of God. For Carl Sagan the "Cosmos," which he always spells with a capital letter, obviously fills the role of a God-substitute. Though all these men profess not to believe in God, they smuggle in a God-substitute through the back door because they cannot bear to live in a universe in which everything is the chance result of impersonal forces.

And it's interesting to see many thinkers betray their views when they're pushed to their logical conclusions. For example, certain feminists have raised a storm of protest over Freudian sexual psychology because it is chauvinistic and degrading to women. And some psychologists have knuckled under and revised their theories. Now this is totally inconsistent. If Freudian psychology is really true, then it doesn't matter if it's degrading to women. You can't change the truth because you don't like what it leads to. But people cannot live consistently and happily in a world where other persons are devalued. Yet if God does not exist, then nobody has any value. Only if God exists can a person consistently support women's rights. For if God does not exist, then natural selection dictates that the male of the species is the dominant and aggressive one. Women would no more have rights than a female goat or chicken have rights. In nature whatever is, is right. But who can live with such a view? Apparently not even

Freudian psychologists, who betray their theories when pushed to their logical conclusions.

Or take the sociological behaviorism of a man like B. F. Skinner. This view leads to the sort of society envisioned in George Orwell's *1984*, where the government controls and programs the thoughts of everybody. If Pavlov's dog can be made to salivate when a bell rings, so can a human being. If Skinner's theories are right, then there can be no objection to treating people like the rats in Skinner's rat-box as they run through their mazes, coaxed on by food and electric shocks. According to Skinner, all our actions are determined anyway. And if God does not exist, then no moral objection can be raised against this kind of programming, for man is not qualitatively different from a rat, since both are just matter plus time plus chance. But again, who can live with such a dehumanizing view?

Or finally, take the biological determinism of a man like Francis Crick. The logical conclusion is that man is like any other laboratory specimen. The world was horrified when it learned that at camps like Dachau the Nazis had used prisoners for medical experiments on living humans. But why not? If God does not exist, there can be no objection to using people as human guinea pigs. A memorial at Dachau says *Nie Wieder*—"Never Again"—but this sort of thing is still going on. It was revealed a few years ago that in the United States several people had been injected, unknown to them, with a sterilization drug by medical researchers. Must we not protest that this is wrong—that man is more than an electro-chemical machine? The end of this view is population control in which the weak and unwanted are killed off to make room for the strong. But the only way we can consistently protest this view is if God exists. Only if God exists can there be purpose in life.

The dilemma of modern man is thus truly terrible. And insofar as he denies the existence of God and the objectivity of value and purpose, this dilemma remains unrelieved for "post-modern" man as well. Indeed, it is precisely the awareness that modernism issues inevitably in absurdity and despair that constitutes the anguish of post-modernism. In some respects, post-modernism just *is* the awareness of the bankruptcy of modernity. The atheistic world view is insufficient to maintain a happy and consistent life. Man cannot live consistently and happily as though life were ultimately without meaning, value, or purpose. If we try to live consistently within the atheistic world view, we shall find ourselves profoundly unhappy. If instead we manage to live happily, it is only by giving the lie to our world view.

Confronted with this dilemma, man flounders pathetically for some means of escape. In a remarkable address to the American Academy for the Advancement of Science in 1991, Dr. L. D. Rue, confronted with the predicament of modern man, boldly advocated that we deceive ourselves by means of some "Noble Lie" into thinking that we and the universe still have value.[20] Claiming that "The lesson of the past two centuries is that intellectual and moral relativism is profoundly the case," Dr. Rue muses that the consequence of such a realization is that one's quest for personal wholeness (or self-fulfillment) and the quest for social coherence become independent from one another. This is because on the view of relativism the search for self-fulfillment becomes radically privatized: each person chooses his own set of values and meaning. "There is no final, objective reading on the world or the self. There is no universal vocabulary for integrating cosmology and morality." If we are to avoid "the madhouse option," where self-fulfillment is pursued regardless of social coherence, and "the totalitarian option," where social coherence is imposed at the expense of personal wholeness, then we have no choice but to embrace some Noble Lie that will inspire us to live beyond selfish interests and so achieve social coherence. A Noble Lie "is one that deceives us, tricks us, compels us beyond self-interest, beyond ego, beyond family, nation, [and] race." It is a lie, because it tells us that the universe is infused with value (which is a great fiction), because it makes a claim to universal truth (when there is none), and because it tells me not to live for self-interest (which is evidently false). "But without such lies, we cannot live."

This is the dreadful verdict pronounced over modern man. In order to survive, he must live in self-deception. But even the Noble Lie option is in the end unworkable. For if what I have said thus far is correct, belief in a Noble Lie would not only be necessary to achieve social coherence and personal wholeness for the masses, but it would also be necessary to achieve one's *own* personal wholeness. For one cannot live happily and consistently on an atheistic world view. In order to be happy, one must believe in objective meaning, value, and purpose. But how can one believe in those Noble Lies while at the same time believing in atheism and relativism? The more convinced you are of the necessity of a Noble Lie, the less you are able to believe in it. Like a placebo, a Noble Lie works only on those who believe it is the truth. Once we have seen through the fiction, then the Lie has lost its power over us. Thus, ironically, the Noble Lie cannot solve the human predicament for anyone who has come to see that predicament.

The Noble Lie option therefore leads at best to a society in which an elitist group of *illuminati* deceive the masses for their own good by perpetuating the Noble Lie. But then why should those of us who are enlightened follow the masses in their deception? Why should we sacrifice self-interest for a fiction? If the great lesson of the past two centuries is moral and intellectual relativism, then why (if we could) pretend that we do not know this truth and live a lie instead? If one answers, "for the sake of social coherence," one may legitimately ask why I should sacrifice my self-interest for the sake of social coherence? The only answer the relativist can give is that social coherence is in my self-interest—but the problem with this answer is that self-interest and the interest of the herd do not always coincide. Besides, if (out of self-interest) I do care about social coherence, the totalitarian option is always open to me: forget the Noble Lie and maintain social coherence (as well as my self-fulfillment) at the expense of the personal wholeness of the masses. Generations of Soviet leaders who extolled proletarian virtues while they rode in limousines and dined on caviar in their country *dachas* found this alternative quite workable. Rue would undoubtedly regard such an option as repugnant. But therein lies the rub. Rue's dilemma is that he obviously values deeply both social coherence and personal wholeness for their own sakes; in other words, they are objective values, which according to his philosophy do not exist. He has already leapt to the upper story. The Noble Lie option thus affirms what it denies and so refutes itself.

THE SUCCESS OF BIBLICAL CHRISTIANITY

But if atheism fails in this regard, what about biblical Christianity? According to the Christian world view, God does exist, and man's life does not end at the grave. In the resurrection body man may enjoy eternal life and fellowship with God. Biblical Christianity therefore provides the two conditions necessary for a meaningful, valuable, and purposeful life for man: God and immortality. Because of this, we can live consistently and happily. Thus, biblical Christianity succeeds precisely where atheism breaks down.

CONCLUSION

Now I want to make it clear that I have not yet shown biblical Christianity to be true. But what I have done is clearly spell out the alternatives. If God does not exist, then life is futile. If the God of the Bible does exist, then life is meaningful. Only the second of these two alternatives enables us to live happily and consistently. Therefore, it seems to me that even if the evidence for these two options were absolutely equal, a rational person ought to choose biblical Christianity. It seems to me positively irrational to prefer death, futility, and destruction to life, meaningfulness, and happiness. As Pascal said, we have nothing to lose and infinity to gain.

PRACTICAL APPLICATION

The foregoing discussion makes clear the role I conceive cultural apologetics to play: it is not one's whole apologetic but rather an introduction to positive argumentation. It serves to lay out in a dramatic way the alternatives facing the unbeliever in order to create a felt need in him. When he realizes the predicament he is in, he will see why the gospel is so important to him; and many a non-Christian will be impelled by these considerations alone to give his life to Christ.

In sharing this material with an unbeliever, we need to push him to the logical conclusions of his position. If I am right, no atheist or agnostic really lives consistently with his world view. In some way he affirms meaning, value, or purpose without an adequate basis. It is our job to discover those areas and lovingly show him where those beliefs are groundless. We need not attack his values themselves—for they are probably largely correct—but we may agree with him concerning them, and then point out only that he lacks any foundation for those values, whereas the Christian has such a foundation. Thus, we need not make him defensive by a frontal attack on his personal values; rather we offer him a foundation for the values he already possesses.

I have found the material on the absence of objective moral value in an atheistic world view to be an especially powerful apologetic to university students. Although students may give lip-service to relativism, my experience is that 95% can be very quickly convinced that objective moral values do exist after all. All you have to do is produce a few illustrations and let them decide for themselves. Ask what they think of the Hindu practice of *suttee* (burning widows alive on the funeral pyres of their husbands) or the ancient Chinese custom of crippling women for life by tightly binding their feet from childhood to resemble lotus-blossoms. Point out that without God to provide a trans-cultural basis for moral values, we're left with socio-cultural relativism, so that such practices are morally unobjectionable—which scarcely anyone can sincerely accept.

Of course, sometimes you find some hard-liners, but usually their position is seen to be so extreme that others are repulsed by it. For example, at a recent meeting of the Society of Biblical Literature, I attended a panel discussion on "Biblical Authority and Homosexuality," in which all the panelists endorsed the legitimacy of homosexual activity. One panelist dismissed scriptural prohibitions against such activity on the grounds that they reflect the cultural milieu in which they were written. Since this is the case for all of Scripture's commands (it wasn't written in a vacuum), he concluded that "there are no timeless, normative, moral truths in Scripture."

In discussion from the floor, I pointed out that such a view leads to socio-cultural relativism, which makes it impossible to criticize *any* society's moral values, including those of a society which persecutes homosexuals. He responded with a fog of theological double-talk and claimed that there's no place outside Scripture where we can find timeless moral values either. "But that just *is* what we mean by moral relativism," I said. "In fact, on your view there's no content to the notion of the goodness of God. He might as well be dead. And Nietzsche recognized that the death of God leads to nihilism." At this point another panelist came in with that knock-down refutation: "Well, if you're going to get pejorative, we might as well not discuss it."

I sat down, but the point wasn't lost on the audience. The next man who stood up said, "Wait a minute. I'm rather confused. I'm a pastor and peo-ple are always coming to me, asking if something they have done is wrong and if they need forgiveness. For example, isn't it always wrong to abuse a child?" I couldn't believe the panelist's response. She replied: "What counts as abuse differs from society to society, so we can't really use the word 'abuse' without tying it to a historical context." "Call it whatever you like," the pastor insisted, "but child abuse is damaging to children. Isn't it wrong to damage children?" And still she wouldn't admit it! This sort of hardness of heart ultimately backfires on the moral relativist and exposes in the minds of most people the bankruptcy of such a world view.

In sharing this material with unbelievers, it's important also to ask our-selves exactly what part of our case his objections are meant to refute. Thus, if he says that values are merely social conventions pragmatically adopted to ensure mutual survival, what does this purport to refute? Not that life without God really is without value, for this the objection admits. Therefore, it would be a mistake to react by arguing that values are not social conventions but are grounded in God. Rather the objection is really aimed at the claim that one cannot live as though values do not exist; it holds that one may live by social conventions alone.

Seen in this light, however, the objection is entirely implausible, for we have argued precisely that man cannot live as though morality were merely a matter of social convention. We believe certain acts to be genuinely wrong or right. Therefore, one ought to respond to the unbeliever on this score by saying, "You're exactly right: if God does not exist, then values are merely social conventions. But the point I'm trying to make is that it is impossible to live consistently and happily with such a world view." Push him on the Holocaust or some issue of popular concern like ethnic cleans-ing, apartheid, or child abuse. Bring it home to him personally and if he's honest and you are not threatening, I think he will admit that he does hold to some absolutes. Thus, it's very important to analyze exactly what the unbeliever's objection actually attacks before we answer.

I believe that this mode of apologetics can be very effective in helping to bring people to Christ because it does not concern neutral matters but cuts to the heart of the unbeliever's own existential situation. I remember that once, when I was delivering a series of talks at the University of Birmingham in England, the audience the first night was very hostile and aggressive. The second night I spoke on the absurdity of life without God. This time the largely same audience was utterly subdued: the lions had turned to lambs, and now their questions were no longer attacking but sincere and searching. The remarkable transformation was due to the fact that the message had penetrated their intellectual facade and struck at the core of their existence. I would encourage you to employ this material in evangelistic dorm meetings and fraternity/sorority meetings, where you can compel people to really *think* about the desperate human predicament in which we all find ourselves.

CHAPTER THREE

The Existence of God

W E'VE SEEN THAT ONLY IF GOD EXISTS can there be hope for a solution to the human predicament. Therefore, the question of the existence of God is vital for us today. Now most people would probably agree that this question does have great existential significance, but at the same time deny that it is a question to which rational argumentation is relevant. Most people would say that it's impossible to "prove" the existence of God and that therefore, if one is going to believe in God, he must "take it by faith" that God exists. I've heard many students say this as an excuse for not believing in God. "Nobody can prove that God exists and nobody can prove that he doesn't," they say with a smile, "so I just don't believe in him." I've already argued that such a blithe attitude fails to appreciate the depth of man's existential predicament in a universe without God. The rational man ought to believe in God even when the evidence is equally balanced, rather than the reverse.

But is it in fact the case that there is no probatory evidence that a Supreme Being exists? This was not the opinion of the biblical writers. The Psalmist said, "The heavens are telling of the glory of God; and their expanse is declaring the work of his hands" (Ps 19:1), and the apostle Paul declared, "Since the creation of the world His invisible attributes, His eternal power and divine nature, have been clearly seen, being understood through what has been made, so that they [men] are without excuse" (Rom 1:20). Nor can it be said that this evidence is so ambiguous as to admit of equally plausible counter-explanations—for then people would not be "without excuse." Thus, people are without excuse for not believing in God's existence, not only because of the internal testimony of the Holy Spirit, but also because of the external witness of nature. I think that there are good reasons for believing that God exists. Accordingly, we shall in this chapter examine various arguments for the existence of God.

This question is extremely important at the present juncture in history. Atheism and agnosticism are widespread in Europe and have become influential in the United States as well, particularly in the universities. Most philosophers would probably adhere to one of those world views. Humanism has become remarkably aggressive in the United States, with an almost evangelical fervor. I'm not talking about low-brow atheists like Madeleine Murray OHair, but sophisticated and intelligent humanists who are opposing theism and Christianity with rational argument. Not only do they publish several magazines in the tradition of free thought, such as *The Humanist* or *The Sceptical Inquirer*, but they have founded a publishing house, appropriately called Prometheus Books, which disseminates anti-theistic literature and has large displays at all major philosophical conventions. They publish both anti-theistic books, which serve to undermine belief in God, and ethics books which aim to undercut absolutist morality. I was saddened to see that they even publish a child's primer aimed at destroying or insulating the child against belief in God. How it broke my heart to watch one woman purchase that book at a philosophical convention to take home, no doubt, to her children! Their approach is rationally argumentative. As Christians, we simply cannot afford to stand by, exhorting people to believe in God, without dealing with the problem on the rational level.

Rational argumentation will not, of course, save people, but as J. G. Machen observed, it serves to provide an intellectual, cultural context in which the gospel cannot be dismissed simply as a logical absurdity and is therefore given an honest chance to be heard.[1] There are signs that point in the direction of such a reshaping of our intellectual milieu. For example, not too long ago *Time* carried a lengthy article on the renewed interest among philosophers in all the traditional arguments for God's existence.[2] There is an ongoing revolution in Anglo-American philosophy which has so transformed the philosophical landscape that today some of the United States' most esteemed philosophers are outspoken Christians and are bringing their faith to bear on their philosophical work. This is an encouraging sign that the question of God's existence will not be abandoned to the fideists and the atheists.

HISTORICAL BACKGROUND

Ever since Plato, philosophers and theologians have tried to provide a rational basis for belief in God. In this section, we shall briefly survey some of the traditional theistic arguments as developed by various thinkers.

ONTOLOGICAL ARGUMENT

The ontological argument attempts to prove from the very concept of God that God exists: if God is conceivable, then he must actually exist. This argument was formulated by Anselm and defended by Scotus, Descartes, Spinoza, Leibniz, and, in modern times, Norman Malcolm, Charles Hartshorne, and Alvin Plantinga, among others. We shall examine the Anselmian argument.

Anselm (1033-1109) wanted to find a single argument that would prove not only that God exists, but also that he has all the superlative attributes Christian doctrine ascribes to him. Having almost given up the project, Anselm landed upon the following reasoning:[3] God is the greatest conceivable being. This is true by definition, for if we could conceive of something greater than God, then *that* would be God. So nothing greater than God can be conceived. It is greater to exist in reality than merely in the mind. Anselm gives the example of a painting. Which is greater, the artist's idea of the painting or the painting itself as it really exists? Obviously the latter; for the painting itself exists not only in the artist's mind, but in reality as well. Similarly, if God existed only in the mind, then something greater than him could be conceived, namely, his existing not only in the mind, but in reality as well. But God is the greatest conceivable being. Hence, he must exist not merely in the mind, but in reality as well. Therefore, God exists.

Another way of putting this, says Anselm, is the following: a being whose non-existence is inconceivable is greater than a being whose non-existence is conceivable. But God is the greatest conceivable being. Therefore, God's non-existence must be inconceivable. There is no contradiction involved in this notion. Therefore, God must exist.

This deceptively simple argument is still hotly debated today.

COSMOLOGICAL ARGUMENT

In contrast to the ontological argument, the cosmological argument assumes that something exists and argues from the existence of that thing to the existence of a First Cause or a Sufficient Reason of the cosmos. This argument has its roots in Plato and Aristotle and was developed by medieval Islamic, Jewish, and Christian thinkers. It has been defended by such great minds as Plato, Aristotle, ibn Sīna, al-Ghāzali, ibn Rushd, Maimonides, Anselm, Aquinas, Scotus, Descartes, Spinoza, Berkeley, Locke, and Leibniz. The cosmological argument is really a family of different proofs, which can be conveniently grouped under three main types.

Al-Ghāzalī

The *kalam* cosmological argument originated in the attempts of Christian thinkers to rebut Aristotle's doctrine of the eternity of the universe and was developed by medieval Islamic theologians into an argument for the existence of God. Let's look at the formulation of this argument by al-Ghāzalī (1058-1111). He reasons, "Every being which begins has a cause for its beginning; now the world is a being which begins; therefore, it possesses a cause for its beginning."[4] In support of the first premise, that every being that begins has a cause for its beginning, Ghāzalī reasons: anything that begins to exist does so at a certain moment of time. But since, prior to the thing's existence, all moments are alike, there must be some cause that determines that the thing comes to exist at that moment rather than earlier or later. Thus, anything that comes to exist must have a cause.

The second premise is that the world, or the universe, began to exist. In support of this premise Ghāzalī argues that it is impossible that there should be an infinite regress of events in time, that is to say, that the series of past events should be beginningless. He gives several reasons for this conclusion. For one thing, the series of past events comes to an end in the present—but the infinite cannot come to an end. It might be pointed out that even though the series of events has one end in the present, it can still be infinite in the other direction because it has no beginning. But Ghāzalī's point may be that if the series is infinite going back into the past, then how could the present moment arrive? For it is impossible to cross the infinite to get to today. So today could never arrive, which is absurd, for here we are!

Second, if the number of past events were infinite, that would lead to infinites of different sizes. For suppose Jupiter completes an orbit once every twelve years and Saturn once every thirty years and the sphere of the stars once every thirty-six thousand years. If the universe is eternal and these planets have been orbiting from eternity, then each of these bodies has completed an infinite number of orbits, and yet one will have completed twice as many or thousands of times as many orbits as another, which is absurd.

Finally, if we take the orbits completed by just one of these planets, we may ask, is the number of orbits it has completed odd or even? It would have to be one or the other, and yet it is absurd to say the infinite is odd or even. For these reasons, the universe must have had a beginning, and it must have a cause of its beginning, which Ghāzalī identifies with God, the Eternal.

Thomas Aquinas

The Thomist cosmological argument is based on the impossibility of an infinite regress of simultaneously operating causes. It seeks a Cause that is

First, not in the temporal sense, but in the sense of rank or source. Although Thomas Aquinas (1225-74) did not originate this line of reasoning, he is famous for his clear summary of it in his Five Ways of proving that God exists.[5] We'll look at his first three ways, which are different versions of the argument for a First Cause.

The First Way is his proof for an Unmoved Mover based on motion. We see in the world that things are in motion. But anything that is in motion is being moved by something else. For a thing that has the potential to move cannot actualize its own potential; some other thing must cause it to move. But this other thing is also being moved by something else, and that is also being moved by something else, and so on. Now this series of things being moved by other things cannot go on to infinity. For in such a series, the intermediate causes have no power of their own but are mere instruments of a first cause.

It is important to keep in mind that Aquinas is thinking here of causes that all act simultaneously like the gears of a machine, not successively like falling dominoes. So if you take away the first cause, all you have left are the powerless instrumental causes. It does not matter if you have an infinity of such causes; they still could not cause anything. Aquinas contends, in effect, that a watch could not run without a spring even if it had an infinite number of gears, or that a train could not move without an engine even if it had an infinite number of box cars. There must be a first cause of motion in every causal series. For all self-moving things—including humans, animals, and plants—this would be the individual soul, which is an unmoved mover. But souls themselves come to be and pass away and thus cannot account for the eternal motion of the heavenly spheres. In order to account for this cosmic motion, we must postulate an absolutely Unmoved Mover, the First Cause of all motion, and this is God.

The Second Way attempts to prove the existence of a First Cause of existence based on causation in the world. We observe that causes are ordered in series. Now nothing can be self-caused, because then it would have to bestow existence on itself, which is impossible. Everything that is caused is therefore caused by something else. Aquinas thinks here of the same sort of simultaneous causal series as he did in the First Way, except that here the causes are of existence, not motion. The existence of any object depends on a whole array of contemporary causes, of which each in turn depends on other causes, and so forth. But such a causal series cannot go on to infinity for the same reason I explained above. Therefore, there must be a First Cause of the existence of everything else, which is simply uncaused; and this everyone calls "God."

The Third Way is the proof for an Absolutely Necessary Being based

on the existence of possible beings. We see in the world beings whose existence is not necessary but only possible. That is to say, these beings do not
have to exist, for we see them come to be and pass away. If they were necessary, they would always exist. But all beings cannot be merely possible
beings, for if everything were merely possible, then at some point in time
everything would cease to exist. Aquinas here presupposes the past eternity of the world and appears to reason that in infinite time all possibilities would be realized. Hence, if every being, including matter itself, were
only a possible being, then it is possible that nothing would exist. Thus,
given infinite past time, this possibility would be realized and nothing
would exist. But then nothing would now exist either, since out of nothing, nothing comes. Since this is obviously absurd, not all beings must be
possible beings. Some being or beings must be necessary. In fact, Aquinas
believed that there were many necessary beings: the heavenly bodies,
angels, even matter itself.

Now he continues, where do these necessary beings get their necessity—
from themselves or from another? Thomas here distinguishes between a
thing's essence and existence. A thing's essence is its nature, that set of
properties which it must possess in order to be what it is. For example, the
essence of man is "rational animality." If anything lacked either of these
properties, it would not be a man. A thing's existence, on the other hand,
is its being. Now if a being is not necessary in itself, this means that its
essence is distinct from its existence. It does not belong to its nature to
exist. For example, I could think of the nature of an angel without ever
knowing whether or not an angel actually exists. Its essence is distinct from
its existence. Hence, if such a being is to exist, something else must conjoin to its essence an act of existence. Then it would exist. But there cannot be an infinite regress of necessary beings that get their existence from
another. (The reasoning is the same as that in the First Way against an infinite regress.) So there must be a First Being, which is absolutely necessary
in itself. In this Being, essence and existence are not distinct; in some mysterious way its nature is existence. Hence, according to Aquinas, God is
Being itself subsisting (*ipsum esse subsistens*). God is pure Being and is the
source of being to everything else, whose essences do not involve their
existing.

G. W. F. Leibniz

The Leibnizian cosmological argument was developed by the German
mathematician and philosopher G. W. F. Leibniz (1646-1716) and is
often confused with the Thomist cosmological argument. But Leibniz
does not argue for the existence of an Uncaused Cause, but for the exis-

tence of a Sufficient Reason for the universe.[6] The difference will become clear as we proceed.

"The first question which should rightly be asked," wrote Leibniz, "will be, *Why is there something rather than nothing?*" That is, why does anything at all exist? There must be an answer to this question, because "*nothing happens without a sufficient reason.*"[7] Leibniz's famous Principle of Sufficient Reason holds that there must be a reason or rational explanation for the existence of one state of affairs rather than another. Why does the universe exist? The reason cannot be found in any single thing in the universe, for these are contingent themselves and do not have to exist. Nor is the reason to be found in the whole aggregate of such things, for the world is just the collection of these contingent beings and is therefore itself contingent. Nor can the reason be found in the prior causes of things, for these are just past states of the universe and do not explain why there are any such states, any universe, at all. Leibniz asks us to imagine that a series of geometry books has been copied from eternity; such an infinite regress would still not explain why such books exist at all. But the same is true with regard to past states of the world: even should these be infinite, there is no sufficient reason for the existence of an eternal universe. Therefore, the reason for the universe's existence must be found outside the universe, in a being whose sufficient reason is self-contained; it is its own sufficient reason for existing and is the reason the universe exists as well. This Sufficient Reason of all things is God, whose own existence is to be explained only by reference to himself. That is to say, God is a metaphysically necessary being.

This proof is clearly different from the Thomist argument: there is no reference to the distinction between essence and existence, nor to the argument against an infinite causal regress. Indeed, Leibniz is not seeking a cause at all, but an explanation for the world. Thomas concludes to an Uncaused Cause, but Leibniz to a Self-Explanatory Being. Many philosophers have confused these and come up with God as a Self-Caused Being, which neither Aquinas nor Leibniz defended.

Thus, there is a variety of cosmological arguments, which need to be kept distinct, for arguments against one version may prove inapplicable to another.

TELEOLOGICAL ARGUMENT

Perhaps the oldest and most popular of all the arguments for the existence of God is the teleological argument. It is the famous argument from design, and it infers an intelligent designer of the universe just as we infer an intelligent designer for any product in which we discern evidence of purposeful adaptation of means to some end (*telos*).

Plato and Aristotle

The ancient Greek philosophers were impressed with the order that pervades the cosmos, and many of them ascribed that order to the work of an intelligent mind who fashioned the universe. The heavens in constant revolution across the sky were especially awesome to the ancients. Plato's Academy lavished extensive time and thought on the study of astronomy because, Plato believed, it was the science that would awaken man to his divine destiny. According to Plato, there are two things that "lead men to believe in the gods": the argument based on the soul, and the argument "from the order of the motion of the stars, and of all things under the dominion of the mind which ordered the universe."[8] What a lovely statement of the divine design evident throughout the universe! Plato employed both of these arguments to refute atheism and concluded that there must be a "best soul" who is the "maker and father of all," the "King," who ordered the primordial chaos into the rational cosmos we observe today.[9]

An even more magnificent statement of divine teleology is to be found in a fragment from a lost work of Aristotle entitled *On Philosophy*. Aristotle, too, was struck with wonder by the majestic sweep of the glittering host across the night sky of ancient Greece. Philosophy, he said, begins with this sense of wonder about the world:

> For it is owing to their wonder that men both now begin and at first began to philosophize; they wondered originally at the obvious difficulties, then advanced little by little and stated difficulties about greater matters, e.g. about the phenomena of the moon and those of the sun, and about the stars and about the genesis of the universe.[10]

Anyone who has personally studied the heavens must lend a sympathetic ear to these men of antiquity who gazed up into the night sky as yet undimmed by pollution and the glare of city lights, and watched the slow but irresistible turn of the cosmos, replete with its planets, stars, and familiar constellations, across their view and wondered, what is the cause of all this? Aristotle concluded that the cause was divine intelligence. He imagined the impact that the sight of the world would have on a race of men who had lived underground and never beheld the sky:

> When thus they would suddenly gain sight of the earth, seas, and the sky; when they should come to know the grandeur of the clouds and the might of the winds; when they should behold the sun and should learn its grandeur and beauty as well as its power to cause the day by shedding light over the sky; and again, when the night had

darkened the lands and they should behold the whole of the sky spangled and adorned with stars; and when they should see the changing lights of the moon as it waxes and wanes, and the risings and settings of all these celestial bodies, their courses fixed and changeless throughout all eternity—when they should behold all these things, most certainly they would have judged both that there exist gods and that all these marvellous works are the handiwork of the gods.[11]

In his *Metaphysics* Aristotle proceeded to argue that there must be a First Unmoved Mover which is God, a living, intelligent, incorporeal, eternal, and most good being who is the source of order in the cosmos. Hence, from earliest times men, wholly removed from biblical revelation, have concluded on the basis of design in the universe that a divine mind must exist.

Thomas Aquinas

We've already seen that Thomas Aquinas in his first three Ways argued for the existence of God via the cosmological argument. His Fifth Way, however, represents the teleological argument. He notes that we observe in nature that all things operate toward some end, even when those things lack consciousness. For their operation hardly ever varies and practically always turns out well, which shows that they really do tend toward a goal and do not hit upon it merely by accident. Thomas is here expressing the conviction of Aristotelian physics that everything has not only a productive cause but also a final cause or goal toward which it is drawn. To use an example of our own, poppy seeds always grow into poppies and acorns into oaks. Now nothing, Aquinas reasons, that lacks consciousness tends toward a goal unless it is under the direction of someone with consciousness and intelligence. For example, the arrow does not tend toward the bull's eye unless it is aimed by the archer. Therefore, everything in nature must be directed toward its goal by someone with intelligence, and this we call "God."

William Paley

Undoubtedly, the high point in the development of the teleological argument came with William Paley's brilliant formulation in his *Natural Theology* of 1804. Paley combed the sciences of his time for evidences of design in nature and produced a staggering catalogue of such evidences, based, for example, on the order evident in bones, muscles, blood vessels, comparative anatomy, and particular organs throughout the animal and plant kingdoms. So conclusive was Paley's evidence that Leslie Stephen in his *History of English Thought in the Eighteenth Century* wryly remarked that "if there were no hidden flaw in the reasoning, it would be impossible to understand, not only how any should resist, but how anyone should ever have overlooked the demonstration."[12] Although most philosophers—who have undoubtedly never read Paley—believe that his sort of argument was dealt a crushing and fatal blow by David Hume's critique of the teleological argument, Paley's argument, which was written nearly thirty years after the publication of Hume's critique, is in fact not vulnerable to most of Hume's objections, as Frederick Ferré has pointed out.[13] Paley opens with a statement of the famous "watch-maker argument":

> In crossing a heath, suppose I pitched my foot against a stone, and were asked how the stone came to be there; I might possibly answer, that, for anything I knew to the contrary it had lain there forever: nor would it perhaps be very easy to show the absurdity of this answer. But suppose I had found a *watch* upon the ground, and it should be inquired how the watch happened to be in that place; I should hardly think of the answer which I had before given, that, for anything I knew, the watch might have always been there. Yet why should not this answer serve for the watch as well as for the stone? Why is it not as admissible in the second case, as in the first? For this reason, and for no other, viz. that, when we come to inspect the watch, we perceive (what we could not discover in the stone) that its several parts are framed and put together for a purpose, e.g. that they are so formed and adjusted as to produce motion, and that motion so regulated as to point out the hour of the day; that if the different parts had been differently shaped from what they are, of a different size from what they are, or placed after any other manner, or in any other order, than that in which they are placed, either no motion at all would have been carried on in the machine, or none which would have answered the use that is now served by it. To reckon up a few of the plainest of these parts, and of their offices, all tending to one result: We see a cylindrical box containing a coiled elastic spring, which, by its endeavor to relax itself, turns round the box. We next observe a flexible chain (artificially wrought for the sake of flexure) communicating the action of the spring from the box to the fusee. We then find a series of wheels, the teeth of which catch in, and apply to each other, conducting the motion from the fusee to the balance, and from the balance to the pointer; and at the same time, by the size and shape of those wheels, so regulating that motion, as to terminate in causing an index, by an equable and measured progression, to pass over a given space in a given time. We take notice that the wheels are made of brass in order to keep them from rust; the springs of steel, no other metal being so elastic; that over

the face of the watch there is placed a glass, a material employed in no other part of the work; but in the room of which, if there had been any other than a transparent substance, the hour could not be seen without opening the case. This mechanism being observed (it requires indeed an examination of the instrument, and perhaps some previous knowledge of the subject, to perceive and understand it; but being once, as we have said, observed and understood), the inference, we think, is inevitable; that the watch must have had a maker; that there must have existed, at some time, and at some place or other, an artificer or artificers, who formed it for the purpose which we find it actually to answer; who comprehended its construction, and designed its use.[14]

This conclusion, Paley continues, would not be weakened if I had never actually seen a watch being made nor knew how to make one. For we recognize the remains of ancient art as the products of intelligent design without having ever seen such things made, and we know the products of modern manufacture are the result of intelligence even though we may have no inkling how they are produced. Nor would our conclusion be invalidated if the watch sometimes went wrong. The purpose of the mechanism would be evident even if the machine did not function perfectly. Nor would the argument become uncertain if we were to discover some parts in the mechanism that did not seem to have any purpose, for this would not negate the purposeful design in the other parts. Nor would anyone in his right mind think that the existence of the watch was accounted for by the consideration that it was one out of many possible configurations of matter and that some possible configuration had to exist in the place where the watch was found. Nor would it help to say that there exists in things a principle of order, which yielded the watch. For one never knows a watch to be so formed, and the notion of such a principle of order that is not intelligent seems to have little meaning. Nor is it enough to say the watch was produced from another watch before it and that one from yet a prior watch, and so forth to infinity. For the design is still unaccounted for. Each machine in the infinite series evidences the same design, and it is irrelevant whether one has ten, a thousand, or an infinite number of such machines—a designer is still needed.

Now the point of the analogy of the watch is this: just as we infer a watchmaker as the designer of the watch, so ought we to infer an intelligent designer of the universe:

> For every indication of contrivance, every manifestation of design, which existed in the watch, exists in the works of nature, of being

greater and more, and that in a degree which exceeds all computation. I mean, that the contrivances of nature surpass the contrivances of art, in the complexity, subtilty, and curiosity of the mechanism; and still more, if possible, do they go beyond them in number and variety: yet, in a multitude of cases, are not less evidently contrivances, not less evidently accommodated to their end, or suited to their office, than are the most perfect products of human ingenuity.[15]

Here Paley begins his cataloging of the contrivances of nature bespeaking divine design. He concludes that an intelligent designer of the universe exists, and closes with a discussion of some of the attributes of this cosmic architect.

MORAL ARGUMENT

The moral argument for the existence of God argues for the existence of a Being that is the embodiment of the ultimate Good, which is the source of the objective moral values we experience in the world. The reasoning at the heart of the moral argument goes all the way back to Plato, who argued that things have goodness insofar as they stand in some relation to the Good, which subsists in itself. With the advent of Christian theism, the Good became identified with God himself.

Thomas Aquinas

Aquinas's Fourth Way is a type of moral argument. He observes that we find in the world a gradation of values: some things are more good, more true, more noble, and so forth, than other things. Such comparative terms describe the varying degrees to which things approach a superlative standard: the most good, most true, and so forth. There must therefore exist something that is the best and truest and noblest thing of all. Aquinas believed that whatever possesses a property more fully than anything else is the cause of that property in other things. Hence, there is some being that is the cause of the existence, goodness, and any other perfection of finite beings, and this being we call "God."

William Sorley

Perhaps the most sophisticated development of the moral argument is that of William Sorley (1855-1935), professor of moral philosophy at Cambridge University until 1933, in his Gifford Lectures, *Moral Values and the Idea of God* (1918). Sorley believed that ethics provides the key to metaphysics, and he argues that God as the ground of the natural and moral orders best provides for a rational, unified view of reality. He begins by arguing that reality is characterized by an objective moral order, which is as real and independent of our recognition of it as the natural order of things is. He admits that in a sense one cannot prove that objective values exist, but insists that in this same sense one cannot prove that the external world exists either! Thus, the moral order and the natural order are on equal footing. On the same ground that we assume the reality of the world of objects, we assume the reality of the moral order of objective value. Now obviously Sorley does not mean we perceive value with our five senses in the way we do physical objects. We discern value in some non-empirical way, and just as we are rational to assume that some objective natural order lies behind our sense perceptions, so we are rational to assume that some objective moral order lies behind our perceptions of value. Our perceptions of both value and physical objects are simply givens of experience.

Our perception of a realm of objective value does not mean for Sorley that everyone has an innate and accurate knowledge of specific moral values. In his *The Ethics of Naturalism* (1885) he had refuted the historical, evolutionary approach to ethics, and now he turns to refute psychological, sociological explanations of value. The fundamental error of all these approaches is that they confuse the subjective origin of our moral judgments and the objective value to which the judgments refer. Just because the origin of our moral judgments can be historically or sociologically explained does not mean there are no objective, corresponding values in reality. In fact, Sorley argues that our moral judgments are not infallible and that we do not know the content of the moral ideal that we ever seek to approach.

Where, then, does objective moral value reside? Sorley answers: in persons. The only beings that are bearers of intrinsic moral value are persons; non-personal things have merely instrumental value in relation to persons. Only persons have intrinsic value, because meaningful moral behavior requires purpose and will.

The foregoing analysis of moral value provides the ground for Sorley's moral argument for God. We have seen that the natural order and the moral order are both part of reality. Therefore, the question is: what world view can combine these two orders into the most coherent explanatory form? According to Sorley, there are three competing world views: theism, pluralism, and monism.

Turning first to theism, Sorley believes that the most serious objection to this world view is the problem of evil. Basically, the problem here is that the natural order and the moral order seem to be working at cross-purposes with each other: the natural order often fails to realize the good that ought to be realized. Sorley, however, thinks this objection is answerable. The objection, he says, tends to confuse moral purpose with personal happiness; because personal happiness is often not realized, it is assumed that moral purpose has been frustrated. But Sorley points out that the realization of moral purpose cannot be equated with the realization of personal happiness. In other words, just because we are not happy about some situation does not imply that the situation ought not to be. In general, Sorley argues that suffering and evil are possible in a theistic world view if finite minds are gradually recognizing moral ends that they are free to accept or reject.

Indeed, Sorley argues that the theistic account of the natural and moral orders is the superior world view. For we have seen that moral values or ideals are an objective part of reality and that they reside in persons. The problem is that no finite person has ever fully realized all moral value. The moral ideal is nowhere fully actualized in the finite world, though it is presently valid, that is, binding and obligatory for the finite world. But how can something be objective and valid if it does not exist? Physical laws, by contrast, are fully realized in the world. So no further explanation of their validity is required. Therefore, if the moral ideal is to be valid for reality, it must be fully realized in an existent that is both personal and eternal, that is, God.

Sorley then proceeds to refute the other two alternatives, pluralism and monism. Against pluralism, which holds that the moral ideal resides in a plurality of finite beings, Sorley argues that the moral values are eternally valid and so cannot reside in temporally finite persons. Against monism, which holds that the universe is constituted by a single nonpersonal reality of which minds are mere modes, Sorley maintains that it leaves no room for purposeful endeavor or real freedom, because "is" and "ought to be" are identical and everything simply is as it is.

Hence, although not a rigid demonstration, this reasoning, concludes Sorley, shows that theism offers the most reasonable and unified explanation of reality. The moral order is the order of an infinite, eternal Mind who is the architect of nature and whose moral purpose man and the universe are slowly fulfilling.

ASSESSMENT

All of these arguments have been both criticized and defended by modern philosophers. The ontological argument was rejected by Immanuel Kant, and many thinkers have followed him in this regard. On the other hand, Alvin Plantinga defends the argument against Kant's criticisms via the notion of possible worlds. Plantinga contends that God is by definition a being who exists supremely, with maximum greatness, in all possible worlds; and since the actual world is a possible world, God must actually exist. So, if God's existence is possible, he must exist.

The teleological argument is widely regarded as having been refuted by Hume, with the Darwinian theory of evolution supplying the nails in the coffin. But F. R. Tennant and Stuart Hackett, in full cognizance of Hume's objections, have argued that on the very assumption of evolution, there is a cosmic teleology that points to a divine designer. In any case, there is something of a crisis in origin of life studies today, as all the traditional scenarios of the origin of the first living cell in the primordial organic soup have broken down. Moreover, the gradualism of classical evolutionary theory based upon the mechanism of minor mutations and natural selection has been radically called into question by the proponents of "punctuated equilibrium," who argue that the transitional forms are absent from the fossil record because they never existed. Rather, they say evolution occurs by intermittent bursts from one form to another. Insofar as this new theory fails to account for these bursts and must appeal to "hopeful monsters"—massive mutations that produce new forms without transitional forms—the hypothesis of design becomes more plausible. On a broader scope, current science is wrestling with the so-called "Anthropic Principle," according to which the entire universe and its history are fine-tuned from its inception with incredible precision to produce man on earth. By appealing to the inconceivably improbable balance of physical constants and cosmological quantities given in the Big Bang itself, thinkers like John Leslie have argued for divine design wholly apart from the controverted question of biological origins.

While I am not aware of any contemporary defender of the moral argument of the stature of a William Sorley, there are nonetheless a good many philosophers who are defending the viability and even superiority of a theistically-based system of ethics over against non-theistic systems, and insofar as they are successful, their arguments constitute a sort of moral argument for God.

In addition to these traditional arguments, new arguments—often very creative, like Adams's argument from colors and flavors—are being put forward. Plantinga has presented a paper "Two Dozen (or So) Theistic Arguments," and complains that philosophers have too often been preoccupied with traditional arguments and have not availed themselves of the wider resources that support a theistic world view.

DEFENSE OF THE *KALĀM* COSMOLOGICAL ARGUMENT

I find quite a number of the proffered theistic arguments to be sound and persuasive and together to constitute a powerful cumulative case for the existence of God. In particular, I find the *kalām* cosmological argument for a temporal first cause of the universe to be one of the most plausible arguments for God's existence. I have defended this argument in two books, *The Kalām Cosmological Argument* and *Theism, Atheism, and Big Bang Cosmology*, the latter being a debate with Quentin Smith, an atheist philosopher. Students who want to go deeper can consult those works. The argument is basically this: both philosophical reasoning and scientific evidence show that the universe began to exist. Anything that begins to exist must have a cause that brings it into being. So the universe must have a cause. Philosophical analysis reveals that such a cause must have several of the principal theistic attributes.

The argument may be formulated in three simple steps:

1. Whatever begins to exist has a cause.
2. The universe began to exist.
3. Therefore, the universe has a cause.

The logic of the argument is valid and very simple; the argument has the same logical structure as the argument: "All men are mortal; Socrates is a man; therefore, Socrates is mortal." So the question is, are there good reasons to believe that each of the steps is true? I think there are.

Whatever Begins to Exist Has a Cause

The first step is so intuitively obvious that I think scarcely anyone could sincerely believe it to be false. I therefore think it somewhat unwise to argue in favor of it, for any proof of the principle is likely to be less obvious than the principle itself. And as Aristotle remarked, one ought not to try to prove the obvious via the less obvious. The old axiom that "out of nothing, nothing comes" remains as obvious today as ever. When I first wrote *The Kalām Cosmological Argument*, I remarked that I found it an attractive feature of this argument that it allows the atheist a way of escape: he can always deny the first premiss and assert that the universe sprang into existence uncaused out of nothing. I figured that few would take this option, since I believed they would thereby expose themselves as persons interested only in an academic refutation of the argument and not in really discovering the truth about the universe. To my surprise, however, atheists seem to be increasingly taking this route. For example, Quentin Smith, commenting that philosophers are too often adversely affected by Heidegger's dread of "the nothing," concludes that "the most reasonable belief is that we came from nothing, by nothing, and for nothing"[16]—a nice ending to a sort of Gettysburg address of atheism, perhaps.

Similarly, the late J. L. Mackie, in refuting the *kalām* cosmological argument, turns his main guns on this first step: "there is *a priori* no good reason why a sheer origination of things, not determined by anything, should be unacceptable, whereas the existence of a god [*sic*] with the power to create something out of nothing is acceptable."[17] Indeed, he believes *creatio ex nihilo* raises problems: (i) If God began to exist at a point in time, then this is as great a puzzle as the beginning of the universe. (ii) Or if God existed for infinite time, then the same arguments would apply to his existence as would apply to the infinite duration of the universe. (iii) If it be said that God is timeless, then this, says Mackie, is a complete mystery.

Now notice that Mackie never *refutes* the principle that whatever begins to exist has a cause. Rather, he simply demands what good reason there is *a priori* to accept it. He writes, "As Hume pointed out, we can certainly conceive an uncaused beginning-to-be of an object; if what we can thus conceive is nevertheless in some way impossible, this still requires to be shown."[18] But, as many philosophers have pointed out, Hume's argument in no way makes it plausible to think that something could really come into being without a cause. Just because I can imagine an object, say a horse, coming into existence from nothing, that in no way proves that a horse really could come into existence that way. The defender of the *kalām* argument is claiming that it is *really* impossible for something to come uncaused from nothing. Does Mackie sincerely believe that things can pop into existence uncaused, out of nothing? Does anyone in his right mind really believe that, say, a raging tiger could suddenly come into existence uncaused, out of nothing, in this room right now? The same applies to the universe: if prior to the existence of the universe, there was absolutely nothing—no God, no space, no time—how could the universe possibly have come to exist?

In fact, Mackie's appeal to Hume at this point is counterproductive. For Hume himself clearly believed in the causal principle. In 1754 he wrote to John Stewart, "But allow me to tell you that I never asserted so absurd a Proposition as *that anything might arise without a cause*: I only maintain'd, that our Certainty of the Falsehood of that Proposition proceeded neither from Intuition nor Demonstration, but from another source."[19] Even Mackie confesses, "Still this [causal] principle has some plausibility, in that it is constantly confirmed in our experience (and also used, reasonably, in interpreting our experience)."[20] So why not accept the truth of the causal principle as plausible and reasonable—at the very least more so than its denial?

Because, Mackie thinks, in this particular case the theism implied by affirming the principle is even more unintelligible than the denial of the principle. It makes more sense to believe that the universe came into being uncaused out of nothing than to believe that God created the universe out of nothing.

But is this really the case? Consider the three problems Mackie raises with *creatio ex nihilo*. Certainly, the proponent of the *kalām* argument would not hold (i) that God began to exist or (ii) that God has existed for an infinite number of, say, hours, or any other unit of time. But what is wrong with (iii), that God is, without creation, timeless? I would argue that God exists timelessly without creation and in time subsequent to creation. This may be "mysterious" in the sense of "wonderful" or "awe-inspiring," but it is not, so far as I can see, unintelligible; and Mackie gives us no reason to think that it is. Moreover, there is also an alternative which Mackie failed to consider: (iv) prior to creation God existed in an undifferentiated time in which hours, seconds, days, and so forth simply do not exist. Because this time is undifferentiated, it is not incompatible with the *kalām* argument that an infinite regress of events cannot exist. It seems to me, therefore, that Mackie is entirely unjustified in rejecting the first step of the argument as not being intuitively obvious, plausible, and reasonable.

The Universe Began to Exist

If we agree that whatever begins to exist has a cause, what evidence is there to support the crucial second step in the argument, that the universe began to exist? I think that this step is supported by both philosophical arguments and scientific confirmation of those arguments.

Philosophical Arguments: (1) Argument from the Impossibility of an Actually Infinite Number of Things

An actually infinite number of things cannot exist because this would involve all sorts of absurdities, which I'll illustrate in a moment. And if the universe never had a beginning, then the series of all past events is actually infinite. That is to say, an actually infinite number of past events exists. Because an actually infinite number of things cannot exist, then an actually infinite number of past events cannot exist. The number of past events is finite; therefore, the series of past events had a beginning. Since the history of the universe is identical to the series of all past events, the universe must have begun to exist. This argument can also be formulated in three steps:

1. An actually infinite number of things cannot exist.
2. A beginningless series of events in time entails an actually infinite number of things.
3. Therefore, a beginningless series of events in time cannot exist.

Let's examine each step individually.

1. *An actually infinite number of things cannot exist.* In order to understand this first step, we need to understand what an actual infinite is. There is a difference between a potential infinite and an actual infinite. A potential infinite is a collection that is increasing toward infinity as a limit but never gets there. Such a collection is really indefinite, not infinite. For example, any finite distance can be subdivided into potentially infinitely many parts. You can just keep on dividing parts in half forever, but you will never arrive at an actual "infinitieth" division or come up with an actually infinite number of parts. By contrast, an actual infinite is a collection in which the number of members really is infinite. The collection is not growing toward infinity; it *is* infinite, it is "complete." This sort of infinity is used in set theory to designate sets that have an infinite number of members, such as {1, 2, 3...}. Now I am arguing, not that a potentially infinite number of things cannot exist, but that an actually infinite number of things cannot exist. For if an actually infinite number of things could exist, this would spawn all sorts of absurdities.

Perhaps the best way to bring this home is by means of an illustration. Let me use one of my favorites, Hilbert's Hotel, a product of the mind of the great German mathematician David Hilbert.[21] Let's imagine a hotel with a finite number of rooms. Suppose, furthermore, that all the rooms are full. When a new guest arrives asking for a room, the proprietor apologizes, "Sorry, all the rooms are full." But now let us imagine a hotel with an infinite number of rooms and suppose once more that *all the rooms are full*. There is not a single vacant room throughout the entire infinite hotel. Now suppose a new guest shows up, asking for a room. "But of course!" says the proprietor, and he immediately shifts the person in room #1 into room #2, the person in room #2 into room #3, the person in room #3 into room #4, and so on, out to infinity. As a result of these room changes, room #1 now becomes vacant and the new guest gratefully checks in. But remember, before he arrived, all the rooms were full!

Equally curious, according to the mathematicians, there are now no more persons in the hotel than there were before: the number is just infinite. But how can this be? The proprietor just added the new guest's name to the register and gave him his keys—how can there not be one more person in the hotel than before? But the situation becomes even stranger. For suppose an infinity of new guests show up at the desk, asking for a room. "Of course, of course!" says the proprietor, and he proceeds to shift the person in room #1 into room #2, the person in room #2 into room #4, the person in room #3 into room #6, and so on out to infinity, always putting each former occupant into the room number twice his own. Because any natural number multiplied by two always equals an even number, all the guests wind up in even-numbered rooms. As a result, all the odd numbered rooms become vacant, and the infinity of new guests is easily accommodated. And yet, before they came, all the rooms were full! And again, strangely enough, the number of guests in the hotel is the same after the infinity of new guests check in as before, even though there were as many new guests as old guests. In fact, the proprietor could repeat this process *infinitely many times* and yet there would never be one single person more in the hotel than before.

But Hilbert's Hotel is even stranger than the German mathematician made it out to be. For suppose some of the guests start to check out. Suppose the guest in room #1 departs. Is there not now one less person in the hotel? Not according to the mathematicians—but just ask the woman who makes the beds! Suppose the guests in rooms # 1, 3, 5 . . . check out. In this case an infinite number of people have left the hotel, but according to the mathematicians, there are no less people in the hotel—but don't talk to that laundry woman! In fact, we could have every other guest check out of the hotel and repeat this process infinitely many times, and yet there would never be any less people in the hotel.

Now suppose the proprietor doesn't like having a half-empty hotel (it looks bad for business). No matter! By shifting occupants as before, but in reverse order, he transforms his half-vacant hotel into one that is jammed to the gills. You might think that by these manoeuvres the proprietor could always keep this strange hotel fully occupied. But you would be wrong. For suppose that the persons in rooms #4, 5, 6 . . . checked out. At a single stroke the hotel would be virtually emptied, the guest register would be reduced to three names, and the infinite would be converted to finitude. And yet it would remain true that the *same* number of guests checked out this time as when the guests in rooms # 1, 3, 5 . . . checked out! Can anyone believe that such a hotel could exist in reality?

Hilbert's Hotel is absurd. As one person remarked, if Hilbert's Hotel could exist, it would have to have a sign posted outside: NO VACANCY—GUESTS WELCOME. The above sorts of absurdities show that it is impossible for an actually infinite number of things to exist. There is simply no way to avoid these absurdities once we admit the possibility of the existence of an actual infinite. Students sometimes react to such absurdities as Hilbert's Hotel by saying that we really don't understand the nature of infinity and, hence, these absurdities result. But this attitude is simply mistaken. Infinite set theory is a highly developed and well-understood branch of mathematics, so that these absurdities result precisely because we *do* understand the notion of a collection with an actually infinite number of members.

William J. Wainwright has suggested that we could reduce the force of these absurdities by translating them into mathematical terms; for example, an actually infinite set has a proper subset with the same cardinal number as the set itself.[22] But this amounts only to a way of *concealing* the absurdities; it was to bring out the paradoxical character of these mathematical concepts that Hilbert came up with his illustration in the first place. And the whole purpose of philosophical analysis is to bring out what is entailed by unanalyzed notions and not to leave them at face value.

But does the possibility of an actual infinite really *entail* that such absurdities are possible, or could an actual infinite be possible, as Wainwright suggests, without thereby implying that such absurdities are possible? The answer to that question is simple: the possibility of the existence of an actual infinite *entails*, that is, necessarily implies, that such absurdities could exist. Hilbert's illustration merely serves to bring out in a practical and vivid way what the mathematics necessarily implies; for if an actually infinite number of things is possible, then a hotel with an actually infinite number of rooms must be possible. Hence, it logically follows that if such a hotel is impossible, then so is the real existence of an actual infinite.

These considerations also show how superficial Mackie's analysis of this point is.[23] He thinks that the absurdities are resolved by noting that for infinite groups the axiom that *the whole is greater than its part* does not hold, as it does for finite groups. But far from being the solution, this is precisely the problem. Because in infinite set theory this axiom is denied, one gets all sorts of absurdities, like Hilbert's Hotel, when one tries to translate that theory into reality. And the contradictions that result when guests check out of the hotel are not even *prima facie* resolved by Mackie's analysis. (In trans-finite arithmetic, subtraction is against the rules because it leads to contradictions; but in reality, you can't stop people from checking out of the hotel if they want to!) Hence, I conclude that an actually infinite number of things cannot exist.[24]

2. A beginningless series of events in time entails an actually infinite number of things. This second point is pretty obvious. If the universe never began to exist, then the series of events would be infinite. If the universe never began to exist, then prior to the present there have existed an actually infinite number of previous events. Thus, a beginningless series of events in time entails an actually infinite number of things, namely, events.

3. Therefore, a beginningless series of events in time cannot exist. If the above two premises are true, then the conclusion follows logically. The series of past events must be finite and have a beginning. Since, as I said, the universe is not distinct from the series of events, the universe therefore began to exist.

Philosophical Arguments: (2) Argument from the Impossibility of Forming an Actually Infinite Collection of Things by Adding One Member After Another

It is very important to note that this argument is distinct from the forego-ing argument, for it does not deny that an actually infinite number of things can exist. It denies that a collection containing an actually infinite number of things can be *formed* by adding one member after another. Basically, the argument goes like this: you cannot form an actually infinite collection of things by adding one member after another, because it would be impossible to get to infinity. The series of past events is a collection that has been formed by adding one event after another. Therefore, the series of past events up till now can only be finite, not infinite. Otherwise, it would be an actually infinite collection formed by adding one member after another. This argument, too, can be formulated in three steps:

1. The series of events in time is a collection formed by adding one member after another.
2. A collection formed by adding one member after another cannot be actually infinite.
3. Therefore, the series of events in time cannot be actually infinite.

Let's take a look at each step.

1. *The series of events in time is a collection formed by adding one member after another.* This is rather obvious. The past did not spring into being whole and entire but was formed sequentially, one event occurring after another. Notice, too, that the direction of this formation is "forward," in the sense that the collection grows with time. Although we sometimes speak of an "infinite regress" of events, in reality an infinite past would be an "infinite progress" of events with no beginning and its end in the present.

2. *A collection formed by adding one member after another cannot be actu-ally infinite.* This is the crucial step. It's important to realize that this impossibility has nothing to do with the amount of time available: no mat-ter how much time one has available, an actual infinite cannot be formed. No matter how many numbers you count, you can always add one more before arriving at infinity.

Now someone might say that while an infinite collection cannot be formed by beginning at a point and adding members, nevertheless an infinite collection could be formed by never beginning but ending at a point, that is to say, ending at a point after having added one member after another from eternity. But this method seems even more unbelievable than the first method. If one cannot count to infinity how can one count down from infinity? If one cannot traverse the infinite by moving in one direction, how can one traverse it by moving in the opposite direction?

Indeed, the idea of a beginningless series ending in the present seems absurd. To give just one illustration: suppose we meet a man who claims to have been counting from eternity and who is now finishing: . . ., -3, -2, -1, 0. We could ask, why didn't he finish counting yesterday or the day before or the year before? By then an infinite time had already elapsed, so that he should already have finished. Thus, at no point in the infinite past could we ever find the man finishing his countdown, for by that point he should already be done! In fact, no matter how far back into the past we go, we can never find the man counting at all, for at any point we reach he will already have finished. But if at no point in the past do we find him counting, this contradicts the hypothesis that he has been counting from eternity. This illustrates that the formation of an actual infinite by never beginning but reaching an end is as impossible as beginning at a point and trying to reach infinity.

Hence, set theory has been purged of all temporal concepts; as Russell says, "classes which are infinite are given all at once by the defining properties of their members, so that there is no question of 'completion' or of 'successive synthesis.'"[25] The only way an actual infinite could come to exist in the real world would be by being created all at once, simply in a moment. It would be a hopeless undertaking to try to form it by adding one member after another.

Mackie's objections to this step are off the target.[26] He thinks that the argument illicitly assumes an infinitely distant starting point in the past and then pronounces it impossible to travel from that point to today. If we take the notion of infinity "seriously," he says, we must say that in the infinite past there would be no starting point whatever, not even an infinitely distant one. Yet from any given point in the past, there is only a finite distance to the present.

Now I know of no proponent of the *kalām* argument who assumed that there was an infinitely distant starting point in the past. On the contrary, the beginningless character of the series of past events only serves to underscore the difficulty of its formation by adding one member after another. The fact that there is *no beginning at all*, not even an infinitely distant one, makes the problem worse, not better. It is not the proponent of the *kalām* argument who fails to take infinity seriously. To say the infinite past could have been formed by adding one member after another is like saying someone has just succeeded in writing down all the negative numbers, ending at - 1. And, we may ask, how is Mackie's point that from any given moment in the past there is only a finite distance to the present even relevant to the issue? The defender of the *kalām* argument could agree to this without batting an eye. For the issue is how the *whole* series can be formed, not a finite portion of it. Does Mackie think that because every *finite* segment of the series can be formed by adding one member after another the whole *infinite* series can be so formed? That is as logically fallacious as saying because every part of an elephant is light in weight, the whole elephant is light in weight. Mackie's point is therefore irrelevant. It seems that this step of the argument, that an actually infinite collection cannot be formed by adding one member after another, remains unrefuted.

3. *Therefore, the series of events in time cannot be actually infinite.* Given the truth of the premises, the conclusion logically follows. If the universe did not begin to exist a finite time ago, then the present moment would never arrive. But obviously it has arrived. Therefore, we know that the universe is finite in the past and began to exist.

We thus have two separate arguments to prove that the universe began to exist, one based on the impossibility of an actually infinite number of things and one on the impossibility of forming an actually infinite collection by successive addition. If one wishes to deny the beginning of the universe, he must refute, not one, but both of these arguments.

Scientific Confirmation

Now some people find philosophical arguments difficult to follow; they prefer empirical evidence. So I now turn to an examination of two remarkable scientific confirmations of the conclusion already reached by philosophical argument alone. This evidence comes from what is undoubtedly one of the most exciting and rapidly developing fields of science: astronomy and astrophysics.

1. *Confirmation from the Big Bang model of the universe.* Prior to the 1920s, scientists had always assumed that the universe was stationary. But in 1929 an alarming thing happened. An astronomer named Edwin Hubble discovered that the light from distant galaxies appears to be redder than it should. The startling conclusion to which Hubble was led was that the light is redder because the universe is *growing apart*; it is expanding! The light from the galaxies is affected because they are moving away from us. But this is the interesting part: Hubble not only showed that the universe is expanding, but that *it is expanding the same in all directions*.

To get a picture of this, imagine a balloon with buttons glued on its surface. As you blow up the balloon, the buttons get farther and farther apart. Now those buttons are just like the galaxies in space. Everything in the universe is expanding outward. The staggering implication of this is that at some point in the past *the entire known universe was contracted down to a single mathematical point*, from which it has been expanding ever since. The further back one goes in the past, the denser the universe becomes, so that one finally reaches a point of infinite density called the singularity from which the universe began to expand. That initial event has come to be known as the "Big Bang."

How long ago did the Big Bang occur? In a very important series of nine articles published over the course of three decades, two scientists, Allan Sandage and G. A. Tammann, estimated that the Big Bang occurred about 15 billion years ago. Therefore, according to the Big Bang theory the universe began to exist with a great explosion from a state of infinite density about 15 billion years ago. Four of the world's most famous astronomers describe that event in these words:

> The universe began from a state of infinite density. . . . Space and time were created in that event and so was all the matter in the universe. It is not meaningful to ask what happened before the Big Bang; it is like asking what is north of the North Pole. Similarly it is not sensible to ask where the Big Bang took place. The point-universe was not an object isolated in space; it was the entire universe, and so the only answer can be that the Big Bang happened everywhere.[27]

Thus, the term "Big Bang" and the terminology associated with an explosion can be misleading, because it is not correct to suppose that the expansion can be visualized from the outside. There is no external vantage point from which the expansion could be observed, because what is expanding is the entire universe. Space itself is expanding in the sense that the separation between any two galaxies grows with time.

The event that marked the beginning of the universe becomes all the more amazing when one reflects on the fact that it implies the origin of the universe out of nothing. As the British physicist P. C. W. Davies explains,

> If we extrapolate this prediction to its extreme, we reach a point when all distances in the universe have shrunk to zero. An initial cosmological singularity therefore forms a past temporal extremity to the universe. We cannot continue physical reasoning, or even the concept of spacetime, through such an extremity. For this reason most cosmologists think of the initial singularity as the beginning

of the universe. On this view the big bang represents the creation event; the creation not only of all the matter and energy in the universe, but also of spacetime itself.[28]

Similarly, another pair of physicists conclude, "At this singularity, space and time came into existence; literally nothing existed before the singularity, so, if the Universe originated in such a singularity, we would truly have a creation *ex nihilo*."[29] Thus, as astronomer Fred Hoyle points out, the Big Bang theory requires the creation of the universe from nothing. This is because as one goes back in time, one reaches a point at which, in Hoyle's words, the universe was "shrunk down to nothing at all."[30] So what the Big Bang model implies is that the universe had a beginning and was created out of nothing.

Now some people were deeply disturbed with the idea that the universe began from nothing.[31] Einstein wrote privately, "This circumstance of an expanding universe irritates me. . . . To admit such possibilities seems senseless." Another scientist, Arthur Eddington, wrote, "I have no axe to grind in this discussion, but the notion of a beginning is repugnant to me. . . . I simply do not believe that the present order of things started off with a bang. . . . The expanding universe is preposterous . . . incredible. . . . It leaves me cold." The German chemist Walter Nernst declared, "To deny the infinite duration of time would be to betray the very foundations of science." Phillip Morrison of the Massachusetts Institute of Technology said, "I find it hard to accept the Big Bang theory; I would like to reject it, but I have to face the facts."

Alternative models. But if one rejects the Big-Bang model, the alternatives are not very convincing. Let's examine the major kinds of competing theories.

The *steady state model* holds that the universe never had a beginning, but has always existed in the same state. As the galaxies mutually recede, new matter comes into existence in the voids left by the retreating galaxies, so that the overall state of the universe remains the same. Ever since this model was first proposed in 1948, it has never been very convincing. According to S. L. Jaki, this theory never secured "a single piece of experimental verification." It always seemed to be trying to explain away the facts rather than explain them. According to Jaki, the proponents of this model were actually motivated by "openly anti-theological, or rather anti-Christian motivations."[32]

Against this theory is the fact that a count of galaxies emitting radio waves indicates that there were once more radio sources than there are today. Therefore, the universe is not in a steady state after all. But the theory was decisively discredited when in 1965 two scientists working for the Bell Telephone Laboratory, A. A. Penzias and R. W. Wilson, discovered that the entire universe is bathed with a background of microwave radiation. This radiation background shows that the universe was once in a very hot and very dense state. In the steady state model no such state could have existed, since the universe is supposed to have been the same from eternity. Therefore, the steady state model has been abandoned by virtually everyone. According to Ivan King, "The steady-state theory has now been laid to rest, as a result of clear-cut observations of how things have changed with time."[33]

A second alternative model is the *oscillating model*. John Gribbin describes this model:

> The biggest problem with the Big Bang theory of the origin of the universe is philosophical—perhaps even theological—what was there before the bang? This problem alone was sufficient to give a great initial impetus to the steady state theory; but with that theory now sadly in conflict with the observations, the best way round this initial difficulty is provided by a model in which the universe expands, collapses back again, and repeats the cycle indefinitely.[34]

According to this model, the universe is sort of like a spring, expanding and contracting from eternity. This model became a sort of "Great White Hope" for atheistic scientists, who terribly wanted it to be true so as to avoid an absolute beginning of the universe. You may have seen Carl Sagan, for example, in his popular "Cosmos" program on public television propounding this model and reading from the Hindu scriptures about cyclical Brahman years in order to illustrate the oscillating universe.[35]

There are, however, at least two very well-known difficulties with the oscillating model, which Sagan did not mention. First, the oscillating model is physically impossible. That is to say, for all the talk about such a model, the fact remains that it is only a *theoretical* possibility, not a *real* possibility. You can draft such models on paper, but they cannot be descriptive of the real universe, because they contradict the known laws of physics. As the late Professor Tinsley of Yale explains, in oscillating models "even though the mathematics *says* that the universe oscillates, there is no known physics to reverse the collapse and bounce back to a new expansion. The physics seems to say that those models start from the Big Bang, expand, collapse, then end."[36] More recently, four other scientists, themselves obviously in sympathy with the oscillating model, admitted, in describing the contraction of the universe, "there is no understanding of how a bounce can take place. . . . We have nothing to contribute to the question of whether and/or how the universe bounces."[37] In order for the oscillating model to be correct, the known laws of physics would have to be revised.

Second, the observational evidence is contrary to the oscillating model. Let me explain two respects in which the observational evidence does not support the oscillating model. The first is that there is no way to account for the observed even distribution of matter in the universe on the basis of an oscillating model. This is because as the universe contracts, black holes begin to suck everything up, so that matter becomes very unevenly distributed. But when the universe (supposedly) rebounds from its contracting phase, there is no mechanism to "iron out" these lumps and make the distribution smooth. Hence, the scientists cited above confess that even if there is some unknown mechanism that could cause the universe to bounce back to a new expansion, it is still not clear that it would prevent the unevenness that would result from the black holes formed during the contraction phase.[38] The present evenness of matter distribution simply cannot be explained by using models in which the universe begins with matter unevenly distributed.[39] The oscillating model therefore cannot satisfactorily account for the presently observed evenness of the distribution of matter in the universe.

A second respect in which the observational evidence is contrary to the oscillating model concerns the question of whether the universe will someday re-contract or continue to expand forever. If the first alternative is correct, the expansion will reach a certain point, halt, and then gravity will pull everything back together again. But if the second alternative is right, the force of the expansion is greater than the force of gravity so that the expansion will never stop but will just go on and on forever.

An illustration of this difference concerns the escape velocity needed by a rocket to escape earth's gravity. If a certain speed is not attained, the force of gravity will pull the ship back to earth again. But if the rocket attains or exceeds escape velocity, then the force of the earth's gravity cannot prevent its flying off into space. Similarly, if the universe is expanding, so to speak, at escape velocity or faster, then it will overcome the internal pull of its own gravity and will expand forever. Now clearly, the oscillating model, even in order to be a *possibility*, must posit a closed universe, one that is expanding slower than escape velocity. But is it?

The crucial factor in answering that question is the density of the universe. For density determines the gravitational force of an object. Scientists have estimated that if there are more than about three hydrogen atoms per cubic meter on the average throughout the universe, then the universe will re-contract. Now that may not sound like very much, but remember that most of the universe is just empty space. I won't go into all the technicalities of how scientists measure the density of the universe, but let me simply report their conclusions. If all matter were luminous, visible matter associated with galaxies, then the universe would possess only a trifling 1% of the density necessary to bring about re-contraction. But undoubtedly there is dark, non-luminous matter surrounding the galaxies and galactic structures and perhaps in inter-galactic space. Repeated measurements on ever-widening scales of the effects of this dark matter on galactic motion and of the constraints placed on it by the abundance of the lightest elements in the universe (which would not have been produced were the universe too dense) vindicate earlier estimates that even taking all luminous and non-luminous matter together, the density of the universe is still only about 10% of what is necessary for re-contraction.[40] In order for the universe to recontract, 99% of the matter in the universe would have to be invisible, which is, as Sandage muses, "a bizarre requirement."[41]

Theoretical physicists bent on finding the "missing" 90% have proposed that it may take the form of exotic matter rather than ordinary matter. Two scenarios have been proposed. *Hot Dark Matter* theories hold that sub-atomic particles like neutrinos (particles which have no electrical charge, no rest mass, and which travel at the speed of light) may have a mass after all and exist in sufficient quantities to bring the density up to the 100% necessary for re-contraction. These scenarios have now been widely abandoned because the evidence supports the traditional picture of neutrinos as massless, and especially because such scenarios predict a large-scale structure of the universe which is completely at odds with what is observed.[42]

The *Cold Dark Matter* theories postulate the existence of unknown particles of weakly interacting matter (facetiously called WIMPs) which exist in sufficient abundance to make the universe re-contract. But there is no evidence that WIMPs even exist; theorists have to simply invent such particles and their masses. Worse still, Cold Dark Matter scenarios have to say that this exotic matter exists mainly in intergalactic space, so as not to disrupt the measured motion of galaxies. But the existence of vast amounts of exotic matter in intergalactic space is incompatible with the recent measurements by the COBE satellite of the primordial fluctuations in the microwave background radiation.[43] The fact is that nobody knows where the so-called "missing mass" of 90% is supposed to come from. Astronomer Joseph Silk reflects, "If the hidden mass is completely unobservable, anything is permissible. Suggestions for the missing mass have ranged from snowflakes to rocks, planets, black holes, even to excess issues of the

Astrophysical Journal." ". . . in the absence of observable evidence, any suggestions must lack credibility."[44]

The observational evidence thus supports a low density universe destined to indefinite expansion. Sandage and Tammann conclude: "Hence, we are forced to decide that . . . it seems inevitable that the Universe will expand forever."[45] This conclusion may be strengthened. For Sandage and Tammann in a later discussion go on to point out that in order to fit the observational evidence, even high density universes (which are typically thought to re-contract) may also have to expand forever. They conclude, "Hence, the one certain conclusion is that in all models of either high or low density, . . . the Universe will not stop its expansion. *This means it has happened only once.* The creation event was unique."[46]

The oscillating model, therefore, is seriously flawed. It contradicts both the known laws of physics and the current observational evidence. It therefore provides no plausible escape from the beginning of the universe.

In recent years theoretical cosmology has become increasingly speculative, obscuring the boundary between physics and metaphysics. The marriage of the General Theory of Relativity (upon which the Big Bang model is based) to Quantum Theory (sub-atomic physics) has resulted in the conception of a third alternative to the standard Big Bang model: *quantum models* of the universe. One should say the "would-be marriage," for the fact is that these two great theories of modern physics are mutually inconsistent, and nobody knows how to reconcile them. Quantum models grow out of the attempt at one such reconciliation. Prior to 10^{-43} second after the Big Bang (that's .0000000000000000000000000000000000000000001 of a second) quantum physics must be employed to describe the universe, and the goal of the union of Relativity Theory and Quantum Theory is to describe this brief moment. Unfortunately, this period is so poorly understood that one commentator has compared it with the regions on the maps of ancient cartographers marked "Here there be dragons!"—it can be filled with all sorts of fantasies. The fact is that these theories are as much speculation as science.

The first class of models appealing to quantum effects to explain the origin of the universe were *vacuum fluctuation models.* These theories hold that what we have thus far taken to be the expansion of the *whole* universe is really only the expansion of a *part* of it, or, in other words, that our observable universe is just a tiny part of a wider Universe-as-a-whole. The Universe-as-a-whole is itself a vacuum in a steady state. But throughout this vacuum sub-atomic energy fluctuations are conceived to be occurring, by means of which material particles are created out of the energy contained in the vacuum. These then grow into separate mini-universes within the whole. All we can observe is the expansion of our mini-universe, and we have no knowledge whatsoever of what is going on in other similar mini-universes.

Our universe thus never went back to an initial singularity, but emerged by an uncaused fluctuation from the vacuum of a wider background space—a view that is often expressed by saying that the universe is a "free lunch" because in this case we got something for nothing.

Such a congenial way of talking is, however, completely misleading. In popular presentations of these models it is often not explained that they require the postulation of some sort of specially fine-tuned, background space on the analogy of a quantum mechanical vacuum from which the universe emerges via a fluctuation. Thus, the origin of the observable universe out of this wider space-time is not at all a free lunch, but requires an elaborately set table in advance.

Such models face formidable theoretical difficulties which are so severe that even some of the original proponents of these models have now abandoned them. Brout and Spindel, for example, have moved beyond such models, commenting that the theoretical foundations of the particle production mechanisms as well as the instability of the background space to fluctuations "are flimsy at best."[47]

In any case such models have been shown to be incompatible with observational cosmology.[48] On such scenarios, there is no way to specify exactly when and where a fluctuation in the primordial vacuum will occur which will grow into a universe. Within any finite interval of time there is a positive probability of such a fluctuation occurring at any point in space. It follows that given infinite past time, universes will spring into being at every point in the vacuum and, as they expand, will begin to collide and coalesce with one another. But we do not observe anything of this sort happening in nature.

Isham comments that this problem is "fairly lethal" to vacuum fluctuation models and that they therefore "have not found wide acceptance."[49] About the only way to avoid the difficulty of colliding universes is to postulate that the background vacuum space is itself expanding—but then we're forced to posit some origin of the wider Universe itself, and we're right back where we started from.

I mentioned that vacuum fluctuation models have been abandoned as plausible accounts of the origin of the universe by some of their original expositors and to that extent are already somewhat passé. Brout and Spindel now contend that an explanation of the origin of the universe "must await the yet-to-come quantum theory of gravity."[50] That brings us to the second class of quantum models.

In addition to vacuum fluctuation models, there are also *quantum gravity models*. The particular quantum gravity model of the origin of the universe which has drawn the most attention in recent years is the Hartle-Hawking model, popularized by Stephen Hawking, the brilliant mathematical theorist of Cambridge University, who has received wide publicity of his views in the popular press. One of the most interesting features of Hawking's best-selling *Brief History of Time*, in which he expounds his views, is its overtly theological orientation. Although Hawking does not deny the existence of God, he does deny that there is a Creator in the sense of a temporal First Cause of the origin of the universe.

In discussing whether a Creator exists, Hawking admits that if the universe began to exist, then one could identify the Big Bang as the instant at which God created the universe.[51] In fact, he thinks that a number of attempts to avoid the Big Bang were probably motivated by the feeling that a beginning of time "smacks of divine intervention."[52] Although it is not clear if Hawking shares this same motivation, he does tout his model as preferable to the Big Bang, because there would be no edge of space-time at which one "would have to appeal to God."[53]

Hawking's theory is perhaps most easily understood by contrasting it to the standard Big Bang model. In the standard model, the universe sprang from an initial singularity which marked the origin of all matter and energy, indeed, of physical space and time themselves. Nothing existed before this point; hence, the singularity cannot have any natural cause.

Hawking hopes that by introducing quantum physics into the description of the earliest stage of the universe, prior to 10^{-43} seconds after the Big Bang, one can eliminate the singularity. In order to accomplish this, however, Hawking must introduce imaginary numbers for the time variable in his equations, that is to say, numbers like $\sqrt{-1}$. Since any real number squared always equals a positive number, it is evident that there can be no real number which is the square root of -1. Therefore, mathematicians call such numbers "imaginary."

By using imaginary numbers for the time variable, one eliminates the singularity all right, but one also thereby eliminates the difference between time and space in the equations describing the universe. As Hawking says, ". . . the distinction between time and space disappears completely."[54] This is a very peculiar feature of the model, since in both the Special and General Theories of Relativity, time and space are distinct in virtue of their variables' having different mathematical signs (+ or -) in the equations. But in Hawking's model, this difference in sign disappears, because he is using imaginary numbers for the time variable. By means of this device, Hawking proposes a model in which time becomes imaginary prior to 10^{-43}

second, so that the singularity is rounded off. Space-time in this early region is geometrically the four-dimensional analogue of the two dimensional surface of a sphere. Any point on a sphere which one chooses to be an "initial" or "beginning" point, such as the North Pole, is really just like every other point on the sphere's surface. In particular, it does not constitute an edge or boundary to that surface. Thus, on Hawking's model, the past is finite, but boundless. Moreover, since imaginary time is not distinguishable from space, it would be improper to regard any point on this sphere-like surface as actually *earlier* than any other point on that surface, just as it would be improper to think of any point on the surface of a ball as earlier than any other similar point. Hawking comments,

> There would be no singularities at which the laws of science broke down and no edge of space-time at which one would have to appeal to God or some new law to set the boundary conditions for space-time. . . . The universe would be completely self-contained and not affected by anything outside itself. It would be neither created nor destroyed. It would just BE.[55]

In saying that the universe on his theory would not begin to exist, but would just BE, Hawking expresses the timeless existence of this four-dimensional space-time in which time is imaginary. He is not at all reluctant to draw theological conclusions from his model:

> The idea that space and time may form a closed surface without boundary . . . has profound implications for the role of God in the affairs of the universe. . . . So long as the universe had a beginning, we could suppose it had a creator. But if the universe is really completely self-contained, having no boundary or edge, it would have neither beginning nor end. What place, then, for a creator?[56]

In assessing Hawking's proposed model, one could criticize it effectively merely on the physical level alone. It is on the face of it highly speculative, and, according to Isham, it is most unlikely that it is even mathematically consistent.[57] Moreover, it is now generally recognized that the Hartle-Hawking approach fails to predict uniquely our universe; consequently, why this universe exists rather than one of an infinite number of alternatives cannot be explained.

But I prefer to leave such criticisms aside; perhaps better, more consistent models can be devised. Rather my objections strike much deeper, at the philosophical or metaphysical foundations of such theories. Hawking's quantum cosmology is rife with unexamined philosophical assumptions which are, at best, unproven and, at worst, false. Given his claim to have eliminated the need for a Creator, it's evident that Hawking does not take his theory to be merely some mathematical model which is useful for facilitating scientific predictions but which makes no pretense to be a realistic description of the world. Such a non-realist (or instrumentalist) understanding of the theory would not be incompatible with the claim that in actual fact the universe began to exist in real time and was created. Hawking's model would in that case be a sort of symbolic description of the real origin of the universe using the mathematical formalism of quantum physics. The fact that there is no beginning of the universe *in the model* would do nothing to eliminate the beginning of the universe *in reality*. Since Hawking wants to avoid a beginning of the universe and the attendant need for a Creator, he must (and does) take his model to be a realistic description of the early universe. But this is precisely where the problems arise. It seems quite evident that Hawking faces acute difficulties in commending his theory as a realistic account of the origin of the universe.

Take just one example: his use of so-called "imaginary time." Two problems arise in connection with this notion. First, it is physically unintelligible. If he is to commend his theory as a realistic description of the universe, then Hawking has the burden to explain what "imaginary time" means. Otherwise it is a meaningless combination of words. But it is no more evident what an imaginary interval of time is anymore than, say, the imaginary volume of a box or the imaginary area of a field or the imaginary number of people in a room. Hawking insists that imaginary time is "a well-defined mathematical concept."[58] But that's not the question; rather the question is whether that mathematical concept corresponds to any physical reality. The fact that something can be defined mathematically is no guarantee that any physical reality corresponds to it, as the late Sir Herbert Dingle so vividly illustrated:

> Suppose we want to find the number of men required for a certain job under certain conditions. Every schoolboy knows such problems, and he knows that he must begin by saying: "Let x = the number of men required." But that substitution introduces a whole range of possibilities that the nature of the original problem excludes. The mathematical symbol x can be positive, negative, integral, fractional, irrational, imaginary, complex, zero, infinite, and whatever else the fertile brain of the mathematician may devise. The number of men, however, must be simply positive and integral. Consequently, when you say, "Let x = the number of men required" you are making a quite invalid substitution, and the result of the cal-

culation, though entirely possible for the symbol, might be quite impossible for the men.

Every elementary algebra book contains such problems that lead to quadratic equations, and these have two solutions, which might be 8 and -3, say. We accept 8 as the answer and ignore -3 because we know from experience that there are no such things as negative men, and the only alternative interpretation—that we could get the work done by subtracting three men from our gang—is obviously absurd. . . .

So we just ignore [one] of the mathematical solutions, and quite overlook the significance of that fact—namely, that in the language of mathematics we can tell lies as well as truths, and *within the scope of mathematics itself there is no possible way of telling one from the other.* We can distinguish them *only by experience* or *by reasoning outside the mathematics,* applied to the possible relation between the mathematical solution and its supposed physical correlate.[59]

The point is that a "well-defined mathematical concept" may in fact be a metaphysical impossibility and that the only way to determine this is by getting outside the mathematics to consult what experience or extra-mathematical reasoning tells us reality is like. Time is one of those aspects of reality with which we are most intimately acquainted by experience and which has received extensive philosophical analysis as well. We simply have no comprehension of what it would be for time to be "imaginary" in the mathematical sense. Putting in imaginary numbers for the time variable appears to make no more sense than using negative numbers for the number of men required to do a job. It is a mere mathematical artifice.

Such a use of imaginary numbers for the time coordinate is nothing new. Already in 1920, Sir Arthur Eddington said that readers who found it difficult to understand curved space-time could evade the difficulty by using the "dodge" of imaginary numbers.[60] But, he said, it is "not very profitable" to speculate on the implications of this, because "it can scarcely be regarded as anything more than an analytical device." Imaginary time was only an illustrative tool, "which certainly does not correspond to any physical reality."[61]

Imaginary numbers are useful as mathematical devices which help in the computation of certain equations; but one always converts back to real numbers at the end in order to have some physically meaningful result. Hawking himself admits, "As far as everyday quantum mechanics is concerned, we may regard our use of imaginary time . . . as a merely mathematical device (or trick) to calculate answers about real space-time."[62] But Hawking in his model simply declines to take the final step of re-converting to real numbers. When you do that, the singularity suddenly reappears. Hawking states,

> Only if we could picture the universe in terms of imaginary time would there be no singularities. . . . When one goes back to the real time in which we live, however, there will still appear to be singularities.[63]

Thus, Hawking does not really eliminate the singularity; he only conceals it behind the physically unintelligible artifice of imaginary time.

Secondly, the use of imaginary numbers for the time variable makes time a spatial dimension, which is just bad metaphysics. Space and time are essentially different. Space is ordered by a relation of *betweenness*: for three points x, y, and z on a spatial line, y is between x and z. But time is ordered in addition by a unique relation of *earlier/later than*: for two moments t_1 and t_2 in time, t_1 is earlier than t_2, and t_2 is later than t_1. Spatial points are not related by any such relation; but this relation is essential to the nature of time, as the philosopher George Schlesinger points out: "The relations 'before' and 'after' have generally been acknowledged as being the most fundamental temporal relations, which means that time deprived of these relations would cease to be time."[64] Thus, it is impossible for time to be a dimension of space. Moreover, time is also ordered by the relations *past/future* with respect to the present. For example, my eating breakfast this morning was once present; but now it is past. There is nothing even remotely similar to this relation among points in space. Thus, space and time are essentially distinct.

But perhaps Hawking can be interpreted as holding, not that time in the earliest stage of the universe is a dimension of space, but that as one goes back in time, time ceases to exist and is replaced by a spatial dimension. But such an interpretation makes no sense. It would mean that the early history of the universe was timeless. But this assertion is contradictory to the claim that this era existed *before* the point that time began. For *before/after* is precisely a temporal relation, as we have seen. Thus, to say that this timeless segment existed *before* time is to presuppose a time before time, which is self-contradictory.

Hawking seems to realize the impossibility of having two successive stages of the universe, one timeless and the other temporal, and so he is driven to the position that our universe's existing in real time is just an illusion! He asserts,

This might suggest that the so-called imaginary time is really the real time, and that what we call real time is just a figment of our imaginations. In real time, the universe has a beginning and an end at singularities that form a boundary to spacetime and at which the laws of science break down. But in imaginary time, there are no singularities or boundaries. So maybe what we call imaginary time is really more basic, and what we call real is just an idea that we invent to help us describe what we think the universe is like.[65]

But as Smith points out, such an interpretation is "preposterous . . . at least observationally, since it is perfectly obvious that the universe in which we exist lapses in real rather than imaginary time."[66] If Hawking were right, we could not even correctly say, for example, that Lincoln's assassination occurred after his birth, since this is to assert a temporal relation between these two events.

Significantly, this philosophical critique applies not to the Hartle-Hawking model alone, but to all quantum gravitational models, since they all share the common feature of having real space-time originate in a quantum mechanical region which is a four-dimensional space involving imaginary time.[67] The metaphysical inadequacy of such scenarios is not a deficiency which can be solved through scientific advance precisely because the deficit is metaphysical, not physical. Of course, if some such model is interpreted non-realistically, then no metaphysical objection arises. On a non-realist interpretation, the real beginning of the universe at an initial singularity can be re-described in the language of quantum physics as a non-singular point existing in imaginary time. But the advance here is scientific (in the instrumental sense), not metaphysical. Such a model would not abrogate the fact the universe really began to exist.

It seems evident, therefore, that quantum models of the origin of the universe avoid the beginning of the universe only at the expense of making enormous and unjustified metaphysical assumptions about reality, assumptions which in the end deny the reality of time and temporal becoming and thus vitiate the models based on them as realistic descriptions of the universe. Thus, it appears that none of the alternatives to the Big Bang model of the origin of the universe is plausible. The best scientific evidence available confirms that the universe began to exist.

2. Confirmation from thermodynamics. Now if this were not enough, there is a second scientific confirmation for the beginning of the universe, the evidence from thermodynamics. According to the second law of thermodynamics, processes taking place in a closed system always tend toward a state of equilibrium. In other words, unless energy is constantly being fed into a system, the processes in the system will tend to run down and quit. For example, if I had a bottle that was a sealed vacuum inside, and I introduced into it some molecules of gas, the gas would spread itself out evenly inside the bottle. It is virtually impossible for the molecules to retreat, for example, into one corner of the bottle and remain. This is why when you walk into a room, the air in the room never separates suddenly into oxygen at one end and nitrogen at the other. It's also why when you step into your bath you may be confident that it will be an even temperature instead of frozen solid at one end and boiling at the other. It is clear that life would not be possible in a world in which the second law of thermodynamics did not operate.

Now our interest in the law is what happens when it is applied to the universe as a whole. The universe is, on the atheistic view, a gigantic closed system, since it is everything there is and there is nothing outside it. What this seems to imply then is that, given enough time, the universe and all its processes will run down, and the entire universe will come to equilibrium. This is known as the heat death of the universe. Once the universe reaches this state, no further change is possible. The universe is dead.

There are two possible types of heat death for the universe. If the universe will eventually re-contract, it will die a "hot" death. Dr. Tinsley describes such a state:

> If the average density of matter in the universe is great enough, the mutual gravitational attraction between bodies will eventually slow the expansion to a halt. The universe will then contract and collapse into a hot fireball. There is no known physical mechanism that could reverse a catastrophic big crunch. Apparently, if the universe becomes dense enough, it is in for a hot death.[68]

If the universe is fated to re-contraction, then as it contracts the stars gain energy, causing them to burn more rapidly so that they finally explode or evaporate. As everything in the universe grows closer together, the black holes begin to gobble up everything around them, and eventually begin themselves to coalesce. In time, "All the black holes finally coalesce into one large black hole that is coextensive with the universe,"[69] from which the universe will never re-emerge.

But suppose, as is more likely, that the universe will expand forever. Dr. Tinsley describes the fate of this universe:

> If the universe has a low density, its death will be cold. It will expand forever at a slower and slower rate. Galaxies will turn all of their gas into stars, and the stars will burn out. Our own sun will become a

cold, dead remnant, floating among the corpses of other stars in an increasingly isolated Milky Way.[70]

At 10^{30} years the universe will consist of 90% dead stars, 9% supermassive black holes formed by the collapse of galaxies, and 1% atomic matter, mainly hydrogen. Elementary particle physics suggests that thereafter protons will decay into electrons and positrons, so that space will be filled with a rarefied gas so thin that the distance between an electron and a positron will be about the size of the present galaxy. At 10^{100} years, some scientists believe that the black holes themselves will dissipate by a strange effect predicted by quantum mechanics. The mass and energy associated with a black hole so warp space that they are said to create a "tunnel" or "worm-hole" through which the mass and energy are ejected in another region of space. As the mass of a black hole decreases, its energy loss accelerates, so that it is eventually dissipated into radiation and elementary particles. Eventually all black holes will completely evaporate and all the matter in the ever-expanding universe will be reduced to a thin gas of elementary particles and radiation. Equilibrium will prevail throughout, and the entire universe will be in its final state, from which no change will occur.

Now the question that needs to be asked is this: if given enough time the universe will reach heat death, then why is it not in a state of heat death now, if it has existed forever, from eternity? If the universe did not begin to exist, then it should now be in a state of equilibrium. Its energy should be all used up. My wife and I have a very loud wind-up alarm clock. If I hear that the clock is ticking—which is no problem, believe me—then I know that at some point in the recent past it was wound up and has been running down since then. It's the same with the universe. Since it has not yet run down, this means, in the words of one baffled scientist, "In some way the universe must have been *wound up*."[71]

Some scientists have tried to escape this conclusion by arguing that the universe oscillates back and forth from eternity, and so never reaches a final state of equilibrium. Now I've already observed that such a model of the universe is a physical impossibility. But suppose it were possible. The fact is that the thermodynamic properties of this model imply the very beginning of the universe that its proponents seek to avoid. For as several scientists have pointed out, each time the model universe expands it would expand farther than before. Therefore, if you traced the expansions back in time they would get smaller and smaller and smaller. One scientific team explains, "The effect of entropy production will be to enlarge the cosmic scale, from cycle to cycle. . . . Thus, looking back in time, each cycle generated less entropy, had a smaller cycle time, and had a smaller cycle expansion factor then [*sic*] the cycle that followed it."[72] Therefore, in the words of another scientific team, "the multicycle model has an infinite future, but only a finite past."[73] Indeed, Silk estimates on the basis of the current level of entropy in the universe that it could not have gone through more than 100 previous oscillations.[74] Gribbin reluctantly concludes that this implies that the oscillating model of the universe still requires an origin of the universe prior to the smallest cycle.

So whether you choose a re-contracting model, an ever-expanding model, or an oscillating model, thermodynamics implies that the universe had a beginning. According to the English scientist P. C. W. Davies, the universe must have been created a finite time ago and is in the process of winding down. Prior to the creation, the universe simply did not exist. Therefore, Davies concludes, even though we may not like it, we must conclude that the universe's energy was somehow simply "put in" at the creation as an initial condition.[75]

So we have two scientific confirmations that the universe began to exist. First, the expansion of the universe implies the universe had a beginning. Second, thermodynamics shows the universe began to exist. Therefore, on the basis of both philosophical argument and scientific evidence, I think we are justified in accepting our second premiss, that the universe began to exist.

Therefore, the Universe Has a Cause of Its Existence

From the first premise—that *whatever begins to exist has a cause*—and the second premise—that *the universe began to exist*—it follows logically that *the universe has a cause.* This conclusion ought to stagger us, to fill us with awe, for it means that the universe was brought into existence by *something* which is greater than and beyond it.

But what is the nature of this first cause of the universe? It seems to me quite plausible that it is a personal being who created the universe. This thesis is supported by both philosophical argument and scientific confirmation.

Philosophical Argument

Consider the following puzzle: we've concluded that the beginning of the universe was the effect of a first cause. By the nature of the case that cosmic cause cannot have any beginning of its existence nor any prior cause. Nor can there have been any changes in this cause, either in its nature or operations, prior to the beginning of the universe. It just exists changelessly without any beginning, and a finite time ago it brought the universe into existence. Now this is exceedingly odd. The cause is in some sense eternal and yet the effect which it produced is not eternal, but began to exist a finite time ago. How can this be? If the necessary and sufficient conditions for the production of the effect are eternal, then why isn't the effect eternal? How can all the causal conditions sufficient for the production of the effect be changelessly existent and yet the effect not also be existent along with the cause? How can the cause exist without the effect?

Let me illustrate what I mean: Let's say the cause of water's freezing is sub-zero temperatures. Whenever the temperature falls below zero degrees Centigrade, the water freezes. Once the cause is given, the effect must follow, and if the cause exists from eternity, the effect must also exist from eternity. If the temperature were to remain below zero degrees from eternity, then any water around would be frozen from eternity. But this seems to imply that if the cause of the universe existed eternally, the universe would also have existed eternally. And this we know to be false.

One might say that the cause came to exist or changed in some way just prior to the first event. But then the cause's beginning or changing would be the first event, and we must ask all over again for its cause. And this cannot go on forever, for we know that a beginningless series of events cannot exist. There must be an absolutely first event, before which there was no change, no previous event. We know that this first event must have been caused. The question is: How can a first event come to exist if the cause of that event exists changelessly and eternally? Why isn't the effect as co-eternal as the cause?

It seems that there is only one way out of this dilemma, and that is to infer that the cause of the universe is a personal agent who chooses to create a universe in time. Philosophers call this type of causation "agent causation," and because the agent is free, he can initiate new effects by freely bringing about conditions which were not previously present. For example, a man sitting from eternity could will to stand up; thus, a temporal effect arises from an eternally existing agent. Similarly, a finite time ago a Creator endowed with free will could have willed to bring the world into being at that moment. In this way, God could exist changelessly and eternally but choose to create the world in time. By "choose" one need not mean that the Creator changes his mind about the decision to create, but that He freely and eternally intends to create a world with a beginning. By exercising his causal power, he therefore brings it about that a world with a beginning comes to exist. So the cause is eternal, but the effect is not. In this way, then, it is possible for the temporal universe to have come to exist from an eternal cause: through the free will of a personal Creator.

The Anthropic Principle

This purely philosophical argument for the personhood of the cause of the origin of the universe receives powerful scientific confirmation from the observed fine-tuning of the universe, which bespeaks intelligent design. Without wanting to go into a discussion of the teleological argument, let me simply say that in recent years the scientific community has been stunned by its discovery of how complex and sensitive a balance of initial conditions must be given in the Big Bang in order for the universe to permit the origin and evolution of intelligent life on Earth. The universe appears, in fact, to have been incredibly fine-tuned from the moment of its inception for the production of intelligent life on Earth at this point in cosmic history.

The incredibly complex and delicately balanced nexus of initial conditions necessary for intelligent life seems to be most plausibly explained if that nexus is the product of intelligent design, that is to say, if the cause of the beginning of the universe is a personal Creator.[76] The scientific evidence thus serves to underscore the conclusion to which philosophical argument has led us. More than that, however: the evidence also suggests a special relationship between the Creator and human beings. For man truly is the crown of creation. Though diminutive in size in comparison with the cosmos, a human being is nonetheless the most complex structure in the universe. After listing a minimum of ten crucial steps in the evolution of *Homo sapiens*, each of which is so improbable that the sun would have ceased to be a main sequence star and so incinerated the Earth before it would occur, Barrow and Tipler estimate that the odds against the assembly of the human genome are between $4^{-180(110,000)}$ and $4^{-360(110,000)}$![77] They also point out that far from showing the unimportance of human life, the vast size of the universe is a prerequisite of the natural production of just those elements which are necessary to life: ". . . for there to be enough time to construct the constituents of living beings, the Universe must be at least ten billion years old and therefore, as a consequence of its expansion, at least ten billion light years in extent."[78] That the entire universe should thus be so designed as to culminate in man as its most marvelous creation is highly suggestive of some special care of the Creator for human creatures in particular. Indeed, the Creator might be properly understood to be a Cosmic Parent of whom we are the children. The contemporary debate surrounding the Anthropic Principle thus not only confirms the personhood of the Creator, but is also quite suggestive theologically.

So we have both good philosophical and scientific reasons for regarding the cause of the universe as a personal Creator. What more can be known about his nature? On the basis of our philosophical arguments for the beginning of the universe, we know that he must be uncaused and changeless (since an infinite regress of events is impossible). Even if God was causally active prior to the creation of the universe in some sort of metaphysical time (say, creating spiritual realms), there must still be a beginning point to his activity and, hence to change; otherwise, one would have an infinite regress of events, which is impossible. Since we know nothing about God's having been active prior to physical creation, we may assume for simplicity's sake that time (or at least differentiated time) begins at creation and that God without creation is changeless. Since he is changeless without creation, he must be either timeless without creation, or at least "relatively timeless," to borrow the expression of one philosopher; that is, he exists in an undifferentiated time prior to creation. Since he is causally related to the world, he must be in time subsequent to creation (given that the "flow" of time is in some sense real). Since he is changeless without creation, he must be immaterial, since matter inherently involves change. Being immaterial, he must be spaceless as well as timeless. Since he created the universe from nothing, we know that he must be enormously powerful, if not omnipotent. Since he brought the universe into being without any antecedently determining conditions and fine-tuned it with a precision that literally defies comprehension, he must be both free and unimaginably intelligent, if not omniscient. Moreover, the fact that the entire known universe, from the smallest elementary particles to the most distant stars, was designed in such a way as to be a suitable environment for the existence of human life on Earth suggests the astounding conclusion that he may have some special concern for us. These properties constitute the central core of what theists mean by "God."

The book of Genesis declares, "In the beginning God created the heavens and the earth." For thousands of years, muses Robert Jastrow, people who have believed this statement have known the truth which scientists have discovered only within the last fifty years. For the rationalistic scientist (and, we may add, philosopher), the story ends, smiles Jastrow, like a bad dream:

> He has scaled the mountains of ignorance; he is about to conquer the highest peak; as he pulls himself over the final rock, he is greeted by a band of theologians who have been sitting there for centuries.[79]

The beginning of the universe—declared by revelation, established by philosophy, and confirmed by science—thus points beyond itself to God, its Personal Creator.

Objections. Now certain thinkers have objected to the intelligibility of this conclusion. For example, Adolf Grünbaum, a prominent philosopher of space and time and a vociferous critic of theism, has marshaled a whole troop of objections against inferring God as the Creator of the universe.[80] As these are very typical, a brief review of his objections should be quite helpful. Grünbaum's objections fall into three groups. Group I seeks to cast doubt upon the concept of "cause" in the argument for a cause of the universe. (1) When we say that everything has a cause, we use the word "cause" to mean something that transforms previously existing materials from one state to another. But when we infer that the universe has a cause, we must mean by "cause" something that creates its effect out of nothing. Since these two meanings of "cause" are not the same, the argument is guilty of equivocation and is thus invalid. (2) It does not follow from the necessity of there being a cause that the cause of the universe is a conscious agent. (3) It is logically fallacious to infer that there is a *single* conscious agent who created the universe.

But these objections do not seem to present any insuperable difficulties: (1) The univocal concept of "cause" employed throughout the argument is the concept of something which brings about or produces its effects. Whether this production involves transformation of already existing materials or creation out of nothing is an incidental question. Thus, the charge of equivocation is groundless. (2) The personhood of the cause does not follow from the cosmological argument proper, but from an analysis of the notion of a first cause of the beginning of the universe, confirmed by Anthropic considerations. (3) The inference to a single cause of the origin of the universe seems justified in light of the principle, commonly accepted in science, that one should not multiply causes beyond necessity. One is justified in inferring only causes such as are necessary to explain the effect in question; positing any more would be gratuitous. Since the universe is a single effect originating in the Big Bang event, we have no grounds for inferring a plurality of causes.

The objections of Group II relate the notion of causality to the temporal series of events: (1) Causality is logically compatible with an infinite, beginningless series of events. (2) If everything has a cause of its existence, then the cause of the universe must also have a cause of its existence.

Both of these objections, however, seem to be based on misunderstandings. (1) It is not the concept of causality which is incompatible with an infinite series of past events. Rather the incompatibility, as we have seen, is between the notion of an actually infinite number of things and the series of past events. That causality has nothing to do with it may be seen by reflecting on the fact that the philosophical arguments for the beginning of the universe would work even if the events were all spontaneous, causally non-connected events. (2) The argument does not presuppose that everything has a cause. Rather the operative causal principle is that *whatever begins to exist has a cause*. Something that exists eternally and, hence, without a beginning would not need to have a cause. This is not special pleading for God, since the atheist has always maintained the same thing about the universe: it is beginningless and uncaused. The difference between these two hypotheses is that the atheistic view has been shown to be untenable.

Group III objections are aimed at the alleged claim that creation from nothing surpasses all understanding: (1) If creation out of nothing is incomprehensible, then it is irrational to believe in such a doctrine. (2) An incomprehensible doctrine cannot explain anything.

But with regard to (1), creation from nothing is not incomprehensible in Grünbaum's sense. By "incomprehensible" Grünbaum appears to mean "unintelligible" or "meaningless." But the statement that a finite time ago a transcendent cause brought the universe into being out of nothing is clearly a meaningful statement, not mere gibberish, as is evident from the very fact that we are debating it. We may not understand *how* the cause brought the universe into being out of nothing, but then it is even more incomprehensible, in this sense, how the universe could have popped into being out of nothing without *any* cause, material or productive. One cannot avert the necessity of a cause by positing an absurdity. (2) The doctrine, being an intelligible statement, obviously does constitute a purported explanation of the origin of the universe. It may be a metaphysical rather than a scientific explanation, but it is no less an explanation for that.

Grünbaum has one final objection against inferring a cause of the origin of the universe: the cause of the Big Bang can be neither *after* the Big Bang (since backward causation is impossible) nor *before* the Big Bang (since time begins at or after the Big Bang). Therefore, the universe's beginning to exist cannot have a cause.[81] But this argument pretty clearly confronts us with a false dilemma. For why couldn't God's creating the universe be *simultaneous* (or coincident) with the Big Bang? On the view I've defended, God may be conceived to be timeless or relatively timeless without creation and in time at and subsequent to the first moment of creation.

None of Grünbaum's objections, therefore, seems to undermine the credibility of our argument for God as the Personal Creator of the universe.

Hence, amazing as it may seem, the most plausible answer to the question of why something exists rather than nothing is that God exists. That means, in turn, that the first and most fundamental condition for meaning to life and the universe is supplied.

PRACTICAL APPLICATION

Having just completed this section, some of you may wonder "How could I possibly share all this in an evangelistic contact?" Here we must simply exercise a little common sense and be sensitive to where the other person is in his thinking. Of course, you don't lay all this material about actual and potential infinity, the expanding universe, infinite density, thermodynamics, quantum fluctuations, and imaginary time on the poor non-Christian at once! You need to understand how deep his thinking and background concerning these subjects are in order to know just what to relate to him. You start simple and go deep as he has further questions. I know this material is effective, because I have seen God use it when it is communicated with sensitivity.

For example, my wife, Jan, was once talking to a gal in the student union who said that she did not believe in God. Jan replied, "Well, what do you think of the argument for a first cause?" "What's that?" said the gal. My wife explained, "Everything we see has a cause, and those causes have causes, and so on. But this can't go back forever. There had to be a beginning and a first cause which started the whole thing. This is God." Now that was obviously a very simple statement of the argument we've been discussing. The young woman responded, "I guess God exists after all." She was not ready to receive Christ at that point, but at least she had moved one step closer, away from her atheism.

On another occasion I was talking to a guy who thought he was very clever; he said smugly, "If God created the universe, then where did God come from?" (I think he thought this was an unanswerable question.) So I replied, "God didn't come from anywhere. He is eternal and has always existed. So he doesn't need a cause. But now let me ask you something. The universe has not always existed but had a beginning. So *where did the universe come from?*" He was utterly dumbfounded. Again, he did not become a Christian, but I hope that at least he was shaken out of his intellectual lethargy so as to be more open to the gospel. Here again the insights of the argument we have been discussing were capable of being shared in a very simple way to speak to the man in the street on his own level.

When one talks with a person who has a deeper understanding of these issues, then of course one must go deeper. For example, when we were studying in Germany on a research fellowship, we met a Polish physicist who was in Germany on a similar fellowship. As we chatted, she mentioned that physics had destroyed her belief in God and that life had become meaningless to her. "When I look out at the universe all I see is blackness," she explained, "and when I look in myself all I see is blackness within." (What a poignant statement of the modern predicament!) Well, at that point my wife volunteered, "Oh, you should read Bill's doctoral dissertation! He uses physics to prove God exists." So we lent her my dissertation on the cosmological argument to read. Over the ensuing days, she became progressively more excited. When she got to the section on astronomy and astrophysics, she was positively elated. "I *know* these scientists that you are quoting!" she exclaimed in amazement. By the time she reached the end, her faith had been restored. "Thank you for helping me to believe that God exists," she said. We answered, "Would you like to know him in a personal way?" Then we made an appointment to meet her that evening at a restaurant. Meanwhile we prepared from memory our own hand-printed Four Spiritual Laws. After supper we opened the booklet and began, "Just as there are physical laws that govern the physical universe, so there are spiritual laws that govern your relationship to God. . . ." "Why, physical laws! Spiritual laws!" she exclaimed. "This is just for me!" When we got to the circles at the end representing two lives and asked her which circle represented her life, she put her hand over the circles and said, "Oh, this is so personal! I cannot answer now." So we encouraged her to take the booklet home and to give her life to Christ. When we saw her the next day, her face was radiant with joy. She told us of how she had gone home and in the privacy of her room prayed to receive Christ. She then flushed all the wine and tranquilizers that she had been on down the toilet. She was a truly transformed individual. We gave her a *Good News for Modern Man* and explained the importance of maintaining a devotional life with God. Our paths then parted for several months. But when we saw her again she was still enthusiastic in her faith, and her most precious possessions were her Good News Bible and her hand-made Four Spiritual Laws. So it was a great victory for God. It was one of the most vivid illustrations I've seen of how the Holy Spirit can use arguments and evidence to draw people to a saving knowledge of God.

One final practical tip in sharing this material: I've learned from experience that one must be extremely sensitive in talking with science students, because they tend to come to a discussion with a deeply held belief in the mutual irrelevancy of science and religion. This belief is rarely thought through; it's just a presupposition of much of their scientific sub-culture which they've absorbed, and they tend to react emotionally when it's challenged. Thus, on the one hand, they resent any attempt to enlist scientific evidence on behalf of theism (though, inconsistently, many are quite content to allow science to criticize religion). In response to the material of this chapter, one is apt to hear responses like "Physics can't prove that God exists" or "The Big Bang theory might be proven to be wrong." On the other hand, they are scandalized that a religious person should criticize scientific theories, even though that critique is based on philosophical argument and empirical evidence, rather than theology. In particular, Stephen Hawking has become something of an icon to many students, and any critique of his views is taken as an affront, if not irreverent.

I've found the most effective way of dealing with this problem is to head it off at the pass. Right at the beginning, I raise this issue myself and confront it squarely, usually by saying something like: "Now before we begin, let me try to diffuse an emotional time bomb that may be ticking in your mind." I then explain two things: "(1) The issues I'm raising are primarily philosophical in nature, not scientific. I'm not proposing some sort of creation science whereby God becomes a part of a scientific theory.[82] I'm just saying that scientific evidence shows that the universe had a beginning. That's a religiously neutral statement. Any further questions are philosophical, not scientific, in character. *As scientists* we can refuse to ask such questions, but surely as *human beings* seeking to find meaning to life and the universe we can legitimately pose such philosophical questions. (2) I'm not claiming that I can *prove* God exists. All I'm saying is that the evidence makes it more probable than not that the universe began to exist and that to the extent that this is probable, it is also probable that God exists."[83]

Should students persist in arguing about this, I often point out the double standard involved: whenever people think that science and religion conflict (for example, Darwinian evolution and Genesis), people jump on the bandwagon of science and proclaim another victory in the "warfare between science and religion," but the minute scientific evidence confirms the Bible, people start jumping off the bandwagon, and one is apt to hear all sorts of grave intonations about how uncertain science is or its irrelevancy to religion. You can't have it both ways.

In dealing with the scandal of criticizing certain scientific theories, I've found it useful to explain to students the distinction between criticizing a person and criticizing a person's views. I praise Hawking's brilliance and courage in the face of Lou Gehrig's disease, but go on to point out that as a scientist Hawking himself would be the first to say that no one's views are sacrosanct and above criticism. I emphasize that I am criticizing only his metaphysical views. It's surprising how making this elementary distinction up front can prevent a hostile reaction later.

So I encourage you to master this material and learn to communicate with sensitivity. As one of my apologetics teachers once remarked to us, "We should know our subject profoundly and share it simply." If you cannot answer an unbeliever's objection on some point, admit it and refer him to literature on the subject that can satisfy his question. In an age of increasing atheism and agnosticism, we cannot afford to forgo an apologetic for this most basic of all Christian beliefs: the existence of God.

CHAPTER FOUR

The Problem of Miracles

BEFORE WE CAN EVEN EXAMINE the evidence to see whether the Creator God of the universe has revealed himself in some special way in the world in order to offer man the promise of immortality which is so necessary for meaningful existence now, we must first deal with the problem of whether such divine action is possible in the first place. And if it is, how can it be identified? That is to say, we are confronted with the problem of miracles.

Undoubtedly, one of the major stumbling blocks to becoming a Christian for many people today is that Christianity is a religion of miracles. It asserts that God became incarnate in Jesus of Nazareth, being born of a virgin, that he performed various miracles, exorcised demonic beings, and that, having died by crucifixion, he rose from the dead. But the problem is that these sorts of miraculous events seem to belong to a world view foreign to modern man—a pre-scientific, superstitious world view belonging to the ancient and middle ages.

Some theologians have been so embarrassed by this fact that many of them, following Rudolf Bultmann, have sought to demythologize the Bible, thereby removing the stumbling block to modern man. According to Bultmann, no one who uses the radio or electric lights should be expected to believe in the mythological world view of the Bible in order to become a Christian. He insists that he is not trying to make Christianity more palatable to modern man, but is trying merely to remove a false stumbling block so that the true stumbling block—the call to authentic existence symbolized by the cross—might become evident. But in so doing, Bultmann reduces Christianity to little more than the existentialist philosophy of Martin Heidegger. Indeed, some Bultmann disciples like

Herbert Braun or Schubert Ogden have pushed Bultmann's views to their logical conclusion and have propounded a Christless and even atheistic Christianity. Such theologies offer man no hope of immortality. If the Christian hope of immortality through eschatological resurrection is to be believed, then contemporary thinkers may well demand of Christians some defense of miracles.

HISTORICAL BACKGROUND

DEIST OBJECTIONS TO MIRACLES

The skepticism of modern man with regard to miracles arose during the Enlightenment, or Age of Reason, which dawned in Europe during the seventeenth century. Thereafter, miracles simply became unbelievable for most of the intelligentsia. The attack upon miracles was led by the Deists. Although Deists accepted the existence of God, his conservation of the world in being, and his general revelation in nature, they strenuously denied that he had revealed himself in any special way in the world. They were therefore very exercised to demonstrate the impossibility of the occurrence of miracle, or at least of the identification of miracle. They were countered by a barrage of Christian apologetic literature defending the possibility and evidential value of miracle. Let us examine now the principal arguments urged by the Deists against miracles and the responses offered by their Christian opponents.

The Newtonian World-Machine

Although the most important philosophical opponents of miracles were Spinoza and Hume, much of the debate was waged against the backdrop of the mechanical world view of Newtonian physics. In his *Philosophiae naturalis principia mathematica* (1687), Isaac Newton formulated his famous three laws of motion, from which, together with some definitions, he was able to deduce the various theorems and corollaries of his physics. In regarding the world in terms of masses, motions, and forces operating according to these laws, Newton's *Principia* seemed to eliminate the need for God's providence and gave rise to a picture of the universe appropriately characterized as the "Newtonian world-machine."

Newton's model of mechanical explanation was enthusiastically received as the paradigm for explanation in all fields; this attitude reached its height in Pierre Simon de Laplace's belief that a Supreme Intelligence, equipped with Newton's *Principia* and knowing the present position and velocity of every particle in the universe, could deduce the exact state of the universe at any other point in time. Such a world view promoted the Deist conception of God as the creator of the world-machine, who wound it up like a clock and set it running under the laws of matter and motion, never to interfere with it again.

Indeed, this harmoniously functioning world-machine was thought to provide the best evidence that God exists. The eighteenth-century French *philosophe* Diderot exclaimed, "Thanks to the works of these great men, the world is no longer a God; it is a machine with its wheels, its cords, its pulleys, its springs, and its weights."[1] But equally it was thought that such a world system also made it incredible that God should interfere with its operation via miraculous interventions. Diderot's contemporary Voltaire said it was absurd and insulting to God to think that he would interrupt the operations of "this immense machine," since he designed it from the beginning to run according to his divinely decreed, immutable laws.[2] For eighteenth-century Newtonians, such miraculous interventions could only be described as violations of the laws of nature and were therefore impossible.

Benedict de Spinoza

The philosophical attack upon miracles, however, actually preceded the publication of Newton's *Principia*. In 1670 Benedict de Spinoza in his *Tractatus theologico-politicus* argued against both the possibility and evidential value of miracles. Two of his arguments are of special significance for our discussion.

Miracles Violate the Unchangeable Order of Nature

First, Spinoza argues that nothing happens contrary to the eternal and unchangeable order of nature. He maintains that all that God wills is characterized by eternal necessity and truth. For since there is no difference between God's understanding and his will, it is the same to say that God knows a thing or that God wills a thing. Thus, the same necessity that characterizes God's knowledge characterizes his will. Therefore, the laws of nature flow from the necessity and perfection of the divine nature. If some event that was contrary to these laws could occur, then the divine will and knowledge would stand in contradiction to nature, which is impossible. To say God does something contrary to the laws of nature is to say God does something contrary to his own nature. Therefore, miracles are impossible.

Miracles Insufficient to Prove God's Existence

Second, Spinoza believed that a proof of God's existence must be absolutely certain. It is by the unchangeable order of nature that we know that God exists. By admitting miracles, Spinoza warns, we break the laws of nature and thus create doubts about the existence of God, leading us right into the arms of atheism!

Spinoza also develops two sub-points under this objection. First, a miracle could not in any case prove God's existence, since a lesser being such as an angel or demon could be the cause of the event. Second, a so-called miracle is simply a work of nature not yet discovered by man. Our knowledge of nature's laws is limited, and just because we cannot explain the cause of a particular event does not mean it is a miracle having God as its supernatural cause.

David Hume

While Spinoza attacked the possibility of the occurrence of a miracle, the eighteenth-century Scottish skeptic David Hume attacked the possibility of the identification of a miracle. In his essay "Of Miracles" he presents a two-pronged assault against miracles, which takes the form of an "Even if . . . but in fact . . ." argument; that is to say, in the first half he argues against miracles while granting certain concessions, and in the second half he argues on the basis of what he thinks is in fact the case. We may differentiate the two halves of his argument by referring to the first as his "in principle" argument and to the second as his "in fact" argument.

"In Principle" Argument

Hume maintains that it is impossible in principle to prove that a miracle has occurred. A wise man, he says, proportions his belief to the evidence. If the evidence makes a conclusion virtually certain, then we may call this a "proof," and a wise man will give whole-hearted belief to that conclusion. If the evidence makes a conclusion more likely than not, then we may speak of a "probability," and a wise man will accept the conclusion as true with a degree of confidence proportionate to the probability. Now, Hume argues, even if we concede that the evidence for a particular miracle amounts to a *full proof*, it is still in principle impossible to identify that event as a miracle. Why? Because standing opposed to this proof is an equally full proof, namely the evidence for the unchangeable laws of nature, that the event in question is not a miracle.

Hume seems to imagine a scale in which the evidence is being weighed. On the one side of the scale is the evidence for a particular miracle, which (he concedes for the sake of argument) amounts to a full proof. But on the other side of the scale stands the evidence from all people in all the ages for the regularity of the laws of nature, which also amounts to a full proof. He writes, "A miracle is a violation of the laws of nature, and as a firm and unalterable experience has established these laws, a proof against miracle, from the very nature of the fact, is as entire as any argument from experience can possibly be imagined."[3] Thus, proof stands against proof, and the scales are evenly balanced. Since the evidence does not incline in either direction, the wise man cannot hold to a miracle with any degree of confidence.

Indeed, Hume continues, to prove a miracle has taken place, one would have to show that it would be an even *greater* miracle for the testimony in support of the event in question to be false. Thus, with regard to the resurrection, Hume asks, which would be the greater miracle: that a man should rise from the dead or that the witnesses should either be deceived or try to deceive? He leaves no doubt as to his answer: he asserts that even if all historians agreed that on January 1, 1600, Queen Elizabeth publicly died and was buried and her successor installed, but that a month later she reappeared, resumed the throne, and ruled England for three more years, Hume would not have the least inclination to believe so miraculous an event. He would accept the most extraordinary hypothesis for her pretended death and burial rather than admit such a striking violation of the laws of nature. Thus, even if the evidence for a miracle constituted a full proof, the wise man would not believe in miracles.

"In Fact" Arguments

But in fact, says Hume, the evidence for miracles does not amount to a full proof. Indeed, the evidence is so poor, it does not even amount to a probability. Therefore, the decisive weight falls on the side of the scale containing the full proof for the regularity of nature, a weight so heavy that no evidence for miracle could ever hope to counter-balance it.

Hume gives four reasons why in fact the evidence for miracles is negligible: First, no miracle in history is attested by a sufficient number of educated and honest men, who are of such social standing that they would have a great deal to lose by lying. Second, people crave the miraculous and will believe the most absurd stories, as the abundance of false tales of miracles proves. Third, miracles occur only among barbarous peoples. And fourth, miracles occur in all religions and thereby cancel each other out, since they support contradictory doctrines.

Hume concludes that miracles can never be the foundation for any system of religion. "Our most holy religion is founded on *Faith*, not on reason," pontificates Hume, all the while laughing up his sleeve:

> The Christian Religion not only was at first attended with miracles, but even at this day cannot be believed by any reasonable person

without one. Mere reason is insufficient to convince us of its veracity: And whoever is moved by *Faith* to assent to it, is conscious of a
continued miracle in his own person, which subverts all the principles of his understanding, and gives him a determination to believe
what is most contrary to custom and experience.[4]

In other words, it is a miracle that anyone could be stupid enough to believe
in Christianity!

CHRISTIAN DEFENSE OF MIRACLES

As I indicated earlier, the Christians of the seventeenth and eighteenth
centuries were far from lax in responding to the Deists' attacks. Let us look,
therefore, at their answers to Spinoza and Hume, as well as to the general
Newtonian world view.

Contra Spinoza

First, we shall consider the response to Spinoza's two objections by several
of the leading Christian thinkers of that era.

Jean Le Clerc

One of the earliest progenitors of biblical criticism, the French theologian
Jean Le Clerc, presented in his *Sentimens de quelques theologiens* (1685) an
apologetic for Christianity that, he maintained, was invulnerable to
Spinoza's attacks. He asserts that the empirical evidence for Jesus' miracles and resurrection is simply more convincing than Spinoza's *a priori*
philosophical reasoning. Specifically, against Spinoza's contention that
miracles may simply be natural events, Le Clerc rejoins that nobody could
sincerely believe Jesus' resurrection and ascension to be natural events com-
parable to, say, a man's birth. Nor does it suffice to say these events could
be caused by unknown natural laws, for why then are not more of these
events produced, and how is it that at the very instant Jesus commanded a
paralyzed man to walk "the Laws of Nature (unknown to us) were prepared
and ready to cause the . . . Paralytic Man to walk"?[5] Both of these considerations serve to show that the miraculous events in the gospels, which can
be established by ordinary historical methods, are indeed of divine origin.

Samuel Clarke

Considerable analysis was brought to the concept of miracle by the English
philosopher-theologian Samuel Clarke in his Boyle lectures of 1705.
Reflecting Newtonian influence, Clarke asserts that matter only has the
power to continue in either motion or rest. Anything that is *done* in the
world is done either by God or by created intelligent beings. The so-called

natural forces of matter, like gravitation, are properly speaking the effect of God's acting *on* matter at every moment. The upshot of this is that the so-called "course of nature" is a fiction—what we call the course of nature is in reality nothing other than God's producing certain effects in a continual and uniform manner. Thus, a miracle is not contrary to the course of nature, which does not really exist; it is simply an unusual event that God does. Moreover, since God is omnipotent, miraculous events are no more difficult for him than regular events. So the regular order of nature proves the existence and attributes of God, and miracles prove the interposition of God into the regular order in which he acts.

From the miracle itself taken as an isolated event, it is impossible to determine whether it was performed directly by God or by an angel or a demonic spirit. But, according to Clarke, the key to distinguishing between demonic miracles and divine miracles (whether done directly or indirectly by God) is the doctrinal context in which the miracle occurs. If the miracle is done in support of a doctrine that is contrary to moral law, then we may be sure it is not a divine miracle. Thus, in order to be a divine miracle, the *doctrinal context* of the event must be at least morally neutral. If two miracles are performed in support of two contrary doctrines, each morally neutral in itself, then the doctrine supported by the greater miracle ought to be accepted as of divine origin. Hence, the correct theological definition of a miracle is: "a work effected in a manner unusual, or different from the common and regular Method of Providence, by the interposition of God himself, or of some intelligent Agent superior to Man, for the proof or Evidence of some particular Doctrine, or in attestation to the Authority of some particular Person." Jesus' miracles thus prove that he was "a Teacher sent from God" who had "a Divine Commission."[6]

Jacob Vernet

The finest apologetic work written in French during the eighteenth century was in my opinion J. Alphonse Turrettin and Jacob Vernet's multi-volume *Traité de la vérité de la religion chrétienne* (1730-88). Turrettin, an esteemed professor of Protestant theology at Geneva, wrote the first volume in Latin; Vernet, also a member of the theological faculty at Geneva after 1756, translated Turrettin's volume and added nine of his own. The result was a sophisticated and informed response to French Deism based on internal and external Christian evidences.

Vernet defines a miracle as "a striking work which is outside the ordinary course of nature and which is done by God's all-mighty will, such that witnesses thereof regard it as extraordinary and supernatural."[7] Vernet does not, like Clarke, deny that there is a course of nature, but he does insist that the so-called course or order of nature is really composed of incidental states of events, not necessary states. They depend on the will of God, and it is only the constant and uniform procession of events that leads us to think the course of nature is invariable. But God can make exceptions to the general order of things when he deems it important. These miraculous events show that the course of nature "is not the effect of a blind necessity but of a free Cause who interrupts and suspends it when He pleases."[8]

Against the objection that miracles may be the result of an as yet undiscovered law of nature, Vernet replies that when the miracles are diverse and numerous, this possibility is minimized because it is hardly possible that all these unknown, marvelous operations of nature should occur at the same time. One might be able to explain away a single, isolated miracle on this basis, but not a series of miracles of different sorts.

Claude François Houtteville

The French Abbé Claude François Houtteville also argued for the possibility of miracles against Spinoza in his treatise *La religion chrétienne prouvée par les faits* (1740). He defines a miracle as "a striking action superior to all finite power" or more commonly as "a singular event produced outside the chain of natural causes."[9] Given the existence of God, it is at once evident that he can perform miracles, since he not only created the world but preserves it in being and directs all the laws of its operation by his sovereign hand. Against Spinoza's charge that miracles are impossible because natural law is the necessary decree of God's immutable nature, Houtteville responds that natural law is not necessary, but that God is free to establish whatever laws he wills. Moreover, God can change his decrees whenever he wishes. And even if he could not, miracles could be part of God's eternal decree for creation just as much as the natural laws, so that they represent no change in God. Houtteville even suggests that miracles may not be contrary to nature but only to what we know of nature. From God's perspective they could conform to certain laws unknown to us.

Contra Hume

Thomas Sherlock

The Christian response to Hume's arguments was as variegated as the response to Spinoza's. Thomas Sherlock, the Bishop of London, wrote his immensely popular *Tryal of the Witnesses* (1729) against the Deist Thomas Woolston, but his arguments are relevant to Hume's later critique of miracles. He presents a mock trial in which the apostles are accused of hoaxing the resurrection of Jesus. Woolston's attorney argues that because the resurrection violates the course of nature, no human testimony could possibly establish it, since it has the whole witness of nature against it. Sherlock has a multifaceted reply.

First, on that principle many natural matters of fact would have to be pronounced false. If we admit testimony only when it accords with our prior conceptions, then a man living in a hot climate, for example, would never believe the testimony of others that water could exist in a solid state as ice. Second, the resurrection is simply a matter of sense perception. If we met a man who claimed to have been dead, we would be admittedly suspicious. But of what? Not that he is now alive, for that is evident to our senses, but that he was ever dead. But would we say it is impossible to prove by human testimony that this man died a year ago? Such evidence is admitted in any court of law. Conversely, if we saw a man executed and later heard he was alive again, we would be suspicious. But of what? Not that he had been dead, but that he was now alive. But again, could we say that it is impossible for human testimony to prove that a man is alive? The point is, we are suspicious in these cases not because the facts in question cannot be proved by evidence, but because we tend to believe our own senses rather than reports of others that go contrary to our preconceived opinions of what can and cannot happen. But as a historical fact, the resurrection requires no more ability in the witnesses than to be able to distinguish between a dead man and a living man. Sherlock is willing to grant that in miraculous cases we may require more evidence than usual; but it is absurd to say that such cases admit of no evidence.

Third and finally, the resurrection contradicts neither right reason nor the laws of nature. Similarly to Houtteville, Sherlock maintains that the so-called course of nature arises from the prejudices and imaginations of men. Our senses tell us what the usual course of things is, but we go beyond our senses when we conclude that it cannot be otherwise. The uniform course of things runs contrary to the resurrection, but that is no proof that it is absolutely impossible. The same Power that created life in the first place can give it to a dead body again—the latter feat is no greater than the former.

Gottfried Less

Less, a German theologian at the University of Göttingen, discusses Hume's objections at length in his *Wahrheit der christlichen Religion* (1758). He defines a miracle as a work beyond the power of all creatures. There are two types of miracles: first degree miracles, which are performed directly by God; and second degree miracles, which are beyond human power but are done by finite spirit beings. Less admits that only second degree miracles can be proved, since one cannot be sure when God is acting directly. Miracles are both physically and morally possible: physically because God is the Lord of nature, and morally because miracles constitute part of his plan to confirm divine teaching.

There are two steps in proving that a miracle has occurred. First, one must prove the historicity of the event itself. Second, one must prove that the event is a miracle. Less argues that the testimony of the disciples to Jesus' miracles meets even the stringent conditions laid down by Hume, and that therefore, even he should accept the historicity of the gospel accounts. Although the apostles were unlearned men, all one needs in order to prove that something happened (say, a disease's being cured at a sheer verbal command) is five good senses and common sense. More specifically, Less argues that the miracles of Jesus were witnessed by hundreds of people, friends and enemies alike; that the apostles had the ability to testify accurately to what they saw; that the apostles were of such doubtless honesty and sincerity as to place them above suspicion of fraud; that the apostles, though of low estate, nevertheless had comfort and life itself to lose in proclaiming the Gospel; and that the events to which they testified took place in the civilized part of the world under the Roman Empire, in Jerusalem, the capital city of the Jewish nation. Thus, there is no reason to doubt the apostles' testimony concerning the miracles and resurrection of Jesus.

But were these events miracles? Less maintains that they were and turns to a refutation of Hume's arguments. In response to the "in principle" argument, Less argues: first, because nature is the freely willed order of God, a miracle is just as possible as any other event. Therefore, it is just as believable as any other event. Second, testimony to an event cannot be refuted by prior experiences and observations. Otherwise, we should never be justified in believing something outside our present experience; no new discoveries would be possible. Third, there is no contradiction between miracles and experience. Miracles are different events (*contraria*) from experience in general, but not contradictory events (*contradictoria*) to experience in general. For example, the contradiction to the testimony that Jesus raised certain people from the dead and himself so rose three days after his death must necessarily be the exact opposite of this statement, namely, that Jesus never raised anyone from the dead and never himself so rose. This latter statement would have to be proved in order to destroy the evidence for the gospels. But it would hardly be sufficient to assert that experience in general shows that dead men do not rise, for with this the Christian testimony is in full agreement. Only when the exact opposite is proved to be true could the Christian testimony be said to contradict experience.

As for Hume's "in fact" arguments, these are easily dismissed. First, it has already been shown that the witnesses to the gospel miracles were abundant and qualified. Second, the fact that people tend to believe miracle stories without proper scrutiny only shows that our scrutiny of such stories ought to be cautious and careful. Third, Jesus' miracles did not occur among a barbarous people, but in Jerusalem. Fourth, Hume's allegation that all religions have their miracles is not in fact true, for no other religion claims to be able to prove its teachings through miracles. Less also examines in considerable detail the examples furnished by Hume and finds in each case that the evidence does not approach that for the gospel miracles.

William Paley

Paley's two-volume *A View of the Evidences of Christianity* (1794) is undoubtedly the finest apologetic work of that era in English, and it exercised such considerable influence that it remained compulsory reading for any applicant to Cambridge University right up until the twentieth century. Primarily a studious investigation of the historical evidence for Christianity from miracles, Paley's treatise constitutes an across-the-board refutation of Hume's arguments. It will be remembered that it was Paley who so masterfully expounded the teleological argument, and he makes clear that in this work he presupposes the existence of God as proved by that argument.

Given the existence of God, miracles are not incredible. For why should it be thought incredible that God should want to reveal himself in the natural world to men, and how could this be done without involving a miraculous element? Further, any antecedent improbability in miracles is not so great that sound historical testimony cannot overcome it. Paley discerns the same fallacy in Hume's argument as did Less. A narrative of a fact can only be said to be contrary to experience if we, being at the time and place in question, observe that the alleged event did not in fact take place.

What Hume really means by "contrary to experience" is simply the lack of similar experience. (To say a miracle is contrary to universal experience is obviously question-begging, since it assumes in advance the miracle in question did not occur.) But in this case the improbability that results from our not having similar experiences is equal to the probability that we should have similar experiences. But what probability is there for that? Suppose God wished to inaugurate Christianity with miracles. What is the probability that we should also experience similar events today? Clearly, any such

probability is negligible. Conversely then, any improbability resulting from
our lack of such experiences is also negligible. According to Paley, Hume's
argument assumes either that the course of nature is invariable or that if it
is variable, these variations must be frequent and general. But what
grounds are there for either of these assumptions? If the course of nature
is the work of an intelligent Being, should we not expect that he would vary
the course of nature only infrequently at times of great importance?

As for determining whether a miracle has occurred, Paley considers
Hume's account of the matter a fair one: which is more probable in any
given case, that the miracle be true or the testimony be false? In answering this question, Paley reminds us, we must not remove the miracle from
its theistic and historical context, nor can we ignore how the testimony and
evidence arose. According to Paley, the real problem with Hume's skepticism becomes clear when we apply it to a test case: suppose twelve men,
whom I know to be honest and reasonable people, were to assert that they
saw personally a miraculous event in which it was impossible for them to
have been tricked; furthermore, the governor called them before him for
an inquiry and sentenced them all to death unless they were to admit the
hoax; and they all went to their deaths rather than say they were lying.
According to Hume, we should still not believe such men. But such
incredulity, says Paley, would not be defended by any skeptic in the world.

Against Hume's "in fact" arguments, Paley maintains that no parallel
to the gospel miracles exists in history. Like Less, he examines Hume's
examples in considerable detail and concludes that it is idle to compare
such cases with the miracles of the gospels. Even in cases not easily
explained away, there is no evidence that the witnesses have passed their
lives in labor and danger and have voluntarily suffered for the truth of
what they reported. Thus, the circumstance of the gospel accounts is
unparalleled.

Summary

Christian apologists thus contested Spinoza's and Hume's objections to
miracles from a variety of standpoints. It is noteworthy that virtually all the
Christian thinkers presupposed the existence of God in their argument. It
must be remembered that it was not a case of theism versus atheism, but
of Christian theism versus Deism. Moreover, God's existence was not
always just assumed: Clarke and Paley formulated sophisticated arguments
to justify belief in God. The Christians argued that given the existence of
God, miracles are possible because of God's omnipotence (Clarke),
because of his conservation of the world in being (Houtteville), and
because of his sovereign freedom to act as he wills (Less).

Against the mechanistic Newtonian world-view, they argued variously that the course of nature is really only the regular pattern of the operation of God's will (Clarke), or that it is subject to God's freedom to alter it (Vernet, Houtteville, Less, Paley), or even that it may include within itself the capacity for miraculous events (Sherlock, Houtteville).

Against Spinoza's first objection, the apologists argued that miracles do not contradict God's nature, because the laws of nature do not flow in necessitarian fashion from the being of God, but are freely willed and therefore alterable (Vernet); and miracles as well as the laws could be willed by God from eternity so that their occurrence represents no change in God's decrees (Houtteville). Against his second objection, they maintained that miracles, while not proof of the existence of God, are proof of the *Christian* God. Hence, it is correct to say that the regular order of nature proves God's existence; but it is equally true to say that a miracle proves the action of God in the world (Clarke, Paley).

The Christian thinkers sometimes granted freely that one could not know whether God or a lesser being was at work in the miracle; but here they urged that it was the religious, doctrinal context that allowed one to determine if the miracle was divine (Clarke, Less).

As for Spinoza's charge that a supposed miracle may be caused by an unknown law of nature, Le Clerc responded that it then becomes inexplicable why such events do not recur and why these mysterious laws operated coincidentally at the moment of Jesus' command. Vernet replied that this possibility is negligible when numerous and various miracles occur. And others (Sherlock, Houtteville) granted that such unknown laws might be God's means of acting within the course of nature.

In response to Hume's "in principle" argument they argued: Given God's existence, miracles are as possible as any other event (Less); and the probability that God would reveal himself nullifies any inherent improbability in miracles (Paley). A miracle is a matter of sense perception like any other event, and is therefore capable of being supported by historical testimony (Sherlock). A miracle is not contrary to experience as such, and therefore, the testimony to a miracle cannot be nullified by the testimony to the regular order of other experiences (Less, Paley). The improbability that a miracle should occur in the past is equal to the probability that we should experience such events today, a probability that is slight or nonexistent (Paley). Hume's argument, if equally applied, would eliminate not only miracles but many natural matters of fact as well (Sherlock, Less). Hume's argument leads to an indefensible skepticism regarding events amply established by reliable testimony (Paley).

In response to Hume's "in fact" argument, the Christian apologists simply sought to prove that in the case of Jesus' miracles and resurrection, the factual evidence was strong enough to establish the credibility of these events, in contrast to other stories of purported miracles (Less, Paley). In short, miracles are neither impossible nor unidentifiable.

ASSESSMENT

We've seen that the problem of miracles occupied a central place in the Deist controversy of the seventeenth and eighteenth centuries. Although the Christians argued vigorously on behalf of miracles, it was undoubtedly the arguments of Spinoza, Hume, and the Deists that posterity gave an eye to, for in the next century D. F. Strauss was able to proceed in his investigation of the life of Jesus on the *a priori* assumption that miracles are impossible. According to Strauss, this is not a presupposition requiring proof; on the contrary, to assume that miracles are possible is a presupposition requiring proof. Strauss asserts that God's interposition in the regular course of nature is "irreconcilable with enlightened ideas of the relation of God to the world."[10] Thus, any supposedly historical account of miraculous events must be dismissed out of hand; "indeed no just notion of the true nature of history is possible, without a perception of the inviolability of the chain of finite causes, and of the impossibility of miracles."[11]

This presupposition governed the remainder of the nineteenth-century Life of Jesus movement. According to Albert Schweitzer, the historian of that movement, by the mid-1860s the question of miracles had lost all importance. He reports, "The exclusion of miracle from our view of history has been universally recognized as a principle of criticism, so that miracle no longer concerns the historian either positively or negatively."[12] This might lead one to think that the Deists had won the debate. But is this in fact the case?

THE NEWTONIAN WORLD-MACHINE VERSUS QUANTUM PHYSICS

It will be remembered that the backdrop for the Deist controversy was a view of the universe as a Newtonian world-machine that bound even the hands of God. With the advent of quantum physics, however, twentieth-century scientists have abandoned so iron-clad a view of natural law.

In quantum physics there is an ineradicable element of indeterminacy in the behavior of systems described by those laws, whether those systems be sub-atomic or macro-scopic. For example, in classical physics, if the kinetic energy of an elementary particle is less than its potential energy, then the particle will be unable to surmount a potential barrier which it confronts. But in quantum physics, if the kinetic and potential energies are close, then through a phenomenon called "quantum tunneling" the particle can surmount or pass through the barrier. Whether the particle is stopped by or overcomes the barrier cannot be determined on the basis of information obtainable concerning its state prior to its encountering the barrier. It appears to be entirely random whether or not similar particles breach the barrier, and where they end up is a matter of probability. Similarly, an elementary particle fired at a screen cannot be predicted to strike the screen at a specific determined point, as in Newtonian physics. Rather, there is a probability curve describing the various points where it might strike which is highest in a certain area and becomes vanishingly low as one moves away from that area. Theoretically, the particle could end up anywhere. Now since macro-scopic objects, like a human body, for example, are composed of sub-atomic particles governed by quantum laws, there is some non-zero probability that each of the particles composing the body should travel to some distant location, and if all the particles did this in concert, the whole body would be "miraculously" transported to another location. Natural laws then become statistical in nature, describing what generally occurs in a number of cases.

This would appear to bring some comfort to the modern defender of miracles, for he may now argue that it is illegitimate to exclude *a priori* a certain event that does not conform to known natural law, since that law cannot be rigidly applied to individual cases. Given quantum indeterminacy, there is at least *some* chance of an event's occurring, regardless of how bizarre it might be.

It seems to me, however, that this does not settle the problem of miracles. In the first place, not all of nature's laws are affected by quantum indeterminacy. Relativity theory, which, together with quantum theory, underpins the structure of modern physics, enunciates laws which are not statistical or based on indeterminacy. Miracles violating such laws would still be impossible. Secondly, it is not evident that all the gospel miracles could be explained in conformity to quantum laws. Water might be changed into wine by a spontaneous rearrangement of its sub-atomic constituents, but no such explanation could account for the resurrection of Jesus, which was not simply the resuscitation of a corpse, but the transformation of the body to an immortal and glorified existence.

More importantly, however, quantum indeterminacy and the statistical character of certain natural laws only show that one cannot *absolutely* rule out in advance an event not conforming to known laws. Although quantum physics has opened a crack in the door for the defender of miracles, it is not wide enough for him to put his whole case through. As one philosopher of science explains:

There is no question that most events regarded as significantly "miraculous" in religious contexts would, if they violate Newtonian laws, also be excessively improbable on well-established quantum laws, and therefore would be regarded as violations of these also. Thus, if we consider only the currently accepted theories of physics, the credibility of such miracles is no greater than in Newtonian theory.[13]

It would be crazy, for example, for a person accused of murder, who was known to have been alone in the room with the victim at the time the murder occurred, to offer as his defense the claim that another man quantum tunneled into the room spontaneously, shot the victim dead, and then, before he could be apprehended, spontaneously quantum tunneled back out again. (Come to think of it, maybe such a defendant could get off by being declared not guilty by reason of insanity!) We cannot sidestep the problem of miracles, then, by a disingenuous appeal to quantum indeterminacy or the statistical character of nature's laws. We are still confronted with the question whether violations of nature's laws are possible.

But are miracles in fact "violations of the laws of nature," as Newtonian mechanists claimed? Here it would seem to be of no avail to answer with Clarke that matter has no properties and that the course of nature is simply God's regular action. Not only does modern physics hold that matter does possess certain properties and that certain forces like gravitation and electro-magnetism are real forces operating in the world, but Clarke's view also leads to the strange doctrine of occasionalism, which holds that fire does not really burn wood, for example, but that God causes wood to burn merely upon the occasion of its coming into contact with fire. Nor would it help to answer with Sherlock and Houtteville that nature may contain within itself the power to produce certain effects contrary to its normal operation. For this explanation is unconvincing in cases where the natural laws are sufficiently well-known so as to preclude with a high degree of probability the event's taking place. Moreover, this solution threatens to reduce the event in question to a freak of nature, the result of chance, not an act of God.

A better tack, I think, is to ask whether in fact miracles should be characterized as "violations of the laws of nature," as Newtonian mechanists assumed. (It would be well if we could rid ourselves of this characterization, since it is very prejudicial psychologically, smacking of the breaking of a civil law, so that God takes on the appearance of a cosmic criminal or divine rapist of Mother Nature.) An examination of the chief competing schools of thought concerning the notion of a natural law in fact reveals that on each theory the concept of a violation of a natural law is incoherent and that miracles need not be so defined. Broadly speaking, there are three main views of natural law today: the regularity theory, the nomic necessity theory, and the causal dispositions theory.[14]

According to the regularity theory, the "laws" of nature are not really laws at all, but just descriptions of the way things happen in the world. They describe the regularities which we observe in nature. Now since on such a theory a natural law is just a generalized description of *whatever* occurs in nature, it follows that no event which occurs can violate such a law. Instead, it just becomes part of the description. The law cannot be violated, because it just describes in a certain generalized form everything that does happen in nature.

According to the nomic necessity theory, natural laws are not merely descriptive, but tell us what can and cannot happen in the natural world. They allow us to make certain contrary-to-fact conditional judgments, such as "If the density of the universe were sufficiently high, it would have re-contracted long ago," which a purely descriptivist theory would not permit. Again, however, since natural laws are taken to be universal inductive generalizations, a violation of a natural law is no more possible on this theory than on the regularity theory. So long as natural laws are *universal* generalizations based on experience, they must take account of anything that happens and so would be revised should an event occur which the law did not permit.

Of course, in practice proponents of such theories do not treat natural laws so rigidly. Rather, natural laws are assumed to have implicit in them the assumption "all things being equal." That is to say, the law states what is the case under the assumption that no other natural factors are interfering. When a scientific anomaly occurs, it is usually assumed that some unknown natural factors are interfering, so that the law is neither violated nor revised. But suppose the law fails to describe or predict accurately because some *supernatural* factors are interfering? Clearly the implicit assumption of such laws is that no supernatural factors as well as no natural factors are interfering. Thus, if the law proves inaccurate in a particular case because God is acting, the law is neither violated nor revised. If God brings about some event which a law of nature fails to predict or describe, such an event cannot be characterized as a violation of a law of nature, since the law is valid only under the tacit assumption that no supernatural factors come into play apart from the natural factors.

On such theories, then, miracles ought to be defined as naturally impossible events, that is to say, events which cannot be produced by the natural causes operative at a certain time and place. Whether an event is a miracle is thus relative to a time and place. Given the natural causes operative at a certain time and place, for example, rain may be naturally inevitable or necessary, but on another occasion, rain may be naturally impossible. Of course, some events, say, the resurrection, may be absolutely miraculous in that they are at every time and place beyond the productive capacity of natural causes.

According to the causal dispositions theory, things in the world have different natures or essences, which include their causal dispositions to affect other things in certain ways, and natural laws are metaphysically necessary truths about what causal dispositions are possessed by various natural kinds of things. For example, "Salt has a disposition to dissolve in water" would state a natural law. If, due to God's action, some salt failed to dissolve in water, the natural law is not violated, because it is still true that salt has such a disposition. As a result of things' causal dispositions, certain deterministic natural propensies exist in nature, and when such a propensity is not impeded (by God or some other free agent), then we can speak of a natural necessity. On this theory, an event which is naturally necessary must and does actually occur, since the natural propensity will automatically issue forth in the event if it is not impeded. By the same token, a naturally impossible event cannot and does not actually occur. Hence, a miracle cannot be characterized on this theory as a naturally impossible event. Rather, a miracle is an event which results from causal interference with a natural propensity which is so strong that only a supernatural agent could impede it. The concept of miracle is essentially the same as under the previous two theories, but one just cannot call a miracle "naturally impossible" as those terms are defined in this theory; perhaps we can adopt instead the nomenclature "physically impossible" to characterize miracles.

On none of these theories, then, should miracles be understood as violations of the laws of nature. Rather they are naturally (or physically) impossible events, events which at certain times and places cannot be produced by the relevant natural causes.

Now the question is, what could conceivably transform an event that is naturally impossible into a real historical event? Clearly, the answer is the personal God of theism. For if a transcendent, personal God exists, then he could cause events in the universe that could not be produced by causes within the universe. It is precisely to such a God that the Christian apologists appealed. Given a God who is omnipotent, who conserves the world in being, and who is capable of acting freely, Christian thinkers seem to be entirely justified in maintaining that miracles are possible. Indeed, only if atheism were proved to be true could one rationally deny the possibility of miracles. For if it is even possible that a transcendent, personal God exists, then it is equally possible that he has acted in the universe. Therefore, it seems to me that the Christian apologists argued in the main correctly against their Newtonian opponents, and that the natural (or physical) impossibility of miracles in no way precludes their reality.

SPINOZA'S OBJECTIONS

Turning to Spinoza's objections, again it seems to me that the Christian thinkers argued cogently.

Objection Based on the Immutability of Nature

It would be tempting to dismiss Spinoza's objections simply on the grounds that he was a pantheist, for whom "God" and "Nature" were interchangeable terms. So, of course, a violation of nature's laws would be a violation of God's nature, since they are the same. The question is not whether miracles are possible on a pantheistic world view, but on a theistic world view.

But such a refutation would be too easy. The *Tractatus* is a Deistic, not a pantheistic, work, and Spinoza presupposes the traditional understanding of God. In particular, his argument is based on the classic doctrine of divine simplicity, which states that God's knowledge, will, goodness, power, and so forth are all really identical and one with his essence. The question Spinoza raises is, in effect, how can God's knowledge be necessary and his will be contingent, if these are identical? Now contrary to Spinoza, classical theology did not claim that God's knowledge is characterized by necessity. For example, God knows the truth "The universe exists." But God was under no obligation to create the universe. Since creation is a free act, he could have refrained from creating anything at all. If God had not created the world, then he would instead know the truth "No universe exists." Necessarily, then, whatever God knows is true; but it is not necessary that the content of God's knowledge be what it is. Had he created a different world or no world at all, the content of his knowledge would be different. Hence, just as God is free to will differently than he does, so he is able to have different knowledge than he does.

The laws of nature, then, are not known by God necessarily, since, as Vernet said, they depend on God's will. Even if we hold that the laws of nature are necessary truths, God could have willed to create a universe operating according to a different set of laws by creating things having different natures from the things he created. By the same token, the miracles he performs could, as Less and Houtteville pointed out, have been willed by God just as eternally and immutably as the laws. There is just no reason, then, to think that when he causes a naturally impossible event, God's knowledge and will come into conflict.

Spinoza's objection does raise one important point, though. It is very difficult to see how God's knowledge, for example, can be contingent and yet be identical with his essence, which includes necessary existence. How can God be utterly simple if he is in some respects necessary and in others contingent? What this calls into question, however, is not the possibility of miracles, but the doctrine of divine simplicity. This is a doctrine which is fortunately extra-biblical and is rejected as incoherent by the majority of Christian philosophers today.

Objection Based on the Insufficiency of Miracles

Spinoza's second objection was that miracles are insufficient to prove God's existence. As it is stated, the objection was simply irrelevant for most of the Christian apologists, for virtually all of them used miracles not as a proof for the existence of God, but as a proof for his action in the world. Hence, Spinoza was really attacking a straw man.

Nevertheless, the supporting reasoning of the objection was relevant to the Christians' position. Spinoza's main point was that a proof for God must be absolutely certain. Since we infer God's existence from the immutable laws of nature, anything that casts doubt on those laws casts doubt on God's existence. Two assumptions seem to underlie this reasoning: first, that a proof for God's existence must be demonstratively certain; and second, that God's existence is inferred from natural laws. But Christian apologists denied both of these assumptions. The more empirically-minded of them held that a cogent argument for God's existence need not be demonstratively certain. Think, for example, of Paley's teleological argument: while not reaching absolute certainty, it claimed to make it more plausible to believe in God than not. Modern philosophers agree that if we were justified in accepting only those conclusions proved with demonstrative certainty, then we should know very, very little indeed. The second assumption fails to take account of the fact that there are other arguments for the existence of God not based on natural laws. For example, Clarke, while sharing Spinoza's concern for demonstrative certainty, nevertheless believed that the ontological and cosmological arguments provided rational grounds for accepting God's existence. So even if natural law were uncertain, that would not for Clarke call into question God's existence.

But is Spinoza's objection in fact true? He seems to think that the admission of a genuine miracle would overthrow the natural law violated by the miracle. But Clarke and Paley argue more persuasively that a miracle need not overthrow the general regularity of nature; it only shows God's intervention at that particular point. As Richard Swinburne argues, a natural law is not abolished because of one exception; the exception must occur repeatedly whenever the conditions for it are present. If the event will not occur again under identical circumstances, then the law will not be abandoned. A natural law will not be reformulated unless a new version will yield better predictability of future events without being more complicated than the original law. But if the new version does no better in predicting the phenomena and explaining the event in question, then the event will simply remain an unexplained exception to the natural law. Thus, Spinoza's fear that miracles would destroy the fabric of natural law appears to be unjustified. Rather than leading us into the arms of atheism, exceptions to natural laws could lead us to discern the action of God in the world at that point.

Spinoza's sub-point that miracles could not prove the existence of God, but only of a lesser being, did not strike against most of the Christian apologists, because they were not trying to prove the existence of God. Having proved or presupposed God's existence, they used miracles chiefly to show that Christian theism was true.

But they were very concerned about how to show in any particular case that a miracle was not demonic but divine. I think that their answer to this problem constitutes one of their most important and enduring contributions to the discussion of miracles. They held that the doctrinal context of the miracle makes it evident if the miracle is truly from God. In this way they drew attention to the religio-historical context in which the miracle occurred as the key to the interpretation of that miracle. This is very significant, for a miracle without a context is inherently ambiguous. This is the problem with Hume's example of the revivification of Queen Elizabeth: the event lacks any religious context and appears as a bald and unexplained anomaly. Hence, one feels a degree of sympathy for Hume's skepticism. But how different it is with the case of Jesus' resurrection! It occurs in the context of and as the climax to Jesus' own unparalleled life and teachings and produced so profound an effect on his followers that they called him Lord and proclaimed salvation for all men in his name. It ought, therefore, to give us serious pause, whereas the resuscitation of Queen Elizabeth would occasion only perplexity. The religio-historical context is crucial to the interpretation of a miraculous event.

Spinoza's concern with lesser spiritual beings like angels and demons would probably not trouble many contemporary minds. Such beings are part of the furniture, so to speak, of a wider theistic world view, so that no atheist today would seriously concede the gospel miracles and yet maintain they were performed by angels. It would not seem unwarranted to infer that if such events are genuine miracles, then they were wrought by God.

Spinoza's final sub-point, that a supposed miracle may really be the effect of an unknown law of nature, is not really an objection against the occurrence of miracles, but against the identification of miracles. Granted that miracles are possible, how can we know when one has occurred? This problem has been persuasively formulated in our day by the English philosopher Antony Flew:

> We simply do not have, and could not have, any natural . . . criterion which enables us to say, when faced with something which is found to have actually happened, that here we have an achievement which nature, left to her own unaided devices, could never encompass. The natural scientist, confronted with some occurrence inconsistent with a proposition previously believed to express a law of nature, can find in this disturbing inconsistency no ground whatever for proclaiming that the particular law of nature has been supernaturally overridden![15]

The response of Sherlock and Houtteville to this objection, that an unknown law of nature is God's means of producing the event, is surely inadequate. For it could just as easily be the case that the event is no act of God at all, just a spontaneous accident of nature without religious significance. Rather I think Le Clerc and Vernet have taken a better tack: when the miracles occur at a momentous time (for example, a man's leprosy vanishing when Jesus spoke the words "Be clean") and do not recur regularly in history, and when the miracles in question are numerous and various, then the chance of their being the result of unknown natural causes is minimal. Since, as we shall see, most critics now acknowledge that Jesus did perform what we may call miracles, this answer to Spinoza and Flew seems to be a cogent defense of the supernatural origin of the gospel miracles.

But even if we leave Jesus' miracles aside and focus our attention on his resurrection from the dead, I think the supernatural nature of that event alone may be successfully defended. We're not asking here whether the facts of the case, such as the empty tomb or resurrection appearances, might be explained in a natural manner. The question is, if Jesus actually did rise from the dead, would we then be justified in inferring a supernatural cause for that event? Here the overwhelming majority of people would say yes. Those who argue against the resurrection try to explain away the facts of the case without allowing that Jesus rose from the dead. I know of no critic who argues that the best explanation of the historical facts is that Jesus rose from the dead, but that his resurrection was no miracle but a perfectly natural occurrence. That would appear to be a somewhat desperate obstinacy.

Two factors undergird this reasoning. First, the resurrection so exceeds what we know of natural causes that it seems most reasonable to attribute it to a supernatural cause. Hume himself asserted that it has never in the history of the world been heard of that a truly dead man (in Jesus' case for a night, a day, and a night) has been raised from the dead. Given the length of time that Jesus had been dead, it would be idle to compare his resurrection with the resuscitation of persons pronounced clinically dead in hospitals. But more than that: it is very important to understand that the resurrection was more than the resuscitation of a corpse. It was not a return to the earthly mortal life; rather it was the transformation of the body to a new mode of existence, which Paul described as powerful, glorious, imperishable, and Spirit-directed (1 Cor 15:42-44). It is inconceivable that such an event could be the product of natural causes. Moreover, if it were the effect of purely natural causes, then its singularity in the history of mankind becomes very difficult to understand—why has it not happened again? In the nearly two thousand years since that event, no natural causes have been discovered that could explain it. On the contrary, the advance of science has only served to confirm that such an event is naturally impossible.

Second, the supernatural explanation is given immediately in the religio-historical context in which the event occurred. Jesus' resurrection was not merely an anomalous event, occurring without context; it came as the climax to Jesus' own life and teachings. As Wolfhart Pannenberg explains,

> The resurrection of Jesus acquires such decisive meaning, not merely because someone or anyone has been raised from the dead, but because it is Jesus of Nazareth, whose execution was instigated by the Jews because he had blasphemed against God.
>
> Jesus' claim to authority, through which he put himself in God's place, was . . . blasphemous for Jewish ears. Because of this Jesus was then also slandered before the Roman Governor as a rebel. If Jesus really has been raised, this claim has been visibly and unambiguously confirmed by the God of Israel, who was allegedly blasphemed by Jesus.[16]

Thus the religio-historical context furnishes us with the key to the supernatural character of that event.

One final remark on Spinoza's objection against the identification of a miracle: his argument, unlike Hume's, does not spring from the nature of historical investigation. Rather, the very eyewitnesses of the event could press Spinoza's objection. But in this case, the argument leads to an untenable skepticism. There comes a point when the back of skepticism is broken by the sheer reality of the miracle before us. I think, for example, of that delightful scene in Dickens's *Christmas Carol* in which Scrooge is confronted by Marley's ghost, all bound in chains:

"You don't believe in me," observed the Ghost.

"I don't," said Scrooge.

"What evidence would you have of my reality beyond that of your senses?"

"I don't know," said Scrooge.

"Why do you doubt your senses?"

"Because," said Scrooge, "a little thing affects them. A slight disorder of the stomach makes them cheats. You may be an undigested bit of beef, a blot of mustard, a crumb of cheese, a fragment of underdone potato. There's more gravy than grave about you, whatever you are. . . ."

". . . You see this toothpick?" said Scrooge.

"I do," replied the Ghost.

". . . Well!" returned Scrooge, "I have but to swallow this, and be for the rest of my life persecuted by a legion of goblins, all of my own creation. Humbug, I tell you! Humbug!"

At this the spirit raised a frightful cry and shook its chain with such a dismal and appalling noise, that Scrooge held on tight to his chair, to save himself from falling into a swoon. But how much greater was his horror, when the phantom, taking off the bandage round its head . . . its lower jaw dropped down upon its breast!

Scrooge fell upon his knees, and clasped his hands before his face.

"Mercy!" he said. "Dreadful apparition, why do you trouble me?"

"Man of worldly mind!" replied the Ghost, "do you believe in me or not?"

"I do," said Scrooge. "I must."[17]

Such studied skepticism as Scrooge's becomes untenable when confronted with the evident reality of such a striking miracle. Can we imagine, for example, doubting Thomas, when confronted with the risen Jesus, studiously considering whether what he saw palpably before him might not be the effect of an unknown natural cause? Had Jesus himself encountered such skepticism, would he not have attributed it to hardness of heart? In this light, such skepticism need not be demonstratively refuted but is self-condemned. Perhaps Pascal was right in saying that God has given evidence sufficiently clear for those with an open heart, but sufficiently vague so as not to compel those whose hearts are closed.

HUME'S OBJECTIONS

"In Principle" Argument

The "in principle" argument, it seems to me, is either question-begging or confused. As Hume presents the argument, it appears to be clearly question-begging. To say that uniform experience is against miracles is to implicitly assume already that miracles have never occurred. It seems almost embarrassing to refute so sophisticated an objection by such a simple consideration, but nevertheless, this answer seems to me to be entirely correct. The only way Hume can place uniform experience for the regularity of nature on one side of the scale is by assuming that the testimony for miracles on the other side of the scale is false. And that, quite simply, is begging the question.

But suppose we give Hume the benefit of the doubt and relax the meaning of the term "uniform experience" to mean merely "general experience." It seems to me that the argument so interpreted is still fallacious, because it embodies a fundamental confusion. Hume confuses the realms of science and history. In the realm of science the general experience of mankind has enabled us to formulate certain laws that describe the physical universe. That dead men do not rise is a generally observed pattern in our experience. But at most it only shows that a resurrection is naturally impossible. That's a matter of science. But it doesn't show that such a naturally impossible event has not in fact occurred. That is a matter of history. It is only by means of this category mistake that Hume is able to weigh evidence for a particular miracle in the same scale with evidence for natural laws. But as Less and Paley correctly pointed out, one cannot counterbalance the evidence for a particular miracle with evidence for the regularity of nature in general. If the historical evidence makes it reasonable to believe Jesus rose from the dead, then it is illegitimate to suppress this evidence because all other men have always remained in their graves.

Nor can it be objected that the evidence for a miracle must be spurious because the event in question is naturally impossible. It may well be the case that history proves that a naturally impossible event has occurred. As Sherlock argued, a miraculous event is just as much a matter of sense perception as an ordinary event and can therefore be proved by historical testimony in the same way as a non-miraculous event. As history, they are on a par. As Paley further pointed out, Hume's principle could lead us into situations where we would be forced to deny the testimony of the most reliable witnesses because of general considerations; and this is an unrealistic skepticism. And that goes not only for miraculous events, but, as Sherlock and Less urged, for non-miraculous events as well. There are all sorts of events that make up the stuff of popular books and television shows on unexplained mysteries (such as levitations, disappearing persons, spontaneous human combustions, and so forth) that have not been scientifically explained, but—judging by their pointless nature, sporadic occurrence, and lack of any religious context—are not miracles. It would be folly for a historian to deny the occurrence of such events in the face of good eyewitness

evidence to the contrary, simply because they do not fit in with known natural laws. Yet Hume's principle would require the historian to say that these
events never occurred, which is indefensible.

Flew has sought to redefend Hume's "in principle" argument. He
writes:

> It is only and precisely by presuming that the laws that hold today
> held in the past and by employing as canons all our knowledge . . .
> of what is probable or improbable, possible or impossible, that we
> can rationally interpret the detritus of the past as evidence and from
> it construct our account of what actually happened. But in this con-
> text, what is impossible is what is physically, as opposed to logically
> impossible. And "physical possibility" is, and surely has to be,
> defined in terms of inconsistency with a true law of nature. . . .
>
> Our sole ground for characterizing a reported occurrence as
> miraculous is at the same time a sufficient reason for calling it phys-
> ically impossible.[18]

Now Flew's objection appears to be actually inconsistent with his
defense of Spinoza's objection. There he asserted that our knowledge of
nature is so incomplete that we can never regard any event as miraculous,
since it could conform to an unknown law of nature. This would force us
to take a totally open attitude toward the possibility of any event, for virtually anything could be possible in nature. But now he asserts precisely the
opposite, namely, that our knowledge of natural law is so complete that not
only can we determine which events are naturally impossible, but we are
also able to impose this standard over the past to expunge such events from
the record. The two positions are incompatible. Flew thus seems to have
worked himself into the following dilemma:

> Either naturally impossible events can be specified or not.
>
> If they can be specified, then the occurrence of such events could
> be identified as miracles.
>
> If they cannot be specified, then we must be open to anything's
> happening in history, including miracles.

Now I have argued that naturally impossible events can sometimes be
specified and that Jesus' resurrection is such an event. Does this therefore
mean, as Flew alleges, that I must regard this event as unhistorical? Not at
all; Flew has made an unwarranted identification between natural (or as he
puts it, physical) possibility and real, historical possibility. The assumption
hidden behind this identification is that naturally impossible events can-

not occur or, in other words, that miracles cannot happen, which is question-begging, as that is precisely the point to be proved. Thus, despite the apparent sophistication of his argument, Flew is actually arguing in a circle. If one wishes to talk about historical possibility or impossibility at all, these terms ought not to be defined in terms of scientific law, but in terms of historical evidence. Thus, for example, it is historically possible that Nietzsche's insanity resulted from venereal disease; it is historically impossible that Napoleon won the battle of Waterloo. On this basis, only the evidence itself can tell us whether it is possible that Jesus rose from the dead.

What really lies behind Flew's objection is the conviction that in order to study history, one must assume the impossibility of miracles. This viewpoint is simply a restatement of the nineteenth-century German theologian Ernst Troeltsch's principle of analogy. According to Troeltsch, one of the most basic historiographical principles is that the past does not differ essentially from the present. Though the events of the past are obviously not the same events as those of the present, they must be the same kind of events if historical investigation is to be possible. Troeltsch realized that this principle was incompatible with the miraculous events of the gospels and therefore held that they must be regarded as unhistorical.

In our own day, however, Pannenberg has persuasively argued that Troeltsch's principle of analogy cannot be legitimately employed to banish all non-analogous events from history. According to Pannenberg, analogy, when properly defined, means that in an unclear historical situation we should interpret the facts in terms of known experience. Troeltsch, however, uses analogy to constrict all past events to purely natural events. But, Pannenberg maintains, the fact that an event bursts all analogies to the present cannot be used to dispute its historicity. When, for example, myths, legends, illusions, and the like are dismissed as unhistorical, it is not because they are unusual but because they are analogous to present forms of consciousness to which no historical reality corresponds. When an event is said to have occurred for which no present analogy exists, we cannot automatically dismiss its historicity; to do that we must have an analogy to some known form of consciousness to which no reality corresponds that would suffice to explain the situation.

Pannenberg has thus reformulated Troeltsch's principle of analogy in such a way that it is not the *lack* of an analogy that shows an event to be unhistorical, but the *presence* of a positive analogy to known thought forms that shows a purported miracle to be unhistorical. Hence, he has elsewhere affirmed that if the Easter narratives were shown to be essentially secondary constructions analogous to common comparative religious phenomena, if the Easter appearances were shown to correspond completely to the model of hallucinations, and if the empty tomb tradition were shown to be a late legend, then the resurrection should be evaluated as unhistorical. In this way the lack of an analogy to present experience says nothing for or against the historicity of an event. Pannenberg's use of the principle preserves the analogous structure of the past to the present or to the known, thus making the investigation of history possible without thereby forcing the past into the mold of the present. It would therefore seem that Hume's "in principle" argument fares no better than Spinoza's objections.

"In Fact" Arguments

If, then, there is no "in principle" objection to the identification of miracles, what may be said of Hume's "in fact" arguments? All of his points have force, but the fact remains that these general considerations cannot be used to decide the historicity of any particular miracle. They serve to make us cautious in the investigation of any miracle, but the only way the question of historicity can be solved is through such an investigation. Hume's fourth point (that miracles occur in all religions and thereby cancel each other out) does try to preclude an investigation, but it still remains an empirical question whether the evidence for any miracle supporting a counter-Christian claim is as well (or better) attested as the evidence for Jesus' miracles and resurrection. And if the latter should prove to be genuine, then we can forgo the investigation of every single counter-Christian miracle, for most of these pale into insignificance next to the gospel miracles.

CONCLUSION

Hence, I think that for the most part the Christian apologists argued correctly against their Deist opponents; and it is sad that the nineteenth century failed to discern this fact. The presupposition against miracles survives in theology only as a hangover from an earlier Deistic age and ought now to be once for all abandoned.

PRACTICAL APPLICATION

The material shared in this chapter and the next does not, I must confess, admit of much practical application in evangelism. I've never encountered a non-Christian who rejected the gospel because of an overt objection to miracles.

Nevertheless, this section is extremely important, because the presupposition of modern biblical criticism has been the impossibility of miracles in history, so that a conservative approach to the Scriptures necessitates a prior defense of the possibility of miracles. Thus, the material in this section is critical to a reform of biblical scholarship, without which we evangelicals cannot win in the theological community.

Moreover, I've been surprised to find how often Deistic thinking underlies the flowering dialogue between science and religion on the contemporary scene. For example, in a recent conference at Notre Dame on "Science and Religion in the Post-Positivist Era," Arthur Peacocke claimed that modern cell biology has "radically undermined" the credibility of the virgin birth because it would require God's making a Y-chromosome *de novo* in Mary's ovum—in other words, it would have to be a miracle! Similarly, the stern remonstrances one often hears from theologians and physicists against inferring a supernatural cause for the origin and order of the universe often conceal a presuppositional bias against miracles, since such acts of God are essentially miracles on a cosmic scale.

In addition, however, I do think that people whom we talk to about Christ do sometimes have covert problems with miracles. They do not formulate their misgivings into an argument; they just find it hard to believe that the miraculous events of the gospel really occurred. Insofar as we sense this is the case, we need to bring this presupposition out into the open and explain why there are no good grounds for it. Show unbelievers that they have no reasons for rejecting the possibility of miracles and challenge them with the thought that the universe may be a much more wonderful place than they believe. In my own case, the virgin birth was a stumbling block to my coming to faith—I simply could not believe such a thing. But when I reflected on the fact that God had created the entire universe, it occurred to me that it wouldn't be too difficult for him to create the genetic material necessary for a virgin birth! Once the non-Christian understands who God is, then the problem of miracles should cease to be a problem for him.

CHAPTER FIVE

The Problem of
Historical Knowledge

THE UNIQUENESS AND THE SCANDAL of the Christian religion," writes George Ladd, "rest in the mediation of revelation through historical events." Christianity is not a code for living or a philosophy of religion; rather it is rooted in real events of history. To some this is scandalous, because it means that the truth of Christianity is bound up with the truth of certain historical facts, such that if those facts should be disproved, so would Christianity. But at the same time, this makes Christianity unique because, unlike most other world religions, we now have a means of verifying its truth by historical evidence.

This, however, brings us face to face with the problem of historical knowledge; that is to say, how is it possible to learn anything about the human past with any degree of assurance? On the popular level, this expresses itself in the attitude that history is uncertain and irrelevant to us today. It has been said that history is a series of lies that everyone has decided to agree on. On the scholarly level, the problem finds expression in the outlook of historical relativism, which denies the objectivity of historical facts. This outlook has profound implications for Christian theology in the areas of apologetics, hermeneutics, and the doctrine of revelation, to name a few. It would make it impossible to demonstrate historically the accuracy of the biblical narratives, since the past cannot be objectively established. One would be free to impose whatever meaning one chose upon the narratives, since facts have no meaning. And one could leave aside the doctrine of the inerrancy of Scripture, since it would be meaningless to speak of "errors" if historical relativism were true.

Therefore, it is imperative that the Christian scholar handle certain critical issues in the philosophy of history as a prelude to an examination of the biblical documents themselves.

HISTORICAL BACKGROUND

Though people have written histories from earliest times, historiography as a science is a product of the modern age.

MEDIEVAL PERIOD

To understand the development of this science and its impact upon apologetics, let's turn back to the Middle Ages.

Medieval Dearth of Historiography

After the Patristic age, the West, in contrast to the Byzantine lands, lapsed into a period of intellectual and cultural decline that lasted from the fifth to the eleventh centuries. Only in ecclesiastical circles were literacy and learning retained, for the masses were to a great extent illiterate. Most of the medieval histories of this time consisted of chronicles that simply listed events and their dates. Around A.D. 900 historiography almost completely disappeared. For the medieval historians, the biblical writers and the Church Fathers on the one hand, together with the classical writers and poets on the other, were considered "authors" or authorities, whose testimony was not questioned. Their successors counted as mere "writers" or "compilers," who adduced the testimony of authorities. Thus, verbatim reiteration became a virtue, and a writer describing the history of the recent past, for which no authorities could be adduced, often felt obliged to apologize to his readers for writing in his own words.

The character of medieval historical writing as reiteration of authorities was largely determined by Isidore, Bishop of Seville (d. 636), who argued in his *Etymologies* that since history, as contrasted to both fable and myth, narrates what truly took place, it must be an eyewitness account. Therefore, the narration of past events is simply a matter of compilation of the testimonies of authorities, who were taken to be eyewitnesses. Writing history consisted of copying one's sources. This historiographical method has been called the "scissors and paste" method by modern historians such as R. G. Collingwood, who emphasize the historian's liberty to criticize his sources.

Although the eleventh and twelfth centuries experienced a revival of culture and learning, this had little effect on historiography. With important exceptions, history continued in the main to be a recapitulation of authorities; and by the thirteenth century history as a literary form had collapsed back into chronicle. It is instructive to note that when in 1286 the administration of the University of Paris drew up a booklist of all the texts necessary for basic reading at the university, only three out of 140 were historical in nature. It was not until the fifteenth century that modern historiography was born, and not until even later that history became a widely read literary genre.

Impact on Apologetics

Given this circumstance, it would be unrealistic to expect a historical apologetic for the Christian faith from medieval thinkers. What then could be done to commend rationally the Christian faith to unbelievers? Some thinkers, epitomized by Anselm, sought to prove the deity and incarnation of Christ (and hence the truth of the biblical books authorized by him) by *a priori* reasoning alone. At the conclusion of *Cur Deus Homo* Anselm's dialogue partner confesses:

> All things you have said seem to me reasonable and incontrovertible. And by the solution of the single question proposed, do I see the truth of all that is contained in the Old and New Testament. For, in proving that God became man by necessity, leaving out what was taken from the Bible . . . you convince both Jews and Pagans by the mere force of reason. And the God-man himself originates the New Testament and approves the Old. And, as we must acknowledge him to be true, so no one can dissent from anything contained in these books.[1]

Anselm's deductive approach circumvented the need for any historical investigation of the facts, because everything was proved by deductive reasoning from intuitively obvious premisses.

On the other hand, we find very early on, and then with increasing sophistication in the thirteenth century, the development of a philosophical framework well-suited for historical argumentation, even if it was itself devoid of such argumentation. According to this approach, one supported the authority of Scripture by the empirical signs of credibility, mainly miracle and prophecy. Those were the chief signs employed by Augustine to justify belief in the authority of Scripture. Although early scholasticism tended to follow Anselm's *a priori* approach, during the thirteenth century this approach became less convincing, and increasing weight was given instead to the external signs.

According to Thomas Aquinas, the truths of faith, while unprovable directly, can nevertheless be confirmed or proved indirectly by means of miracle and prophecy. For Aquinas, miracle is the most important sign of credibility. It confirms the truths of faith in two ways: it confirms the truth of what the miracle worker teaches, and it makes known God's presence in the miracle worker. Hence, he says with regard to Christ's miracles: "Christ wrought miracles in order to confirm his teaching, and in order to demonstrate the divine power that was his."[2] I have argued in the last chapter that this approach to the interpretation of miracle is essentially correct. For Aquinas, therefore, the crucial problem is *historical*: How do I know that the miracles in question ever occurred? Here there is danger of reasoning in a circle: miracles confirm that the Scripture is from God; therefore, what it teaches is authoritatively true; therefore, the miracles recorded in Scripture really occurred. Now Aquinas himself never so reasons—he just leaves the historical question unanswered. But the philosophical framework he constructs is well-suited to historical argumentation for the events in question, thus filling the gap and avoiding circularity.

Because the medievals lacked the historical method, they could not argue in any substantial way for the historicity of the events recorded in the gospels. About the only proof they offered for the historicity of the miracles and fulfilled prophecies was the origin and growth of the Christian Church. But with the rise of historical consciousness, that deficit could be remedied and the medieval framework could be filled out with historical evidences.

MODERN PERIOD

Modern apologetics has been to a great extent historical apologetics. Let's examine briefly how this came to pass.

Rise of Historical Consciousness

It is probably no coincidence that the rise of historical apologetics parallels the rise of modern historiography. The modern science of historical study was born in the Italian Renaissance. The first stirrings of the Renaissance spirit in Italy found expression in the search for ancient manuscripts. The humanists cultivated the use of classical Latin and Greek and found their greatest delight in the discovery of documents of antiquity in those languages. They developed the skills of historical criticism; on the basis of internal criteria alone Lorenzo Valla was able to expose the famous Donation of Constantine, on the basis of which the Catholic church claimed secular authority over Italy, as a forgery. Despite this embarrassment, for nearly a century the papacy supported the humanist writers, and learning and the arts flourished in Rome. In search of ancient manuscripts, Italian humanists visited the monasteries of Northern Europe, and the new learning spread, eventually making its way into the university chairs of Germany and into cultivated circles elsewhere. France, after its invasion of

Italy in 1494, thoroughly imbibed the spirit of the Italian Renaissance. Before the end of the fifteenth century, Oxford University was already offering courses in classical Greek and Latin, and Cambridge University soon followed suit.

The embodiment of the ideal Renaissance humanist was Erasmus, who occupied much of his life translating classical works into Latin and editing the Greek NT. Lorenzo Valla sought to restore the original Greek text of the NT through the use of ancient manuscripts. Erasmus published Valla's corrections as annotations on the NT in 1505, and they provided the model for Erasmus's edition of the Greek NT in 1516.

The Protestant Reformation spurred the development of the science of history by turning attention to the Patristic age in order to accentuate the Roman Catholic church's departures from the faith of the Fathers. In their effort to demonstrate that Catholic doctrines and institutions were not of divine origin, but were human accretions not present in the early church, the Reformers stimulated historical research. And, of course, the Catholic Counter-reformers had a tremendous stake in the study of history, because for the Catholic church a defense of a historical tradition was a defense of the Catholic faith.

By the end of the seventeenth century, the most successful practitioners of the science of history were Catholics of the scholarly orders. Historical writing also became popular literature. Every class in European society took interest in the new historical scholarship and sought to use it to support its own point of view. During the sixteenth and seventeenth centuries, historical writing became one of the most popular literary forms, avidly sought by a growing reading public. Between 1460 and 1700 it has been estimated that more than 2.5 million copies of seventeen of the most prominent ancient historians were published in Europe. During the eighteenth century this interest intensified. According to J. Westfall Thompson, "No other age had such a voracious interest in historical literature as the eighteenth century. Everyone read and talked history."[3]

Impact on Apologetics

Without the rise of modern historical consciousness the development of historical apologetics would have been impossible. Protestant apologists were especially effective during the seventeenth and eighteenth centuries in their use of historical arguments for the faith. The course of this development is quite interesting. Although Hugo Grotius may rightly be called the father of modern apologetics, he had important precursors in Juan Luis Vives and Philippe de Mornay.

Vives was a Spanish humanist educated in Paris. He lived very much in the mainstream of European life and traveled so frequently to England and throughout the Continent that Erasmus called him an amphibious animal! After his fifth stay in England, he left for the Netherlands, never to return to Spain. From 1538-40 he worked on his apology *De veritate fidei christianae*. He died in 1540, and the book was published in 1543. In Vives we find a blend of medieval theology with humanist methodology. That is to say, Vives was a Thomist who accepted the framework of the signs of credibility, but as a humanist he began to provide historical reasons for the credibility of Scripture.

His work tries to deal critically with the question of why Christ is mentioned primarily in Christian sources. He speaks of the true history of Christ and provides a list of historical facts about Jesus. He provides both internal and external evidence for the authenticity of the gospels. His arguments are primitive and amount to little more than assertion, but they are the first glimmerings of a historical approach to the credibility of Scripture. Vives is significant because in him we see the links between modern historical apologetics and the Renaissance rise of historical consciousness on the one hand, and the medieval framework of the signs of credibility on the other.

Mornay, one of the most important Reformed leaders of the late sixteenth century, was a veteran of the Huguenot persecution in France and founder of the Protestant Academie de Saumur. In 1581, writing in French instead of Latin, Mornay penned his treatise *De la vérité de la religion chrestienne*. Although never quoting Vives, Mornay nonetheless appears to have been influenced by him, judging by parallel structure and passages between their works.

Mornay makes explicit his appeal to history: he claims that one can prove the divinity of Christ by means of philosophy and history. He says, "The philosopher thinks only of nature; the historian only of his documents. And from the two we have concluded the deity of Christ and the truth of our Scriptures."[4] Hence, his case is based on what he calls arguments and testimonies. The historical material is brought to bear in the final chapter, demonstrating that "the Gospel truly contains the history and doctrine of Jesus, Son of God."[5] Here he argues for the reliability of the gospel accounts on the basis of the disciples' unwavering witness even unto death. He appeals to the great number of witnesses, to the changed lives of the disciples, and to the conversion of Paul as evidence for the historicity of the resurrection. Again, his arguments are not sophisticated by modern standards; but they represent an important advance over his predecessors in the development of historical apologetics.

A renowned expert in international law and himself a historical writer,

Hugo Grotius was the first to provide a developed historical argument for Christianity in his *De veritate religionis christianae* (1627). He openly expressed his appreciation of the works of his predecessors, Vives and Mornay. *De veritate* is divided into six books: book one defends a cosmological argument and demonstrates God's revelation in Israel's history; book two contains historical proofs for Jesus' miracles and resurrection; book three treats the authority of Scripture; book four demonstrates Christianity's superiority to paganism; book five contains the proof from prophecy to show Christianity's superiority to Judaism; and book six refutes the Islamic religion.

Grotius clearly understood the importance of the science of history for the truth of the Christian faith. He discriminates between the methods employed in mathematics, physics, ethics, and history. In historical proofs we must rely on testimony free from all suspicion of falsity—otherwise the whole structure and use of history collapses. He notes that many historical narrations are commonly accepted as true on no other ground than authority; but the history of Christ is attested by strong proofs that declare it to be true.

Grotius begins by pointing out that it is certain that Jesus of Nazareth was an actual historical person living in Judea under the reign of Tiberius. This fact is acknowledged in historical writings from Christians, Jews, and pagans alike. Further, he was put to death and thereafter worshiped by men. The reason for this worship was that he had performed various miracles during his life. Many of the early Christians such as Polycarp, Irenaeus, Athenagoras, Origen, Tertullian, Clement of Alexandria, and so forth were raised in other religions, yet came to worship this man Jesus as God, because they had made a diligent inquiry and discovered that he had wrought many miraculous deeds. Moreover, none of their opponents— neither Celsus nor Julian nor the Rabbinic doctors—could deny that Jesus had done these miracles. It is not possible to explain away Jesus' miracles as either wrought by nature or by the devil. With regard to the first of these possibilities, it is not naturally possible that terrible diseases and infirmities should be cured by the sound of a man's voice or his mere touch. As to the second, Christ's teaching was diametrically opposed to Satan, so that his miracles could hardly be attributed to demonic power.

Grotius then argues that Christ's resurrection can also be proved by credible reasons. He points out that the apostles claimed to be eyewitnesses of the risen Christ. They even appealed to the testimony of five hundred brethren who had seen Jesus after his resurrection. Now it would have been impossible for so many to conspire together to perpetrate such a hoax. And what was there to gain by lying? They could expect neither honor, nor wealth, nor worldly profit, nor fame, nor even the successful propagation of their doctrine. If they lied, says Grotius, it had to be for the defense of their religion. But in this case, they either sincerely believed that this religion was true or they did not. If not, then they would never have chosen it for their own and rejected the safer, more customary religions. But if they believed it to be true, then the resurrection of Jesus cannot be avoided. For had he not risen, contrary to his prediction, that would have destroyed the very foundation of any faith the disciples had. Moreover, their own religion prohibited lying and any bearing of false witness. And besides this, no one, and especially so many, would be willing to die for a lie that they themselves had made up, a lie that would bring them absolutely no worldly good. And it is clear from their writings that the apostles were not madmen. Finally, the conversion of the apostle Paul bore witness to the reality of the resurrection.

Grotius concludes by handling two theoretical problems. First, to those who object that the resurrection is impossible, Grotius simply replies that it involves no logical contradiction to say that a dead man has been restored to life. Second, the significance of the resurrection Grotius finds in its confirming the new doctrine taught by Jesus, especially in light of Jesus' prediction that he would rise from the dead.

In his argument for Jesus' resurrection, Grotius presents his opponents with a dilemma. Given the authenticity of the gospels and 1 Corinthians, the apostolic testimony to the event of the resurrection can only be denied if the apostles were either lying or sincerely mistaken. But neither of these are reasonable. Therefore, the resurrection must be a historical event. We find here in rudimentary form the dilemma that would be sharpened and pressed by subsequent generations of Christian apologists against their Deist opponents.

The period between Blaise Pascal (d. 1662) and Pierre Bayle's skeptical *Dictionnaire historique et critique* (1695) has been called the golden age of classical French apologetics. This period included thinkers such as Malebranche, Huet, Bossuet, and Abbadie. The tone for this era—and indeed for that of the next century—was set by Pascal's disciple Filleau de la Chaise in his *Discours sur les preuves des livres de Moyse* (1672). He was important because he inaugurated as a self-conscious methodology in apologetics the method of proof *par les faits* (by the facts).

Filleau held that the proper method of persuading people of the truth of the Christian religion does not consist in trying to make its theological mysteries comprehensible or reasonable, but in showing that the mysteries are entailed in the truth of certain indisputable historical facts. He states:

> If men know anything with assurance, it is the facts; and of everything that falls within their knowledge, there is nothing in which it would be more difficult to deceive them and over which there would be less occasion for dispute. And thus, when one will have made them see that the Christian religion is inseparably attached to facts whose truth cannot be sincerely contested, they must submit to all that it teaches or else renounce sincerity and reason.[6]

This method of proving Christianity by the facts was in French apologetics a logical extension of the function of the signs of credibility in attesting the truths of faith coupled with the historical method. Because truths of faith are above reason, they cannot be directly proved, but can nevertheless be indirectly confirmed by miracle and prophecy. Similarly, Filleau contended that we may prove the mysteries of the faith, not directly, but indirectly by the historical facts that entail their truth.

Thus, French apologists began to make a bifurcation between the *contenant* and the *contenu* of the faith. Roughly rendered, the distinction contrasted the "container" of the faith to the "content" of the faith. Though the content of the Christian religion, that is, the body of theological doctrines, may be above reason, nonetheless the container of this religion, that is, the historical events of the gospel story, is demonstrable by the facts; hence, the *contenu* is indirectly proved by historical verification of the *contenant*. Under the influence of this conception, there was during the seventeenth and eighteenth centuries a marked swing in French apologetics toward historical apologies.

In eighteenth-century England there was a similar turn toward empirical, historical proofs of Christianity. Although John Locke set the pattern for English thought in this century by his defense of the reasonableness of Christianity on the basis of Jesus' miracles, it was Charles Leslie who enunciated clearly the method of proving Christianity by the facts in his *Short and Easie Method with the Deists* (1697).

The short and easy method recommended by Leslie is the historical proof of the matters of fact on which Christianity is founded. He argues that when one examines the biblical narratives as one would any matter of fact, one will find them to be historically reliable. Hence, he maintains that one must either reject all the historical works of classical antiquity or else admit the gospel accounts along with them. Following in Locke's footsteps, Leslie helped to set the tone for the hundreds of historical apologies published in England during the next century.

There was a subtle, yet decisive, difference between French and English historical apologetics. Both agreed that revelation may be discerned by what the medievals called the signs of credibility (miracle and prophecy), but they differed in the following way. By making a distinction between the *contenant* and the *contenu*, the French thinkers underscored the bifur-cation between truths of reason and truths of faith, the latter being in themselves rationally incomprehensible and only indirectly verifiable; the English apologists tended to dissolve the distinction between truths of rea-son and truths of faith, the upper story collapsing down into the lower, so that all truths became in a sense truths of reason, demonstrable by philos-ophy, science, history, and so forth. When English writers spoke of truths above reason, they did not generally mean mysterious or incomprehensi-ble truths, as did their French counterparts; rather they meant simply truths that we lack the necessary facts to prove. But in both cases, it was the methodology of history that they counted on to carry the weight of the case for the truth of the Christian faith.

NINETEENTH AND TWENTIETH CENTURIES

During the nineteenth and twentieth centuries the parallel development of historiography and historical apologetics was disrupted.

Historicism and Relativism

The nineteenth century saw the greatest advances in the science of history that had theretofore occurred. The climax of this development came in the school of historicism, shaped by the prodigious influence of the German historian Leopold von Ranke. Von Ranke, through his doctoral students and in turn through their students, was responsible for shaping a whole generation of great historians. The earmark of nineteenth-century his-toricism was objectivity. The task of the historian was to uncover the objec-tive facts, and let those facts speak for themselves. The subjective element—the historian's own personality, biases, outlook, milieu, and so forth—did not enter the historical equation. Von Ranke's goal in doing history, to use his famous phrase, was to describe the past "*wie es eigentlich gewesen ist*" (as it actually was). He apparently saw no reason, given the enormous industry that he brought to his research and that he instilled in his students, why this goal could not be achieved.

During the twentieth century there came a sharp reaction to von Ranke's naive objectivism. The school of historical relativism emphasized the inextricable subjective element in the writing of history. In the United States, relativism was associated particularly with the historians Charles Beard and Carl Becker. Against von Ranke, they denied that historical facts are "out there," waiting to be discovered. Facts do not bear their own meaning piggy-back; it is the historian who must ascribe meaning to the facts. And the historian, who is himself a product of his time and place in history, cannot assume the point of a neutral observer in writing history. The personal element is always in the equation. Von Ranke's goal of describing the past as it really was is illusory; rather, the historian must himself reconstruct the past on the basis of the present. Ironically, the viewpoint of historical relativism is often referred to today as historicism, so that this term now means exactly the opposite of what it meant in the nineteenth century.

During the 1970s the post-modernist critique of objective canons of rationality and truth revitalized the old debate between historical objectivists and relativists. Rooted in Continental philosophy and hermeneutics and in the anti-realism of Wittgenstein, there has emerged a powerful post-modernist current of relativism which flows through virtually every academic field, including history. Calling the conflict between objectivism and relativism the "central cultural opposition of our time," Richard Bernstein remarks, "Relativism, a stream in the philosophy of the past two hundred years that began as a trickle, has swelled in recent times into a roaring torrent."[7] As a result, he observes, "There is an uneasiness that has spread throughout intellectual and cultural life. It affects almost every discipline and every aspect of culture."[8] In 1986, writing in the journal *History and Theory*, F. R. Ankersmit called for the abandonment of what he termed the old "epistemological," or objectivist, philosophy of history.[9] The objectivist approach aimed at specifying the conditions under which we are justified in believing the historian's statements about the past to be true, whereas the narrative approach is concerned only with the interpretation of texts and makes no distinction between the historian's language and what that language is about. The narrative approach tends to ignore the intent of the original author and evaluates texts only on aesthetic or noncognitive grounds, while the objectivist hermeneutical approach seeks to discern the author's intent and so to penetrate more deeply into the past. Narrative non-realists are thus unconcerned with historical truth of narratives or with what actually happened. Indeed, it is not clear whether there really is such a thing as the past on a thoroughgoing post-modernist view, since the multiplicity of historical reconstructions and texts seems to lead to multiple pasts, none of which is privileged. A more moderate non-realist like Leon Goldstein affirms the existence of the unique, actual past, but denies that it concerns him as a historian. As Goldstein puts it, "the standpoint of God does not enter into the work of historians attempting to constitute the human past."[10] Goldstein remains objectivist in affirming that ultimately there is one interpretation of the past which best accords with the evidence, but he is non-realist or constructionist in that it is a matter of indifference to him whether the historian's construction corresponds to reality as it actually was in the past. Contemporary historical relativism thus comprises two challenges to any claim to know the past as it actually happened: (1) non-realism, or constructionism, the view that all we know are historical reconstructions of the past, rather than the past itself, and (2) non-objectivism, or subjectivism, the view that no historical reconstruction can legitimately claim to be superior to alternative reconstructions.

Impact on Apologetics

One might expect that during the nineteenth century the historical apologetic for Christianity would flower. Seeing instead that it withered away, we might suspect that the historical method had simply gotten too big for its theological britches and had exposed the gospels as historically unreliable documents. That would, however, be misleading. The chief obstacle to a historical case for the gospels, as we have seen, was the nineteenth century's conviction that miracles had no place in a historical narrative. Because this presupposition was accepted into biblical criticism, the historical method assumed great importance there, whereas it did not take hold in apologetics. The nineteenth century's enthusiasm for the historical may be seen in the old quest for the historical Jesus. One after another life of Jesus appeared during this century, each trying to rediscover the non-miraculous Jesus behind the supernatural figure of the gospels. Indeed, in that movement one may see the greatest weakness of von Ranke's method exemplified: apparently unaware of the personal element they all brought to their research, each writer reconstructed a historical Jesus after his own image. There was Strauss's Hegelian Jesus, Renan's sentimental Jesus, Bauer's non-existent Jesus, Ritschl's liberal Jesus, and so forth. As one observer remarked, each one looked down the long well of history and saw his own face reflected at the bottom. The movement finally ground to a halt in skepticism, since no non-miraculous Jesus could be uncovered in the gospel traditions. Rather than accept the supernatural Jesus as historical, however, biblical critics ascribed that belief to the theology of the early church, which they said so overlaid the traditions about the historical Jesus that he was no longer recoverable.

During the twentieth century, the historical method—usually called the historical-critical method—has continued to play the decisive role in biblical exegesis. But both dialectical and existential theology severed the theological truth of the gospel from the facts concerning the historical Jesus. Hence, any historical apologetic was conceived to be worse than useless, since it focused on the historical Jesus instead of the Christ of faith—a distinction introduced by the German theologian Martin Kähler at the close of the nineteenth century and subsequently taken up into dialectical and existential theology. It is only since the second half of this century that a new quest of the historical Jesus has begun, this time more cautious and chastened; and once more historical apologetics is beginning to reassert itself. Whether this new movement will be engulfed by post-modernist relativism remains yet to be seen.

ASSESSMENT

RELATIVIST OBJECTIONS TO THE OBJECTIVITY OF HISTORY

If a historical apologetic for the Christian faith is to be successful, the objections of historical relativism need to be overcome. This does not mean a return to naive von Rankian historicism. Of course, the subjective element cannot be eliminated. But the question is whether this subjective element need be so predominant that the study of history is vitiated. In order to answer this question, let us examine more closely the objections of historical relativism. They may be summarized under two main points: first, we cannot know anything about the past as it actually happened, because we cannot directly observe the past; and second, we cannot reconstruct the past objectively, because we are not neutral observers, but rather products of our time, place, culture, circumstances, and so forth. Let me explain each of these objections in turn.

The Problem of Lack of Direct Access

The things and events of the past no longer exist or are happening today, except in the peculiar sense that events of the recent past may be continuing in the present (a war, say, or a scoring drive) and some things existing in the past may have endured to the present (for example, the pyramids). But for the most part, events of the past have ceased, and things of the past no longer exist. Having slipped through our grasp, they are no longer available for direct inspection. At best all we have of the past are the remains and memories of the past, which are in the present. All we seem to know, then, is what exists in the present. How, then, can one avoid skepticism about the past? As historian Patrick Gardiner asks,

> In what sense can I be said to know an event which is in principle unobservable, having vanished behind the mysterious frontier which divides the present from the past? And how can we be sure that anything really happened in the past at all, that the whole story is not an elaborate fabrication, as untrustworthy as a dream or a work of fiction?[11]

Even if one admits the reality of the past, of what relevance is it to the historian? Goldstein points out that historical realism doesn't add anything factually to the historian's store of information; he is still wholly dependent on the present evidence for his reconstructions and inferences about the past.[12] Since past events and things are forever gone, the historian has no way to check if his reconstructions correspond to reality, that is to say, are true. Historical realism and historical truth are otiose for the historian and should therefore be ignored.

Old-line relativists often emphasized the contrast between history and science on this score. The scientist has the objects of his research right in front of him and is free to experiment repeatedly upon them in order to test his hypotheses. By contrast, the historian's objects of research no longer exist and so are not subject to either observation or experiment. Historical knowledge thus fails to measure up to the standards of objectivity set by scientific knowledge.

More recently, however, post-modern relativism has invaded science as well, threatening to undermine the objectivity of the scientific enterprise. Old-line historical relativists prized the objectivity of science because it served them well as a foil for exposing what they considered to be the comparative non-objectivity of historical constructions. But during the 1960s proponents of so-called *Weltanschauung* analyses of scientific theories, such as Thomas Kuhn and Paul Feyerabend, radically challenged the old, positivistic view of science. According to these thinkers, scientific work takes place within the context of an all-embracing world view (*Weltanschauung*) or paradigm, which is so intimately linked with a given scientific theory that for scientists working within that paradigm, their observations are not neutral, but theory-laden; the very meanings of terms used by them are determined by the theory, so that scientists working within a different paradigm aren't even talking about the same things; and what counts as a fact is determined by a scientist's *Weltanschauung*, so that there are no neutral facts available for assessing the adequacy of two rival theories. On this analysis, scientific change from one theory to another becomes fundamentally arational and is to be explained sociologically. On *Weltanschauung* analyses, scientists find themselves in the same boat with historical relativists, for scientific theories are constructions which are not based on objective facts and cannot claim to describe the world as it actually is. Ironically, then, the old-line relativist complaint that the scientist (unlike the historian) has direct access to the objects of his study has been undercut by post-modernist relativists who challenge the positivist idea that scientists neutrally observe the uninterpreted world around them. The scientist's understanding of the present is just as much a theoretical construction as is the historian's understanding of the past, a construction which cannot be checked for its correspondence with the objective facts, since one's *Weltanschauung* determines what the facts are. The implication is that science and history alike are anti-realist and non-objective.

Now, according to historical relativists, our lack of direct access to the past has two important implications. First, it affects how one views historical facts. According to one famous relativist, Carl Becker, it means that historical facts are only in the mind. The event itself is gone, so all we have are the historian's statements about the event. It is those statements that are historical facts. If one were to reply that the event itself is a historical fact because it had an enduring impact on the course of history, Becker would say it had an impact only because people had "long memories." If everyone forgot the event, it would no longer be a historical fact. Thus, historical events really only exist in your mind, not in the past. Two notions are in turn implied by this implication; I'll call them sub-implications.

The first sub-implication is that facts have no meaning and that the historian must put his own meaning onto the facts. Because the event itself is gone and the facts are only in the historian's mind, this means, in Becker's words, that "even if you could present all the facts, the miserable things wouldn't say anything, would say nothing at all." Therefore, the historian must put his own meaning on the facts. As Becker further says, "the event itself, the facts, do not say anything, do not impose any meaning. It is the historian who speaks, who imposes a meaning."[13]

The second sub-implication is that history is largely a result of the historian's own biases, personality, interest, and so forth. Because the historian determines the meaning of the facts himself, the history he writes will be just a reflection of himself. In this way the past is really the product of the present.

There is a second important implication of the historian's not having direct access to the past. There seems to be no way to test the truth of historical facts. A scientist has the method of experimentation to test his hypotheses. But the historian cannot do that, because the events are gone. The scientist at least has the advantage of predictability and repeatability which the historian lacks. So how can the historian test his hypotheses? As historian Patrick Gardiner says,

> We cannot reproduce what we believe to have been the conditions that determined the collapse of the Roman Empire and then watch for the consequences, in the fashion in which we can combine certain chemicals and then see whether the result agrees or disagrees with a prediction of the result of such a combination.[14]

So because the historian cannot directly observe the facts, there is the unsolved problem of how to test for truth in history.

Thus, the problem of the lack of direct access to the past raises two challenges to those who want to learn something from history: first, what is the nature of historical facts, and second, how can one test the truth of historical facts?

The Problem of Lack of Neutrality

The second objection of historical relativists to knowledge of the past as it actually happened is that we cannot reconstruct the past objectively because we are not neutral observers, but are the products of our time, place, culture, and so forth. The historian cannot "stand back" and observe what has happened from a neutral perspective because the historian, too, is caught up in the historical flow of events. Henri Pirenne makes the point:

> Historical syntheses depend to a very large degree not only upon the personality of their authors, but upon all the social, religious, or national environments which surround them. It follows, therefore, that each historian will establish between the facts relationships determined by the convictions, the movements, and the prejudices that have molded his own point of view.[15]

Because of this, each new generation must rewrite history in its own way. The history written today will be judged inferior and obsolete by the historians of the next generation. But their work will also be shaped by their culture and so forth. Thus, in the words of philosopher Karl Popper, "There can be no history of the past as it actually did happen; there can only be historical interpretations; and none of them final; and every generation has a right to frame its own."[16] Therefore, history can never be objectively written. The historian always looks at the past through the colored glasses of the present, as determined by his society and environment.

CRITIQUE OF HISTORICAL RELATIVISM

These two basic objections, then, need to be answered before we examine the historical foundations of Christianity: first, the problem of the lack of direct access to the past, which issues in anti-realism; and second, the problem of the lack of neutrality, which issues in subjectivism.

The Problem of Lack of Direct Access

The things and events of the past are obviously for the most part gone; the question is whether our lack of direct access to them forces us to become historical constructionists or narrative non-realists. Here it will be helpful to distinguish between constructionism as a methodology and constructionism as a philosophy.[17] Post-modern relativism at its most radical takes constructionism philosophically as an ontological thesis about how reality is constituted. Ontological constructionism holds that the historian actually constitutes the past events themselves via his reconstruction; that there really is not nor ever was a past-in-itself, but only a past-for-me, relative to each person. As such, this view implies a fantastic subjective idealism which flies in the face of our common sense beliefs that things and events of the past really existed independently of oneself before one arrived on the scene, that we share together a common past issuing in a shared present, that after we die the world will go on without us. Given the radical nature of this thesis, Nowell-Smith is surely right when he states that the burden of proof lies on the person who claims that what the historian constructs is not an *account* of past events, but rather the past events themselves. Moreover, ontological constructionism has some bizarre implications, as Plantinga points out in his biting satire of post-modernist Richard Rorty's claim that "truth is what my peers will let me get away with saying":

> Although this view is very much *au courant* and with-it in the contemporary intellectual world, it has consequences that are peculiar, not to say preposterous. For example, most of us think that the Chinese authorities did something monstrous in murdering those hundreds of young people in Tiananmen Square, and then compounded their wickedness by denying that they had done it. On Rorty's view, however, this is an uncharitable misunderstanding. What the authorities were really doing, in denying that they had murdered those students, was something wholly praiseworthy: they were trying to bring it about that the alleged massacre never happened. For they were trying to see to it that their peers would let them get away with saying that the massacre never happened; that is, they were trying to make it *true* that it never happened; and who can fault them for that? The same goes for those contemporary neo-Nazis who claim that there was no holocaust; from a Rortian view, they are only trying to see to it that such a terrible thing never happened; and what could be more commendable than that? This way of thinking has real possibilities for dealing with poverty and disease: if only we let each other get away with saying that there isn't any poverty and disease—no cancer or AIDS, let's say—then it would be true that there isn't any; and if it were true that there isn't any, then of course there wouldn't *be* any.[18]

The serious point in this justifiably deserved satire is that ontological constructionism is not only obviously ridiculous, but even sinister, in that it
lends itself to wicked and self-justifying distortions of history.

A constructionist who is not also a subjectivist might insist that one's
reconstruction of the past must be constrained by present evidence. Not
only would this not solve the moral problem (destroying present evidence
so as to bring about a different past), but a moment's reflection exposes the
untenability of such a view. For it is clearly impossible to act only on present evidence, since this would necessitate abandonment of all memory
beliefs, including everything we have learned in our research. The very
notion of "present evidence" is past-infected, for it has been assembled,
digested, catalogued, remembered, and so on. The only present evidence
we have is our immediate sensory awareness, which cannot restrain ontological constructionism. Lionel Rubinoff is therefore amply warranted in
his observation that post-modern relativism "risks succumbing to all the
pitfalls and skeptical implications of the epistemological anarchism that
follow from unqualified, radical relativism or subjectivism. . . ."[19]

But suppose the philosophical constructionist adopts a more moderate
line such as Goldstein's, who holds, it will be remembered, that the past is
real independent of our reconstructions, but that we cannot or do not come
to know that past. The untenability of even this moderate philosophical
constructionism may be seen by reflecting on a case in which every statement in a historian's reconstruction of the past corresponds to what actually happened in the past. In such a case those statements are true,
according to a view of truth as correspondence, and if the evidence justi-
fies belief in that historian's theory, as Goldstein admits it may, then how
could we be said to have knowledge only of the historian's theory and not
of the past itself? Perhaps Goldstein would say that in such a case we do
not know that the reconstruction corresponds with the past and so we do
not have true knowledge of the past, but only a sort of unwitting true belief.
But then consider the case of a detective who on the basis of the evidence
independently offers a reconstruction of a crime which an eyewitness
knows to be correct. Wouldn't the detective be said to know what really
happened, since he believes exactly what the eyewitness believes and does
so on the basis of the evidence? In general, the claim that in order to know
something we must be able to know that we know it, that is, to justify our
justification, is an epistemological principle which should be rejected.[20]

Admittedly, Goldstein is right that historical realism doesn't contribute
factually to the historian's work in the sense of adding one more event to
our knowledge of the past which we otherwise would have missed. But
realism is a philosophical thesis which lends to science and history a sig-

nificance they would otherwise lack, for on the realist view such enterprises really do tell us something about the world we live in, as opposed to historical or science fiction. Indeed, on Goldstein's view it is hard to see a qualitative difference between the writing of history and the writing of historical novels, since the latter cohere with all known evidence, too. He might insist that history is limited to what the evidence *requires* us to believe; but then what is the rationale for such a limitation if not the fact that history aims at truth about the real past whereas historical novels do not?

Moreover, as W.H. Dray points out, historical realism serves a quasi-methodological function in that a real past cannot have incompatible properties, and realism thus serves as a restraint on the anti-realist tendency toward acceptance of multiple, incompatible reconstructions of the past.[21]

But if historical constructionism fails as a philosophy, what about constructionism as a methodology? As a historiographical methodology, constructionism may be interpreted as the thesis that the historical past should be regarded as what the evidence indicates that it was. The historian reasons, "The evidence is such and such; it would not be such and such unless my theory were true; therefore, my theory is true." So understood there is no incompatibility between historical realism and methodological constructionism. On the contrary, it is precisely the historian's goal, using all his critical skills, to determine what happened in the past by reconstructing it on the basis of the evidence. Of course, in many cases, various proferred reconstructions will be underdetermined by the evidence, so that one does not know which one, if any, is correct; but that in no way implies that there is no objective past or that in other cases where the evidence is clear we cannot know with confidence what really happened. Nowell-Smith points out,

> Some results of historical thinking are so well established that it would be madness to doubt them; others have only the status of being a more probable explanation of the evidence than any rival hypothesis. This is a point on which it is worth while to dwell. Why is it still reasonable to doubt whether there ever was such a person as King Arthur but utterly unreasonable to question the existence of George Washington? The reason is not far to seek. If we took *seriously* the hypothesis that there never was any such person as George Washington, we should be faced with the problem of accounting for the existence of such a vast body of evidence—not testimony, but *evidence*, documents of whose existence and nature we are now aware—that it would soon become obvious that the task is impossible. To put it mildly, the hypothesis that there was no such person

is in a very weak position vis-a-vis the hypothesis that there was; and that is all that the standard of proof in history requires.[22]

We shall have more to say below about how the historian weighs the evidence for his hypotheses; but for now the point seems clear that while constructionism fails as a philosophical thesis, it is a vital part of historical methodology aimed at recovering the real past.

Turning then to the traditional relativist claim that the historian finds himself in a disadvantaged position compared to the scientist due to the greater inaccessibility of the objects of historical study, let me say two things. First, it is naive to think that the scientist always has direct access to his objects of study. Not only is the scientist largely dependent on the reports of others' research (which, interestingly, constitute for him historical documents) for his own work, but furthermore, the objects of the scientist's research are often only indirectly accessible, especially in the highly theoretical fields like physics. Such theoretical entities as black holes, quarks, and neutrinos are postulated as the best explanations for the observable data, but they themselves cannot be directly observed. It might be thought that this point actually serves to reinforce the relativist's objection, since it is precisely in the case of such theoretical entities that a non-realist interpretation of scientific theories is most plausible. The plausibility of non-realism in the case of high-level theoretical entities, such as those postulated in particle physics, need not be disputed; but what this retort fails to appreciate is that scientific theories also populate the world with very low-level theoretical entities whose real existence is far more difficult to deny, entities such as dinosaurs, Ice Age glaciers, and even galaxies! The relativist will have to swallow hard before denying that such things are real simply because they are not susceptible to direct observation.

Secondly, while the historian does not have direct access to the past, the residue of the past, things that have really existed, is directly accessible to him. The modern historian is not simply dependent on the reports of earlier historians. For example, archaeological data furnish direct access to the objects of the historian's investigation. The renowned English historian R. G. Collingwood states,

> scissors and paste (is) not the only foundation of historical method. Archaeology has provided a wonderfully sensitive method for answering questions to which not only do literary sources give no direct answer but which cannot be answered even by the most ingenious interpretation of them.[23]

Thus, the historian, like the scientist, often has direct access to things he is investigating. Now, I'm not confusing the evidence with the events themselves, which are admittedly past; but I am saying, in Van der Dussen's words, that "from the epistemological point of view evidence has the peculiar feature of being itself directly observable and accessible for inspection, while the knowledge it may lead to is not."[24] And archaeology is only one of the means to secure such evidence. As OT scholar R. K. Harrison explains, modern historians are not so heavily dependent on subjective literary sources as before, because the sciences of linguistics, sociology, anthropology, numismatics, and archaeology have become so developed.[25]

In fact, we can at this point draw a very instructive analogy: what history is to the humanities, geology is to the sciences. The major difference between history and geology is the human factor, not the accessibility of the data. Whereas the subject matter of the geologist is the earth's history, the subject matter of the historian is human history. Basically their task is the same. As Collingwood states, "The historian's real work is the reconstruction in thought of a particular historical event; the geologist's, the reconstruction in thought of a particular geological epoch at a particular place."[26]

If this is the case, then the relativists' argument based on the inaccessibility of the past loses all its punch. For the subject matter of the geologist is every bit as indirect as that of the historian, and yet geology is part of science, which has traditionally been the model of objectivity to the relativist. Since lack of direct access cannot preclude geological knowledge, neither can it preclude historical knowledge.

But what, then, of the post-modern relativist's claim that science, as well as history, is non-realist and subjective? It does not appear to be widely appreciated outside the field of philosophy of science—especially by postmodernist theologians who continue to invoke the authority of Thomas Kuhn and to talk freely of paradigms, as though this notion were accepted or even well-defined—that after an initial stir *Weltanschauung* analyses had already been widely discredited by philosophers of science by the late 1970s.[27] Contemporary philosophy of science is post-positivist, post-Kuhnian, and generally realist.

Consider the anti-realist claim that all observation is theory-laden. Taken in the radical sense that our theory actually determines the way the world is, this thesis leads at once to the same subjective idealism implied by ontological constructionism, which is, as Scheffler says, the *reductio ad absurdum* of such a thesis.[28] What about a more moderate claim, that our *Weltanschauung* determines how we observe the independently existing world? Here one need not dispute that observation is theory-laden in the sense that it involves "seeing that something is the case" or "seeing something as a certain kind of thing," which is relative to the observer's background knowledge. For example, if a scientist and a layman enter a laboratory together, the scientist may see an interferometer on the table, while the layman sees only a piece of machinery. Or again, a baseball fan may leap to his feet at seeing a home run at the ballpark, while someone ignorant of the game sees only a ball going over the fence. This sort of theory-ladenness characterizes historical observation and writing as well: when a historian describes the history of primitive man in terms of "magic" and "mythology," for example, this is only possible because he is writing from the standpoint of a scientific culture for whom the distinction between science and magic is meaningful.[29]

Now I think it is obvious that this sort of theory-ladenness does nothing to undermine the objectivity of science or history or to support antirealism. As the great historian of philosophy Frederick Copleston argues, to say that I experience something as x is not to imply that it is not in fact x. "Why should it?" he asks. "I am aware of an object lying on my table. I see it as a pencil. It by no means follows that the object is not a pencil." Similarly, "It is reasonable to claim that the people who were present at the beheading of King Charles I saw the course of events as the beheading of the king. It by no means follows that this was a purely subjective interpretation or reading of the events."[30] Nor does the failure of someone else to see something as I see it do anything to suggest that either of us fails to see correctly. If an aboriginal fails to see the slender, yellow object on the table as a pencil, that in no way proves that it is not a pencil as I see it to be. Now, of course, I may be mistaken in seeing x as a pencil. But I can discover my mistakes. I can pick up x and try to write with it and find that what I thought was a pencil isn't one after all. Here we return to the notion of evidence. "Sometimes," observes Copleston, "the available evidence is such as to eliminate any reasonable doubt about the validity of an interpretation."[31] (Recall the case of George Washington; similarly no scientist could today justifiably hold to a pre-Copernican cosmology or a pre-Harveyian theory of blood circulation.)

Now, to be sure, the evidence itself is also seen as such and such. But for people with shared background knowledge, certain observed facts can simply be taken as data. For example, the layman and the scientist both see the interferometer as machinery, so that that fact is for them a datum; but for a very primitive person, say a troglodyte, that fact would not be a datum. What counts as data or interpretation is thus relative, but in order for much of the evidence available to us to count as data the level of shared background beliefs is not very high at all. Even a caveman could not justifiably see the interferometer as, say, his wife or a saber-toothed tiger. Thus, when the historian or scientist assesses the evidence for a theory, he needn't try to justify all over again every datum which he uses. Some data are reasonably taken as given. As Copleston says, "it is foolish to demand uninterpreted experiential data before we are prepared to admit that historiography is not a purely subjective construction."[32]

The evidence which the historian uses will include texts, as well as artifacts, and here, too, his reconstruction will be limited by the data. Copleston states,

> the historian is not free to interpret the texts as he likes. Some statements may be ambiguous; but there are others, the meaning of which is clearly determined independently of the historian's will. For example, he is not at liberty to deny the fact that Marx asserted the priority of matter to spirit or mind. As far as the historian is concerned, the texts constitute something given, something which limits his reconstruction. . . .[33]

Texts have limits to the meanings which can be seen in them. No one employs post-modern hermeneutics in reading the instructions on a medicine bottle. The fact that texts taken as evidence have limits is of particular importance to our project, since most of the evidence which we shall assess involves the texts of the NT.

The above leads to one final point about theory-ladenness. As Suppe explains, it is false that there is a different *Weltanschauung* uniquely correlated with each scientific theory.[34] If the notion of a *Weltanschauung* is defined too broadly, then it just becomes equivalent to one's total-background, experience, beliefs, training, and so forth, in which case the striking fact is that scientists possessing widely different *Weltanschauungen* do employ the same theories and come to agreement on the testing, articulation, and use of such theories. On the other hand, if one tries to narrow the definition of a *Weltanschauung*, then the fact is that scientists involved in research programs on different theories do not necessarily have different *Weltanschauungen*, but clearly understand the competing theory, the observations and evidence that support it, and regularly communicate with one another about such matters. It would be bizarre, for example, to say that all proponents of the standard Big Bang theory have a unique and different *Weltanschauung* than cosmologists who advocated the old Steady State theory, rather than to say that they just disagreed on which theory offered the best explanation of the evidence. Thus, theory-ladenness of observation, insofar as this is a plausible notion, undermines neither science nor history.

The second major thesis of *Weltanschauung* analyses, that the meanings of terms in theories are theory-dependent, has proved even more indefensible.[35] It implies that two different theories could not agree or disagree with each other, in which case it makes no sense to speak of them as alternatives between which a choice is to be made; instead, every theory becomes true by definition and the testing of theories circular (since anything purportedly contradictory to the theory will have a different meaning). This is just a gross distortion of what science is. If one adopts a more moderate thesis to the effect that in our formulations of theories the meanings of some of the terms are partially determined by some of the principles of the theory, then one gives up to characteristic claim of *Weltanschauung* analyses that theories are incommensurable and cannot be adjudicated from outside the paradigm. In any case, it is not clear how the incommensurability thesis for scientific theories would apply to the terms of historians' reconstructions of the past, since the latter do not employ theoretical terms and principles, but are formulated in ordinary language.

Finally, the third major claim of *Weltanschauung* analyses, that what counts as a fact is determined by the *Weltanschauung*, is patient of a radical or a moderate interpretation.[36] Radically construed as the thesis that facts about the world are literally determined by our *Weltanschauung*, it leads once again to a sort of solipsism. A more moderate claim, that what one can entertain as a fact is determined by one's *Weltanschauung*, can only be defended when due consideration is given to the criticisms of the first two theses above. There exists a body of evidence which can serve to adjudicate rival theories. While a theory will shape some of the criteria for its assessment, such as which questions the theory should address or what is the appropriate methodology for testing its assertions, still the requirement that an adequate theory be empirically true guarantees that subjective factors will not nullify the objectivity of science. Similarly, in history, while different reconstructions of the past may be prompted by different questions on the part of the historian and no single methodology exists for testing historical reconstructions, still any acceptable reconstruction must make its peace with the empirical evidence. The appeal of post-modern relativists to *Weltanschauung* analyses of science in order to undermine objectivism in history thus proves vain. According to Suppe, *Weltanschauung* analyses "are not widely viewed as serious contenders for a viable philosophy of science. Contemporary philosophy of science, although strongly influenced by these *Weltanschauungen* views, has gone beyond them and is heading in new directions. The *Weltanschauungen* views, in a word, today are passé, although . . . they continue to be much discussed in the philosophical literature."[37] The turn to realism by contemporary philosophy of science is an encouraging development which can only reinforce historical objectivism.

Nature of Historical Facts

Now it will be remembered that there were two supposed implications of our lack of direct access to the past. First, there's the problem of the nature of historical facts. Becker says that facts exist only in the mind. He says that the facts are merely the historian's statements about events. But this is clearly untenable. For Becker also says the facts have no meaning. Now surely he doesn't want to say that the historian's statements have no meaning! His position is self-refuting. Rather a historical fact is either the historical event itself or a piece of accurate information about that event. Thus, a historian makes statements about the facts.

Seen in this light, Becker's statement that facts exist only in the mind is somewhat silly. His belief forces him to the bizarre conclusion that Lincoln's assassination made a difference in history only because people have long memories, but that if everyone had forgotten Lincoln's death within forty-eight hours, then it would have made no difference at all and would have ceased to be a historical fact! It's difficult to take such an idea seriously. For clearly, Lincoln's death would have made an immense impact on U.S. history whether *anyone* remembered it or not. It was primarily Lincoln's *absence*, not memories of Lincoln, that made such a difference in U.S. history. Even if everyone had forgotten that there even was a Lincoln, the absence created by the death of that great man would still have had its devastating results. In other words, the facts exist independently of our minds and still have their impact even long after they are forgotten.

There were two sub-implications arising from the idea that historical facts are just in one's mind. A little reflection will reveal that the first sub-implication, that historical facts have no meaning, is a preposterous notion. For what do we mean by the phrase *facts without meaning*? What in the world is a "meaningless" fact? This is a notion trembling on the brink of self-contradiction. Meaning is inherent in the very concept of *fact*. To describe a fact is to give its meaning. Thus, if I say "It is a fact that Garfield was the twentieth President of the United States," the meaning of the fact, if not obvious enough, is given by simply defining its terms: It is a fact that a man named Garfield was the twentieth man to be the head of the executive branch of the government of the country named the United States. What the fact is *is* its meaning. The notion of a meaningless fact is absurd;

there can be no such thing. Insofar as a thing is a fact, it has meaning, because meaning is inherent in the concept of fact.

The second sub-implication of the relativists' argument that facts are just in the mind is that history is the product of the historian himself. I plan to deal with this argument when I discuss whether the historian can reconstruct the past objectively or whether what he writes is determined by his society and so forth. I'll argue that because the facts are not just in his mind but are, as it were, out there, subjective influences are constrained by the facts themselves.

Testing for Truth in History

The second major implication of the lack of direct access to the data concerns the testability of historical hypotheses. Since the historian cannot perform experiments like a scientist, how can he test the truth of his theories? It seems to me that the historian's hypotheses are to be tested like any other's: by their systematic consistency. If a historical reconstruction is logically consistent and provides the best explanation of the evidence, then it ought to be accepted.

The problem arises as to how to apply this test in history. I suggest that the historian applies this test in exactly the same way as the scientist. Whatever model of explanation one adopts in the sciences will do nicely for history as well. One popular model is the hypothetico-deductive model. The scientist invents a hypothesis to provide a systematically consistent explanation of the facts, and then he deduces from the hypothesis specific conditions that would either confirm or disprove his hypothesis. Then he performs certain experiments to see which conditions obtain.

The historian can follow the same procedure. He reconstructs a picture of the past. This is his hypothesis. Then he deduces certain conditions from it that will confirm or disprove his hypothesis. He then checks to see which conditions exist. He does this not by experiments, as the scientist does, but by historical evidence. As Collingwood says, "The historian's picture of the past stands in a peculiar relation to something called evidence. The only way in which the historian can judge of its truth is by considering this relation."[38] Collingwood is saying that the historian's hypothesis must be corroborated by the evidence, for example, archaeological evidence. "By treating coins, pottery weapons, and other artifacts as evidence," one historian writes, "the historian raises his study to the level of a science. What happened in the past is what the evidence indicates as having happened."[39]

Alternatively, one may employ the more recently developed model of inference to the best explanation. According to this approach, we begin with the evidence available to us and then infer what would, if true, provide the best explanation of that evidence. Out of a pool of live options determined by our background beliefs, we select the best of various competing potential explanations to give a causal account of why the evidence is as it is rather than otherwise. The scientist can test his proposed explanation by performing experiments; the historian will test his by seeing how well it elucidates the historical evidence.

The process of determining which historical reconstruction is the best explanation will involve the historian's craft, as various factors will have to be weighed. In his recent book *Justifying Historical Descriptions,*[40] C. Behan McCullagh lists the factors which historians typically weigh in testing a historical hypothesis:

1. The hypothesis, together with other true statements, must imply further statements describing present, observable data.
2. The hypothesis must have greater *explanatory scope* (that is, imply a greater variety of observable data) than rival hypotheses.
3. The hypothesis must have greater *explanatory power* (that is, make the observable data more probable) than rival hypotheses.
4. The hypothesis must be *more plausible* (that is, be implied by a greater variety of accepted truths, and its negation implied by fewer accepted truths) than rival hypotheses.
5. The hypothesis must be less *ad hoc* (that is, include fewer new suppositions about the past not already implied by existing knowledge) than rival hypotheses.
6. The hypothesis must be *disconfirmed by fewer accepted beliefs* (that is, when conjoined with accepted truths, imply fewer false statements) than rival hypotheses.
7. The hypothesis must so exceed its rivals in fulfilling conditions (2)-(6) that there is little chance of a rival hypothesis, after further investigation, exceeding it in meeting these conditions.

Since some reconstructions may fulfill some conditions but be deficient in others, the determination of the best explanation requires skill and may often be difficult. But if the strength and scope of any explanation are very great, so that it explains a large number and variety of facts, many more than any other competing explanation, then, advises McCullagh, it is likely to be true.

In his process of formulating and testing hypotheses the historian is very much like the scientist, especially the geologist, who also lacks direct access to his data and the opportunity of lab experiments on past events. Collingwood gives the conclusion: "The analysis of science in epistemological terms is identical with the analysis of history and the distinction between them as separate kinds of knowledge is an illusion."[41]

One final point needs to be made. The goal of historical knowledge is to obtain probability, not mathematical certainty. An item can be regarded as a piece of historical knowledge when it is related to the evidence in such a way that any reasonable person ought to accept it. This is the situation with all of our inductive knowledge: we accept what has sufficient evidence to render it probable. Similarly, in a court of law, the verdict is awarded to the case that is made most probable by the evidence. The jury is asked to decide if the accused is guilty—not beyond all doubt, which is impossible—but beyond all reasonable doubt. It is exactly the same in history: we should accept the hypothesis that provides the most probable explanation of the evidence.

To summarize, then, we test for truth by systematic consistency, and the method of applying this test is the same in history as it is in science. The historian should accept the hypothesis that best explains all the evidence. Thus, the supposed lack of direct access to the data is no stumbling block to testing for truth in history and so gaining an accurate knowledge of the past.

Problem of Lack of Neutrality

Let's move now to the second major objection to our gaining knowledge from the past: the lack of neutrality. Relativists argue that because we are all shaped by personality and environment, no historian can objectively reconstruct the past. In what I've said already we have begun to expose the fallacies of this objection.

When we judge the truth of a historical work, it is not so important how the knowledge of the past was learned, as *what* the content of that knowledge is. As the historian Maurice Mandelbaum explains, if we say a historical work is false, we say it is false because it does not accord with the facts, not because of sociological factors surrounding the historian.[42] As long as historical realism is correct and historical hypotheses must square with the evidence, then the cultural conditioning of the historian is secondary. As long as the content of the historian's knowledge accords with the facts, then how he got that knowledge is unimportant.

Another way of putting this is that it is not so important how the historian comes to arrive at his hypothesis as how his hypothesis is tested. So long as it is tested by the objective facts, it is of secondary importance what factors influenced the historian to come up with his hypothesis in the first place. Thus, Morton White emphasizes that although a number of psychological and social factors may influence the formulation of a hypothesis, the historian still has to submit to objective tests that have nothing to do with personality, milieu, or general world view.[43] This is just the same as in science. The scientist who discovered the chemical structure of the benzine molecule hit upon the idea from a dream he had of a snake holding its own tail, thus forming a circular structure. I don't mean to say that there isn't a "logic of discovery" that the scientist (or historian) follows in framing fruitful hypotheses. The point is that so far as the truth of the hypothesis is concerned, it doesn't matter how the historian or scientist comes up with his hypothesis—he could have learned it at his mother's knee, for all that matters. So long as the hypothesis is tested by the facts, there is no danger of sacrificing objectivity.

In reality, relativists recognize that our knowledge of history is not awash in subjectivism. For although they deny historical objectivity, they do not really treat history in so roughshod a manner. This is evident in three ways:

1. *A common core of indisputable historical facts exists.* Thus, one relativist confesses that "there are basic facts which are the same for all historians," facts which it is "the duty" of the historian to present accurately.[44] Even Becker, while saying that facts have no meaning, admits that "some things, some 'facts' can be established and agreed upon"—examples include the date of the Declaration of Independence, Caesar's crossing the Rubicon, the sale of indulgences in 1517, Lincoln's assassination, and so forth.[45] Not even the most radical relativist is prepared to abandon history as a hopeless bog of subjectivism. As historian Isaiah Berlin puts it, if someone were to tell us that *Hamlet* was written at the court of Genghis Khan in outer Mongolia, we would not think that he was merely wrong, but that he was out of his mind![46]

But if there is a common, incontrovertible core of historical facts, then the relativist has surrendered his point that the facts do not speak for themselves or that historical objectivity is vitiated. It is a simple truth that, in historian Christopher Blake's words, there "is a very considerable part" of history that is "acceptable to the community of professional historians beyond all question," be they Marxists or liberals, Catholics or Protestants, nineteenth-century Germans or twentieth-century Englishmen.[47] If one were to ask me what some of the facts are which make up this backbone of history, I think few historians would disagree with very much of what has been catalogued in a book such as Langer's *Encyclopedia of World History*. Thus, the existence of a common core of historical facts shows that even relativists believe that lack of neutrality does not obviate the objectivity of history.

2. *It is possible to distinguish between history and propaganda.* "All rep-

utable historians," states W. H. Walsh, make a distinction between history and propaganda. The latter may serve some purpose, says Walsh, but, he insists, it is "emphatically not history."[48] A good example of such propaganda was the Soviet practice of "rewriting" history to serve their political purposes. According to Morton White, when Stalin came to power, he had Russian history rewritten so that it was he and Lenin who led the Bolshevik Revolution instead of Lenin and Trotsky. According to White,

> It has been shown by students of the Russian Revolution that mountains of books, newspapers, pamphlets, decrees, and documents had to be consigned to the "memory hole," mashed to pulp, or brought out in corrected editions in order to substitute for Lenin-Trotsky a new duality-unity, Lenin-Stalin.[49]

White charges that the most dangerous thing about historical relativism is the way it can be used to justify historical distortions. The ultimate result of this totalitarian fiddling with the past is envisioned by George Orwell in *1984*:

> "There is a Party slogan dealing with control of the past," he said. "Repeat it, if you please."
> "Who controls the past controls the future; who controls the present controls the past," repeated Winston obediently.
> "Who controls the present controls the past," said O'Brien, nodding his head with slow approval. . . .
> "I tell you, Winston, that reality is not external. Reality exists in the human mind, and nowhere else. Not in the individual mind, which can make mistakes, and in any case soon perishes; only in the mind of the Party, which is collective and immortal. Whatever the Party holds to be truth *is* truth."[50]

If the facts have no meaning and can be made to say whatever the historian wants, then there is no way to protest this propagandizing of history. On relativist grounds, there is no way to distinguish history from propaganda. But again, no relativist could countenance such a notion. They want to say that the facts *do* make a difference and that propagandists cannot distort them at will. But the only way to do that is to acknowledge that historical objectivity is in some measure attainable.

3. *It is possible to criticize poor history.* All historians distinguish good history from poor. A good example is Immanuel Velikovsky's attempt to rewrite ancient history on the basis of world-wide catastrophes caused by extra-terrestrial forces in the fifteenth, eighth, and seventh centuries B.C.

Velikovsky completely reconstructs ancient history, dismissing entire ancient kingdoms and languages as fictional. In a meticulously documented essay on Velikovsky's theories, archaeologist Edwin Yamauchi incisively criticizes the proposed reconstruction, relentlessly plucking out one support after another by a detailed analysis of ancient documents, archaeology, and philology until the whole structure tumbles down in ruin. His conclusion is succinct: "Velikovsky's reconstruction is a catastrophic history in a double sense. It is a history based on catastrophe, and it is a disastrous catastrophe of history."

Now no relativist could make such a statement. If history is simply the subjective product of the historian's own biases and background, then Velikovsky's views are as good as anybody's. Yet, as Yamauchi observes, the reaction of historians to Velikovsky's proposals was "quite hostile."[51] In saying that such a rewrite is poor history or biased or inaccurate, historians implicitly admit that the facts themselves do say something and are not like a wax nose that can be pulled and twisted about to suit any historian's whim. So in criticizing poor history the relativist acknowledges the objectivity of history.

Finally, the objection based on lack of neutrality fails to realize that the historian can make it plain what his point of view is. Karl Popper says that the best way out of the problem of having unconscious points of view is to state clearly one's view and to recognize that there are also other points of view.[52] Raymond Aron states that "relativism is transcended as soon as the historian ceases to claim a detachment which is impossible, recognizes what his point of view is, and consequently puts himself in a position to recognize the points of view of others."[53] Thus, there is simply the need to be forthright in writing history.

Why, then, are histories rewritten each generation? In his classic book *The Problem of Historical Knowledge,* Maurice Mandelbaum provides seven reasons.[54] None of these count against historical objectivity. Some of the reasons are: new sources and evidence are discovered; recent history always needs to be reworked as we gain perspective on what has happened; new appreciation of a certain form of art, music, literature, and so forth may arise in one generation after another. Far from eliminating knowledge of the past as it actually was, the rewriting of history serves to advance our knowledge of the past as new discoveries are made.

One aspect of the problem of lack of neutrality is of special interest for our inquiry: the presupposition of naturalism or supernaturalism on the part of the historian. Naturalism, in contrast to supernaturalism, holds that every effect in the world is brought about by causes which are themselves also part of the natural order (the space-time realm of matter and energy).

It follows that no naturalist as such can accept the historicity of the miraculous events of the gospels, such as Jesus' resurrection: he must deny either their miraculous nature or their historicity. The presupposition of naturalism will thus affect the historian's assessment of the evidence of the gospels. R. T. France has commented:

> at the level of their literary and historical character we have good reasons to treat the gospels seriously as a source of information on the life and teaching of Jesus, and thus on the historical origins of Christianity. . . . Beyond that point, the decision as to how far a scholar is willing to accept the record they offer is likely to be influenced more by his openness to a "supernaturalist" world-view than by strictly historical considerations.[55]

We have seen, for example, that in inferring to the best explanation, one chooses from a pool of live options a candidate to serve as one's explanation for the evidence. For the naturalist historian confronted with, say, the evidence of the empty tomb and resurrection appearances, the hypothesis that Jesus rose from the dead would most probably not even be a live option.[56] If a supernaturalistic historian were to offer such an explanation of the evidence, his naturalistic colleague would probably find it incredible.

But on what grounds? In a fascinating comment on the criteria for assessing historical hypotheses, McCullagh actually considers the Christian hypothesis of the resurrection of Jesus and observes, "This hypothesis is of greater explanatory scope and power than other hypotheses which try to account for the relevant evidence, but it is less plausible and more *ad hoc* than they are. That is why it is difficult to decide on the evidence whether it should be accepted or rejected."[57] Whether the resurrection hypothesis is more *ad hoc* than its rivals can be deferred until our discussion of that event, but for now we may ask why this hypothesis should be considered less plausible than rival hypotheses. Degree of plausibility is defined by McCullagh as the degree to which a hypothesis is implied by accepted knowledge, including both background knowledge and the specific relevant evidence for the hypothesis. Now with respect to the background knowledge alone, the supernaturalist may agree with the naturalist that the resurrection hypothesis has virtually zero plausibility in McCullagh's sense, for nothing in that information alone implies that the resurrection occurred (for the sake of argument, we set aside our experience of the Risen Lord). But by the same token, the hypotheses that the disciples stole the body or that Jesus was taken down from the cross alive, and so forth, also have zero plausibility with respect to the background information alone, for nothing in that information implies that any of these events took place either. That means that the greater plausibility enjoyed by naturalistic hypotheses must derive from the specific evidence itself. But here it is very hard to see how the specific evidence confers greater plausibility on any naturalistic hypothesis than on the resurrection hypothesis; on the contrary, these rival hypotheses, far from being rendered plausible by the evidence, are usually thought to be made implausible by the evidence.

Perhaps McCullagh's claim, then, should have been that the resurrection hypothesis is *more implausible* than rival hypotheses. *Degree of implausibility* is defined as the degree to which our present knowledge implies the falsity of a hypothesis. Now, again dividing present knowledge into background information and specific evidence for the hypothesis, it cannot be that the specific evidence renders the resurrection hypothesis more implausible than its competitors, for that evidence in no way implies the falsity of the resurrection hypothesis. Hence, there must be something in our background knowledge that renders the resurrection hypothesis more implausible than its rivals. I strongly suspect that the reason the naturalist finds the resurrection implausible is because included in our background knowledge of the world is the fact that dead men do not rise, which he takes to be incompatible with Jesus' resurrection. In other words, we are right back to the old Humean argument against miracles! We may agree that our background knowledge makes the hypothesis of the natural revivification of Jesus from the dead enormously implausible, in that the causal powers of nature are insufficient to return a corpse to life; but such considerations are simply irrelevant to assessing the implausibility of the hypothesis of the resurrection of Jesus, since according to that hypothesis God raised Jesus from the dead. In light of our discussion of the problem of miracles, I should say that the hypothesis that God raised Jesus from the dead has about zero implausibility with respect to our background knowledge—leaving aside any implausibility thought to attend to the hypothesis of God's existence. Only if the naturalist has good reasons to think that God's existence is implausible or his intervention in the world implausible could he justifiably regard the resurrection hypothesis as implausible.

The upshot of this discussion is that the objective facts can lead a historian to abandon his naturalistic stance if a miraculous hypothesis should clearly exceed any naturalistic hypothesis in fulfilling the conditions of a best explanation. Of course, a historian could be so deeply prejudiced in favor of naturalism that he resolutely refuses to accept any miraculous hypothesis. But that is just a fact of psychology, which does not undermine the objectivity of history, any more than does the case of a Marxist historian who shuts his eyes to un-economic causes of historical development or a Confederate historian who refuses to acknowledge any responsibility of the South in bringing on the Civil War. The point is that naturalism (or supernaturalism) does not inevitably determine how one weighs the evidence. Indeed, one's naturalism might be very lightly held, a sort of unconscious assumption unreflectively embraced as a result of one's upbringing, and quickly abandoned upon the presentation of powerful evidence for a miraculous hypothesis.

All this has been said concerning metaphysical naturalism. But it has been argued, even by Christian thinkers, that there is a sort of methodological naturalism which must be adopted in science and history. According to methodological naturalism, science and, by implication, history just don't deal with supernatural explanations, and so these are left aside. Now in this case the issue does not concern a lack of neutrality; it is merely a question of methodology. For my part, I see no good reason for methodological naturalism in either science or history.[58] But we may simply sidestep the issue, since our purpose is not to show that the historian *qua* historian should accept the miraculous events of the gospels, any more than our aim was to show that the scientist *qua* scientist should accept the existence of a Creator. A methodological naturalist will simply remain agnostic when speaking professionally about such issues, but acknowledge that as a human being he accepts the supernaturalistic explanations.

CONCLUSION

Therefore, we can conclude that neither the supposed problem of lack of direct access to the past nor the supposed problem of the lack of neutrality can prevent us from learning something from history. And if Christianity's claims to be a religion rooted in history are true, then history may lead us to a knowledge of God himself.

PRACTICAL APPLICATION

Like the material in the previous chapter, the content of this chapter has little direct applicability to evangelism. I have never met a non-Christian who overtly objected to the gospel message because of historical relativism. But in an age self-consciously post-modern, historicism and subjectivism are rampant. As people who believe in an objective revelation mediated through historical events, Christians cannot afford to sacrifice the objectivity of history. Otherwise, the events of the life, death, and resurrection of Jesus cannot be said to be part of the objective past because the gospels do not represent objective history. It is critical if we are not to lapse into mere mythology that we defend the objectivity of history and, thus, of the gospels.

Moreover, when sharing the gospel, one does occasionally encounter non-Christians who seem very skeptical about history. With such persons I think it would be especially effective to share the three ways in which relativists implicitly concede the objectivity of history. If they insist on a complete historical skepticism, then we should explain to them the utter unliveability of such a view. If we are to get along in this world, we need a method of sorting out to the best of our ability what has and has not happened. The results of this procedure will allow for the possibility that the historical foundations of the Christian faith will be as well established as many other purely natural events. Therefore, it would be hypocrisy to admit the one but not the other. Insist on this fundamental dilemma in dealing with the non-Christian.

CHAPTER SIX

The Historical Reliability of the New Testament

by Craig L. Blomberg

INTRODUCTION

Central to a Christian world and life view are the teachings of that collection of writings which has come to be known as the Bible. The portion of the Bible which separates Christianity from Judaism and which describes the core events and beliefs that led to its development as a distinct religion is, of course, the NT. But how trustworthy is the NT? Phrasing the question this way, however, leaves undisclosed an inquirer's particular area of interest. Some people doubt the substantial accuracy of the transmission of the NT documents after they were first written. Others challenge the scientific or philosophical assumptions of its world view. Still others wonder about the theological validity of the doctrine which appears on its pages.

None of these questions need detain us long here. It is true, for example, that Mormons and Muslims allege that the NT documents were substantially corrupted in their transmission, but there is overwhelming evidence which proves these claims wrong. Textual criticism, the science of comparing and classifying the manuscript evidence for an ancient document, demonstrates such allegations to be utterly without foundation. Scholars of almost every theological stripe attest to the profound care with which the NT books were copied in the Greek language, and later translated and preserved in Syriac, Coptic, Latin and a variety of other ancient European and Middle Eastern languages.[1] In the original Greek alone, over 5,000 manuscripts and manuscript fragments of portions of the NT have been preserved from the early centuries of Christianity. The oldest of these is a scrap of papyrus (p^{52}) containing John 18:31-33, 37-38, dating from A.D. 125-130, no more than forty years after John's Gospel was most probably written. More than thirty papyri date from the late second through early third centuries, including some which contain good chunks of entire books and two which cover most of the gospels and Acts (p^{45}) or the letters of Paul (p^{46}). Four very reliable and nearly complete NTs date from the fourth and fifth centuries ($\aleph$, B, A, C).

All kinds of minor variations distinguish these manuscripts from one another, but the vast majority of these variations have to do with changes in spelling, grammar, and style, or accidental omissions or duplications of words or phrases. Only about 400 (less than one per page of English translation) have any significant bearing on the meaning of the passage, and most of these are noted in the footnotes or margins of modern translations and editions of Scripture (unlike the KJV). The only textual variants which affect more than a sentence or two (and most affect only individual words or phrases) are John 7:53—8:11 and Mark 16:9-20. Neither of these passages is very likely to be what John or Mark originally wrote, though the story in John (the woman caught in adultery) still stands a fairly good chance of being true.[2] But overall, 97-99% of the NT can be reconstructed beyond any reasonable doubt, and no Christian doctrine is founded solely or even primarily on textually disputed passages.[3]

The significance of the manuscript evidence for the NT books becomes clearer when we compare it with similar evidence for other writings in antiquity. For Caesar's *Gallic War* (ca. 50 B.C.) there are only nine or ten good manuscripts, and the oldest dates from 900 years after the events it records. Only thirty-five of Livy's 142 books of Roman history survive, in about twenty manuscripts, only one of which is as old as the fourth century. Of Tacitus's fourteen books of Roman history, we have only four and one-half, in two manuscripts dating from the ninth and eleventh centuries. Examples could be multiplied at length.[4] The point is simply that the textual evidence for what the NT authors wrote far outstrips the documentation we have for any other ancient writing, including dozens which we believe have been preserved relatively intact. There is absolutely no support for claims that the standard modern editions of the Greek NT[5] do not very closely approximate what the NT writers actually wrote.

The scientific and philosophical challenges to the NT's world view usually surround its "supernaturalism," particularly its belief in the possibility of miracles. These questions have already been dealt with in a previous chapter of this book. Questions of the theological validity of Scripture's claims focus on the interpretations given to the events recorded. It is one thing to acknowledge as historical fact that Jesus of Nazareth died—most likely in either A.D. 30 or 33. It is a quite different kind of statement to claim that "Jesus died for my sins." The latter requires a discussion of how one interprets the significance of a historical fact. Key theological issues of the Christian faith have also been treated throughout this volume, though space has precluded discussing all but a select handful.

Sooner or later, however, the core question concerning Scripture's trust-worthiness must be raised—*are its historical portions factual?* Or to ask the question another way, where the Bible purports to be relating things that happened on this earth at a particular period of its history, is it conveying accurate or reliable information about what was said and done? In the case of the NT, this means focusing primarily on the gospels and Acts. Now, theoretically, there could be various minor errors of historical detail which would not call into question the main contours of the lives of Jesus and the apostles and the theological claims built on their words and works. Plenty of other ancient historians are not inerrant but still considerably reliable. It is not a case of all or nothing. Many Bible readers find certain periph-eral historical problems insuperable, although the authors of this book do not believe they are. Unfortunately, many would-be believers have been discouraged from accepting Christianity because they have been misled into thinking that they have to have satisfactory resolutions of all of their questions before they can commit themselves to Christ.[6] On the other hand, it is not possible for any of the principal theology of the NT to be true if a significant portion of its central historical claims is false. Or, in the words of Graham Stanton,

> at least some aspects of the portrait of Jesus are essential to faith, for if historical research were ever able to prove conclusively that the historical Jesus was quite unlike the Jesus of the gospels, then faith would certainly be eroded. The gospel is concerned with history: not in that it stands if its claims could be verified by the historian, but in that it falls if the main lines of the early church's portrait of Jesus of Nazareth were to be falsified by historical research.[7]

As noted in an earlier chapter, it is this historical nature of Christianity which sets it off from many other world religions, particularly the Eastern religions. The moral wisdom of Confucianism or Buddhism does not depend on the founders of those religions having even lived. Someone else could just have easily spoken the teachings attributed to Confucius or Buddha, and they would remain equally true (or false). But Christianity's claims are bound up with the historical Jesus' having done and said certain things on this earth at identifiable times and places, things which disclose the meaning and significance of his person and work and which may not be jettisoned without undermining the very heart of Christian faith.

HISTORICAL BACKGROUND

PRE-ENLIGHTENMENT

Before the rise of modern biblical criticism in the eighteenth century, Christians widely assumed the historical reliability of Scripture as a logical corollary of their nearly universal belief in its infallibility or inerrancy.[8] Closely bound to these beliefs was the view that most or all of the biblical books could be ascribed to a prophetic or apostolic writer, whose inspiration and veracity was secure. The apparent contradictions within Scripture were well-known from the earliest years of the Church's history onwards. Sometimes they were dealt with in ways which Christians today would generally not accept. For example, allegorical interpretation often allowed one to bypass thorny problems. Origen of Alexandria, writing approximately two centuries after the events of the life of Christ, solved the problem of the two temple cleansings (cf. John 2:14-22; Matt 21:12-13) by assuming that John's more "spiritual" account is not the description of a literal action of Jesus in Jerusalem. Rather, he understood it to be a symbolic narrative about the need for Jesus' followers to put away unrighteousness from their midst and to stop exploiting those who like oxen and sheep are senseless or like doves are empty and unstable![9]

In other cases, the Church adopted methods which more conservative scholars today still applaud but which more liberal ones ridicule, most notably the method of harmonization. The most famous harmony of the Gospels in the early years was Tatian's late second-century *Diatessaron* (a name formed from two Greek words meaning "through four"). In explaining the apparent discrepancy in location between Matthew's Sermon on the Mount (Matt 5—7) and Luke's Sermon on the Plain (Luke 6:17-49), for example, Tatian arranged the introductory verses in the order, Matt 5:1, Luke 6:13-17, Mark 3:14-15, and Matt 5:2ff., to underline the fact that Luke's Jesus was also in the mountains but then descended to speak to the crowds at a place sufficiently level to accommodate everyone comfortably. This view remains defensible today.[10]

In still other instances, Christian commentators employed methods which would anticipate the approaches of modern biblical criticism. In the Patristic period, St. Augustine emphasized that the Gospels often fail to give a clear indication of the location or sequence of the events they are reporting and that one is to assume continuity of time and place only when it is explicitly mentioned in the text.[11] Centuries later, during the Protestant Reformation, John Calvin would write the next most famous harmony of the Gospels and entertain the suggestion that Matthew's Sermon on the Mount might in fact be a composite construction gathering together Jesus' teaching from several different occasions in his ministry.[12] This is the dominant view among scholars today, although it is still plausible that Matthew and Luke each abstracted from a much longer, unified sermon.[13]

Once in a while, solutions were suggested which were quite far-fetched. For example, the sixteenth-century harmonist Andreas Osiander failed to see that the same episode could be narrated in more than one gospel with a fair amount of stylistic and conceptual variation. This led him to make the implausible suggestion that Jesus raised Jairus's daughter at least twice, or that Jesus was crowned with thorns on at least two different occasions.[14] But for the most part, Christians were satisfied that the apparent problems with the historical reliability of Scripture could be given reasonable solutions and that its authority could remain intact.

MODERN BIBLICAL CRITICISM

With the dawn of the Enlightenment, the Bible began to be treated more like any other great religious book of human composition. Traditional claims for the authorship of the biblical books were almost all called into question. Harmonizations became suspect, the trustworthiness of Scripture was increasingly rejected, and an antisupernaturalist world view came more and more into vogue, at least in scholarly circles. Other chapters of this book treat the contributions of leading figures in these eighteenth- and nineteenth-century developments; we may outline here the contours of the three major critical tools which the twentieth-century has spawned: form criticism, redaction criticism, and literary criticism.

Form Criticism

Pioneered first by turn-of-the century OT scholars Herman Gunkel and Julius Wellhausen, form criticism postulated a long period of oral transmission of biblical materials, during which they circulated in relatively discrete, isolated literary units such as miracle stories, proverbs, legends, and so on. Rudolf Bultmann put NT form criticism on the map with his *Die Geschichte der synoptischen Tradition* in 1921.[15] Using elaborate analysis based on analogies from primitive European folklore in a variety of cultures, Bultmann believed that only a small portion of the words and deeds attributed to Jesus in the Gospels could be said to be authentic—that is, to have actually been uttered or accomplished by Christ in the way that the evangelists narrated them. He applied "laws" for the development of the tradition, which assumed that later gospel writers would embellish and add unhistorical details to earlier, briefer accounts.

Hence, early form critics believed that the early church had increasingly turned Jesus into a divine wonder-worker making grandiose claims for himself, when in fact he had originally been little more than a great, human teacher who did not put himself forward nearly so pretentiously. Later Christian prophets, unconcerned to distinguish between the words they believed they were being inspired to proclaim by their Risen Lord, added all kinds of additional unhistorical material to the Jesus-tradition. Only after the first generation of Christianity was dying off and believers had come to realize that Christ might not be coming back as quickly as they first expected, did people become concerned to write down the teachings and events of Jesus' life. By then, the more liberal scholars claimed, it was too late to produce an accurate account.

Not all form critics proved as radical as Bultmann and his German colleagues. English scholarship, for example, produced relatively conservative form criticism from men like Vincent Taylor and C. H. Dodd.[16] Some concentrated more on analyzing the discrete literary units of material which circulated by word of mouth than on writing the history of the transmission of the tradition. But all agreed that the seemingly historical information found in the Gospels and Acts, like that in corresponding "historical" portions of the OT, was actually a complex and somewhat unstable mixture of fact and fiction, history and legend, sober narrative and fanciful embellishment. Hence, one spoke of "getting back to" the historical Jesus, as if one had to strip away layers of unhistorical accretion which the gospel writers had superimposed over the core of historical fact.[17]

Redaction Criticism

In the 1950s, several of Bultmann's disciples began to move in a slightly more conservative direction. They also recognized that the model of the gospel writers as scissors-and-paste editors of isolated units of materials which they had inherited was not an entirely accurate description of the composition of the writings of the four evangelists. Utilizing the German word for "editing" (*Redaktion*), scholars like Günther Bornkamm, Willi Marxsen, and Hans Conzelmann fashioned the tool of critical analysis of the Scriptures known as redaction criticism.[18] Here the study focused not nearly so much on some postulated oral pre-history of discrete forms, but on the editorial activity of Matthew, Mark, Luke, and John, as they imposed their own theological stamp on each of the Gospels and Acts. Redaction critics sought to "lay bare the theological perspectives of a

Biblical writer by analyzing the editorial (redactional) and compositional techniques and interpretations employed by him in shaping and framing the written and/or oral traditions at hand."[19]

The end result was to stress the theological diversity of the four evangelists by means of painstaking attention to the differences among parallel accounts of the same episode from Jesus' life and by means of careful analysis of the sequence of events, including what stories were uniquely omitted or included in any one individual Gospel. Hence, for example, Matthew was seen to portray the disciples in a more positive light than did Mark. Luke's propensity for focusing on Jesus' ministry to the outcasts of his society was highlighted. And John's uniquely high Christology became the object of much attention. But redaction criticism did not so much reject form criticism as build on it. Its practitioners tended to be a little less skeptical about the amount of authentic, historical information which was recoverable from the texts, but one still spoke of the "quest of the historical Jesus" and assumed that much of the material on the surface of the Gospels had to be removed in order to find that Jesus.[20]

Literary Criticism

Since the 1970s, many biblical critics have been calling for a paradigm shift in the analysis of Scripture. The type of historical study reflected in both form and redaction criticism has seemed increasingly sterile to many. For those still tied into a Christian tradition of some sort, it has become clear that such criticism "will not preach." For many critics, unconcerned with such matters, it simply seems that the old tools have been used as much as they can be. Now appreciation is being recovered for the need to look at literary works in their entirety, as stories with a discernible plot, theme, characterization, development, climax, and so on.[21]

As with the move from form to redaction criticism, many literary critics simply presuppose the results of the earlier methodologies. Literary criticism is for them not a tool by which one becomes any more confident of the historical reliability of the text. On the other hand, concern to accept the "canonical shape" of the text as it stands has allowed more conservative scholars to re-enter the dialogue without compromising fundamental presuppositions about the text which form and redaction criticism challenged and without having to combat them at each stage of the discussion. And to the extent that the text can be explained as a coherent unity, the need for parceling it out into bits of tradition vs. redaction is diminished. Literary criticism has proved particularly significant in demonstrating the unity of the Gospel of John, against an older form of historical tradition which confidently parceled it out into numerous sources.[22]

A growing awareness of the influence any given reader of a text has on the production of that text's meaning has further enabled a diversity of readings of a particular passage of Scripture to challenge cherished interpretations of traditional male, Eurocentric scholarship and Christian life. Thus, one increasingly encounters a feminist literary criticism or an African-American (or African) or Latin American or Asian reading of a passage, and so on. To the extent that some of these cultures remain closer in various ways to the biblical cultures, belief in the historicity of Scripture may at times be supported in surprising ways. For example, Matthew's miracle-laden birth narrative (Matt 1—2) fits squarely within the volatile political milieu of Herodian Palestine, once one recognizes the sociopolitical threats latent in Matthew's description of the circumstances surrounding Christ's birth. Here is a theme helpfully emphasized (though at times overemphasized) by contemporary liberation theology, spawned in the Two-Thirds World by readers who have seen striking parallels to their contemporary situations of oppression. In light of their experience, Herod's "massacre of the innocents," often lampooned as historically improbable, becomes perfectly understandable and historically likely.[23] On the other hand, most non-evangelical feminism still finds the views of women in home and church attributed to Paul in Eph 5:22-33 and 1 Tim 2:11-15 intolerable, and this becomes one important reason for assuming that Paul did not write either Ephesians or the Pastoral Epistles.[24]

The Current State of the Art

Two current scholarly trends may be discerned which utilize all three of the above methods and impinge directly on an evaluation of the historical writings of the four Evangelists. On the one hand, there is what has been called the "third quest" for the historical Jesus (following the nineteenth-century "lives of Christ" and the post-Bultmannian "new quest").[25] Numerous recent historical analyses of Jesus have moved in an increasingly positive direction, believing that we can recover substantial amounts of information about what he did and said. These studies tend to set Jesus and the gospels squarely within the milieu of ancient Judaism much more so than did their predecessors. Two prolific contributors to this third quest, E. P. Sanders and James Charlesworth, agree that "the dominant view today seems to be that we can know pretty well what Jesus was out to accomplish, that we can know a lot about what he said, and that those two things make sense within the world of first-century Judaism."[26] The one main area, however, that these writers generally fail most to come to grips with is the miraculous, and especially the resurrection.

Unfortunately, it is not true that the third quest is "the dominant view" today. Equally influential is a far more skeptical collection of scholars who read Jesus more against a Greco-Roman background, believe much less of what the gospels say about him, and view him as a wise Oriental sage who spoke in pithy aphorisms and subversive parables. He probably had the ability to heal people of some physical and many psychological maladies, through powers of suggestion and his radical transgression of the social boundaries of purity in his world. But he did not see himself as Messiah (much less divinity) and did not teach about a coming kingdom or end of the age that was potentially "imminent." By far the most prolific contributor to this school of thought is John Dominic Crossan, whose voluminous work *The Historical Jesus* is ambitiously but inaccurately labeled on its cover as "the first comprehensive determination of who Jesus was, what he did, what he said."[27] Sadly, Crossan interacts with almost none of the "third questers" and similarly pretends that his view dominates the field.

By far the most famous outgrowth of this more radical line of thought is the work of the Jesus Seminar. Culminating fifteen years of conferences and research, seventy-four contemporary academicians and pastors, mostly American and mostly representing scholarship's radical fringe, have created *The Five Gospels*, a book which prints all of the passages from the canonical gospels (and from the Gnostic Gospel of Thomas) and colors each of Jesus' sayings red, pink, gray, or black, according to the probability of Jesus' having actually spoken the words contained in them.[28] Red means "Jesus undoubtedly said this or something very like it"; pink, "Jesus probably said something like this"; gray, "Jesus did not say this, but the ideas contained in it are close to his own"; and black, "Jesus did not say this; it represents the perspective or content of a later or different tradition."[29] Only about twenty percent of all of Jesus' teaching turns up red or pink, and over half turns out to be black.

EVANGELICAL RESPONSES

When skeptical biblical criticism first gained a serious foothold in the academy and more liberal Christian circles in the nineteenth-century, more conservative scholars generally tried to engage that skepticism with serious, carefully reasoned responses. In Germany, E. Hengstenberg wrote voluminously in the area of OT studies. C. F. Keil and F. Delitzsch authored a multivolume commentary series on the OT from a conservative yet scholarly perspective. In the early twentieth-century, Adolf Schlatter did much the same for a good portion of the NT. In America, the old Princeton Seminary produced many staunch defenders of the faith in both biblical and systematic studies (most notably A. A. and C. Hodge,

B. B. Warfield, R. D. Wilson, and J. G. Machen), who engaged critical scholarship in discussion, seeking as much common ground as possible. With the fundamentalist-modernist controversy climaxing in the 1920s, conservative American Christianity tended to retreat into its own cloister, not engage in as much serious scholarship, and simply complain that infidels were bringing destructive methodologies into their biblical analysis which made dialogue difficult and even undesirable.[30]

After World War II, many neo-fundamentalists began calling themselves evangelicals and re-engaging the academy, led particularly by British conservatives who had never retreated nearly to the extent that the Americans had. Today evangelical biblical scholarship has made great strides, but often by starting its own publishing houses and academic institutions, so that the broader university world has not been as influenced as it might have been. On the other hand, secular and mainline Christian schools and presses until quite recently have remained remarkably closed to conservatives. With respect to the trustworthiness of the gospels, perhaps the most significant scholarship in recent years has been the six-volume *Gospel Perspectives* series produced by the Cambridge-based Tyndale Fellowship's Gospels Project—an international team of evangelical scholars exploring questions of historicity from numerous angles.[31] Now the Tyndale Fellowship has an even more ambitious series on the book of Acts underway, with Colin Hemer's magisterial defense of the historicity of major portions of that biblical document already published, and other collections of essays beginning to appear.[32]

On the other hand, a minority of evangelicals continues to support retrenchment and isolationism. Often this occurs when certain individuals have been particularly "burned" by their own personal encounters with the academy. One recent, striking example is the former Bultmannian, Eta Linnemann. Since experiencing a charismatic conversion, she has repudiated her former scholarly writing, literally urges people to throw her previous works into the trash, denies any value to the historical-critical method, and sees enterprises such as postulating literary dependence of one gospel upon another as inherently anti-Christian.[33] Not nearly as extreme but more widespread is the legacy of Cornelius van Til, longtime professor at Westminster Seminary and champion deluxe of the presuppositional approach to apologetics. Exponents of his perspective reject the kind of "evidentialist" apologetics of the Tyndale House Projects (or, for that matter, of substantial portions of this book) as misguided, because they think that one cannot demonstrate the probability of Christianity apart from presupposing its truth.[34]

ASSESSMENT

Although the very nature of historical inquiry precludes an apodeictic proof (one which entails its conclusions with the logical certainty of mathematical reasoning), we do believe that historical analysis is capable of establishing an inherent probability of the trustworthiness of the historical portions of the NT. To be sure, apart from the convicting work of the Holy Spirit, such discussion will lead no one to saving faith in Jesus. But as with the other myriad of ways God works through human agency, evidentialist apologetics can be an important means by which his Spirit brings men and women to himself. For those open to the logic of the case, a demonstration of the general historical trustworthiness of the NT, particularly of the gospels and Acts, impels one to respond to the claims of Christ which confront us on almost every page. And if one accepts the NT's portrait of who Jesus is, then one ought to believe his teachings, not least with respect to *his* high view of the Scriptures.[35]

As with scientific or historical research more generally, the biblical scholar is engaged in hypothesis verification. One formulates a hypothesis and then tests to see how well the data fit it, particularly in comparison with competing hypotheses. This chapter has room merely to sketch the contours of such an approach with respect to the historicity of the NT, but fortunately the more detailed work has been and is being done elsewhere (see the literature cited in notes 31-32 above). Here I hope to show, first, that the writers of the historical portions of the NT were *able* to record reliable history; second, that it was their *intention* to record reliable history within the literary genres they used; and, third, that they in fact *did* record reliable history insofar as this can be tested, all of which warrants a presumption of accuracy in untestable instances. Traditional approaches to the gospels are particularly relevant to the first of these concerns, modern methods to the second and third. Accordingly, we shall examine each in turn.

TRADITIONAL APPROACHES

Apostolicity, Authorship, and Date

Modern biblical criticism has made two different kinds of claims about the authorship of the gospels and Acts. On the one hand, it has rightly pointed out that these five books are, strictly speaking, anonymous. None of the gospels or the Book of Acts originally had a writer's name attached to it. Titles (for example, "The Gospel according to . . .") were most likely added early in the second century when the fourfold gospel collection circulated as a unit.[36] On the other hand, modern scholarship has more speculatively also questioned the accuracy of the traditional ascriptions of the authorship of these books to Matthew, Mark, Luke, and John. There are no dissenting traditions whatever in the first centuries of the Church's history concerning the authorship of the first three gospels and Acts and concerning the repeated claims that these books were indeed written by Matthew, Mark, and Luke. Given that two of these men were not apostles (Mark and Luke), and that Matthew would have been one of the most "suspect" of the apostles, in light of his background as a tax collector, it seems unlikely that the first Christians would have invented these authorship claims if they were merely trying to enhance the credibility of the documents attributed to these writers. Later apocryphal gospels and acts are consistently attributed to less suspect writers—for example, Peter, James, Philip, Thomas, Bartholomew, Andrew, even Mary.[37] There *is* some uncertainty in the early centuries about the Gospel of John, but it surrounds which "John" was behind the Fourth Gospel (John the apostle or a later John the elder), not whether or not the book was written by someone named John.[38] And the clear majority opts for the apostle.

This early external evidence—the testimony of the early Church Fathers—should be taken more seriously than many modern scholars take it. The oldest evidence, the testimony of Papias (preserved and cited by the later Christian historian Eusebius in the early 300s) dates from the beginning of the second century. Papias's testimony affirms that Matthew originally compiled the oracles or sayings of Jesus in the Hebrew (or Aramaic) language and that Mark was Peter's interpreter, writing accurately though "not in order" what he learned from that apostle (*Historia Ecclesiae* 3:39.14-16). The reliability of Papias has often been questioned because no ancient Hebrew gospels or gospel sources have ever been discovered and because internal evidence makes it likely that canonical (Greek) Matthew was written after Mark, in partial literary dependence on him.[39] Why, the critics continue, would Matthew the apostle depend on the work of a non-apostolic writer in his composition?

In fact, it is precisely when we are prepared to give Papias serious credence that an answer to this question emerges. If Peter reflects the apostolic authority behind Mark, then Matthew would have been quite interested in seeing how a gospel stemming from him was put together. For, first, Peter was the informal leader of the Twelve from the earliest days on. Second, he, with James and John, was present for a variety of episodes in the life of Christ from which the other apostles were excluded—for example, the Transfiguration (Mark 9:2) and Jesus' prayers in Gethsemane (14:33).[40] As for the tradition that Matthew originally wrote something in Hebrew, this is so extremely persistent in the early church that there is probably something to it. The use of the term *logia* ("oracles" or sayings") suggests something less than a full-fledged narrative, perhaps along the lines of the hypothetical Q document which scholars postulate to account for the similarities in sayings of Jesus found in Matthew and Luke but not in Mark. A plausible case can even be made for Matthew being the author of such a collection of teachings of Jesus, first preserved in a Semitic tongue, later translated into Greek, and finally combined with other information Matthew got from Mark, other traditions, and his own memory to produce what we know as the Gospel of Matthew.[41]

The internal evidence of Luke-Acts certainly fits the early church's claim that these two books were written by Paul's traveling companion and "beloved physician" (Col 4:14). In Acts 16:10-17; 20:5-16; 21:1-18; and 27:1—28:16, the writer shifts from third-person to first-person narrative, repeatedly speaking of what "we" did. The most natural explanation of these "we-passages" is that they reflect the eyewitness testimony of one of Paul's traveling companions who was not present for the remaining events narrated in the Gospel and Acts.[42] Information for those portions of Luke's work would have been acquired from eyewitness testimony and other written documents (Luke 1:1-2), no doubt including Mark and Q. Particularly during Paul's two-year stay in Palestine, much of it in prison under Felix and Festus (Acts 21—26), Luke would have had ample opportunity to acquire this information from those who had been with Jesus during his life and had experienced the early years of the apostolic church. The most common objection to Lukan authorship of Luke-Acts revolves around apparent discrepancies between the picture of Paul in Acts and the portrait which emerges from Paul's epistles. But these differences merely prove that Paul did not write Acts! The two portraits are complementary, not contradictory. Tellingly, a detailed chronology of the life of Paul can be discerned by comparing Acts and the epistles; numerous items dovetail with each other, and there are no insuperable problems.[43]

In modern times, the classic case for the apostolic authorship of the Fourth Gospel was articulated in detail by B. F. Westcott.[44] The argument has never been refuted, though it has often been ignored. Westcott amassed detailed evidence to zero in on successively smaller targets by demonstrating that the author of this gospel was a Jew (with his detailed knowledge of the Hebrew feasts, customs, and Scriptures), a Palestinian (with his impressive grasp of local geography and topography), an eyewitness (with repeated, compelling references to details of people, time, place), an apostle (from his intimate acquaintance with the actions and thoughts of the Twelve), and the apostle John—as the "beloved disciple" of 13:23; 19:26; and 21:20, he was probably one of the inner three.

Interestingly, John the Baptist is just called "John" in this gospel, whereas in the Synoptics he is called "the Baptist" to distinguish him from John the apostle. Only if John the apostle wrote the Fourth Gospel to people who knew he was the author is this practice fully understandable.

In short, an excellent case can be made for the gospels and Acts being written by people who were in a position to know what happened in the lives of Jesus and the apostles. But were they likely to remember it accurately? At this point, the date of the gospels and Acts becomes significant. If these books were written by their traditional claimants, then all must date from the first century (a point generally conceded even by most who suspect the traditional ascriptions of authorship). Among liberal scholars, it is fashionable to date all five of these works after A.D. 70, although Mark is sometimes put just before that landmark year in which Jerusalem fell to the Romans. The more dominant early Christian tradition agrees with this verdict, at least with respect to John, assigning it to the decade of the 90s, when the apostle was an old man ministering in Asia Minor.

Dates for the writings of Matthew, Mark, and Luke, however, should probably all be placed in years prior to the fall of Jerusalem. The curiously abrupt ending of Acts, with Paul awaiting word on his appeal to Caesar, is still best explained by the assumption that Luke was writing during the very house-arrest with which his book ends. He does not tell us what happened to Paul because he does not yet know.[45] But that two-year period of Paul's stay in Rome (Acts 28:30-31), coming after Festus's accession to power in Judea (24:27—in A.D. 59), can be precisely dated to A.D. 60-62. Because Luke-Acts shows every sign of being conceived as a two-volume unity,[46] separated only by the need to begin a new scroll, both of Luke's works should most probably be dated to the beginning of the 60s.

Because Luke shows clear signs of dependence on Mark, Mark must have written earlier. Clement of Alexandria claims that Mark wrote while Peter was preaching in Rome (cited in Eusebius, *Historia Ecclesiae* 6.14.6-7). We know Peter left Jerusalem shortly after his imprisonment there in A.D. 44 (Acts 12:17), presumably ministered in Asia Minor and nearby provinces (1 Pet 1:1), and made it to Rome at least by the early sixties (5:13). So a date for Mark in the mid- to late fifties seems quite plausible.[47] Matthew, as we have already seen, relies on Mark, so his gospel must come some time later. Irenaeus asserts it was written "while Peter and Paul were preaching and founding the church in Rome." This would require a date in the early to mid-sixties. Objections to pre-70 dates for the Synoptic Gospels usually revolve around alleged references to the fall of Jerusalem (for example, in Matt 24, Mark 13, and Luke 21) and the belief that Jesus could not have predicted this event in advance. But these objections depend on an unjustified anti-supernaturalist world view. What is more, after-the-fact "prophecies" are usually far more explicit than those we allegedly find in the gospels.[48]

The most probable dates for the historical writings of the NT thus bolster our case for their containing reliable history.[49] Three of four gospels were written within thirty years or so of the events they narrated, since Jesus was crucified in either A.D. 30 or 33. The Book of Acts begins with events thirty years old but becomes increasingly contemporary as its narrative unfolds. John is two generations distant. But all of these data compare extremely favorably with the other Jewish and Greco-Roman histories and biographies available from antiquity. Legends in the ancient world seldom grew so quickly. For example, the two relatively reliable biographers of Alexander the Great (Arrian and Plutarch) wrote more than four hundred years after his death in 323 B.C. Yet it was only in the centuries *after* these two writers that most of the more fictitious stories about Alexander developed.[50]

Harmonization

Despite being lampooned in many liberal circles, harmonization remains a tried and trustworthy method which should be retained. Historians of other ancient literature regularly rely on it. Again the study of Alexander's biographers proves instructive. Commentators on Plutarch and Arrian disclose the same range of suggestions for solving apparent discrepancies among parallel accounts of episodes in Alexander's life as evangelical biblical scholars apply to the historical texts of the NT.[51] And far more study has gone into solving the so-called contradictions among the gospels or between Acts and the letters of Paul.

Many of these discrepancies disappear once we judge ancient historians by the standards of their day rather than ours! In a world which did not even have a symbol for a quotation mark, no one expected a historian to reproduce a speaker's words verbatim. Rather they were expected to be faithful to the gist of what he or she said. Many of the differences between Jesus' teaching in one gospel and in a parallel account, like many of the questions surrounding the speeches in Acts, are explained once we realize this simple fact.[52] In other instances, we need to come to grips with the expectation that historians and biographers would write selectively, choosing material which suited the distinctive purposes of their work. The modern quest for dispassionate objectivity (now abandoned in "postmodernist" circles) was largely unknown to the ancients and would have been viewed as pointless. Why write about the past unless you had a good cause to promote?

I have elsewhere sampled a substantial, representative selection of the so-called contradictions among the Synoptics and between the Synoptics and John and offered what I believe are plausible resolutions of each.[53] Limitations of space prevent discussion of all but a handful of samples here. Was the Last Supper celebrated on the night of the Passover meal (so apparently Mark 14:12-16 and parallels) or before it (so apparently John 18:28 and 19:14)? No doubt it was on Passover, since John 18:28 probably alludes to the week-long Passover festival and 19:14 can be taken as the Day of Preparation *for the Sabbath* during Passover week (as in the NIV rendering). Does the centurion himself come to Jesus to ask healing for his servant (Matt 8:5-13) or does he send the elders of the Jews to make the request (Luke 7:1-10)? Probably the latter, since in the ancient world actions taken by one's emissaries could be considered one's own. We preserve the same convention today when the newspapers write, "The President today said that . . . ," when in fact his speech writers created the copy and his press secretary delivered the address. Did Jesus send the demons into the swine in Gerasa (Mark 5:1; Luke 8:26) or in Gadara (Matt 8:28)? Probably near Khersa—a city on the east bank of the Sea of Galilee, whose spelling in Greek could easily yield Gerasa—in the *province* of Gadara. Additional examples abound.

Hemer has offered a similar overview in even greater detail of the issues involved in harmonizing Acts and Paul and also surveyed the criteria for good history-writing employed in antiquity.[54] Did Paul go to Jerusalem right away after his conversion (so seemingly Acts 9:19-26) or wait three years (so clearly Gal 1:17-18)? Almost certainly the latter. Acts 19:26 does not say that Paul went straight from Damascus to Jerusalem, and the highly selective nature of Luke's writing makes it very plausible to believe that he passes over a three-year period without comment. Was Paul unknown to the Jerusalem Christians even after that visit (so apparently Gal 1:22) or well-known (so apparently Acts 9:27-30)? Probably somewhere in between. Galatians uses an idiom which literally reads, "not being known to the face," that is, intimately acquainted, while Acts describes Paul's ministry in Jerusalem as primarily witnessing to *non-Christian* Jews. How does the Apostolic Council (Acts 15:2-32) fit in with Paul's rebuke of Peter in Antioch (Gal 2:11-14)? Probably as its aftermath, with Acts 15:1 corresponding to the event Paul narrates in Galatians. Again we could give many other examples. Not all proposed harmonizations are equally plausible, and some problems admit of several possible solutions. But the large number of common-sense explanations available for almost every so-called contradiction that has ever been pointed out must surely be considered before glibly dismissing the NT as hopelessly contradictory.[55]

To the dominant methods of form, redaction, and literary criticism could be added many other subdisciplines of historical and literary tools. Today, biblical scholarship has fragmented into a bewildering array of interdisciplinary studies, applying insights from sociology, cultural anthropology, structuralist and deconstructionist literary criticism, and so forth. At times one wonders if anything good can come out of the use of a particular avant-garde method, but on closer inspection something of benefit invariably emerges. Almost each method has its pitfalls, too, however, so the interpreter must proceed with caution.[56] A survey of these methods will help to demonstrate that the gospel writers had not only the ability, but also the intention of writing reliable history within the parameters of their chosen literary genres.

Form Criticism

Studying the oral pre-history of the gospel forms actually reinforces the likelihood that many of the traditions were quite carefully preserved. Unlike models which Bultmann and others relied on from cultures as far afield as Icelandic folklore, the ancient Mediterranean cultures, particularly Judaism, relied heavily on memorization of sacred traditions. Studies by the Scandinavian scholars Harald Riesenfeld and Birger Gerhardsson demonstrated this in programatic fashion in the late 1950s and early 1960s and have been bolstered by the writings of the German scholar Rainer Riesner in more recent years.[57] To the extent that Jesus' disciples venerated his teachings and viewed their master as at the very least a prophet from God, one could have expected them to take great care in the oral transmission of his instruction. Up to 90% of his teaching was poetic in structure and memorable in form. Both Jewish and Greco-Roman sources attest to the use of note-taking and a kind of shorthand to record the key thoughts a teacher gave in his public discourse. The disciples might well have relied on precisely such notes and memorization on their own "solo missions" preaching about Jesus and the kingdom already during his lifetime (Matt 10; Luke 10).[58] J. A. Baird applies a detailed comparative analysis of the Synoptic Gospels and other ancient non-Christian and Christian literature and concludes that Jesus' words and deeds

> bear all the marks of data that was [*sic*] immediately holy in the minds of an escalating number of his disciples, and therefore treasured and preserved with a carefulness second to nothing observed in the literature of the Ancient Near East. Here, it would seem, is a major stabilizing force in the early Synoptic tradition.[59]

Notwithstanding the enormous feats of memorization attested to in antiquity, the gospels cannot be merely the product of rote memory. There still remain the numerous divergences among parallel accounts in the Synoptics which simultaneously show signs of literary dependence. Some other factors must also be at work. Here, research by other students of ancient folklore proves helpful. A. B. Lord, for example, has pointed out how memorization in antiquity often did not preclude variation of a substantial amount of more peripheral detail in the oral "performance" of a sacred tradition by the folkteller or singer. Such variation is remarkably consistent with the types of differences as well as similarities which we find among the four gospels, and particularly among the first three.[60] Kenneth Bailey, lifelong American missionary and educator in the Middle East, has documented the persistence of these phenomena in twentieth-century peasant villages. Bailey likens the variation among the gospels to what he calls "informal controlled oral tradition." Members of the community would correct storytellers who erred on important details as they recounted their traditions but allow them flexibility to vary their presentation of portions of the accounts which did not affect the main contours or lessons of their stories.[61]

As for Bultmann's contention that oral traditions naturally attracted unhistorical and supernatural embellishments, a fair amount of study of the use of the gospels in later Gnostic and aberrant Jewish-Christian sources, as well as in the more orthodox Apostolic Fathers, suggests that at least as commonly, lengthy narratives were abbreviated and streamlined in their transmission.[62] This is true even within the canon as one compares parallel narratives in Mark and Matthew and in Mark and Luke (on the assumption that Mark is the earliest of the three), even though Matthew and Luke are longer overall by virtue of including more total episodes from the life of Christ.[63] The presence of dissenting eyewitnesses, the control exercised by the apostolic leadership as the church grew and proliferated throughout the book of Acts, and the lack of reference within the gospels to later church controversies (such as speaking in tongues or circumcision) all support the relative care with which the oral tradition must have been preserved. Conversely, refusal to eliminate the "hard sayings" of Jesus (for example, Matt 10:5-6 or Mark 13:30) attests to a conservatism of the tradition which did not feel free to rewrite the story of Christ's life apart from the constraints of historical fact.

The form-critical arguments from the nature of early Christian prophecy and the so-called delay of Christ's return also fail. There is not a shred of hard evidence that first-century prophets felt free to mingle their revelations with the words of the earthly Jesus; the form-critics' claims are largely based on the practices of Greco-Roman religion. The NT references to Christian prophecy, on the other hand, clearly distinguish their speakers' words from those of the historical Jesus (Rev 2:1—3:22; Acts 11:28; 21:10-11).[64] It is true that the vibrant hope for a quick return of Christ gradually faded as the Church moved into its second generation, but this would not have likely spurred any sudden change in theology or newfound interest in history-writing. Jews for centuries had been holding in tension the OT's claims that the Day of the Lord was at hand (for example, Joel 2:1; Obad 15; Hab 2:3) with the reality that world history continued, and they had already used Psalm 90:4 (as 2 Pet 3:8-9 does) to account for the "delay."[65] In short, investigation of the period of oral tradition behind the writings of Matthew, Mark, Luke, and John actually bolsters confidence that these authors had both the *ability* and *desire* to preserve accurate history, according to the standards and practices of their day.

Redaction Criticism

What then of the differences among gospel parallels which are seemingly theologically motivated? At this point, it is important to stress that ideological and historical motivations do not cancel each other out. One of the most firmly entrenched fallacies of modern redaction criticism is that an author cannot be writing theology and history simultaneously. Authors passionately devoted to a cause inevitably distort their historical accounts, it is alleged. This claim is patently false. Some of the most meticulous chroniclers of the Holocaust in World War II were Jews, passionately committed to seeing that such atrocities never occurred again. But it is not they, but the revisionist historians, who slanderously alleged that the Holocaust never happened (or was greatly exaggerated), who falsified history. In the ancient world, *all* history was ideologically motivated. Many students of ancient history recognize that historical *explanation* is not a necessary condition for *reliability*. The latter depends on an author's access to accurate reports of the past or to a trustworthy memory of his or her own experiences. The former depends on one's ability to synthesize data and perceive the significance of events.[66] Historians of the Roman Empire often refer to "Caesar's crossing the Rubicon" as an undisputed fact of historic significance, even though it is attested only by four ancient writers, two to three generations after the event, all dependent on one eyewitness account, and preserved in significantly different forms corresponding to the various authors' ideologies, including one which attributes Caesar's decision to enlarge his frontiers to supernatural guidance.[67] Some of the accounts thus try to *explain* the significance of Caesar's crossing, some do not. And the explanations themselves vary, yet all historians agree Caesar crossed the Rubicon. The gospels' evidence to the main contours of the life of Christ is even better attested, at an earlier date, based on more eyewitnesses, and it, too, attributes certain events to supernatural guidance. Little wonder that the secular historian A. N. Sherwin-White, not known for any inclination to promote Christianity, once marveled, "it is astonishing that while Graeco-Roman historians have been growing in confidence, the twentieth-century study of the Gospel narratives, *starting from no less promising material*, has taken so gloomy a turn."[68]

When we can overcome this false dichotomy between theology and history, redaction criticism can prove quite valuable. As with form criticism, there is both a valid use and an abuse of the method. For example, redaction criticism reveals that Mark highlights the failure of the disciples, while Matthew stresses how Jesus' life and teaching fulfilled the Law and the Prophets. Luke is the consummate theologian of social concern, and John's Christology does strike us as consistently more explicit and exalted.[69] But these distinctives have often been turned into contradictions, and hidden agendas have been found behind all kinds of minor stylistic differences among gospel parallels. When stripped of these excesses, however, redaction criticism can actually work with traditional harmonization to explain *why* the gospel accounts differ as they do and thus reinforce our belief in their historical reliability.

For example, Mark concludes his account of Jesus' walking on the water by stressing that the disciples "were completely amazed, for they had not understood about the loaves; their hearts were hardened" (Mark 6:51). Quite differently, Matthew ends his version of the same incident with "those who were in the boat" worshiping Jesus, "saying, 'Truly you are the Son of God'" (Matt 14:33). A sympathetic reader trying to imagine his or her own reaction to such a wondrous event can doubtless believe that the same group of disciples mingled fear, amazement, worship, and disbelief all at once. But such a "harmonization" still sounds a bit forced until one understands why Matthew and Mark have chosen to record different elements of the disciples' reactions. As noted earlier, Matthew consistently stresses the more positive side of the disciples' faith, faltering though it often was, probably to encourage Christians to whom he was writing. On the other hand, Mark for much the same motives is probably writing to a Roman Christian church under Nero in the days shortly before persecution would break out with intensity. Tempted to lose heart, they needed to be reminded of the disciples' failures, to be encouraged that God can use them, too, despite their feelings of inadequacy. Only when we understand each of these perspectives and recognize that they fit a consistent motif in each of the gospels in which they appear is a harmonization likely to seem plausible. The oral tradition did not accidentally falsify the accounts; the Evangelists did not arbitrarily distort them. Rather the same events are retold from complementary perspectives to highlight those themes that were most relevant for their respective audiences.[70]

E. E. Lemcio has recently written an important work which highlights how the Evangelists clearly distinguish "the past of Jesus in the Gospels" from the post-resurrection era of church history.[71] Mark summarizes Jesus' message as preaching the gospel (good news) about God and his government (Mark 1:14-15), but recognizes that by his day it is appropriate to speak of the gospel about *Jesus Christ* (1:1). Matthew stresses the centrality in John's and Jesus' preaching of the kingdom of heaven drawing near (Matt 3:2; 4:17; 10:5), but epitomizes the apostles' post-resurrection ministry as discipling nations in the observance of Jesus' commandments (28:18-20). Luke stresses Christ's pre-crucifixion proclamation of release for the captives and his social concern (Luke 4:16-30), but his post-resurrection command that forgiveness of sins be preached to the nations (24:46-47). In the gospels, Jesus is pre-eminently Savior; in Acts he is primarily Lord. John's recognition of Jesus' "theocentricity" (John 5:24; 12:44) gives way to a post-Easter Christocentricity (1:1-18; 20:31). None of these shifts is inherently contradictory, but each recasts the nature of discipleship and belief significantly enough to make us doubt that the Evangelists were reading post-Easter theology back into the pre-Easter portions of their narratives. Redaction criticism thus can actually increase our confidence in the trustworthiness of the gospel writers.

Literary Criticism

Some uses of this discipline are actually the least germane to a study of the historical nature of the Bible. Literary and historical methods are often pitted against each other as though they were mutually exclusive. But, as noted above, some of the literary analyses of books of Scripture actually support, or at least are consistent with, conservative historical judgments.[72] One subdiscipline of both historical and literary criticism, however, is extremely crucial for our study. Determinations of author, date, use of sources and tradition, and editorial tendencies can all predispose us favorably to the likelihood of substantial historical accuracy in a given document. But writers of fiction, for example, of historical novels, may also pass all of these tests. It is essential, therefore, to raise the question of genre. What kind of literature did the Evangelists think they were writing? What indications have they left to enable us to determine if they expected us to consider their works as historical, fictitious, or some combination of the two? This issue is of such importance that it deserves an entire section of its own.

Genre Criticism

Every work of literature falls into some genre or mixture of genres. A genre is a combination of features of form, content, and function that sends clues to readers as to what type of writing to expect. In modern literature, we distinguish a sonnet from an ode from lyric poetry. We learn to tell the difference between historical reporting, historical novels, and fantasy stories. The NT contains four main genres—gospels, an "acts," epistles, and an apocalypse.[73] Only the first two of these are usually understood as potentially historical or biographical in form, although biographical and autobiographical details are embedded in the epistles, and Revelation reveals a variety of insights into the historical circumstances of its day.[74]

If, then, it be determined that the gospels or Acts are primarily historical in form or intent, we will have to come to grips with their truth claims in different fashion than if there are good reasons to treat them as historical novels or fiction. And here is where much of the "rub" comes in for modern readers. At first glance, the gospels and Acts do *not* seem to conform to conventional standards of reliable history or biography. Consider, for example, the amount of attention each pays to the various facets of Jesus' life. Only two of the four gospels, Matthew and Luke, refer to any part of his life prior to his adult ministry, and even they omit all but one incident between roughly ages two and thirty. On the other hand, Mark and John spend nearly half of their narratives recounting the events of just the last few weeks of Jesus' earthly existence. In between, material is arranged differently in each gospel, and a comparison of parallel accounts makes it clear that the evangelists have not worried about being overly precise in matters of chronology or in their descriptions of what Jesus did and said.

To complicate matters further, not many of the details of the gospels can be verified by reference to non-Christian historians of the day. Scholars have thus established elaborate "criteria of authenticity" by which they try to sift the genuine from the spurious (see below). When all the evidence is compiled, many would endorse Norman Perrin's list of what can be believed with confidence about Jesus from historical research: baptism by John, proclamation of the Kingdom, power to relieve those believing themselves to be afflicted by demons, gathering disciples, sharing meals with them, combating Jewish sectarianism, arousing the opposition of the Jewish leaders, trial by those religious authorities for blasphemy and by the Romans for sedition, and crucifixion. Some of Jesus' followers then continued his work with certain vestiges of his power and authority.[75] And most of these details are attested by or can be inferred from the handful of non-Christian extra-biblical testimonies to the life of Jesus; so it is clear that Perrin adds little to his database unique to the gospels themselves.[76]

On the other hand, one could argue that such a list of events is remarkably full, given ancient history's propensity to deal almost exclusively with political or military rulers and their doings or to focus on fully accredited, "upper crust" religious and philosophical leaders. Since Jesus fits none of these categories, we should not have expected him to receive more treatment by non-Christian writers than he did. The amount of corroboration in the writing of the Jewish historian, Josephus, alone can be viewed as surprisingly large. In his *Jewish Antiquities*, written in the last third of the first century, we read,

> About this time there lived Jesus, a wise man, if indeed one ought to call him a man. For he was one who wrought surprising feats and was a teacher of such people as accept the truth gladly. He won over many Jews and many of the Greeks. He was the Messiah. When Pilate, upon hearing him accused by men of the highest standing amongst us, had condemned him to be crucified, those who had in the first place come to love him did not give up their affection for him. On the third day he appeared to them restored to life, for the prophets of God had prophesied these and countless other marvellous things about him. And the tribe of the Christians, so called after him, has still to this day not disappeared (18:63-64).

Because Josephus's works were preserved and edited in Christian circles, and because Josephus himself was not a Christian, there is reason to believe that the references to Jesus' dubious humanity, Messiahship, and resurrection were added or altered by later Christian scribes. But there is a fair consensus that the rest of this testimony is what Josephus originally wrote, since it closely fits his style of writing elsewhere.[77] In addition, Josephus contains largely undisputed references to Herod the Great, Herod Archelaus, Antipas's execution of John the Baptist, a summary of the Baptist's message, the reign of the ethnarch Aretas, the death of Agrippa I, the famine in Judea, Gallio in Corinth, the accessions of Felix, Festus, and Agrippa II, and various other details which all basically support the parallel narratives in the gospels and Acts.[78]

How shall we respond to these competing impressions concerning the historical veracity of the Evangelists' writings? To begin with, it is useful to separate the Synoptic Gospels off from John and treat them separately, since they are more like each other than like the fourth gospel. Then we shall look at John and Acts and, much more briefly, the rest of the NT.

The Synoptic Gospels

A crucial observation at the outset is that the features of Matthew, Mark, and Luke which lead us moderns to wonder if the gospels are historical in genre were actually quite common in ancient biographies. Giving disproportionate attention to someone's birth and death, particularly if they were seen to have religious significance, grouping material topically as well as chronologically, paraphrase rather than exact quotation, summarizing and digesting long speeches or stories, and a general freedom to describe events from a variety of perspectives, all regularly characterized ancient biographies, including those which historians of antiquity classify as generally historically trustworthy.[79] Problems emerge primarily when we try to impose modern standards of history or biography onto the ancient writers, but this procedure is clearly anachronistic.

External evidence, particularly from archaeology, is not as useful with the Synoptics as with John or Acts, because the first three gospels do not give us as many details of time, place, or setting. Still, the findings which have been unearthed consistently support the pictures painted by these three writers. We still have not found conclusive proof of a census under Quirinius in the years immediately surrounding Christ's birth (Luke 2:1-2), but there is enough circumstantial evidence to at least make a plausible case for one.[80] The dramatic discovery in 1961 of an inscription referring to Pilate in Caesarea during the time of Tiberius provided for the first time extra-biblical corroboration of the reign of Judea's prefect who sentenced Christ. Discoveries of an ossuary (bone-box) of a crucified man named Johanan from first-century Palestine confirm that nails were driven in his ankles. As recently as 1992, the burial grounds of Caiaphas, the Jewish high priest, and his family were unearthed in Jerusalem. These and many similar data at the very least create a favorable impression of the Synoptists' trustworthiness.[81]

An important indicator of the Synoptists' intentions is the preface of Luke's gospel (Luke 1:1-4). Luke is the only gospel writer to declare so explicitly what he is trying to do. And because Matthew and Mark are more like Luke than like any other ancient writings (and because Matthew and Luke each depended on Mark), what emerges as the genre of Luke will be the most likely genre for the first two gospels as well. The most current and comprehensive analysis of Luke's preface comes from the research of a British scholar, Loveday Alexander. She concludes that Luke's preface most closely resembles the technical prose of prefaces to medical and scientific treatises. This would support the Bible's claim that Luke was a doctor, though Alexander herself does not discuss this point. What she does develop, however, is the similarity between Luke's biography and Greco-Roman writings which describe the life of a founder of a philosophical or scientific "school" of disciples and which therefore give careful respect for the traditions of that founder as they are passed along, a respect which does not, however, preclude the reworking of those traditions for new situations.[82]

Indeed, there is a trend in contemporary scholarship to view the Synoptic Gospels as most closely akin to ancient biographies or histories which were relatively trustworthy by the standards of their day—for example, Herodotus, Tacitus, Arrian, Dio Cassius, Sallust, and Josephus.[83] One writer identifies Luke-Acts as "apologetic historiography," which he defines as "the story of a subgroup of people in an extended prose narrative written by a member of the group who follows the group's own traditions but Hellenizes them in an effort to establish the identity of the group within the setting of the larger world."[84] This would again place Luke in the traditions of Herodotus and Josephus, thus challenging the notion that he was not *trying* to pass on valuable and accurate information. And as we have already seen, his apologetic motives are precisely to be expected and do not in any way impugn his veracity.

At the same time, there are clear distinctives in form, content, and function which set the Synoptic Gospels off from other biographies, even ideological biographies. But these mostly involve the various constituent elements or forms embedded within the gospels and how they are organized, as well as the unique demands related to writing about a unique person such as Jesus. Robert Guelich's definition of the gospel genre thus seems to be the most well balanced.

> *Formally* a gospel is a narrative account concerning the public life and teaching of a significant person that is composed of discreet [*sic*] traditional units placed in the context of Scriptures . . . *materially*, the genre consists of the message that God was at work in Jesus' life, death, and resurrection effecting his promises found in the Scriptures.[85]

Formally, then, the gospels find their closest parallels in other historical and biographical literature, even though materially they prove uniquely Christian in nature. This generic identification does not prove that every detail in the Synoptics must be equally reliable, but it creates an initial ethos favorable to their trustworthiness. The apparent contradictions still need to be examined, one by one, and space obviously precludes such an analysis here. But it has been done exhaustively over the years in the major evangelical studies of the gospels. Today students have a plethora of sources to consult, including important commentary series such as the New International, Word Biblical, Expositor's Bible, Tyndale, Pillar, and New American.[86]

The Gospel of John

Many commentators who are willing to grant a substantial amount of historical trustworthiness to the Synoptics often still balk when they come to the fourth gospel. Here is a story of Jesus which seems quite different. Jesus makes high claims for himself on almost every page, in contrast to the reticence to disclose his identity which he displays in Matthew, Mark, and Luke. Few of the episodes are the same. Jesus regularly speaks in long, connected discourses, often linked with dramatic miracles which he works. How could the Synoptics, for example, have omitted the resurrection of Lazarus if it really had taken place as John describes it (John 11:1-44)? On the other hand, no parables appear anywhere in John, even though they are the most characteristic form of Jesus' teaching in the Synoptics. Further, John's narrative style and language is often indistinguishable from the words he attributes to Christ. Surely this gospel, these scholars would claim, is the product of a much more sophisticated theological reflection on the significance of Jesus and cannot be mined as a historical source to nearly the extent that the Synoptics can.

To be sure, when one compares John with his three predecessors, the differences are noteworthy, although a sizable list of similarities could also be compiled.[87] But when one compares all four gospels as a corpus with other Jewish or Greco-Roman literature of the day, it becomes plain that "for all its differences from the Synoptics, John is far closer to them than to any other ancient writing."[88] Indeed, just as he does with the Synoptics, Richard Burridge compares the fourth gospel with other Hellenistic *bioi* ("lives" or biographies) such as Isocrates's *Evagoras*, Xenophon's *Agesilaus*, Satyrus's *Euripides*, Nepos's *Atticus*, Philo's *Moses*, Tacitus's *Agricola*, Plutarch's *Cato Minor*, Suetonius's *Lives of the Caesars*, Lucian's *Demonax*, and Philostratus's *Apollonius of Tyana*, with respect to such features as prologue, verb subjects, allocation of space, mode of representation, length, structure, scale, literary units, use of sources, methods and quality of characterization, setting, topics, style, atmosphere, social setting and occasion, and authorial intention and purpose. Burridge concludes that John, like his canonical predecessors, remains well within the range of Hellenistic biography.[89] The differences can be accounted for either because John was writing independently of the Synoptics or deliberately supplementing them (and thus avoiding unnecessary repetition), because he embraces a more dramatic sub-genre of biography and imposes a more uniform style of the Greek language onto his sources, and because he has distinctive theological purposes. But the differences are not so great as to require a repudiation of "history" or "biography" as the gospel's primary generic identification.[90]

In fact, one of the interesting features of the fourth gospel, when compared with the Synoptics, is that John consistently gives *more* references to chronology, geography, topography, and the like. These have been demonstrated to be highly accurate, particularly in light of modern archaeological discoveries: the five porticoes of the pool of Bethesda by the Sheep Gate (5:2), the pool of Siloam (9:1-7), Jacob's well at Sychar (4:5), the "Pavement" (*Gabbatha*) where Pilate pronounced judgment on Jesus (19:13), Solomon's porch (10:22-23), and so on.[91] Again, it is only because of John that we know Jesus had at least a three-year ministry; most harmonies of the gospels wind up using John's chronological framework and then fitting the Synoptic material into it.[92] And the argument from historical verisimilitude, always tenuous because of the ability of writers of fiction to produce lifelike narratives, nevertheless carries some particular force with the fourth gospel. E. Stauffer, for example, has catalogued an impressive list of historically realistic elements which appear in John (even more often than they do in the Synoptics): theologically irrelevant notices of geography or topography, historically corroborated details, parallels with the Synoptic traditions, parallels with extra-canonical Jesus tradition, details which fit an early first-century Palestinian Jewish setting, proper order and sequence of the various Jewish festivals, juridical elements corresponding to the legal customs of the time, internal and external theological coherence, and speeches based on historically verifiable kernels of Jesus' teaching.[93]

The Book of Acts

Many of the same debates rage around the book of Acts as around the four gospels. If the gospels are more properly termed theological *biographies* because of their unrelenting focus on Jesus as their main character, then Acts is probably best described as theological *history* as it focuses on a much wider sweep of early Christian characters and events, even while concentrating most of all on the ministries of Peter and Paul. Luke's preface in Acts (1:1-3) resembles and refers back to the opening of the gospel so as to make it obvious that Luke still thinks he is functioning as a historian. When taken by itself, Acts most closely approximates the "historical monograph"—historical writing on a limited topic and period of time, selectively presented, with a prologue, narrative, speeches, other quotations, and a historical survey, presented in an action-packed and interesting style. Again, there are unique features of Acts because of its unique content, but the book finds partial precursors in both Sallust and Cicero.[94]

None of this is to deny that Luke imposes a clear theological stamp onto his redaction of the material he unearths or that, particularly in his second volume, he writes in a lively and entertaining style akin to certain adventure novelists. But when one discerns these elements in representatives of other historical genres as well as in more fictitious writing, and when one reads about Luke's expressed purpose of compiling "an orderly account" of "the things that have been fulfilled among us," so that "you may know the certainty of the things you have been taught" (Luke 1:1-4), it is hard not to believe that Luke thought he was communicating trustworthy historical information in the process.[95]

Indeed, the Book of Acts is quite different from the gospels in one key respect which strongly supports this conclusion. Much of its detail may be confirmed by extra-canonical sources. The plethora of names Luke uses to describe the different kinds of political rule in the various cities of the Roman empire—procurators and proconsuls, magistrates and legates, governors and prefects, even the "chief man" on the island of Malta, all have been shown, despite earlier skepticism, to correspond to precisely the legislative setup in the respective communities into which Luke places them. The detailed references to places through which Paul traveled on his missionary journeys all correspond to the actual terrain. Names of provinces fit the Roman administration of the day, even though some of these were then relatively recent and short-lived. Although some of the dates remain a little uncertain, a synthesis of the events of Acts with the historical information Paul supplies in his epistles enables us to reconstruct a harmonious and relatively detailed chronology of events in the life of the early church, especially related to Paul's travels.[96] Not surprisingly, the celebrated turn-of-the century British archaeologist Sir William M. Ramsay, who began his investigations as a skeptic, became a Christian after exploring the sites of Paul's journeys firsthand and comparing them with the testimony of Acts![97]

The Epistles and Revelation

Many readers of the remaining NT genres are often surprised that reference is not made back to the words and deeds of Jesus more often. This, they argue, is a further reason for assuming that the gospel traditions were not well-known in the early church and hence not as likely to be fully trustworthy. But genre criticism rightly alerts us to the fact that we ought not to expect abundant historical allusions in letters and apocalypses. These writers had their own distinct purposes and unique sense of divinely inspired authority, which did not require regular substantiation from secondary sources. Neither do the epistles very often quote what for them remained an authoritative Scripture (our OT).

Nevertheless, a summary of the biographical information about Jesus that can be pieced together from just the Pauline epistles alone would include his descent from Abraham and David (Gal 3:16; Rom 1:3), his upbringing in the Jewish law (Gal 4:4), his gathering together disciples, including Cephas (Peter) and John, and his having a brother named James (Gal 1:19; 2:9), his impeccable character and exemplary life (for example, Phil 2:6-8; 2 Cor 8:9; Rom 15:3, 8), his Last Supper and betrayal (1 Cor 11:23-35), and numerous details surrounding his crucifixion and resurrection (for example, Gal 3:1; 1 Thess 2:15; 1 Cor 15:4-8).

More widespread are signs of a fairly detailed knowledge of Jesus' teaching, especially in Romans, 1 Corinthians, and 1 Thessalonians, even if it is not often cited verbatim. In Romans we hear clear echoes of Jesus' words on blessing those who persecute you (Rom 12:14; cf. Luke 6:27-28), repaying no one evil for evil (Rom 12:17; cf. Matt 5:39), paying taxes and related tribute (Rom 13:7; cf. Mark 12:17), loving neighbor as summarizing the whole Law (Rom 13:8-9; cf. Gal 5:14; Mark 12:31), and recognizing all foods as clean (Rom 14:14; cf. Luke 11:41; Mark 7:19b). Three times in 1 Corinthians Paul more explicitly quotes the words of Jesus from the gospel tradition: on divorce and remarriage (1 Cor 7:10; cf. Mark 10:10-12), on receiving money for ministry (1 Cor 9:14; cf. 1 Tim 5:18; Luke 10:7), and extensively on the Last Supper (1 Cor 11:23-25; cf. Luke 22:19-20). In 1 Thessalonians fairly close quotations appear in 2:14-16 (on the persecution of Judean Christians by their kinfolk cf. Matt 23:29-38) and 4:15—5:4 (on the return of Christ—cf. Matt 24, esp. v. 43).[98] Moving to the epistle of James, one finds allusions to the Synoptic tradition, and especially the Sermon on the Mount, in almost every paragraph,[99] and a more explicit quotation of the saying on letting your yes be yes and your no, no in James 5:12 (cf. Matt 5:37). Even the Book of Revelation draws on and elaborates imagery from the teaching of Jesus, especially his unique use of the title "Son of man."[100] When we realize that all of these books except for Revelation were written before the canonical gospels were compiled and circulated, this is indeed impressive testimony to the pervasiveness of the gospel traditions in their oral stage.[101]

THE BURDEN OF PROOF AND THE CRITERIA OF AUTHENTICITY

We have argued that the gospels and Acts were written at relatively early dates by their traditional authors and reflect historical genres that disclose their authors' intent to write credible history by the standards of those genres; moreover, we have seen that what references do exist to the same events and teachings in other documents, both inside and outside the canon, consistently corroborate the accuracy of these works.

The Burden of Proof

But if even this much be conceded, then we must further insist on the biblical writings being treated at least as generously as other purportedly historical works of antiquity. One cannot require corroboration of every detail; a substantial majority of the details in any work of history from the ancient world will present information which is unparalleled elsewhere and hence both unfalsifiable and unverifiable. Instead, one has to build an impression of the credibility of writers where they can be tested and then assume that their "track record" is relatively consistent throughout. It may not be, but if it is not, we shall have no way of knowing that.

In other words, in the investigation of questions of historical reliability the tack one takes depends on one's overall impressions of a work. If the evidence supports a general presumption favorable to the trustworthiness of the gospels and Acts, then it is both unfair and impossible to require positive support for each of the constituent details within those volumes. The case will be lost before it is begun because of the unavailability of such information.[102] Rather the burden of proof that any portion of these works is *unhistorical* must rest squarely on the skeptic's shoulders. Here is where the apparent contradictions come back into play. There *are* seeming discrepancies which lead many to assume that the gospels and Acts are not entirely trustworthy. The appropriate methodology, therefore, is to consider these one by one and see if plausible alternatives can be suggested in most instances. If they cannot, one's initial assumption will have to be revised. If they can, that assumption should be allowed to stand. As we have previously observed, we believe there is sufficient evidence for the assumption to stand.[103]

The Criteria of Authenticity

Despite our contention that adequate evidence warrants an initial assumption favorable to the historicity of the gospels and Acts, many would disagree. Can we carry on further discussion in such settings or must the conversation end in an impasse? We would maintain that we can proceed further. For even those scholars who begin with a very skeptical stance toward these books have developed "criteria of authenticity," as they are usually termed, for admitting certain sayings or episodes as historically genuine or authentic.[104] The four most common and widely agreed upon criteria are the criteria of dissimilarity, multiple attestation, Palestinian environment, and coherence. Each of these has its strengths and weaknesses which have been adequately discussed elsewhere.[105] But even if we take them at face value as they are usually employed, a remarkable amount of the canonical traditions about Jesus and the early church may be "recovered."

The criterion of dissimilarity accepts as authentic that which is noticeably distinctive from both a first-century Jewish and an early Christian milieu. It will include traditions which cannot easily be explained as being invented out of conventional Jewish practices and which were not widely reproduced or followed by the first Christians. One thinks, for example, of Jesus' kingdom parables. Jewish leaders regularly told parables, but almost always to exegete Scripture rather than to illustrate God's in-breaking reign. Early Christians, on the other hand, even in the rest of the NT, scarcely ever employed the parable form in their instruction at all. The particular form of parable consistently attributed to Jesus, therefore, does not seem likely to have originated with anyone else. The balance between present and future aspects of the kingdom in Jesus' teaching more generally probably fits under this criterion, too, inasmuch as Jews saw the kingdom as almost wholly future and early Christians quickly began to stress the present aspect in an equally one-sided way.[106]

The criterion of multiple attestation affirms that those details which appear in more than one independent source or layer of the gospel tradition are likely to be authentic. So if a passage appears in both Mark and John, or in both Mark and Q, or in one of the canonical gospels and the collection of Jesus-traditions found at the Gnostic library of Nag Hammadi, Egypt, known as the Gospel of Thomas, then one may add them to our database of more or less reliable details. Examples of each of these three concurrences, respectively, might include the feeding of the 5,000 (found in all *four* canonical gospels—Matt 14:13-21; Mark 6:32-44; Luke 9:10-17; John 6:1-13), the commissioning of the Twelve after Jesus first called them (Mark 6:7-11; but in a substantially different form common to parts of Matt 10:1-16 and Luke 9:1-6), and Jesus' words about the rejected stone's becoming the head of the corner in conjunction with the parable of the wicked tenants (Matt 21:33-46; Mark 12:1-12; Luke 20:9-19; Thos 65-66).

The criterion of Palestinian environment admits as more likely authentic those traditions which seem to require an early Palestinian Jewish-Christian milieu for their genesis. One thinks, for example, of many of Jesus' "Son of Man" sayings, of his use of the Aramaic "Abba" (almost Daddy) for Father, or of his consistent prefacing of particularly solemn asseverations with the Hebrew, "Amen" ("Truly"). Here too would be included his concern for the outcasts of his society, rejection of the purity laws, frequent conflicts with the religious authorities over the Law (especially the Sabbath). And many of these details receive dual corroboration by the dissimilarity criterion.[107]

The criterion of coherence, finally, affirms that we may accept traditions which are not immediately suggested by an application of the previous three criteria but which are profoundly consistent with the meaning and significance of those which do. Examples of some of Jesus' nature miracles come to mind here: the changing of water into wine as illustrating the newness of the kingdom taught by the parable of the wineskins (cf. John 2:1-11 with Mark 2:19-20); or the cursing of the fig tree as an illustration of the nearness of judgment for unrepentant Israel, as in the related parable of the fig tree (cf. Mark 11:12-14, 20-25 with Luke 13:1-9).[108]

The idiosyncratic ways these criteria are employed by some writers leaves the impression that only a small percentage of the gospels and Acts may be accepted as historical.[109] Others use the tools more fairly to recover a substantial portion of these traditions.[110] In fact, even when one adopts a skeptical starting point, a sane application of the criteria of authenticity can lend credence, with varying degrees of confidence, to virtually all of the major themes and forms within the historical narratives of the NT. Among modern writers, René Latourelle displays the greatest optimism and provides a long list of details in the Synoptic Gospels alone which have been accepted as genuine by non-evangelical authors of major critical studies employing the criteria of authenticity. These include the linguistic, social, political, economic, cultural and religious environments depicted; the great events of Jesus' life—baptism, temptation, transfiguration, teaching on the kingdom, call to repentance, parables, beatitudes, teaching on God as Father, the miracles and exorcisms as signs of the kingdom, the betrayal, agony, trial, crucifixion, burial and resurrection; the controversies with the scribes and Pharisees; Jesus' attitudes of simplicity and authority, of purity and compassion; the Christology implied by the sign of Jonah, the sign of the temple, and the "Son of Man" title; the rejection of a spatially or temporally limited kingdom; and the calling and mission of the apostles, coupled with their initial enthusiasm, subsequent lack of understanding, and final betrayal and desertion. Latourelle sums up: "On each of the subjects enumerated, we can invoke the testimony of many exegetes. To the extent that researches [sic] go on, the material acknowledged as authentic grows ceaselessly until it covers the whole Gospel."[111]

Royce Gruenler goes one step further, applying the criteria of coherence to the high Christology of John. He argues that even if one begins by accepting only the minimal core of historical details accepted by Norman Perrin (see above) one can demonstrate the profound coherence of their implicit claims concerning Jesus' uniqueness with the more explicit claims particularly prominent in the fourth gospel.[112] Not all will agree that each of Gruenler's claims is equally convincing, but he surely demonstrates that even a skeptical starting point need not lead to widespread agnosticism about the nature of the historical Jesus or to a reconstruction which substantially distances him from the traditional orthodox understanding of Christ as the God-man. Claims to the contrary consistently disclose a failure to judge the Bible by the same canons applied to other ancient history and biography. The confidence of the "third questers" (see above) is justified and may even be extended to cover a substantial portion of the miracle tradition.[113]

THE JESUS SEMINAR AND RELATED DEVELOPMENTS

What then do we make of the color-coded edition of the five gospels and works of its ilk? How do we respond to writers like Burton Mack, who argues that Mark invented most of the story of Jesus, which radically diverged from the earliest stages of Q?[114] Are Mack and Crossan right in saying that Jesus was just an itinerant, quasi-Cynic guru? How should we assess claims of a huge dichotomy between oral and written tradition, so that Mark's enterprise of writing down gospel traditions almost by definition distorted them?[115] We should reject these claims as eccentric (though widely publicized) even within non-evangelical scholarship and as based on highly unreliable methodology.

There is not a shred of hard evidence to support the claim that Mark made up the major contours of his gospel narrative. Putting Jesus in his Jewish milieu makes it virtually certain that he was influenced by apocalyptic literature and not at all limited to uttering short, cryptic proverbs. The view that Jesus was primarily a wise sage has to invert the standard and commonsensical sequence of historical development—from the Jesus of apocalyptic Judaism to the Christ of Greco-Roman wisdom. It leaves us with a Jesus who would not have alienated the authorities of his day sufficient to trigger his execution.[116] It relies on dating the Gospel of Thomas almost a hundred years earlier (ca. A.D. 50) than we have any reason to locate it, and it assumes against the majority of the evidence that Thomas contains significant independent traditions of Jesus' teachings which predate the canonical gospels.[117] It depends on believing other apocryphal literature which is almost certainly unhistorical and demonstrably much later than the canonical gospels.[118] It employs the criteria of authenticity inconsistently, often only when they bolster its case. It assumes a "revolutionary" rather than an "evolutionary" development between the oral and written stages of the gospel tradition for which there are no close analogies in the ancient world. In fact, the influence of the oral tradition persisted side-by-side with developing written accounts of Jesus and the early church well into the second century. And it resurrects nineteenth-century models for the historical Jesus which were disproved and discarded already in the first half of this century.[119]

SUMMARY AND CONCLUSION

The texts of the NT have been preserved in far greater number and with much more care than have any other ancient documents. The authors of the historical portions of the NT—the gospels and Acts—are quite probably Matthew, Mark, Luke, and John, just as the church has historically claimed. Matthew and John were apostles and eyewitnesses of much they recorded. Mark got much of his information from Peter, Luke from Paul and numerous eyewitnesses in and around Jerusalem. Except for John, their writings should all be dated to about A.D. 60 plus or minus a few years. All this makes it inherently probable that these writers were *able* to record reliable history. A study of the conservative nature of ancient oral tradition—prodigious feats of memory coupled with a flexibility in passing on the tradition within fixed limits—reinforces our belief in this ability. The theological distinctives of the Evangelists do not jeopardize this claim and the apparent contradictions all find plausible solutions.

A careful analysis of the genres of Matthew, Mark, Luke, John, and Acts suggests that their writers were not only able to provide trustworthy history, but that they were *intending to* do so with the historical and biographical genres they utilized. The limited external evidence from non-Christian writers, later Christian writers, and archaeology (especially relevant to John and Acts) almost always confirms that, where they can be tested, the Evangelists *did* record accurate historical information. By the very nature of the data, such external corroboration is simply unavailable for many of the details in the gospels and Acts. But all of the above evidence is adequate to place the burden of proof on the shoulders of anyone who would deny the trustworthiness of untestable data. And even for those who do not accept this methodology, a fair application of the standard criteria of authenticity makes it probable that a substantial *majority* of the details in the gospels and Acts do describe what Jesus and the apostles actually said and did. The very nature of historical research prevents us from making any stronger claims as *historians*. This is as far as the evidence can take us, whether we like it or not. But it creates a better case than we have for almost all other periods and documents of ancient history and should therefore be given serious credence, unless one is prepared to admit wholesale agnosticism about anything that happened 2,000 or more years ago. Belief in the veracity of the words and claims of Jesus and the apostles is the next logical step but takes us beyond the bounds of an investigation of the *historical* reliability of the documents.

PRACTICAL APPLICATION

It is possible in many parts of the United States, particularly in the Bible belt, to live and function effectively as a Christian without often having to confront or master the types of issues discussed in this chapter. But the same is not true in other parts of the country and certainly not in most parts of our world. Wherever Christianity is an embattled minority, believers regularly face the types of issues raised here from adherents of other religions or world views. And it is increasingly impossible to escape them even in the parts of our nation and globe that have had the greatest history of Christian influence. Anyone who wants to be active in sharing his or her faith with unbelievers, particularly among the well-educated middle or upper class, will encounter those who have heard and believed that the Scriptures can't be trusted. Anyone who wants to influence the contemporary college or university scene, or public thought as represented in politics or the media, will find these notions well-entrenched. Tragically, countless Christians go off to school for advanced degrees every year, or enter the marketplace of public discourse in the working world, only to encounter such questions for the first time. And because the church and parachurch have not adequately equipped them for responding to skepticism, they abandon once-cherished beliefs to their own detriment.

My own experience was a pleasant exception to this trend. I was reared in a liberal, mainline Protestant church and taught during my confirmation class as a teenager that the Bible was full of errors. I do not consciously remember ever hearing in that church that the way to salvation was through a personal relationship with Jesus as Savior and Lord. This I first encountered in a parachurch organization that ministered to high schoolers, through which I committed my life to Christ. Another parachurch organization provided my primary Christian nurture during my college days. It was at this college, associated with the church I had grown up in, where I was first exposed to a skeptical, academic study of the Bible and religion in a serious fashion. On the first day of a course in the gospels, my instructor, an ordained Protestant minister, had us read the apocryphal infancy Gospel of Thomas (not to be confused with the Gnostic Gospel by the same name noted earlier), in which the child Jesus works frivolous and even spiteful miracles to amaze and combat his playmates. My professor's point was to have us observe how the trend to embellish the accounts of Jesus' life, which he believed began within the canonical gospels, reached a ludicrous climax in the apocryphal writings. In psychology and sociology class discussions, when I would quote Jesus to try to bring a Christian perspective on various topics, my professors would invariably say, "But of course modern scholarship has demonstrated that Jesus probably never said that." A church history professor once responded in a friendly but firm manner to my appeal to the authority of the NT on a certain point with these words: "You simply cannot be a fundamentalist [his word for all evangelical Christians] and maintain your intellectual integrity."

I was a good enough student that, if that comment were true, I was determined to maintain my intellectual integrity! Fortunately, my parachurch group leader and one or two local pastors were knowledgeable enough to put me in touch with very scholarly literature that disproved my professor's claim. As I rummaged through my college's library, I found other solid, conservative evangelical scholarship tucked away in the stacks where few people had read it. Certainly these books had never appeared on any professor's bibliography during my era. One of those works which was highly influential for me in the early seventies was I. H. Marshall's *Luke: Historian and Theologian*.[120] There I discovered how one could grant that the gospel writers were more interested in theology than pure history without necessarily impugning their historical trustworthiness. My appreciation of Marshall's work led me several years later to apply to study under him in Aberdeen, Scotland, for my doctoral degree. As I have kept in touch with friends at that college and become aware of dozens of other schools like it around the country, I understand that things have not changed much. And at secular colleges and universities the challenges to the trustworthiness of Scripture are even more severe.

But the relevance of our topic is not limited to debates which rage on college and university campuses or during discussions with people who have studied about religion in such schools. About once or twice a year, some biblically-related news story hits all the major media and brings questions of Scripture's trustworthiness into national focus. Easter and Christmas often produce stories in national and local newspapers questioning the reliability of the traditions on which those festivals are based. In 1990, a provocative book by Yale literary critic Harold Bloom suggesting that a woman authored the putative "Book of J," one of the hypothetical sources for Genesis through Deuteronomy, triggered a lengthy discussion in *U.S. News and World Report* on "Who Wrote the Bible?"[121]

The next year saw *Time* feature a cover story on the historical Mary, in light of worldwide resurgence in alleged sightings of and devotion to Jesus' mother.[122] Although both of these articles cited a few conservative scholars as well as numerous other academics, the general impression left was not one of confidence in the historical trustworthiness of Scripture.

At times other stimuli awaken the public interest in such questions. The 1988 film *The Last Temptation of Christ* drew rave reviews from syndicated movie critics and cries of blasphemy and picket-waving protests from evangelical Christians. Unfortunately, most of the latter had never seen the film, and the media's reports uniformly distorted its contents. The final version actually shown to the public merited neither extreme reaction, but it raised afresh all of the questions of what the historical Jesus was actually like, and if the portraits of that Jesus in our canonical gospels can be trusted. The story was again featured in *Time*, and it sparked a lengthy cover story on the authorship, composition, and reliability of the gospels more generally. It even included a garbled reference to the *Gospel Perspectives* series noted earlier in this chapter.[123]

The ongoing translation of the remaining Dead Sea Scroll fragments has often generated similarly unwarranted generalizations and sensationalized media claims. It is hard to decide which is more appalling—how factually inaccurate such reports tend to be or how unprepared the average Bible-believing Christian is to make an intelligent response (or even to realize how distorted the reports are). I recall watching a major network's national news report in the early eighties during which the anchorman referred in the context of one of these reports to the four gospels being written by four of Jesus' twelve apostles, as if Mark and Luke had been among the Twelve! A local Denver news station nearly a decade later reported concerning the latest round of Dead Sea Scrolls translations that these documents were "believed by some scholars to discredit the Bible and undermine the very foundations of Christianity." I know of no reputable scholar, Jew, Christian, or atheist, working on the scrolls who would make such a claim. Worse still, the report referred to copies of the NT being found among the library of the Dead Sea sect, when in fact, as a non-Christian Jewish community, this sect produced only copies of various OT books (as well as their own sectarian literature).[124] Not surprisingly, my students, both in my adult Sunday school class and at the seminary where I teach, peppered me with questions about the report shortly thereafter.

A quite different kind of challenge to Christian belief and witness stems from the ongoing claims of aberrant sects, New Age supporters, and generally uninformed people who periodically put forward some *modern* document as the true account of the life of Christ. Stories about Jesus' hidden years—about his traveling to India to become an Oriental guru or learning Essenism in the Judean wilderness—combine with even more bizarre revisions of Jesus' life to delude the gullible.[125] One recent writer claims to have an English translation of a German translation of a lost Aramaic document shown to a UFOlogist, which rewrites the gospel of Matthew so that Jesus was a visitor from outer space teaching pantheism![126] Christians today need to be aware of the fraudulent nature of these claims so that they can confidently reassure curious friends that there is no historical truth to them and that in this case all reputable scholars, however radical or atheistic, agree. Occasionally, a person or group will get a hold of or promote one of the ancient apocryphal gospels, but their historical trustworthiness has also been demonstrated to be quite meager,[127] even though occasionally a scholar or two create headlines by arguing to the contrary.

The Jesus Seminar's *Five Gospels* has spawned the latest round of public interest. Marketed and hyped by the Westar Institute as a deliberate response to fundamentalists and televangelists, this book is designed to publicize the beliefs of this one group of scholars as widely as possible, pawning itself off as if it were representative of a consensus among contemporary scholars! One of the most balanced popular media assessments of the issues raised by the Jesus Seminar appears in a recent *U.S. News and World Report*.[128] The article balances its references to evangelical, moderate, and radical scholars and represents their views rather fairly. But the Jesus Seminar is now embarked on an assessment of the *deeds* of Jesus, so the semi-annual news releases will no doubt continue, as will their exaggerated claims, conservatives' overreactions, and widespread misrepresentations and misunderstanding on both sides. In each of these instances, believers have an outstanding opportunity to witness to their faith and generate meaningful discussion about the truth of Christianity. But will evangelical Christians be up to the task? Unfortunately, until they are confronted by challenges of this nature, many conservative Christians seem happy to remain ignorant of the historical issues at the foundation of their faith and to protest their irrelevance to daily living.

How should Christians who *do* want to enter into these discussions proceed? Obviously each skeptic has different concerns, and we have to answer him or her accordingly. I try to begin with short answers and let my partners in dialogue take the discussion in directions which will best respond to their questions. For example, I might reply to a general claim of historical skepticism by saying, "You know there actually is a substantial amount of evidence that the gospels are historically reliable." If they ask what that is, I would point out in just a few sentences the conclusions we have discussed about authorship, date, and the conservative nature of the oral tradition. If it becomes clear that the major concerns have to do with the apparent contradictions within the Bible, I'd ask which specific ones trouble them. Sometimes people can't even tell you! Other times they can, and then I discuss possible solutions. Don't be bashful to admit you don't know; promise that you will look up some answers and get back to them. Then consult the relevant works from among those we have recommended in the fairly detailed footnotes of this chapter. As long as you feel you have to have all possible answers prepared in advance, you'll never share your faith. The best stimulus to further study along the lines of this chapter is the need to answer a friend's question which you weren't previously able to.

I close this appeal for the relevance of our topic on an upbeat note. One of my greatest joys in life has been to share the kinds of material examined in this chapter with individuals or with student groups and watch people come to the Lord after realizing that they have been erecting unnecessary obstacles in the middle of their path to faith. I have been thrilled as I have received responses to my writings on the topic which have indicated similar reactions. I have been encouraged as liberal Christians, even pastors, have read about the kind of scholarship which I endorse and have changed their views, often lamenting that they had not been exposed to such perspectives in their own education. I am not claiming that these experiences have happened weekly or even monthly. Nor do I believe that concerns about the reliability of Scripture are in the forefront of every unbeliever's mind. But they are present in the thinking of a large enough number of non-Christians and liberal Christians that all born-again believers should have at least some minimal grasp of the issues involved and the ability to give an account for the hope of their trust in Scripture which is within them. And when the periodic challenges to Scripture's reliability make the front pages of newspapers or news magazines, they can at least know where they may refer their friends for responsible reading for a balancing point of view.

CHAPTER SEVEN

The Self-Understanding of Jesus

THE CHRISTIAN RELIGION STANDS OR FALLS with the person of Jesus Christ. Judaism could survive without Moses, Buddhism without Buddha, Islam without Mohammed; but Christianity could not survive without Christ. This is because unlike most other world religions, Christianity is belief in a person, a genuine historical individual—but at the same time a special individual, whom the Church regards as not only human, but divine. At the center of any Christian apologetic therefore must stand the person of Christ; and very important for the doctrine of Christ's person are the personal claims of the historical Jesus. Did he claim to be God? Or did he regard himself as a prophet? Or was he the exemplification of some highest human quality such as love or faith? Who did Jesus of Nazareth claim to be?

HISTORICAL BACKGROUND

Before we can explore this problem, let's take a brief look at the recent historical background of Jesus research.

LIFE OF JESUS MOVEMENT

During the late eighteenth and nineteenth centuries, European theology strove to find the historical Jesus behind the figure portrayed in the gospels. The chief effort of this quest was to write a life of Jesus as it supposedly really was, without the supernatural accretions found in the gospels. One after another these lives of Jesus appeared, each author thinking to have uncovered the real man behind the mask.

Early lives of Jesus tended to portray him as a spiritual man who was forced to make claims about himself that he knew were false in order to get the people to listen to his message. For example, Karl Bahrdt in his *Ausführung des Plans und Zwecks Jesu* (1784-92) maintained that Jesus belonged to a secret order of Essenes, dedicated to weaning Israel of her worldly messianic expectations in favor of spiritual, religious truths. In order to gain a hearing from the Jews, Jesus claimed to be the Messiah, planning to spiritualize the concept of Messiah by hoaxing his death and resurrection. To bring this about, Jesus provoked his arrest and trial by his triumphal entry into Jerusalem. Other members of the order, who secretly sat on the Sanhedrin, ensured his condemnation. Luke the physician prepared Jesus' body by means of drugs to withstand the rigors of crucifixion for an indefinite time. By crying loudly and slumping his head, Jesus feigned his death on the cross, and a bribe to the centurion guaranteed that his legs would not be broken. Joseph of Arimathea, another member of the order, took Jesus to a cave, where he resuscitated Jesus by his ministrations. On the third day, they pushed aside the stone over the mouth of the cave, and Jesus went forth, frightening away the guards and appearing to Mary and subsequently to his other disciples. Thereafter, he lived in seclusion among the members of the order.

Similar to Bahrdt's theory was Karl Venturini's life of Jesus in his *Natürliche Geschichte des grossen Propheten von Nazareth* (1800-02). As a member of a secret society, Jesus sought to persuade the Jewish nation to substitute the idea of a spiritual Messiah for their conception of a worldly Messiah. But his attempt backfired: he was arrested, condemned, and crucified. However, he was taken down from the cross and placed in the tomb alive, where he revived. A member of the secret society, dressed in white, frightened away the guards at the tomb, and other members took Jesus from the tomb. During forty days thereafter he appeared to various disciples, always to return to the secret place of the society. Finally, his energy spent, he retired permanently.

Much of the early Life of Jesus movement was spent in trying to provide natural explanations for Jesus' miracles and resurrection. The high water-mark of the natural explanation school came in H. E. G. Paulus's *Das Leben Jesu* (1828), in which Paulus devised all sorts of clever explanations to explain away the substance of the gospel miracles while still accepting the form of the factual accounts.

But with his *Das Leben Jesu, kritisch bearbeitet* (1835), D. F. Strauss sounded the death knell for this school. According to Strauss, the miraculous events in the gospels never happened; rather they are myths, legends, and editorial additions. Jesus was a purely human teacher who made such an impression on his disciples that after his death they applied to him the myths about the Messiah that had evolved in Judaism. Thus, out of the Jesus of history evolved the Christ of the gospels—the Messiah, the Lord, the incarnate Son of God. Though such a mythological Jesus never actually existed, nevertheless the myth embodies a profound truth, namely, the Hegelian truth of the unity of the infinite and the finite, of God and man—not, indeed, of God and the individual man Jesus, but of God and mankind as a whole. Strauss was a self-confessed pantheist, and it was this truth that the myth of the God-man embodied.

The reaction in Germany against Strauss was virulent, but the Life of Jesus movement did not return to a supernatural view of Jesus. The question of miracles was dead, and the chief issue that remained was the interpretation of the man behind the myth. With the rise of liberal theology in the second half of the nineteenth century, Jesus became a great moral teacher. The kingdom of God was interpreted by Albrecht Ritschl and Wilhelm Herrmann as an ethical community of love among mankind. Although Jesus employed apocalyptic language, his real meaning, according to Ritschl, was ethical. He lived in complete devotion to his vocation of founding this kingdom and therefore serves as the model of the ethical life for all people. According to Herrmann, Jesus completely identified with the moral ideal of the kingdom of God and is thus God's unique representative among men.

Up until this point all of the researchers shared the optimistic view that a purely human Jesus was discoverable behind the gospel traditions, that indeed a life of Jesus was possible. By this time NT criticism had evolved the two-source theory—that is, that the synoptic problem was to be solved by postulating Matthew and Luke's use of Mark and another source of sayings of Jesus, arbitrarily designated Q. It was believed that in these two most primitive sources the true, historical Jesus was to be found.

This optimism received a crushing blow at the hands of Wilhelm Wrede in his theory of the "Messianic secret." Wrede was exercised by the problem, why does Jesus in Mark always seek to conceal his identity as the Messiah, commanding people to tell no one who he really is? Wrede's ingenious answer was that since Jesus never made such divine claims about himself, Mark had to come up with some reason why people are unaware of Jesus' messianic claims, which the Christian Church had written back into the gospel traditions and had asserted were made by Jesus. To get around this problem Mark invented the "Messianic secret" motif, that is, that Jesus tried to conceal his identity, and he wrote his gospel from the perspective of this motif. The consequence of Wrede's theory was that it now became clear that even the most primitive sources about Jesus were theologically colored and that therefore a biography of the historical Jesus was impossible.

ALBERT SCHWEITZER AND THE END OF THE OLD QUEST

Thus, according to Albert Schweitzer, the historian of this intriguing movement, the old Life of Jesus movement ground to a halt in nearly complete skepticism. The liberal Jesus who went forth proclaiming the ethical kingdom of God and the brotherhood of man never existed, but is a projection of modern theology. We do not know who Jesus really was, says Schweitzer; he comes to us as a man unknown. What we do know about him is that he actually believed the end of the world was near and that he died in his fruitless attempt to usher in the eschatological kingdom of God. Schweitzer intimates that Jesus may have been psychologically deranged; hence his eschatological expectation and suicidal course of action. Schweitzer thus not only pronounced the final rites over the liberal Jesus, but he was instrumental in the rediscovery of the eschatological element in Jesus' preaching.

The net result of the old quest of the historical Jesus was the discovery of theology in even the earliest sources of the gospels. This meant that a biography of the human Jesus could not be written. The theology of the early church had so colored the documents that it was no longer possible to extract the Jesus of history from the Christ of faith.

DIALECTICAL AND EXISTENTIAL THEOLOGY

This conviction characterized theology during the first half of the twentieth century. For dialectical and existential theology, the Jesus of history receded into obscurity behind the Christ of faith. Karl Barth took almost no cognizance of NT criticism regarding Jesus. It is the Christ proclaimed by the church that encounters us today. The events of the gospels are *geschichtlich*, but not *historisch*, a distinction that could be rendered as *historic*, but not *historical*. That is to say, those events are of great importance for history and mankind, but they are not accessible to ordinary historical research like other events. Even though the later Barth wanted to place more emphasis on the historicity of the events of the gospels, he never succeeded in placing them in the ordinary world of space and time. What really mattered to him was not the historical Jesus, but the Christ of faith.

Similarly, Bultmann held that all that could be known about the historical Jesus could be written on a 4" x 6" index card,[1] but that this lack of information was inconsequential. Like Strauss, he held the gospel narratives to be mythologically colored throughout. And he, too, sought by demythologizing to find the central truth expressed in the myth. He turned, not to Hegel, but to Heidegger for the proper interpretation of the Christ-myth in terms of authentic existence in the face of death. It was this Christ-idea that was significant for human existence; as for the historical Jesus, the mere *"dass* seines Gekommenseins"—the *that* of his coming—that is to say, the mere fact of his existence, is enough.

THE NEW QUEST OF THE HISTORICAL JESUS

Some of Bultmann's disciples, however, such as Ernst Käsemann, could not agree with their master that the mere fact of Jesus' existence was enough to warrant our acceptance of the meaning of the Christ-idea as constitutive for our lives today. Unless there is some connection between the historical Jesus and the Christ of faith, then the latter reduces to pure myth, and the question remains why this myth should be thought to embody a truth that supplies the key to my existence. Thus, NT criticism heralded a "new quest for the historical Jesus," but this time considerably more cautious and modest than the old quest.

Those pursuing the new quest are painfully conscious of the presence of theology in the gospel narratives and are reluctant to ascribe to the historical Jesus any element that may be found in the theology of the early church. Indeed, James Robinson actually differentiates between the historical Jesus and the Jesus of history. The latter is the Jesus who really lived; the former is the Jesus that can be *proved* as a result of historical research. Robinson says the new quest concerns only the historical Jesus, not the Jesus of history. Moreover, Robinson believes that because of the presence of theology in the gospels, the burden of proof rests on the scholar who would ascribe some fact to the historical Jesus, not on the scholar who would deny that fact. In other words, we ought to presuppose that unless some putative feature of the historical Jesus can be proven to be authentic, we ought to regard it as inauthentic, as a product of Christian theology.

This attitude seems to underlie a great deal of NT criticism, although it has been sharply criticized.[2] For example, the only way in which the scholars involved in the much publicized Jesus Seminar of the Westar Institute can make the judgment that so much of the Jesus tradition in the gospels is doubtful or inauthentic would seem to be by presupposing an approach much like Robinson's.[3] Otherwise, the greatest percentage of the tradition would have to be classified under the unexciting but forthright label "cannot be proven authentic" (a category which the Seminar does not countenance). For almost all of the typical "criteria of authenticity" employed in such studies—such as dissimilarity to Christian teaching, multiple attestation, linguistic Semitisms, traces of Palestinian milieu, retention of embarrassing material, coherence with other authentic material, and so forth[4]—can only be properly used positively, to demonstrate authenticity; they cannot be legitimately employed negatively, to challenge authenticity—unless, that is, one is tacitly presupposing Robinson's principle that Jesus traditions are to be assumed to be inauthentic unless they are proven to be authentic.

More specifically, one of the more celebrated members of the Seminar, John Dominic Crossan, seems to presuppose Robinson's methodology in his work on the historical Jesus, entitled *The Historical Jesus: The Life of a Mediterranean Jewish Peasant* (1991). After sorting out Jesus traditions into various strata from early to late and determining the number of times a saying of Jesus is attested, Crossan chooses to "bracket the singularities"—that is, to leave out of account any saying only singly attested, even if it is found in the earliest, first stratum. The reason he gives for this procedure is that the saying could have been created by the source itself. Or again, he agrees that in theory a saying singly attested in the later, third stratum might be as original as a fivefold-attested saying in the first stratum. "But," he insists, "in terms of method, that is, of scholarly discipline and investigative integrity, study must begin with the first stratum."[5] Now what is the justification for this assertion? If, "in theory," a saying from the third stratum might be as much a part of the Jesus of history as one from the first, why is this not also possible in fact? Multiple or early attestation of a saying counts positively in favor of its authenticity, but the want of multiple or early attestation cannot be assumed to constitute strikes against authenticity—*unless* one is assuming that sayings are presumed to be inauthentic until proven authentic. Without this assumption there can be no grounds for thinking that the historical Jesus which Crossan reconstructs on the attenuated basis of his demonstrably authentic material alone, while bracketing or ignoring all other traditions about him which cannot be proven authentic, will not be but a pale shadow or lop-sided distortion of the real Jesus of history.

During the past generation the assumption enunciated by Robinson that Jesus traditions are to be ascribed to the theological activity of the early church unless they can be positively proven to have originated in Jesus' life and ministry took on the status of a sort of methodological dogma of critical scholarship. But increasingly this dogma has been called into question. Most scholars today would be reluctant to adopt such a methodological approach to the gospels, even given their theological coloring. The difficulty with the approach in question is that it assumes that history and theology are mutually exclusive categories, such that wherever theology is present in the gospels, that automatically precludes their historical accuracy. But what justification is there for this assumption? Some feature of the gospel portrait of Jesus, such as the dividing of his garments at the crucifixion or the piercing of Jesus' side, could be both historical and regarded by the evangelist as pregnant with theological significance. Since one cannot assume a *priori* that history and theology are mutually exclusive, the only way to justify that conclusion with respect to the gospels would be to carry out a historical examination of the gospels. But since such an investigation aims to discover whether the presence of theology in the gospels precludes their historical credibility, this examination cannot itself be based on the assumption that these categories are mutually exclusive in the gospels. Of course, Robinson would contend that such an examination was carried out in the first quest and yielded a negative verdict concerning the compatibility of history and theology in the gospels. But such an examination was far from conclusive. The Roman historian A. N. Sherwin-White has compared the gospels quite favorably with Roman history with respect to external confirmation of narrated events.[6] In the book of Acts, he asserts, the historicity of the narrative is indisputable.[7] Yet Acts is just as much propaganda as the gospels. Moreover, in the gospels wherever Jesus comes into the Jerusalem orbit, the external confirmation inevitably begins. Therefore, in Sherwin-White's judgment, the historical trustworthiness of the accounts of the Galilean ministry, which is by nature less susceptible to external confirmation, ought to be presumed. Thus, according to Sherwin-White's analysis, not only are the categories of history and theology not mutually exclusive, but the gospels enjoy such external confirmation that their trustworthiness ought to be presumed even in cases where specific confirmation is lacking. It can be safely concluded that the assumption that the gospels' status as theological documents precludes their also being historically reliable narratives has not been substantiated and that therefore the methodological principle of "inauthentic until proven authentic" is unfounded. The pursuit of such a methodology threatens to construct a theoretical and historical Jesus which is in fact very unlike the Jesus of history—in which case the whole enterprise becomes rather pointless.

Sharp-sighted critics have recognized that inability to prove some feature of the gospel portrait of Jesus to be authentic does not constitute sufficient grounds for rejecting it as a historical feature of the teaching of the Jesus of history. Therefore, to distinguish as Robinson does between the historical Jesus and the Jesus of history may be positively misleading. Most scholars are really after the Jesus of history and want to know what he claimed and taught. But in that case, it would be wrong to lay the burden of proof solely on the scholar who sees some authentic element in the Jesus of the gospels. At the very least, one ought to say that scholars claiming to prove *either* authenticity or inauthenticity must bear the burden of proof for their assertions.

A THIRD QUEST

In recent years some biblical scholars have spoken of a third quest of the historical Jesus, a quest which one observer has aptly characterized as "the Jewish reclamation of Jesus."[8] One has reference to a movement of increasing momentum among Jewish scholars studying the NT which assesses Jesus appreciatively and seeks to re-incorporate him as far as possible into the fold of Judaism. Spearheaded by the work of men like C. G. Montefiore (*The Synoptic Gospels*, 1909), Israel Abrahams (*Studies in Pharisaism and the Gospels*, 1917, 1929), and Joseph Klausner (*Jesus of Nazareth: His Life, Times, and Teaching*, 1922), the movement has swelled in recent years and includes among contemporary scholars Samuel Sandmel (*We Jews and Jesus*, 1965), Schalom Ben-Chorin (*Bruder Jesus: Der Nazarener in Jüdischer Sicht*, 1967,) David Flusser (*Jesus*, 1969), Pinchas Lapide (*Der Rabbi von Nazareth*, 1974), and, perhaps most significant, the Qumran scholar Geza Vermes (*Jesus the Jew*, 1973; *The Religion of Jesus the Jew*, 1993). A number of non-Jewish scholars have also devoted themselves to demonstrating the rightful interpretation of Jesus in the context of Jewish thought and culture, principally E. P. Sanders (*Jesus and Judaism*, 1985). Confluent with this movement is the Scandinavian school of thought headed by Birger Gerhardsson (*Memory and Manuscript*, 1961), which sees Rabbinic models of teaching and transmission of tradition as the key to understanding Jesus' teachings, and its extension by the German NT scholar Rainer Riesner (*Jesus als Lehrer*, 1981), who shows that memorization and recitation were commonly employed techniques in the home, synagogue, and elementary school, and finds many typical mnemonic aids in Jesus' teaching, which would facilitate its accurate preservation.

Jewish scholars have for the most part concentrated their attention on the ethical teachings of Jesus, with a view toward emphasizing his continuity, rather than rupture, with Judaism. The new questers' criteria of authenticity are generally eschewed, the gospels' record of Jesus' teaching being treated with much more trust, especially in light of its consonance with Jewish ethical teaching. But even the assimilation of this single facet of the historical Jesus, namely, Jesus as ethical teacher, to first-century Judaism has not been without its difficulties for Jewish scholars. Jesus' sense of personal authority to correct the Torah and contradict Jewish tradition goes down hard for faithful Jews. As Ben-Chorin admits, "The sense of the unique, absolute authority that is evident from this way of acting remains deeply problematic for the Jewish view of Jesus."[9] When Jewish scholars do consider the personal claims or self-understanding of Jesus, the majority conclude that Jesus did believe himself to be the Messiah, though, of course, they consider him to have been tragically deluded in this opinion.

Another interesting feature of contemporary scholarship's understanding of Jesus to which the third quest has contributed significantly is what one critic has called "the eclipse of mythology."[10] From Strauss through Bultmann, the category of myth was taken to be key to the gospel portrait of Jesus, and any historical reconstruction would have to proceed by means of "demythologizing" this portrait. Today, however, scarcely any scholar thinks of myth as an important interpretive category for the gospels. The Jewish reclamation of Jesus has helped to make unnecessary any understanding of the gospels' portrait as significantly shaped by mythology. Although contemporary scholars may be no more prepared to believe in the supernatural character of Jesus' miracles and exorcisms than were scholars of previous generations, they are no longer willing to ascribe such stories to the influence of Hellenistic divine man (*theios anēr*) myths;[11] rather Jesus' miracles and exorcisms are to be interpreted in the context of first century Jewish beliefs and practices. Vermes, for example, has drawn attention to the ministries of the charismatic miracle workers and/or exorcists Honi the Circle-Drawer (first century B.C.) and Hanina ben Dosa (first-century A.D.), and interprets Jesus of Nazareth as a Jewish *hasid* or holy man. In contrast to Schweitzer's assessment of the place of miracle with respect to the old quest, today the consensus of scholarship holds that miracle-working and exorcisms (bracketing the question of their supernatural character) most assuredly do belong to any historically acceptable reconstruction of Jesus' ministry.

ASSESSMENT

As we approach the end of the twentieth century after his death, Jesus of Nazareth, now as always, continues to exert his power of fascination over the minds of men and women. From sensational films and popular level speculations to scholarly debates in academic societies, journals, and monographs, Jesus is a matter of controversy. Who did this first-century Galilean take himself to be? A political or social revolutionary? A practitioner of magical arts? A Jewish rabbi or prophet? The Messiah? The Son of God?

DENIAL OF CHRIST'S DIVINE CLAIMS

A number of years ago a group of seven British theologians, headed by John Hick of the University of Birmingham, caused a great stir in the press and among laymen by publishing a book provocatively entitled *The Myth of God Incarnate*. In it they asserted that today the majority of NT scholars agree that the historical Jesus of Nazareth never claimed to be the Son of God or the Lord or the Messiah or indeed any of the divine titles that are attributed to Christ in the gospels. Rather, these titles developed later in the Christian Church and were written back into the traditions handed down about Jesus, so that in the gospels he appears to claim these divine titles for himself. But in fact, the real Jesus never said any such things at all. The idea of Jesus as divine was developed by the Christian church decades after Jesus himself was dead and buried. Thus, the divine Christ of the gospels who appears as God incarnate is a myth, and ought to be rejected.

In a sense this book was the first break in the dike separating theological academia and the man in the pew. As the authors of the book pointed out, the average layman is almost entirely unaware of what the professional theologians believe or say, and it was quite a shock for many people to learn that the majority of scholars no longer think that Jesus claimed to be the Son of God, and so forth. More recently, the results of the work of the Jesus Seminar on the authenticity of sayings attributed to Jesus has been trumpeted in the press. In their assessment, over 50% of Jesus' sayings are inauthentic, including his use of high Christological titles. So quite naturally many church-going laymen have been quite upset, since the work of such scholars seems to abet incredulity concerning Jesus' divinity.

In particular, these results play havoc with the popular apologetic based on the claims of Christ. According to popular apologetics, Jesus claimed to be God, and his claims were either true or false. If they were false, then either he was intentionally lying or else he was deluded. But neither of these alternatives is plausible. Therefore, his claims cannot be false; he must be who he claimed to be, God incarnate, and we must decide whether we shall give our lives to him or not. Now certainly the majority of scholars today would agree that Jesus was neither a liar nor a lunatic; but that does not mean they acknowledge him as Lord. Rather, as we have seen, most would say that the Jesus who claimed to be God is a legend, a theological product of the Christian Church. Thus, the dilemma posed by traditional apologetics is undercut, for Jesus himself never claimed to be God.

DEFENSE OF CHRIST'S DIVINE CLAIMS

What can be said in response to this critique? To begin with, one will have to admit that what has been alleged is, indeed, partly true: namely, it is true that the majority of NT scholars today do not believe that the historical Jesus ever claimed to be the Son of God, Lord, and so forth. Whether or not they have good reasons for their skepticism is another question.

The Christological Titles

Those who deny that Jesus made any extraordinary personal claims face the very severe problem of explaining how it is that the worship of Jesus as Lord and God came about at all in the early church. It does little good to say the early church wrote their beliefs about Jesus back into the gospels, for the problem is the very origin of those beliefs themselves. Studies by NT scholars such as Martin Hengel of Tübingen University, C. F. D. Moule of Cambridge, and others have proved that within twenty years of the crucifixion a full-blown Christology proclaiming Jesus as God incarnate existed. How does one explain this worship by monotheistic Jews of one of their countrymen as God incarnate, apart from the claims of Jesus himself? The great church historian Jaroslav Pelikan points out that all the early Christians shared the conviction that salvation was the work of a being no less than Lord of heaven and earth and that the redeemer was God himself. He observes that the oldest Christian sermon, the oldest account of a Christian martyr, the oldest pagan report of the Church, and the oldest liturgical prayer (1 Cor 16:22) all refer to Christ as Lord and God. He concludes, "Clearly it was the message of what the church believed and taught that 'God' was an appropriate name for Jesus Christ."[12] But if Jesus never made any such claims, then the belief of the earliest Christians in this regard becomes inexplicable.

For example, it seems to me very likely that Jesus did claim to be the Son of Man.[13] Most laymen think this title refers merely to Jesus' humanity, just as the title *Son of God* refers to his deity. But this fails to take into account the Jewish background of the term. In the book of Daniel, the Son of Man is a divine figure who will come at the end of the world to establish the kingdom of God and judge mankind (7:13-14). This was Jesus' favorite self-description and is the title found most frequently in the gospels (eighty times). Yet remarkably, this title is found only once outside the gospels in the rest of the NT. That shows that the designation of Jesus as "Son of Man" was not a title that arose in later Christian usage and was then read back into the gospels. There seems to be no good reason to deny that Jesus regarded himself as and called himself "the Son of Man."

Now some critics are willing to allow this, but they maintain that in calling himself "Son of Man" Jesus merely meant "a human person," just as the OT prophet Ezekiel referred to himself as "a son of man." But as C. F. D. Moule of Cambridge University points out, with Jesus there is a crucial difference. For Jesus did not refer to himself as "a son of man," like Ezekiel, but as "*the* Son of Man." Many critics have overlooked Jesus' constant use of the definite article with the title. By calling himself "*the* Son of Man," Jesus was directing attention to the divine end-time figure of Daniel 7. It may well be that Jesus preferred this title to "Messiah," because the latter title had become so overlaid with political and temporal considerations in Jewish thinking that to claim to be the Messiah would obscure rather than elucidate the true nature of his mission. By using the oblique, self-referential expression "the Son of Man," Gundry believes that Jesus prevented a prematurely transparent revelation of his superhuman and messianic dignity.

Implicit Christology

So, as I said, one might well question the skepticism of most critics with regard to the titles used by Christ in the gospels. But we may actually leave that aside for now. For the main point I want to make is that although it is true that most critics agree that Jesus did not use the Christological titles found in the gospels, that's only part of the story. For it is also true that most NT critics also agree that Jesus also made other claims about himself, claims that imply virtually the same thing as the titles. In other words, the titles only serve to express *explicitly* what Jesus had already said about himself *implicitly*.

That puts an entirely different face on the matter! Reading *The Myth of God Incarnate*, one would come away with the impression that Jesus thought of himself as a mere man, perhaps a prophet or teacher. But such an impression would be far from the truth. In fact, NT scholarship is agreed that Jesus regarded himself as much more than a mere man, a prophet, or a teacher. Let's therefore review some of the personal claims of Jesus widely accepted in NT scholarship, wholly apart from the question of Christological titles. Though I shall not restrict myself to it, what is remarkable is that the clues sufficient for a high Christological self-understanding of Jesus are present even in the attenuated 20% of Jesus' sayings recognized by the members of the Jesus Seminar as authentic.

1. *Jesus thought of himself as being the Son of God in a unique sense.* This may be seen in his prayer life. Jesus *always* prayed to God as "Abba," the word a Jewish child used for "Papa." For a Jew the very name of God was sacred, and no one would dare to pray to God in so familiar a manner. According to the German NT scholar Joachim Jeremias, "To date nobody has produced one single instance in Palestinian Judaism where God is

addressed as 'my Father' by an individual person. . . . Nowhere in the literature of the prayers of ancient Judaism . . . is this invocation of God as *Abba* to be found, neither in the liturgical nor in the informal prayers."[14] But Jesus always talked to his Father in such a way. It might be said that early Christians also prayed to God as "Abba," for example in Romans 8:15. But such a usage was derived from Jesus' own practice. And notice that although Jesus may have taught his disciples to pray to God as "Abba," he never joined with them in praying "*Our* Father . . ." On the contrary, he always referred to God as "My Father." This distinction leads to an odd circumlocution like John 20:17: "my Father and your Father . . . my God and your God." Jesus' prayer life thus shows that he thought of himself as God's Son in a unique sense that set him apart from the rest of the disciples.

Jesus' self-understanding as God's special Son also comes to expression in his parable of the wicked tenants of the vineyard (Mark 12:1-9). The presence of a non-allegorical version of this parable in Gospel of Thomas 65 has persuaded even skeptical scholars of the authenticity of the parable. In the apocryphal version the owner of the vineyard, after sending two servants to collect the harvest, sends his son, whom the tenants recognize as the heir and so murder him. One cannot delete the figure of the son from the parable as an inauthentic, later addition, for then the parable lacks any climax and point. But Jesus' use of such a parable discloses that he thought of himself as God's special Son, distinct from previous envoys to Israel, God's final messenger, and even the rightful heir to Israel.

Another remarkable indication of Jesus' sense of divine Sonship is his saying concerning the date of the consummation: "But of that day or that hour no one knows, not even the angels in heaven, nor the Son, but only the Father" (Mark 13:32). It seems highly unlikely that this saying could be the manufacture of Christian theology because it ascribes ignorance to the Son. The criterion of embarrassment (the retention of sayings awkward for Christian theology) requires the authenticity of the reference to the Son's ignorance. The saying discloses not only Jesus' sense of divine Sonship, but also presents us with an ascending scale of status from men to angels to the Son to the Father. Thus, amazingly, Jesus' sense of being God's Son involved a sense of proximity to the Father which transcended that of any mortal man (such as a king or prophet) or any angelic being.

Jesus' divine filial self-understanding is clearly expressed in the words of Jesus in Matthew 11:27: "All things have been delivered to me by my Father; and no one knows the Son, except the Father; and no one knows the Father except the Son and any one to whom the Son chooses to reveal him." There is good evidence to show that this is indeed a genuine word of Jesus: (a) it comes from the Q source that is shared by Matthew and Luke; (b) the idea of the mutual knowledge of Father and Son is a Jewish idea, indicating its origin in a Semitic-speaking milieu; (c) early church theology did not work out the Father-Son relationship, indicating that this verse is not the later product of Christian theology; and (d) the verse says the Son is unknowable, which is not true for the post-Easter Church. We *can* know the Son. This strongly implies a pre-Easter origin of the saying. Thus, there is good evidence that this verse records a genuine word of Jesus. But what does the saying tell us about Jesus' self-consciousness? It tells us that Jesus claimed to be the Son of God in an *exclusive* and *absolute* sense. Jesus says here that his relationship of sonship to God is unique. And he also claims to be the *only one* who can reveal the Father to men. In other words, Jesus claims to be the absolute revelation of God. Think of it! The historical Jesus of Nazareth claimed to be the absolute revelation of God himself. As Denaux has rightly emphasized, what we have here is a Johannine Christological affirmation in the earliest stratum of the gospel traditions, an affirmation which forms a bridge to the high Christology of John's gospel and yet, in light of passages like Mark 4:10-12; 12:1-11; 13:32; Matt 16:17-19; 28:18, is also at home in the Synoptic tradition.[15] On the basis of the authenticity of this saying, we may conclude that Jesus thought of himself as God's Son in an absolute and unique sense and as having been invested with the exclusive authority to reveal his Father God to men.

2. *Jesus claimed to act and speak with divine authority.* His personal sense of acting and speaking with the authority of God himself is evident in a number of ways.

First, his authority comes to expression in the content and style of his teaching. These two aspects of his teaching are especially evident in the Sermon on the Mount. The typical rabbinical style of teaching was to quote extensively from learned teachers, who provided the basis of authority for one's own teaching. But Jesus did exactly the opposite. He began, "You have heard that it was said to the men of old . . ." and quoted the Mosaic Law; then he continued, "But I say to you . . ." and gave his own teaching. Jesus thus equated his own authority with that of the divinely given Torah. It's no wonder that Matthew comments, "When Jesus finished these sayings, the crowds were astonished at his teaching, for he taught them as one who had authority, and not as their scribes" (Matt 7:28-29).

But it's not just that Jesus placed his personal authority on a par with that of the divine Law. More than that, he adjusted the Law on his own authority. Although Jewish scholars have attempted valiantly to assimilate

Jesus' ethical teachings to the tradition of Judaism, Jesus' opposition of his own personal authority to the divine Torah given through Moses is the rock upon which all such attempts are finally broken. Take, for example, Jesus' teaching on divorce in Matt 5:31-32 (cf. Mark 10:2-12). Here Jesus explicitly quotes the teaching of the Law (Deut 24:1-4) and opposes to it, on the basis of his own authority, his teaching on the matter. In the Markan passage, he declares that Moses does not represent the perfect will of God on this matter and presumes to correct the Law on his own authority as to what really is the will of God. But no human being, no prophet or teacher or charismatic, has that kind of authority. "Jesus," observes Witherington, "seems to assume an authority over Torah that no Pharisee or Old Testament prophet assumed—the authority to set it aside."[16]

In his provocative dialogue *A Rabbi Talks with Jesus*, the eminent Jewish scholar Jacob Neusner explains that it is precisely on this basis why he, as a Jew, would not have followed Jesus had he lived in first-century Palestine. Explaining that for a Jew the Torah is God's revelation to Moses, he asserts,

> Jews believe in the Torah of Moses . . . and that belief requires faithful Jews to enter a dissent at the teachings of Jesus, on the grounds that those teachings at important points contradict the Torah. . . .
>
> And therefore, because that specific teaching was so broadly out of phase with the Torah and covenant of Sinai, I could not then follow him and do not now either. That is not because I am stubborn or unbelieving. It is because I believe God has given a different Torah from the one that Jesus teaches; and that Torah, the one Moses got at Sinai, stands in judgment of the torah of Jesus, as it dictates true and false for all other torahs that people want to teach in God's name.[17]

Given the supremely authoritative status of the divinely revealed Torah, Jesus' teaching can only appear presumptuous and even blasphemous. In effect, as Robert Hutchinson put it, "Neusner wants to ask Jesus, 'Who do you think you are—God?'"[18] Neusner himself recognizes that "no one can encounter Matthew's Jesus without concurring that before us in the evangelist's mind is God incarnate."[19] But if Jesus' opposition of his personal teaching to the Torah is an authentic facet of the historical Jesus—as even the skeptical scholars of the Jesus Seminar concede—then it seems that Jesus did arrogate to himself the authority of God. According to Robert Guelich, "one must not shy away from the startling antithesis between *God has said to those of old / But I say to you* since here lies not only the key to the antithesis but to Jesus' ministry."[20]

Second, Jesus' use of "amēn" expresses his authority. The expression frequently attributed to Jesus, "Truly, truly I say to you," is historically unique and is recognized on all hands to have been used by Jesus to preface his teaching. It served to mark off his authoritative word on some subject, usually a statement about the inbreaking kingdom of God or about Jesus' own work. Ben Witherington in his acclaimed study of the Christology of Jesus explains the significance of Jesus' use of the phrase "Amen, I say to you":

> It is insufficient to compare it to "thus says the Lord," although that is the closest parallel. Jesus is not merely speaking for Yahweh, but for himself and on his own authority. . . . This strongly suggests that he considered himself to be a person of authority above and beyond what prophets claimed to be. He could attest to his own truthfulness and speak on his own behalf, and yet his words were to be taken as having the same or greater authority than the divine words of the prophets. Here was someone who thought he possessed not only divine inspiration . . . but also divine authority and the power of direct divine utterance. The use of *amen* followed by "I say unto you" must be given its full weight in light of its context—early Judaism.[21]

That Witherington's analysis is correct is evident from the complaint of the orthodox Jewish writer Ahad ha' Am: "Israel cannot accept with religious enthusiasm, as the Word of God, the utterances of a man who speaks in his own name—not 'thus saith the Lord,' but '*I* say unto you.' This 'I' is in itself sufficient to drive Judaism away from the Gentiles forever."[22]

Third, Jesus' authority is especially evident in his role as an exorcist. It may be an embarrassment to many modern theologians, but it is historically certain that Jesus believed he had the power to cast out demons.[23] This was a sign to people of his divine authority. He declared, "But if it is by the finger of God that I cast out demons, then the kingdom of God has come upon you" (Luke 11:20). This saying, which is recognized by NT scholarship as genuine, is remarkable for two reasons. First, it shows that Jesus claimed divine authority over the spiritual forces of evil. Second, it shows that Jesus believed that in himself the kingdom of God had come. According to Jewish thinking, the kingdom of God would come at the end of history when the Lord would reign over Israel and the nations. But Jesus was saying, "My ability to rule the spiritual forces of darkness shows that in me the kingdom of God is already present among you." As Ben Meyer explains in his study of Jesus' aims, "The exorcisms pointed beyond themselves to the dawning of God's reign! In terms of the history of religions, this gives an entirely distinctive profile to the exorcisms of Jesus. They become . . . *signs of the eschaton.*"[24] Jesus' exorcisms signaled that a new era was dawning and that Satan was being decisively cast out. More than that, however; for the advent of God's kingdom was inseparable from the advent of God himself, as Meyer explains:

> Dalman pointed out that in the targumic literature "the reign of God" appears as a reverential circumlocution for "God" (as ruler). Jeremias rightly finds this phenomenon in Jesus' idiom, as well, so that the words "the reign of God is near!" virtually mean "God is near"—at the door or already here![25]

In claiming that in himself the kingdom of God had already arrived, as visibly demonstrated by his exorcisms, Jesus was, in effect, saying that in himself God had drawn near, thus putting himself in God's place.

Finally, Jesus' sense of divine authority comes clearly to expression in his claim to forgive sins. Several of Jesus' parables, which are acknowledged on all hands to have been uttered by the historical Jesus, show that he assumed the prerogative to forgive sins. In parables like the prodigal son, the lost sheep, and so forth, Jesus describes persons who have wandered away from God and are lost in sin. In Jewish thought such a person was irretrievably lost and therefore given up as dead. But Jesus extended forgiveness to such persons and welcomed them back into the fold. The problem is that no one but God had the authority to make such a proclamation. No mere prophet could presume to speak for God on this matter. As Royce Gruenler puts it, Jesus "is consciously speaking as the voice of God on matters that belong only to God. . . . The evidence clearly leads us to affirm that Jesus implicitly claims to do what only God can do, to forgive sins. . . . The religious authorities correctly understood his claim to divine authority to forgive sinners, but they interpreted his claims as blasphemous and sought his execution."[26]

What Jesus taught in his parables, he acted out in real life. One of the most radical features of the historical Jesus was his practice of inviting prostitutes, toll collectors, and other outcasts into fellowship with him around the dinner table.[27] This was a living illustration of God's forgiveness of them and his invitation of them into fellowship in the kingdom of God. It's no wonder that the religious authorities saw this presumptuous activity as blasphemous and sought to have him crucified!

Thus, most NT critics acknowledge that the historical Jesus acted and spoke with a self-consciousness of divine authority and that furthermore, he saw in his own person the coming of the long-awaited kingdom of God and invited people into its fellowship.

3. *Jesus believed himself able to perform miracles.* In a saying widely

acknowledged as authentic, Jesus said to the disciples of John the Baptist, "Go and tell John what you hear and see: the blind receive their sight and the lame walk, lepers are cleansed and the deaf hear, and the dead are raised up, and the poor have good news preached to them" (Matt 11:4-5). James D. G. Dunn, a British NT scholar, comments: "Whatever the 'facts' were, Jesus evidently believed that he had cured cases of blindness, lameness, and deafness—indeed there is no reason to doubt that he believed lepers had been cured under his ministry and dead restored to life."[28]

Moreover, the miracle stories are so widely represented in all strata of the gospel traditions that it would be fatuous to regard them as not rooted in the life of Jesus. Thus, Wolfgang Trilling, a German NT scholar, reports that the consensus of NT scholarship agrees that Jesus did perform "miracles"—however one might want to interpret or explain these. According to Trilling, there is no doubt that Jesus performed the sort of miraculous acts ascribed to him in the gospels. Therefore, it is certain that Jesus at least thought he had the power to perform miracles; and in that the majority of NT critics agree.

The miracles of Jesus take on a Christological significance in light of the fact that they, like his exorcisms, were taken to be signs of the in-breaking of the kingdom of God. This is the sense of Jesus' allusion to Isaiah 35:5-6; 61:1 above.[29] As such, they functioned fundamentally differently from the wonders performed by Hellenistic magicians or Jewish holy men. Moreover, Jesus' miracles differed from those of his compatriots Honi and Hanina in that Jesus rarely prays for a miracle to be done; he simply effects it himself. And he does so in his own name, not God's. Moreover, neither Honi nor Hanina carried out a prophetic ministry, made messianic claims, or brought any new teaching in conjunction with their miracles. Thus, Jesus' self-understanding cannot be reduced simply to that of another charismatic Jewish holy man.

This is remarkable enough in itself; but there is more. For Jesus' claim to be able to heal miraculously all diseases and infirmities also contains an implicit claim to divinity. As Howard Kee, a NT scholar from Boston University who has specialized in the study of the gospel miracles, explains, for OT Judaism God is the one who heals all Israel's diseases. In this light, Jesus' claim to heal miraculously, without use of any medical means, takes on a new significance: Jesus in effect takes God's place as the healer of Israel.[30] No doctors or medicine are necessary for him—he heals as God heals. Jesus thus assumes the place of God in the OT. So his claim to perform miracles is not only amazing in itself, but actually has a deeper significance in implying that Jesus is in fact God.

4. *Jesus claimed to determine people's eternal destiny before God.* Jesus held

that people's attitudes toward himself would be the determining factor in God's judgment on the judgment day. He proclaimed, "I tell you, every one who acknowledges me before men, the Son of man also will acknowledge before the angels of God; but he who denies me before men will be denied before the angels of God" (Luke 12:8-9).[31] I have no doubt that in this passage Jesus is referring to himself as the Son of Man, not referring to some third figure besides himself. But be that as it may, the point is that whoever the Son of Man may be, Jesus is claiming that people will be judged before him on the basis of their response to Jesus. Think of it: people's eternal destiny is fixed on their response to Jesus. Make no mistake: if Jesus were not the divine Son of God, then this claim could only be regarded as the most narrow and objectionable dogmatism. For Jesus is saying that people's salvation depends on their confession to Jesus himself.

CONCLUSION

A discussion of Jesus' personal claims could go on and on. According to Witherington, any adequate theory of Jesus' self-understanding must be able to explain the following thirteen established features of the historical Jesus:

1. His independent approach to the Law
2. His feeding of the 5,000
3. His interpretation of his miracles
4. His proclamation of the kingdom of God as present and inbreaking in his ministry
5. His choosing of 12 disciples
6. His use of "the Son of Man"
7. His use of "amen"
8. His use of "abba"
9. His distinguishing himself from his contemporaries, including John the Baptist, the Pharisees, Jewish revolutionaries, and the disciples
10. His belief that one's future standing with God hinged on how one reacted to his ministry
11. His understanding that his death was necessary to rectify matters between God and His people
12. His sense of mission to the whole of Israel, especially to sinners and outcasts, which led to table fellowship with such people
13. His raising messianic expectations in a repeated pattern of controversy with his contemporaries.[32]

Although we have not discussed all these matters, enough has been said, I think, to indicate the radical self-concept of Jesus. Here is a man who thought of himself as the Son of God in a unique sense, who claimed to act and speak with divine authority, who held himself to be a worker of miracles, and who believed that people's eternal destiny hinged on whether or not they believed in him. Gruenler sums it up: "It is a striking fact of modern New Testament research that the essential clues for correctly reading the implicit christological self-understanding of Jesus are abundantly clear." There is, he concludes, "absolutely convincing evidence" that Jesus did intend to stand in the very place of God himself.[33] So extraordinary was the person who Jesus thought himself to be that Dunn at the end of his study of the self-consciousness of Jesus feels compelled to remark, "One last question cannot be ignored: Was Jesus mad?"[34] Dunn rejects the hypothesis that Jesus was insane because it cannot account for the full portrait of Jesus that we have in the gospels. The balance and soundness of Jesus' whole life and teachings make it evident that he was no lunatic. But notice that by means of these claims of Jesus, wholly apart from the disputed question of Christological titles and on the basis of sayings accepted as authentic by the majority of scholars, we are brought back around again to the same dilemma posed by the traditional apologetic: if Jesus was not who he claimed to be, then he was either a charlatan or a madman, neither of which is plausible. Therefore, why not accept him as the divine Son of God, just as the earliest Christians did?

Horst Georg Pöhlmann in his *Abriss der Dogmatik* reports, "In summary, one could say that today there is virtually a consensus concerning that wherein the historical in Jesus is to be seen. It consists in the fact that Jesus came on the scene with an *unheard of authority*, namely with the authority of God, with the *claim of the authority to stand in God's place and speak to us and bring us to salvation.*"[35] This involves, says Pöhlmann, an implicit Christology. He concludes:

> This unheard of claim to authority, as it comes to expression in the antitheses of the Sermon on the Mount, for example, is implicit Christology, since it presupposes a unity of Jesus with God that is deeper than that of all men, namely a unity of essence. This . . . claim to authority is explicable only from the side of his deity. This authority only God himself can claim. With regard to Jesus there are only two possible modes of behavior: either to believe that in him God encounters us or to nail him to the cross as a blasphemer. *Tertium non datur.*[36]

There is no third way.

PRACTICAL APPLICATION

It is to me intellectually gratifying to see how modern NT criticism has actually served to support rather than undermine a high view of Christ. The refusal of radical critics to draw the obvious Christological implications of unquestionably authentic sayings of Jesus is due not to lack of historical evidence but to their personal anti-metaphysical and, quite frankly, anti-Chalcedonian prejudices. The evidence thus vindicates the approach of the traditional apologetic.

But here a word of caution would be in order. Often one hears people say, "I don't understand all those philosophical arguments for God's existence and so forth. I prefer historical apologetics." I suspect that those who say this think that historical apologetics are easy and will enable them to avoid the hard thinking involved in the philosophical arguments. But this section ought to teach us clearly that this is not so. It is naive and outdated to simply trot out the dilemma "Liar, Lunatic, or Lord" and adduce several proof texts where Jesus claims to be the Son of God, the Messiah, and so forth. The publicity generated by the Jesus Seminar has rendered that approach forever obsolete. Rather, if an apologetic based on the claims of Christ is to work, we must do the requisite spadework of sorting out those claims of Jesus that can be established as authentic, and then drawing out their implications. This will involve not only mastering Greek but also the methods of modern criticism and the criteria of authenticity. Far from being easy, historical apologetics, if done right, is every bit as difficult as philosophical apologetics. The only reason most people think historical apologetics to be easier is because they do it superficially. But, of course, one can do philosophical apologetics superficially, too! My point is that if we are to do a credible job in our apologetics, we need to do the hard thinking and the hard work required, or at least to rely on those who have.

Now in applying this material in evangelism, I think it is often more effective when used defensively than offensively. That is to say, if the unbeliever says Jesus was just a good man or religious teacher, then confront him with Christ's claims. Used offensively to convince someone that Jesus was divine, this apologetic can be derouted on the popular level. Many people will say Jesus was a man from outer space, and the more you argue with them the more they become entrenched in this position. Of course, such a view is hopelessly insane, so that, oddly enough, this apologetic is probably more effective on the scholarly level than on the popular.

I think that a more effective approach is to argue that Jesus' claims provide the religio-historical context in which the resurrection becomes significant, as it confirms those claims. Of course, the non-Christian might still say Jesus was from outer space and came back to life like E.T., in which case the most effective strategy is not to argue with him at all, but just point out that no scholar believes such a thing. If you argue with him, this gives the impression that his view is worth refuting and therefore has some credibility, which it does not. So simply brush it aside, and it is to be hoped that the unbeliever, not wishing to feel intellectually isolated, will not take it too seriously either. Taken in conjunction with evidence for the resurrection—and one might add, with the evidence for Jesus' miracles and with fulfilled prophecy, which I have not discussed—the radical claims of Jesus become a powerful apologetic for the Christian faith.

CHAPTER EIGHT

The Resurrection of Jesus

GOD AND IMMORTALITY: those were the two conditions we saw to be necessary if man is to have a meaningful existence. I have argued that God exists, and now we have come at length to the second consideration, immortality. Against the dark background of modern man's despair, the Christian proclamation of the resurrection is a bright light of hope. The earliest Christians saw Jesus' resurrection as both the vindication of his personal claims and as the harbinger of our own resurrection to eternal life. If Jesus rose from the dead, then his claims are vindicated and our Christian hope is sure; if Jesus did not rise, our faith is futile and we fall back into despair. How credible, then, is the NT witness to the resurrection of Jesus?

HISTORICAL BACKGROUND

The historical apologetic for the resurrection played a central role in the case of the Christian apologists during the Deist controversy. A review of their arguments and of the reasons for the decline of this form of apologetics will be useful in preparing the way for a modern assessment of the resurrection. Too often Christians today employ an apologetic for the resurrection that was suitable for use against eighteenth-century opponents but is today ineffective in dealing with the objections raised by modern biblical criticism.

THE CASE FOR THE RESURRECTION IN THE TRADITIONAL APOLOGETIC

The traditional apologetic may be summarized in three steps.

The Gospels Are Authentic

The point of this step in the argument was to defend the apostolic authorship of the gospels. The reasoning was that if the gospels were actually written by the disciples, then quite simply they were either true accounts or they were lies. Since the Deists granted the apostolic authorship of the gospels, they were reduced to defending the implausible position that the gospels were an issue of deliberate falsehoods. In order to demonstrate the authenticity of the gospels, Jacob Vernet (whom we met in chapter 4) appeals to both internal and external evidence.

Internal Evidence

Under internal evidence, Vernet notes that the style of writing in the gospels is simple and alive, what we would expect from their traditionally accepted authors. Moreover, since Luke was written before Acts, and since Acts was written prior to the death of Paul, Luke must have an early date, which speaks for its authenticity. The gospels also show an intimate knowledge of Jerusalem prior to its destruction in A.D. 70. Jesus' prophecies of that event must have been written prior to Jerusalem's fall, for otherwise the church would have separated out the apocalyptic element in the prophecies, which makes them appear to concern the end of the world. Since the end of the world did not come about when Jerusalem was destroyed, so-called prophecies of its destruction that were really written after the city was destroyed would not have made that event appear so closely connected with the end of the world. Hence, the gospels must have been written prior to A.D. 70. Further, the gospels are full of proper names, dates, cultural details, historical events, and customs and opinions of that time. The stories of Jesus' human weaknesses and of the disciples' faults also bespeak the gospels' accuracy. Furthermore, it would have been impossible for forgers to put together so consistent a narrative as that which we find in the gospels. The gospels do not try to suppress apparent discrepancies, which indicates their originality. There is no attempt at harmonization between the gospels, such as we might expect from forgers. Finally, the style of each particular gospel is appropriate to what we know of the personalities of the traditional authors.

Gottfried Less adds to Vernet's case the further point that the gospels do not contain anachronisms; the authors appear to have been first-century Jews who were witnesses of the events. William Paley adds a final consideration: the Hebraic and Syriac idioms that mark the gospels are appropriate to the traditional authors. He concludes that there is no more reason to doubt that the gospels come from the traditional authors than there is to doubt that the works of Philo or Josephus are authentic, *except* that the gospels contain supernatural events.

External Evidence

Turning next to the external evidence for the gospels' authenticity, Vernet argues that the disciples must have left some writings, engaged as they were in giving lessons to and counseling believers who were geographically distant. And what could these writings be if not the gospels and epistles themselves? Similarly, Paley reasons that eventually the apostles would have needed to publish accurate narratives of Jesus' history, so that any spurious attempts would be discredited and the genuine gospels preserved. Moreover, Vernet continues, there were many eyewitnesses who were still alive when the books were written who could testify whether they came from their purported authors or not. Most importantly, the extra-biblical testimony unanimously attributes the gospels to their traditional authors.

No finer presentation of this point can be found than Paley's extensive eleven-point argument. First, the gospels and Acts are cited by a series of authors, beginning with those contemporary with the apostles and continuing in regular and close succession. This is the strongest form of historical testimony, regularly employed to establish authorship of secular works; and when this test is applied to the gospels, their authenticity is unquestionably established. Paley traces this chain of testimony from the Epistle of Barnabas, the Epistle of Clement, and the Shepherd of Hermas all the way up to Eusebius in A.D. 315. Less presents similar evidence, and concludes that there is better testimony for the authenticity of the NT books than for *any* classical work of antiquity.

Second, the Scriptures were quoted as authoritative and as one-of-a-kind. As proof Paley cites Theophilus, the writer against Artemon, Hippolitus, Origen, and many others.

Third, the Scriptures were collected very early into a distinct volume. Ignatius refers to collections known as the Gospel and the Apostles, what we today call the gospels and the epistles. According to Eusebius, about sixty years after the appearance of the gospels Quadratus distributed them to converts during his travels. Irenaeus and Melito refer to the collection of writings we call the NT.

Fourth, these writings were given titles of respect. Polycarp, Justin Martyr, Dionysius, Irenaeus, and others refer to them as Scriptures, divine writings, and so forth.

Fifth, these writings were publicly read and expounded. Citations from Justin Martyr, Tertullian, Origen, and Cyprian go to prove the point.

Sixth, copies, commentaries, and harmonies were written on these books. Noteworthy in this connection is Tatian's *Diatessaron*, a harmony of the four gospels, from about A.D. 170. With the single exception of Clement's commentary on the Revelation of Peter, Paley emphasizes, no commentary was ever written during the first 300 years after Christ on any book outside the NT.

Seventh, the Scriptures were accepted by all heretical groups as well as by orthodox Christians. Examples include the Valentinians, the Carpocratians, and many others.

Eighth, the gospels, Acts, thirteen letters of Paul, 1 John, and 1 Peter were received without doubt as authentic even by those who doubted the authenticity of other books now in the canon. Caius about A.D. 200 reckoned up about thirteen of Paul's letters, but insisted that Hebrews was not written by Paul. About twenty years later Origen cites Hebrews to prove a particular point, but noting that some might dispute the authority of Hebrews, he states that his point may be proved from the undisputed books of Scripture and quotes Matthew and Acts. Though he expresses doubt about some books, Origen reports that the four gospels alone were received without dispute by the whole Church of God under heaven.

Ninth, the early opponents of Christianity regarded the gospels as containing the accounts upon which the religion was founded. Celsus admitted that the gospels were written by the disciples. Porphyry attacked Christianity as found in the gospels. The Emperor Julian followed the same procedure.

Tenth, catalogues of authentic Scriptures were published, which always contained the gospels and Acts. Paley supports the point with quotations from Origen, Athanasius, Cyril, and others.

Eleventh, the so-called apocryphal books of the NT were never so treated. It is a simple fact, asserts Paley, that with a single exception, no apocryphal gospel is ever even quoted by any known author during the first three hundred years after Christ. In fact, there is no evidence that any inauthentic gospel whatever existed in the first century, in which all four gospels and Acts were written. The apocryphal gospels were never quoted, were not read in Christian assemblies, were not collected into a volume, were not listed in the catalogues, were not noticed by Christianity's adversaries, were not appealed to by heretics, and were not the subject of commentaries or collations, but were nearly universally rejected by Christian writers of succeeding ages.

Therefore, Paley concludes, the external evidence strongly confirms the authenticity of the gospels. Even if it should be the case that the names of the authors traditionally ascribed to the gospels are mistaken, it still could not be denied that the gospels do contain the story that the original apostles proclaimed and for which they labored and suffered.

Taken together, then, the internal and external evidence adduced by the Christian apologists served to establish the first step of their case, that the gospels are authentic.

The Text of the Gospels Is Pure

The second step often taken by the Christian thinkers was to argue that the text of the gospels is pure. This step was important to ensure that the gospels we have today are the same gospels as originally written.

Vernet, in support of the textual purity of the gospels, points out that because of the need for instruction and personal devotion, these writings must have been copied many times, which increases the chances of preserving the original text. In fact, no other ancient work is available in so many copies and languages, and yet all these various versions agree in content. The text has also remained unmarred by heretical additions. The abundance of manuscripts over a wide geographical distribution demonstrates that the text has been transmitted with only trifling discrepancies. The differences that do exist are quite minor and are the result of unintentional mistakes. The text of the NT is every bit as good as the text of the classical works of antiquity.

To these considerations, Less adds that the quotations of the NT books in the early church Fathers all coincide. Moreover, the gospels could not have been corrupted without a great outcry on the part of orthodox Christians. Against the idea that there could have been a deliberate falsifying of the text, Abbé Houtteville argues that no one could have corrupted all the manuscripts. Moreover, there is no precise time when the falsification could have occurred, since, as we have seen, the NT books are cited by the Church Fathers in regular and close succession. The text could not have been falsified before all external testimony, since then the apostles were still alive and could repudiate any such tampering with the gospels. In conclusion, Vernet charges that to repudiate the textual purity of the gospels would be to reverse all the rules of criticism and to reject all the works of antiquity, since the text of those works is less certain than that of the gospels.

The Gospels Are Reliable

Having demonstrated that the gospels are authentic and that the text of the gospels is pure, the Christian thinkers were now in a position to argue that the gospels are historically reliable. Their argument basically boiled down to a dilemma: if the gospel accounts of Jesus' miracles and resurrection are false, then the apostles were either deceivers or deceived. Since both of these alternatives are implausible, it follows that the gospel accounts must be true.

Apostles Neither Deceivers Nor Deceived

Let's turn first to the arguments presented against the second horn of the dilemma: that the apostles were deceived. This alternative embraces any hypothesis holding that Jesus did not rise from the dead, but that the disciples sincerely believed he had.

Humphrey Ditton in his *Discourse Concerning the Resurrection of Jesus Christ* (1712) argues that the apostles could not have been mistaken about the resurrection. In the first place, the witnesses to the appearances were well qualified. There were a great many witnesses, and they had personal knowledge of the facts over an extended period of forty days. It is unreasonable, therefore, to ascribe their experience to imagination or dreaming. Moreover, the disciples were not religious enthusiasts, as is evident from their cool and balanced behavior even in extreme situations. Thomas Sherlock responds to the charge that the evidence for the resurrection consists of the testimony of silly women by pointing out that they, too, had eyes and ears to report accurately what they experienced; and far from being gullible, they were actually disbelieving. He observes also that the women were never in fact used as witnesses to the resurrection in the apostolic preaching. Finally, he adds, the testimony of the men is none the worse off for having the testimony of the women as well. (This exchange obviously took place before the days of feminist consciousness!)

Paley answers the allegation that the resurrection appearances were the result of "religious enthusiasm" (that is, were hallucinations) by arguing that the theory fails on several counts. First, not just one person but many saw Christ appear. Second, they saw him not individually but together. Third, they saw him appear not just once, but several times. Fourth, they not only saw him, but touched him, conversed with him, and ate with him. Fifth and decisively, the religious enthusiasm hypothesis fails to explain the non-production of the body. It would have been impossible for Jesus' disciples to have believed in their master's resurrection if his corpse still lay in the tomb. But it is equally incredible to suppose that the disciples could have stolen the body and perpetrated a hoax. Furthermore, it would have been impossible for Christianity to come into being in Jerusalem if Jesus' body were still in the grave. The Jewish authorities would certainly have produced it as the shortest and completest answer to the whole affair. But all they could do was claim that the disciples had stolen the body. Thus, the hypothesis of religious enthusiasm, in failing to explain the absence of

Jesus' corpse, ultimately collapses back into the hypothesis of conspiracy and deceit, which, Paley remarks, has pretty much been given up in view of the evident sincerity of the apostles, as well as their character and the dangers they underwent in proclaiming the truth of Jesus' resurrection.

With Paley's last remark, we return to the first horn of the dilemma: that the disciples were deceivers. This alternative encompasses any hypothesis holding that the disciples knew that the miracles and resurrection of Jesus did not take place, but that they nevertheless claimed that they did.

One of the most popular arguments against this theory is the obvious sincerity of the disciples as attested by their suffering and death. No more eloquent statement of the argument can be found than Paley's: he seeks to show that the original witnesses of the miraculous events of the gospels passed their lives in labors, dangers, and sufferings, voluntarily undertaken in attestation to and as a consequence of the accounts which they delivered.

Paley argues first from the general nature of the case. We know that the Christian religion exists. Either it was founded by Jesus and the apostles or by others, the first being silent. The second alternative is quite incredible. If the disciples had not zealously followed up what Jesus had started, Christianity would have died at its birth. If this is so, then a life of missionary sacrifice must have been necessary for those first apostles. Such a life is not without its own enjoyments, but they are only such as spring from sincerity. With a consciousness at bottom of hollowness and falsehood, the fatigue and strain would have become unbearable.

There was probably difficulty and danger involved in the propagation of a new religion. With regard to the Jews, the notion of Jesus' being the Messiah was contrary to Jewish hopes and expectations; Christianity lowered the esteem of Jewish law; and the disciples would have had to reproach the Jewish leaders as guilty of an execution that could only be represented as an unjust and cruel murder. As to the Romans, they could have understood the kingdom of God only in terms of an earthly kingdom—thus, a rival. And concerning the heathen, Christianity admitted no other god or worship. Although the philosophers allowed and even enjoined worship of state deities, Christianity could countenance no such accommodation. Thus, even in the absence of a general program of persecution, there were probably random outbursts of violence against Christians. The heathen religions were old and established and not easily overthrown. Those religions were generally regarded by the common people as equally true, by the philosophers as equally false, and by the magistrates as equally useful. From none of these sides could the Christians expect protection. Finally, the nature of the case requires that these early apostles must have experienced a great change in their lives, now involved as they were in preaching, prayer, religious meetings, and so forth.

What the nature of the case would seem to require is in fact confirmed by history. Writing seventy years after Jesus' death, Tacitus narrates Nero's persecution about thirty years after Christ, how the Christians were clothed in the skins of wild beasts and thrown to dogs, how others were smeared with pitch and used as human torches to illuminate the night while Nero rode about in the dress of a charioteer, viewing the spectacle. The testimonies of Suetonius and Juvenal confirm the fact that within thirty-one years after Jesus' death, Christians were dying for their faith. From the writings of Pliny the Younger, Martial, Epictetus, and Marcus Aurelius, it is clear that believers were voluntarily submitting to torture and death rather than renounce their religion. This suffering is abundantly attested in Christian writings as well. Christ had been killed for what he said; the apostles could expect the same treatment. Jesus' predictions in the gospels of sufferings for his followers were either real predictions come true or were put into his mouth because persecution had in fact come about. In Acts, the sufferings of Christians are soberly reported without extravagance. The epistles abound with references to persecutions and exhortations to steadfastness. In the early writings of Clement, Hermas, Polycarp, and Ignatius, we find the sufferings of the early believers historically confirmed.

It is equally clear that it was for a *miraculous* story that these Christians were suffering. After all, the only thing that could convince these early Christians that Jesus was the Messiah was that they *thought* there was something supernatural about him. The gospels are a miraculous story, and we have no other story handed down to us than that contained in the gospels. Josephus's much disputed testimony can only confirm, not contradict, the gospel accounts. The letters of Barnabas and Clement refer to Jesus' miracles and resurrection. Polycarp mentions the resurrection of Christ, and Irenaeus relates that he had heard Polycarp tell of Jesus' miracles. Ignatius speaks of the resurrection. Quadratus reports that persons were still living who had been healed by Jesus. Justin Martyr mentions the miracles of Christ. No relic of a non-miraculous story exists. That the original story should be lost and replaced by another goes beyond any known example of corruption of even oral tradition, not to speak of the experience of written transmissions.

These facts show that the story in the gospels was in substance the same story that Christians had at the beginning. That means, for example, that the resurrection of Jesus was always a part of this story. Were we to stop here, remarks Paley, we have a circumstance unparalleled in history: that in the reign of Tiberius Caesar a certain number of persons set about establishing a new religion, in the propagation of which they voluntarily submitted to great dangers, sufferings, and labors, all for a miraculous story which they proclaimed wherever they went, and that the resurrection of a dead man, whom they had accompanied during his lifetime, was an integral part of this story.

Since it has been already abundantly proved that the accounts of the gospels do stem from their apostolic authors, Paley concludes, then the story must be true. For the apostles could not be deceivers. He asks:

> Would men in such circumstances pretend to have seen what they never saw; assert facts which they had not knowledge of, go about lying to teach virtue; and, though not only convinced of Christ's being an imposter, but having seen the success of his imposture in his crucifixion, yet persist in carrying on; and so persist, as to bring upon themselves, for nothing, and with full knowledge of the consequence, enmity and hatred, danger and death?[1]

The question is merely rhetorical, for the absurdity of the hypothesis of deceit is all too clear.

A second popular argument against the disciples' being deceivers was that their character precludes their being liars. Humphrey Ditton observes that the apostles were simple, common men, not cunning deceivers. They were men of unquestioned moral integrity and their proclamation of the resurrection was solemn and devout. They had absolutely nothing to gain in worldly terms in preaching this doctrine. Moreover, they had been raised in a religion that was vastly different from the one they preached. Especially foreign to them was the idea of the death and resurrection of the Jewish Messiah. This militates against their concocting this idea. The Jewish laws against deceit and false testimony were very severe, which fact would act as a deterrent to fraud. Finally, they were evidently sincere in what they proclaimed. In light of their character so described, asks Ditton bluntly, *why not believe the testimony of these men?*

A third argument pressed by the apologists was that the notion of a conspiracy is ridiculous. Vernet thinks it inconceivable that one of the disciples should suggest to the others that they say Jesus was risen when both he and they knew the precise opposite to be true. How could he possibly rally his bewildered colleagues into so detestable a project? And are we then to believe that these men would stand before judges declaring the truth of this product of their imaginations? Houtteville asserts that a conspiracy to fake the resurrection would have had to have been of such unmanageable proportions that the disciples could never have carried it off. Ditton points out that had there been a conspiracy, it would certainly have been unearthed by the disciples' adversaries, who had both the interest and the power to expose any fraud. Common experience shows that such intrigues are inevitably exposed even in cases where the chances of discovery are much less than in the case of the resurrection.

Yet a fourth argument, urged by Less, was that the gospels were written in such temporal and geographical proximity to the events they record that it would have been almost impossible to fabricate events. Anyone who cared to could have checked out the accuracy of what they reported. The fact that the disciples were able to proclaim the resurrection in Jerusalem in the face of their enemies a few weeks after the crucifixion shows that what they proclaimed was true, for they could never have proclaimed the resurrection under such circumstances had it not occurred.

Fifth, the theft of the body from the tomb by the disciples would have been impossible. Ditton argues that the story of the guard at the tomb is plausible, since the Jews had the ability and motivation to guard the tomb. But in this case, the disciples could not have stolen the body on account of the armed guard. The allegation that the guards had fallen asleep is ridiculous, because in that case they could not have known that it was the disciples who had taken the corpse. Besides, adds Houtteville, no one could have broken into the tomb without waking the guard.

Sixth, even the enemies of Christianity acknowledged Jesus' resurrection. The Jews did not publicly deny the disciples' charge that the authorities had bribed the guard to keep silent. Had the charge been false, they would have openly denounced it. Thus, the enemies of Christianity themselves bore witness to the resurrection.

Seventh and finally, the dramatic change in the disciples shows that they were absolutely convinced Jesus had risen from the dead. They went from the depths of despair and doubt to a joyful certainty of such height that they preached the resurrection openly and boldly and suffered bravely for it.

Thus, the hypothesis of deceit is just as implausible as the hypothesis that the apostles had been deceived. But since neither of these alternatives is reasonable, the conclusion can only be that they were telling the truth and that Jesus rose from the dead.

The Origin of Christianity Proves the Resurrection

In addition to this fundamental dilemma, the Christian apologists also refurbished the old argument from the origin of the church. Suppose, Vernet suggests, that no resurrection or miracles occurred: how then could a dozen men, poor, coarse, and apprehensive, turn the world upside down? If Jesus did not rise from the dead, declares Ditton, then either we must believe that a small, unlearned band of deceivers overcame the powers of the world and preached an incredible doctrine over the face of the whole earth, which in turn received this fiction as the sacred truth of God; or else, if they were not deceivers, but enthusiasts, we must believe that these extremists, carried along by the impetus of extravagant fancy, managed to spread a falsity that not only common folk, but statesmen and philosophers as well, embraced as the sober truth. Because such a scenario is simply unbelievable, the message of the apostles, which gave birth to Christianity, must be true.

THE DECLINE OF HISTORICAL APOLOGETICS

Paley's *View of the Evidences* (1794) constituted the high-water mark of the historical apologetic for the resurrection. During the nineteenth century this approach dramatically receded. Indeed, it would be difficult to find a significant and influential thinker defending the Christian faith on the basis of the evidence for the resurrection. It seems to me that there were two factors that served to undermine the traditional apologetic.

Advance of Biblical Criticism

The first of those was the advance of biblical criticism. In England the Deist controversy subsided, in France it was cut short by the Revolution, but in Germany it was taken up into a higher plane. There is a direct link between Deism and the advance in biblical criticism that began in Germany in the late eighteenth century.

The flood of Deist thought and literature that poured into eighteenth century Germany from England and France wrought a crisis in German orthodox theology. That theology had been characterized by an extremely rigid doctrine of biblical inspiration and infallibility and by a devotional pietism. The critique of the Deists undermined the faith of many in the inerrancy of Scripture, but their piety would not allow them to join themselves to the Deist camp and reject Christianity. This group of scholars, generally called Rationalists, therefore sought to resolve the crisis by forging a new way between orthodoxy and Deism; namely, they loosed the religious meaning of a text from the historicity of the events described therein. The historical events were only the form, the husk, in which some spiritual, trans-historical truth was embodied. What was of importance was the substance, the kernel, not the mere external trappings. In this way, the Rationalists could accept the Deist critique of miracles but at the same time retain the spiritual truth expressed in these stories. With regard to the resurrection we have seen that many Rationalists adopted some form of the apparent death theory to explain away the resurrection; but for most it still retained its spiritual significance and truth.

The Rationalists thus sought a middle ground between the Deists and the supernaturalists. The Deists and supernaturalists agreed that if the events of the gospels did not in fact occur, then Christianity was false. But the Rationalists, while holding with the Deists that the events never occurred, nevertheless held with the supernaturalists that Christianity was true. Let's take a look at two of the principal figures in this radical new direction.

Herrmann Samuel Reimarus, a professor of oriental languages at Hamburg, struggled privately with gnawing doubts about the truth of the biblical revelation. From 1730-1768 he wrote them down, and his writing evolved into an enormous 4,000-page critique of the Bible. He was troubled by the many contradictions he found in the Bible and could not accept the stories of the Flood, the crossing of the Red Sea, and the resurrection of Jesus. He denied miracles and came to accept a Deistic natural religion. Nevertheless, he never published his opinions but only showed his manuscript to a few close friends and two of his children. After his death, Reimarus's daughter gave the manuscript to Gottfried Lessing, who became librarian in Wolfenbüttel. In 1774 Lessing began to publish excerpts from the manuscript, passing them off as anonymous fragments found in the library's archives. In 1777 he published Reimarus's attack on the historicity of Jesus' resurrection, which set German orthodoxy in an uproar.

According to Reimarus, Jesus claimed to have been only an earthly Messiah, and having tried to establish his reign and failed, he was executed. But the disciples stole Jesus' corpse and spread the story of Jesus' resurrection, touting him as a spiritual Messiah so that they could continue the easy life of preaching that they had enjoyed with Jesus while he was alive. Reimarus realized that to maintain this position he must refute the evidence for the historicity of the resurrection. In his mind, this consisted of the witness of the guard at the tomb, the witness of the apostles, and the fulfillment of OT prophecies. Against the testimony of the guard, Reimarus employed the arguments of the English Deists. He argued that the story is improbable in itself and is full of contradictions. He held it to be an invention of Matthew that the other evangelists rejected. In order to undermine the testimony of the apostles, Reimarus capitalized on the inconsistencies and contradictions in the resurrection narratives. If these were not enough, there is the overriding problem of the privacy of Jesus' appearances. The apostles' testimony is suspect because they are the only ones who supposedly saw Christ. Finally, Reimarus made short shrift of the proof from prophecy. The interpretations of the OT passages in question are so strained as to be unconvincing. Besides, the whole procedure begs the question anyway, since it assumes Jesus was in fact raised from the dead and the prophecies thus apply to him! In conclusion, Reimarus summarized his case:

> (1) the guard story is very doubtful and unconfirmed, and it is very probable the disciples came by night, stole the corpse, and said afterward Jesus had arisen; (2) the disciples' testimony is both inconsistent and contradictory; and (3) the prophecies appealed to are irrelevant, falsely interpreted, and question-begging.[2]

Thus, Christianity is quite simply a fraud.

Among the many who undertook to refute Reimarus was Johann Salomo Semler, a conservative Rationalist. In his earlier *Abhandlung von freier Untersuchung des Canon* (1771) Semler had broken the ground for the new Rationalist approach to the Scriptures. Semler had been the assistant at the University of Halle to S. J. Baumgarten, who chronicled the course of Deism in his *Nachrichten von einer Hallischen Bibliothek* (1748-51), reviewing almost every English Deist and apologetic work. Semler actually assisted Baumgarten in the reading and translation of Deist literature, and thus became open to Deist influences.

At the same time, Semler had a background in Pietism and had no desire to undermine Christianity. Therefore, he made a distinction between the timeless, spiritual truths in Scripture and the merely local truths. It was his conviction that only the spiritual truths may properly be called the Word of God. He thus introduced into theology the decisive distinction between the Scriptures and the Word of God. Since only the spiritual truths are the Word of God, it is no longer possible to regard the Scriptures as a whole as divinely inspired. Rather, the Word of God is clothed in fallible, human forms, which have only local importance. These fallible forms represent God's and Jesus' accommodation to human weakness. Included among these accommodations is the miraculous element in Scripture. No Christian can be obligated to believe that such events literally happened, for they are not part of the Word of God. Thus, we are free to examine the historical narratives as we would any other ordinary narrative, since inspiration concerns only the timeless truths they embody. Should the narrative be shown to be unhistorical, that is of little consequence, for that cannot have any effect on the Word of God. The proof that certain events are unhistorical is irrelevant to divine truths.

Given his views of Scripture, it seems somewhat surprising to find Semler writing a refutation of Reimarus in his *Beantwortung der Fragmente eines Ungenannten* (1779). Reimarus's bitter attack seems to have forced him back to the orthodox end of the spectrum. But in the way he defends the resurrection, we can see the beginning of the end for the historical apologetic for the resurrection. He emphatically subordinates the resurrection to the teachings of Jesus and removes from it any apologetic significance. According to Semler, Christianity consists of the spiritual doctrines taught by Christ. Reimarus mistakenly thinks that in refuting the three purported grounds for belief in the resurrection, he has thereby struck down the essential truths of Christianity. But this is far from true, asserts Semler. In the first place, one may be a Christian without believing in the resurrection of Jesus. In the second place, the true ground for belief in the resurrection is the self-evident truth of Christ's teachings. For Semler, belief in Christ's teaching entails belief in Christ's resurrection: "The resurrection of Jesus hangs together with Jesus' life and goal; whoever has experienced his teachings will also believe that God has raised him from the dead."[3] The proof of the resurrection is not the three points mentioned by Reimarus; the proof is the spiritual teachings of Christ. In specific response to Reimarus's refutation of the three purported grounds, Semler grants all three to Reimarus—but for Semler they are simply irrelevant and present no problem once one has abandoned the doctrine of verbal inspiration.

Thus, Semler undercut the traditional apologetic in various ways: while affirming the truth of the resurrection, he nonetheless admitted that belief in the resurrection was not essential to being a Christian; he provided no historical reason to accept the reliability of the gospel accounts with regard to this event; he denied that the resurrection has any power to confirm Christ's teaching; and he instead subordinated the resurrection to the teachings of Christ, the self-evident Word of God, making the latter the proof of the former.

By loosing the Word of God from the Scriptures and making its truth self-attesting, Semler enabled Rational theology to adhere to the doctrines of Christianity while denying their historical basis. During the time between Semler and Strauss, the natural explanation school predominated. The old conspiracy theory of Reimarus was rejected as an explanation for the resurrection of Jesus, and instead the apparent death theory enjoyed popularity among Rationalists. Even F. D. E. Schleiermacher, known as the father of modern theology, accepted this explanation. But the roof really caved in on the traditional apologetic with the advent of David Friedrich Strauss and his hermeneutic of mythological explanation.

Strauss's *Leben Jesu* (1835) marks a watershed in the history of biblical criticism, to which modern form and redaction criticism may be traced. The year 1835 marks a turning point in the history of the Christian faith.

Strauss's approach to the gospels, and to the resurrection in particular, may be seen as an attempt to forge a third way between the horns of the dilemma posed by the traditional apologetic, which says that if the miracles and resurrection of Jesus are not historical facts, then the apostles were either deceivers or deceived, neither of which is plausible. Reimarus had chosen to defend the first horn, arguing that the disciples had hoaxed the resurrection. Paulus had chosen to defend the second horn, arguing that the disciples had been mistaken about Jesus' return from the dead. What Strauss saw clearly was that neither of these alternatives was plausible, and so he sought a third alternative in the mythological explanation. According to this view, the miraculous events of the gospels never happened, and the gospel accounts of them are the result of a long process of legend and religious imagination:

> In the view of the church, Jesus was miraculously revived; according to the deistic view of Reimarus, his corpse was stolen by the disciples; in the rationalistic view, he only appeared to be dead and revived; according to our view the imagination of his followers aroused in their deepest spirit, presented their Master revived, for they could not possibly think of him as dead. What for a long time was valid as an external fact, first miraculous, then deceptive, finally simply natural, is hereby reduced completely to the state of mind and made into an inner event.[4]

Strauss thus denied that there was any external fact to be explained. The gospel accounts of the resurrection were unreliable legends colored by myth. Hence, the dilemma of "deceivers or deceived" did not arise. The fact that the resurrection was unhistorical did not rob it of its religious significance (here we see the change wrought by Semler), for a spiritual truth may be revealed within the husk of a delusion.

Strauss believed that the chief problem in applying the mythical interpretation to the NT is that the first century was no longer an age of myths. But although it was a time of writing, if there was a long period of oral transmission during which no written record existed, then marvelous elements could begin to creep in and grow into historical myths. Strauss recognized as well that adherence to this theory necessitated denying the contemporary authorship of the gospels and the influence of eyewitnesses. Hence, Strauss regarded it as "the sole object" of his book to examine the

internal evidence in order to test the probability of the authors' being eyewitnesses or competently informed writers.[5]

Strauss gave short shrift to the external testimony to the gospels: he
believed Mark to be compiled from Matthew and Luke and hence not
based on Peter's preaching; the Matthew mentioned by Papias is not our
Matthew; Acts so contradicts Paul that its author could not be his companion; the earliest reference to John is in A.D. 172, and the gospel's
authenticity was disputed by the Alogoi. Nor could living eyewitnesses
prevent the accrual of legend: first, the legends could have originated in
areas where Jesus was not well known; second, the apostles could not be
everywhere at once to correct or suppress unhistorical stories; and third,
eyewitnesses themselves would be tempted to fill up the gaps in their own
knowledge with stories. Strauss argued that the Jews lagged behind the
Romans and Greeks in their historical consciousness; even Josephus's
work is filled with marvelous tales. Myths about the Messiah had already
arisen between the exile and Christ's day. All that was wanting was the
application of these myths with some modification to Jesus by the
Christian community.

With regard to the resurrection accounts, Strauss used arguments similar to Reimarus's to demonstrate their unreliability. For example, if the
body was embalmed and wrapped, why do the women return for this
purpose? Was the body placed in the tomb because it was Joseph's or
because it was near? The story of the guard is improbable, and the inconsistencies in the empty tomb narrative are irreconcilable. As for the appearances, why should Jesus command the disciples to go to Galilee when he
was going to appear to them in Jerusalem? And why did he command them
to stay in Jerusalem when he was going to Galilee? For such reasons, no
credence can be given to the gospel stories of the empty tomb or resurrection appearances.

Despite this, Strauss admitted that Paul's challenge in 1 Corinthians 15
concerning living witnesses to an appearance of Jesus before 500 brethren
makes it certain that people were alive at that time who believed they had
seen the risen Christ. How is that to be explained? Certainly not by supernatural intervention, for that is unenlightened. "Hence, the cultivated
intellect of the present day has very decidedly stated the following
dilemma: either Jesus was not really dead, or he did not really rise again."[6]
But that Jesus did not die on the cross is the defunct theory of Rationalism;
therefore, Jesus did not rise. The correct explanation of the appearances is
to be found in the appearance to Paul. His experience makes clear that the
appearances were not external to the mind. What happened is that the disciples, convinced that Jesus was the Messiah, began to search the Scriptures

after his death. There they found the dying and glorified Messiah of Isaiah 53. So Jesus must be alive! Soon they would see him, especially the women. Having hallucinated appearances of Christ, they would naturally infer that his grave was empty, and by the time they returned from Galilee to Jerusalem, which was certainly not as soon as Pentecost, there was no closed tomb to refute them. In this way belief in Jesus' resurrection originated, and eventually the legendary gospel accounts arose.

Strauss's work completely altered the tone and course of German theology. Gone forever was the central dilemma of the eighteenth-century apologetic for the resurrection. Now the evangelists were neither deceivers nor deceived, but stood at the end of a long process in which the original events were completely reshaped through mythological and legendary influences. The dissolution of the apologists' dilemma did not itself entail that the supernaturalist view was false. But for Strauss the supernaturalist view was not only disproved by the inconsistencies and contradictions noted by Reimarus, but was *a priori* ruled out of court because of the presupposition of the impossibility of miracles. Any event that stood outside the inviolable chain of finite causes was *by definition* mythological. Therefore, the resurrection could not possibly be a miraculous and historical event.

This is the challenge that Strauss has left to Christian apologetics. The position of Bultmann in this century with regard to the resurrection is virtually the same as Strauss's. It is no longer effective to argue for the resurrection today simply by refuting theories as to who stole the body or that Jesus did not really die. They are no longer the issue. The issue is whether the gospel narratives are historically credible accounts or unhistorical legends.

The Tide of Subjectivism

The other reason, it seems to me, for the decline in historical apologetics during the nineteenth century is the tide of subjectivism that swept away an objective approach to matters of religious belief. We do not have space to develop this here, but let me say in passing that during the nineteenth century there came a backlash to the Age of Reason, and Romanticism swept Europe. This was spurred on in England by the Great Awakening, which emphasized the subjective, personal experience of faith. In France, the very emotive, subjective side of thinkers such as Rousseau emerged as a widespread reaction to the prior age of the *philosophes*, which ended in Revolution and the Reign of Terror. In Germany the effect of the philosophy of Kant and surging German Romanticism combined to color religious faith with a strong subjectivism. The net result of this tide of subjectivism was that apologetics moved from objective evidences for faith to emphasizing the moral grounds for faith or the beauties of faith itself. This subjective turn also enabled one to live with the destruction that was increasingly being wrought on the biblical narrative by the hammers of biblical criticism.

ASSESSMENT

The case for the historicity of the resurrection of Jesus seems to me to rest upon the evidence for three great, independently established facts: the empty tomb, the resurrection appearances, and the origin of the Christian faith. If these three facts can be established and no plausible natural explanation can account for them, then one is justified in inferring Jesus' resurrection as the most plausible explanation of the data. Accordingly, let us examine the evidence for each of these facts.

THE EMPTY TOMB

Here we wish to look first at the fact of the empty tomb and then at attempts to explain the empty tomb.

The Fact of the Empty Tomb

Here I'll summarize briefly eight lines of evidence supporting the fact that Jesus' tomb was found empty.

1. The Historical Reliability of the Story of Jesus' Burial Supports the Empty Tomb

Now you might ask, how does the fact of Jesus' burial prove that his tomb was found empty? The answer is this: if the burial story is true, then both Jew and Christian alike would have known where the tomb was. But in that case, the tomb must have been empty, when the disciples began to preach that Jesus was risen. Why? First, the disciples could not have believed in Jesus' resurrection if his corpse still lay in the tomb. It would have been wholly un-Jewish, not to say foolish, to believe that a man was raised from the dead when his body was still in the grave. Second, even if the disciples had preached this, no one else would have believed them. So long as the people of Jerusalem thought that Jesus' body was in the tomb, they would never have believed such foolishness as that he had been raised from the dead. And third, even if they had, the Jewish authorities would have exposed the whole affair simply by pointing to Jesus' tomb or perhaps even exhuming the body as decisive proof that Jesus had not been raised. Thus, you see, if the story of Jesus' burial is true, then the story of the empty tomb must be true as well.

And, unfortunately for those who deny the empty tomb, nearly all NT scholars agree that Jesus' burial is one of the best-established facts about Jesus. Now space does not permit me to go into all the details of the evidence for the burial. But let me just mention a couple points: First, Jesus was probably buried by Joseph of Arimathea. According to the gospels, Joseph of Arimathea laid Jesus' body in the tomb. Joseph is described as a rich man, a member of the Jewish Sanhedrin. The Sanhedrin was a sort of Jewish Supreme Court made up of seventy men, which presided in Jerusalem. Its members were the leading men of Judaism. It seems very unlikely that Christian tradition would invent a story of Jesus' honorable burial by his enemies, or even that it could invent Joseph of Arimathea, give him a name, place him on the Sanhedrin, and say he was responsible for Jesus' burial if this were not true. The members of the Sanhedrin were too well-known to allow either fictitious persons to be placed on it or false stories to be spread about one of its actual members' being responsible for Jesus' burial. Therefore, it seems very likely that Joseph was the actual, historical person who buried Jesus in the tomb.

Second, Paul's testimony provides early evidence of Jesus' burial. In 1 Corinthians 15:3-5 Paul quotes an old Christian tradition that he had received from the earliest disciples. Paul probably received this tradition no later than his visit to Jerusalem in A.D. 36 (Gal 1:18), if not earlier in Damascus. It thus goes back to within the first five years after Jesus' death. The tradition is a summary of the early Christian preaching and may have been used in Christian instruction. Its form would have made it suitable for memorization. Here is what it says:

> For I delivered to you as of first importance what I also received, that Christ died for our sins according to the Scriptures, and that He was buried, and that He was raised on the third day according to the Scriptures, and that He appeared to Cephas, then to the Twelve.

Now notice that the second line of this tradition refers to Jesus' burial. When one matches the events of this Christian tradition with the events described in the gospels and in the apostles' preaching in Acts, it is clear that the second line of the tradition is a summary of the story of Jesus' burial in the tomb. Thus, we have here very early evidence for Jesus' burial, evidence that is so early it cannot be explained away as legend. For these and many other reasons, the vast majority of scholars accept the historical reliability of Jesus' burial. But if we accept this, then, as I have explained, it is very difficult to deny the historicity of the empty tomb.

2. Paul's Testimony Implies the Fact of the Empty Tomb

Although Paul does not explicitly mention the empty tomb, two phrases in the old Christian tradition that he cites in 1 Corinthians 15 seem to imply it. First, the expression "He was buried," followed by the expression "He was raised" implies the empty tomb. The idea that a man could be buried and then be raised from the dead and yet his body still remain in the grave is a peculiarly modern notion. For the Jews there would have been no question but that the tomb of Jesus would have been empty. As E. E. Ellis remarks, "It is very unlikely that the earliest Palestinian Christians could conceive of any distinction between resurrection and physical, 'grave-emptying' resurrection. To them an *anastasis* (resurrection) without an empty grave would have been about as meaningful as a square circle."[7] Therefore, when Paul says that Jesus was buried and then was raised, he automatically assumes that an empty tomb was left behind.

Second, the expression "on the third day" implies the empty tomb. Since no one actually saw Jesus rise from the dead, why did the early disciples proclaim that he had been raised "on the third day"? The most likely answer is that it was on the third day that the women discovered the tomb of Jesus empty; and so naturally, the resurrection itself came to be dated on that day. In this case, the expression "on the third day" is a time-indicator pointing to the discovery of the empty tomb.

These two expressions in the early Christian tradition quoted by Paul thus indicate that the early Christian fellowship out of which the tradition sprang adhered to the fact of Jesus' empty tomb. Hence, such belief cannot be written off as a late legendary development.

3. The Empty Tomb Story Is Part of Mark's Source Material and Is Therefore Very Old

In writing the story of Jesus' passion, Mark apparently employed a source of information that is accordingly very early. This pre-Markan passion source in all probability included the empty tomb story. The burial story and empty tomb story form one smooth, continuous narrative. They are linked by grammatical and linguistic ties. It seems unlikely that the early Christians would have circulated a story of Jesus' passion ending in his burial. The passion story is incomplete without victory at the end. Hence, the pre-Markan source probably included and may have ended with the discovery of the empty tomb.

But that means that the empty tomb story is very old. The German commentator on Mark, Rudolf Pesch, argues that since Paul's traditions concerning the Last Supper (1 Cor 11) presuppose the Markan account, that implies that the Markan source goes right back to the early years of the Jerusalem fellowship. Pesch also draws attention to the fact that the pre-Markan passion source never refers to the high priest by name. It is as if I were to refer to something "the President" had done, and I and my listeners both knew whom I was referring to, namely, the man currently in power. Pesch believes that this is the case as well in the pre-Markan passion source. Since Caiaphas held office from A.D. 18-37, this means that at the latest Mark's source dates from within seven years of Jesus' crucifixion. This is incredibly early and makes the hypothesis of legend with regard to the empty tomb an idle theory.

4. The Phrase "The First Day of the Week" Is Very Ancient

This goes to confirm the previous point. According to the Markan account, the empty tomb was discovered by the women "on the first day of the week." We've already learned from the Christian tradition quoted by Paul that the earliest Christians proclaimed the resurrection of Jesus "on the third day." As E. L. Bode explains, if the empty tomb story were a late legend, it would almost certainly have been formulated in terms of the accepted and widespread third day motif. The fact that Mark uses "on the first day of the week" confirms that his tradition is very old, even antedating the third day reckoning. This fact is confirmed by the linguistic character of the phrase in question. For although "the first day of the week" is very awkward in the Greek, when translated back into Aramaic it is perfectly smooth and normal. This suggests that the empty tomb tradition reaches all the way back to the original language spoken by the first disciples themselves. Once again, this makes the legend hypothesis extremely unlikely.

5. The Story Is Simple and Lacks Legendary Development

The Markan account is straightforward and shows no signs of legendary embellishment. To appreciate this fact, all you have to do is compare Mark's account of the empty tomb with the account found in the so-called Gospel of Peter, a forgery from around A.D. 125. In this account, the tomb is not only surrounded by Roman guards but also by all the Jewish Pharisees and elders, as well as a great multitude from all the surrounding countryside who have come to watch the resurrection. Suddenly, in the night there rings out a loud voice in heaven, and two men descend from heaven to the tomb. The stone over the door rolls back by itself, and they go into the tomb. Then three men come out of the tomb, two of them holding up the third man. The heads of the two men reach up into the clouds, but the head of the third man reaches up beyond the clouds. Then a cross comes out of the tomb, and a voice from heaven asks, "Have you preached to them that sleep?" And the cross answers, "Yes." In another forgery called the Ascension of Isaiah, Jesus comes out of the tomb sitting on the shoulders of the angels Michael and Gabriel! This is how legends look: they are colored by theological and other developments. By contrast, the gospel account is simple and seems to be pretty much a straightforward report of what happened.

6. The Tomb Was Probably Discovered Empty by Women

In order to see why this is so, we need to understand two things about the place of women in Jewish society. First, women were not qualified to serve as legal witnesses. The testimony of a woman was regarded as so worthless that they could not even testify in a court of law. If a man committed a crime and was observed in the very act by some women, he could not be convicted on the basis of their testimony, since their testimony was regarded as so worthless that it could not even be admitted into court.

Second, women occupied a low rung on the Jewish social ladder. Compared to men, women were second-class citizens. Consider these Jewish texts: "Sooner let the words of the Law be burnt than delivered to women!" and again: "Happy is he whose children are male, but unhappy is he whose children are female!"

Now, given their low social status and inability to serve as witnesses, it is quite amazing that it is women who are the discoverers and principal witnesses of the empty tomb. If the empty tomb story were a legend, then it is most likely that the male disciples would have been made the first to discover the empty tomb. The fact that despised women, whose testimony was deemed worthless, were the chief witnesses to the fact of the empty tomb can only be plausibly explained if, like it or not, they actually were the discoverers of the empty tomb. Hence, the gospels are most likely giving an accurate account of this matter.

7. The Disciples Could Not Have Preached the Resurrection in Jerusalem Had the Tomb Not Been Empty

One of the most amazing facts about the early Christian belief in Jesus' resurrection was that it originated in the very city where Jesus was crucified. The Christian faith did not come into existence in some distant city far from eyewitnesses who knew of Jesus' death and burial. No, it came into being in the very city where Jesus had been publicly crucified, under the very eyes of its enemies. If the proclamation of Jesus' resurrection were false, all the Jewish authorities would have had to do to nip the Christian heresy in the bud would have been to point to his tomb or exhume the corpse of Jesus and parade it through the streets of the city for all to see.

Had the tomb not been empty, then it would have been impossible for the disciples to proclaim the resurrection in Jerusalem as they did.

8. The Earliest Jewish Propaganda Against the Christians Presupposes the Empty Tomb

In Matt 28:11-15 we have the earliest Christian attempt to refute the Jewish propaganda against the Christian proclamation of the resurrection:

> While they were going, behold, some of the guard went into the city and told the chief priests all that had taken place. And when they had assembled with the elders and taken counsel, they gave a sum of money to the soldiers and said, "Tell people, 'His disciples came by night and stole him away while we were asleep.' And if this comes to the governor's ears, we will satisfy him and keep you out of trouble." So they took the money and did as they were directed; and this story has been spread among the Jews to this day.

Now, our interest is not so much in the evangelist's story of the guard at the tomb as in his incidental remark at the end, "This story had been spread among the Jews to this day." This remark reveals that the author was concerned to refute a widespread Jewish explanation of the resurrection. Now what were the Jews saying in response to the disciples' proclamation that Jesus was risen? That these men are full of new wine? That Jesus' body still lay in the tomb in the hillside? No. They were saying, "The disciples stole away his body." Think about that. "The disciples stole away his body." The Jewish propaganda did not deny the empty tomb, but instead entangled itself in a hopeless series of absurdities trying to explain it away. In other words, the Jewish propaganda that the disciples stole the body presupposes that the body was missing. Thus, the Jewish propaganda itself shows that the tomb was empty. This is historical evidence of the highest quality, since it comes not from the Christians but from the very enemies of the early Christian faith.

Taken together these eight considerations constitute a powerful case that Jesus' tomb was indeed found empty on the first day of the week by a group of his women followers. As a historical fact, this seems to be well-established. According to D. H. Van Daalen, "It is extremely difficult to object to the empty tomb on historical grounds; those who deny it do so on the basis of theological or philosophical assumptions."[8] But those assumptions cannot alter the facts themselves. NT scholars seem to be increasingly aware of this. According to Jacob Kremer, a NT critic who has specialized in the study of the resurrection: "By far most exegetes hold firmly to the reliability of the biblical statements about the empty tomb," and he furnishes a list of twenty-eight scholars to which his own name may be added: Blank, Blinzler, Bode, von Campenhausen, Delorme, Dhanis, Grundmann, Hengel, Lehmann, Léon-Dufour, Lichtenstein, Manek, Martini, Mussner, Nauck, Rengstorff, Ruckstuhl, Schenke, Schmitt, Schubert, Schwank, Schweizer, Seidensticker, Strobel, Stuhlmacher, Trilling, Vögtle, and Wilckens.[9] I can think of at least sixteen more that he failed to mention: Benoit, Brown, Clark, Dunn, Ellis, Gundry, Hooke, Jeremias, Klappert, Ladd, Lane, Marshall, Moule, Perry, Robinson, and Schnackenburg. Perhaps most amazing of all is that even two Jewish scholars, Lapide and Vermes, have declared themselves convinced on the basis of the evidence that Jesus' tomb was empty.

Explaining The Empty Tomb

Now if this is the case, that leads us to our second main point: explaining the empty tomb. Down through history, those who denied the resurrection of Jesus have been obligated to come up with a convincing alternative explanation. In fact, they have come up with only about three:

Conspiracy Theory

According to this explanation, the disciples stole the body of Jesus, thus faking the resurrection. This was, as we say, the first counter-explanation for the empty tomb, and it was revived by the Deists during the eighteenth century. Today, however, this explanation has been completely given up by modern scholarship. At least three considerations undergird this consensus:

1. It is morally implausible. Whatever the disciples were, they were not charlatans and hoaxers. They were genuinely devout people who tried to pursue the righteousness that Jesus had taught them. But this theory forces us to regard them as cheap frauds.

2. It is psychologically implausible. It does not take seriously the catastrophe that the crucifixion was for the disciples. After that event they were broken, doubtful, and fearful men—not bold perpetrators of some cleverly hatched and daringly executed conspiracy.

3. It cannot account for the disciples' evident sincerity. The sudden change in their lives and their subsequent suffering for what they proclaimed show clearly that these men were not hypocritical hoaxers, but sincerely believed what they preached.

I can't emphasize enough that no modern scholar would defend such a theory today. The only place you read about such things is in the popular, sensationalist press or in former propaganda from behind the Iron Curtain.

Apparent Death Theory

A second theory was the apparent death explanation. Critics around the beginning of the nineteenth century such as Heinrich Paulus or Friedrich Schleiermacher defended the view that Jesus was not completely dead when he was taken down from the cross. He revived in the tomb and escaped to convince his disciples he had risen from the dead. Once again, today this theory has been almost completely given up. Again, one can mention three factors supporting this consensus:

1. It is physically implausible. First, what the theory suggests is virtually physically impossible. The extent of Jesus' tortures was such that he could never have survived the crucifixion and entombment.

2. It is religiously implausible. Even if Jesus had survived, his appearing to the disciples half-dead and desperately in need of medical attention would not have evoked their worship of him as Lord. The conviction of the earliest disciples was that Jesus rose gloriously and triumphantly from the grave, not as one who had managed to barely escape death.

3. It is biographically implausible. The theory says that Jesus tricked the disciples into believing in his resurrection. But this is a tawdry caricature of all that we know of the real Jesus, whose life and teachings belie such an interpretation of his character.

Wrong Tomb Theory

First proposed by Kirsopp Lake in 1907, this theory holds that the belief in Jesus' empty tomb was based on a simple mistake. According to Lake, the women lost their way that Sunday morning and happened upon a caretaker at an unoccupied tomb in the garden. He said something like, "You're looking for Jesus of Nazareth. He is not here." The women, however, were so unnerved that they fled. After the disciples had experienced visions of Jesus alive, the women's story developed into the account of their discovery of Jesus' empty tomb. Unlike the previous two theories considered, Lake's theory generated virtually no following, but was dead almost upon arrival:

1. The theory treats the evidence selectively and arbitrarily. For example, Lake regards the women's visit to the tomb with the intention of anointing the body as historical, but must discount their noting, precisely because of that intention, where the body was laid (Mark 15:47; 16:1). But why accept the one but not the other? Or again, Lake regards the angel's words ascribed to the caretaker above as authentic, but passes over the words, "He is risen!" But all of the angel's message is the language of Christian proclamation if any of it is. Similarly, there are no grounds for taking Mark's "young man" to be a human rather than angelic figure, the

Greek word used here being often used of angels and the man's white robe being typical for the Jewish portrait of angels. Moreover, the women's fear and astonishment is a characteristic Markan motif which presupposes the angelic confrontation, so that one cannot regard the women's reaction as traditional and historical while historically excising the angel as a legendary accretion. Lake is trying to have his cake and eat it, too.

2. Most decisively, however, any later check of the tomb would have revealed the women's error. After their initial fright, wouldn't the women have attempted to retrace their steps by the light of day? Certainly the disciples themselves would have wanted to verify the empty tomb. The state of the actual tomb could not have remained a matter of complete indifference to a movement in the same locale based on belief in the resurrection of the dead man interred there. And in any case, since the burial site was known to Jew and Christian alike, the Jewish opponents of the Christians would have been only too happy to point out the women's error. Hence, the wrong tomb theory is quite implausible.

Again, I want to emphasize that scarcely any modern historian or biblical critic would hold to these theories. They are almost completely passé. You may say to yourselves at this point, "Well, then, what explanation of the empty tomb do modern critics offer who deny the resurrection?" The fact is that they are self-confessedly without any explanation to offer. There simply is no plausible natural explanation available today to account for how Jesus' tomb became empty. If we deny the resurrection of Jesus, we are left with an inexplicable mystery.

Conclusion

We have seen that multiple lines of historical evidence indicate that Jesus' tomb was found empty on Sunday morning by a group of his women followers. Furthermore, no convincing natural explanation is available to account for this fact. This alone might cause us to believe that the resurrection of Jesus is the best explanation. But there is even more evidence to come.

THE RESURRECTION APPEARANCES

In 1 Corinthians 15:3-8, Paul writes:

> For I delivered to you as of first importance what I also received, that Christ died for our sins in accordance with the scriptures, that he was buried, that he was raised on the third day in accordance with the scriptures, and that he appeared to Cephas, then to the twelve. Then he appeared to more than five hundred brethren at one time, most of whom are still alive, though some have fallen asleep. Then

> he appeared to James, then to all the apostles. Last of all, as to one
> untimely born, he appeared also to me.

This is a truly remarkable claim. We have here the testimony of a man personally acquainted with the first disciples, and he reports that they actually saw Jesus alive from the dead. More than that, he says that he himself also saw an appearance of Jesus alive after his death. What are we to make of this claim? Did Jesus really appear to people alive after his death?

To answer this question, let's again consider two major points: first, the fact of the resurrection appearances of Jesus; and second, explaining the resurrection appearances.

The Fact of the Resurrection Appearances

Let's consider together the first point: the fact of the appearances of Jesus. Once again, space will not allow me to examine in detail all the evidences for Jesus' post-resurrection appearances. But I'd like to examine three main lines of evidence.

1. Paul's Testimony Proves the Disciples Saw Appearances of Jesus

We saw that in 1 Corinthians 15 Paul gives a list of witnesses to Jesus' resurrection appearances. Let's look briefly at each appearance to see whether it is plausible that such events actually took place.

a. Appearance to Peter. We have no story in the gospels telling of Jesus' appearance to Peter. But the appearance is mentioned here in the old Christian tradition, and it is vouched for by the apostle Paul himself. As we know from Galatians 1:18, Paul spent about two weeks with Peter in Jerusalem three years after his Damascus Road experience. So Paul would know personally whether Peter claimed to have had such an experience or not. In addition to this, the appearance to Peter is mentioned in another old Christian tradition found in Luke 24:34: "The Lord has really risen, and has appeared to Simon!" So although we have no detailed story of this appearance, it is quite well attested. As a result, even the most skeptical NT critics agree that Peter saw something that he called an appearance of Jesus alive from the dead.

b. Appearance to the Twelve. This is the best-attested resurrection appearance of Jesus. We have independent stories of this appearance in Luke 24:36-42 and John 20:19-20. Undoubtedly, the most notable feature of this appearance is the physical demonstrations of Jesus' showing his wounds and eating before the disciples. The purpose of the physical demonstrations is to show two things: first, that Jesus was raised *physically*; and second, that he was the *same Jesus* who had been crucified. Thus, they served to demonstrate both *corporeality* and *continuity* of the resurrection body. There can be little doubt that such an appearance occurred, for it is attested in the old Christian tradition, vouched for by Paul, who had personal contact with the Twelve, and is described by both Luke and John.

c. Appearance to 500 brethren. The third appearance comes as somewhat of a shock: "then he appeared to more than five hundred brethren at one time!" This is surprising, since we have no mention whatsoever of this appearance elsewhere in the NT. This would make one rather skeptical about this appearance, but it comes from old information that Paul had received, and Paul himself apparently had personal contact with these people, since he knew that some had died. This is seen in Paul's parenthetical comment, "most of whom remain until now, but some have fallen asleep." Why does Paul add this remark? The great NT scholar of Cambridge University, C. H. Dodd, replies, "There can hardly be any purpose in mentioning the fact that the most of the 500 are still alive, unless Paul is saying, in effect, 'The witnesses are there to be questioned.'"[10] Notice: Paul could never have said this if the event had not occurred. He could not have challenged people to ask the witnesses if the event had never taken place and there were no witnesses. But evidently there were witnesses to this event, and Paul knew that some of them had died in the meantime. Therefore, the event must have taken place.

I think that this appearance is not related in the gospels because it probably took place in Galilee. As one puts together the various appearances in the gospels, it seems that they occurred first in Jerusalem, then in Galilee, and then in Jerusalem again. The appearance to the 500 would have to be out of doors, perhaps on a hillside outside a Galilean village. Since the gospels focus their attention on the appearances in Jerusalem, we do not have any story of this appearance to the 500, because it probably occurred in Galilee.

d. Appearance to James. The next appearance is one of the most amazing of all: he appeared to James, Jesus' younger brother. What makes this amazing is that apparently neither James nor any of Jesus' younger brothers believed in Jesus during his lifetime. (See Mark 3:21, 31-35; John 7:1-10.) They didn't believe he was the Messiah, or a prophet, or even anybody special. But after the resurrection, all of a sudden Jesus' brothers pop up in the Christian fellowship in the upper room in Jerusalem (Acts 1:14). There is no further mention of them until Acts 12:17. This is the story of Peter's deliverance from prison by the angel. What are Peter's first words? "Report this to *James*." In Galatians 1:19 Paul tells of his two-week visit to Jerusalem about three years after his Damascus Road experience. He says that besides Peter, he saw none of the other apostles *except James* the Lord's brother. Paul at least implies that James was now being reckoned as an apostle. When Paul visited Jerusalem again fourteen years later, he says there were three "pillars" of the church in Jerusalem: Peter, John, and *James* (Gal 2:9). Finally, in Acts 21:18 James is the sole head of the Jerusalem church and of the council of elders. We hear no more about James in the NT; but from Josephus, the Jewish historian, we learn that James was stoned to death illegally by the Sanhedrin sometime after A.D. 60 for his faith in Christ.[11] Not only James but also Jesus' other brothers became believers and were active in Christian preaching, as we see from 1 Corinthians 9:5: "Do we not have the right to be accompanied by a wife, as the other apostles and the brothers of the Lord and Cephas?"

Now, how is this to be explained? On the one hand, it seems certain that Jesus' brothers did not believe in him during his lifetime. On the other hand, it is equally certain that they became ardent Christians, active in the church. Many of us have brothers. What would it take to make you believe that your brother is the Lord, so that you would die for this belief, as James did? Can there be any doubt that the reason for this remarkable transformation is to be found in the fact that "then he appeared to James"? Even the skeptical NT critic Hans Grass admits that the conversion of James is one of the surest proofs of the resurrection of Jesus Christ.[12]

e. Appearance to "all the apostles." This appearance was probably to a limited circle somewhat wider than the Twelve. For such a group, see Acts 1:21-22. Once again, the facticity of this appearance is guaranteed by Paul's personal contact with the apostles themselves.

f. Appearance to Saul of Tarsus. The final appearance is just as amazing as the appearance to James: "last of all," says Paul, "he appeared to me also." The story of Jesus' appearance to Saul of Tarsus (or Paul) just outside Damascus is related in Acts 9:1-9 and is later told again twice. That this event actually occurred is established beyond doubt by Paul's references to it in his own letters.

This event changed Saul's whole life. He was a rabbi, a Pharisee, a respected Jewish leader. He hated the Christian heresy and did everything in his power to stamp it out. He was even responsible for the execution of Christian believers. Then suddenly he gave up everything. He left his position as a respected Jewish leader and became a Christian missionary: he entered a life of poverty, labor, and suffering. He was whipped, beaten, stoned and left for dead, shipwrecked three times, in constant danger, deprivation, and anxiety. Finally, he made the ultimate sacrifice and was martyred for his faith at Rome. And it was all because on that day outside Damascus, he saw "Jesus our Lord" (1 Cor 9:1).

From this evidence what should we conclude? We can call these appearances hallucinations if we want to, but we cannot deny that they occurred. The late NT critic of the University of Chicago, Norman Perrin, states, "The more we study the tradition with regard to the appearances, the firmer the rock begins to appear upon which they are based."[13] Paul's testimony makes certain that on separate occasions different groups and individuals had experiences of seeing Jesus alive from the dead. This conclusion is virtually indisputable.

2. The Gospel Accounts of the Resurrection Appearances Are Historically Reliable

Like the reports of Jesus' exorcisms and miracles, the appearance traditions occupy so wide and important a place in the NT testimony to Jesus that the disciples' experience of Jesus' resurrection appearances in all probability belongs, like the exorcisms and miracles, to history. The question then concerns the historical credibility of the narratives of those appearances. Are they fundamentally accurate accounts or have they become so corrupted by legendary accretions and embellishments that they are no longer historically informative? Although it may be impossible to prove the historical reliability of any specific resurrection account, there are nonetheless good reasons to regard the gospels and, by implication, the resurrection appearance stories which occupy so central a position in them as fundamentally historically reliable accounts: (1) the relatively short interval of time between Jesus' crucifixion and the composition of the gospel narratives precludes those narratives' being wholesale legendary accumulations; (2) legends drawn from folk literature or even contemporary "urban legends" seldom concern historical events and personages to the same degree (if at all) as do the gospels; (3) the earliest Christians would have passed on the Jesus traditions with the care and respect for that tradition which was typical of Jewish transmission of traditions, which renders analogies drawn from folk literature or "urban legends" irrelevant; (4) various factors—such as the presence of eyewitnesses and apostolic control of the Jesus tradition—would act as a restraint upon embellishment and legendary accretion; and (5) the demonstrated reliability of the Synoptic evangelists (particularly Luke in Acts) where external verification is possible supports their historical credibility. Space does not permit me to go into all these reasons, so let me comment on only the first: *there was insufficient time for legend to accumulate significantly*. Perhaps the greatest difficulty for those who say that the resurrection accounts are legendary is that the time period between the events and the writing of the gospels was too short to allow legend to substantially accrue. Julius Müller's critique has never been answered:

Most decidedly must a considerable interval of time be required for such a complete transformation of a whole history by popular tradition, when the series of legends are formed in the same territory where the heroes actually lived and wrought. Here one cannot imagine how such a series of legends could arise in an historical age, obtain universal respect, and supplant the historical recollection of the true character and connexion of their heroes' lives in the minds of the community, if eyewitnesses were still at hand, who could be questioned respecting the truth of the recorded marvels. Hence, legendary fiction, as it likes not the clear present time, but prefers the mysterious gloom of grey antiquity, is wont to seek a remoteness of age, along with that of space, and to remove its boldest and most rare and wonderful creations into a very remote and unknown land.[14]

Müller's critique is still valid today and is confirmed by A. N. Sherwin-White, a historian of Greek and Roman times.[15] Professor Sherwin-White is not a theologian; he is a professional historian of times prior to and contemporaneous with Jesus. According to Sherwin-White, the sources for Roman and Greek history are usually biased and removed one or two generations or even centuries from the events they record. Yet, he says, historians reconstruct with confidence the course of Roman and Greek history. When Sherwin-White turns to the gospels, he states that for the gospels to be legends, the rate of legendary accumulation would have to be "unbelievable." More generations would be needed. The writings of Herodotus enable us to determine the rate at which legend accumulates, and the tests show that even two generations is too short a time span to allow legendary tendencies to wipe out the hard core of historical facts. Julius Müller challenged scholars of the mid-nineteenth century to show anywhere in history where within thirty years a great series of legends had accumulated around a historical individual and had become firmly fixed in general belief. Müller's challenge has never been met.

Because there was not sufficient time for legend to accumulate, the gospel accounts of the resurrection appearances must be substantially accurate historically. That brings us to our third point:

3. The Resurrection Appearances Were Physical, Bodily Appearances

In support of this point, I want to examine two supporting sub-points.

a. Paul implies that the appearances were physical. He does this in two ways. First, he conceives of the resurrection body as physical. In 1 Corinthians 15:42-44 Paul describes the differences between the present, earthly body and the future, resurrection body, which will be like Christ's.

He draws four essential contrasts between the earthly body and the resurrection body:

The earthly body is:	*But the resurrection body is*:
mortal	immortal
dishonorable	glorious
weak	powerful
physical	spiritual

Now only the last contrast would make us think that Paul did not believe in a physical resurrection body. But what does he mean by the words translated here as "physical/spiritual"? The word translated "physical" literally means "soul-ish." Now obviously, Paul does not mean that our present body is made out of soul. Rather, by this word he means "dominated by or pertaining to human nature." Similarly, when he says the resurrection body will be "spiritual," he does not mean "made out of spirit." Rather, he means "dominated by or oriented toward the Spirit." It is the same sense of the word "spiritual" as when we say someone is a spiritual person. In fact, look at the way Paul uses exactly those same words in 1 Corinthians 2:14-15:

> The natural man does not receive the gifts of the Spirit of God, for they are folly to him, and he is not able to understand them, because they are spiritually discerned. The spiritual man judges all things but is himself to be judged by no one.

Natural man does not mean "physical man," but "man oriented toward human nature." And *spiritual man* does not mean "intangible, invisible man" but "man oriented toward the Spirit." The contrast is the same in 1 Corinthians 15. The present, earthly body will be freed from its slavery to sinful human nature and become instead fully empowered and directed by God's Spirit. Thus, Paul's doctrine of the resurrection body implies a physical resurrection.

Second, Paul, and indeed all the NT, makes a conceptual (if not linguistic) distinction between an appearance of Jesus and a vision of Jesus. The appearances of Jesus soon ceased, but visions continued in the early church. Now the question is: what is the difference between an appearance and a vision? The answer of the NT would seem to be clear: a vision, though caused by God, was purely in the mind, while an appearance took place "out there" in the real world. The difference between a vision and a hallucination would be that the latter is not induced by God, but is the result of natural or human causes, whereas a vision is caused by God. But a vision, as opposed to a genuine appearance, is in the mind, despite its veridicality. It is instructive to compare here Stephen's vision of Jesus in Acts 7 with the resurrection appearances. What Stephen saw was a vision, for no one else present experienced anything at all. By contrast the resurrection appearances took place in the world "out there" and could be experienced by anybody. Paul could rightly regard his experience on the Damascus Road an appearance, even though it took place after the ascension, because it involved real manifestations in the world, which Paul's companions also experienced. Thus, the conceptual distinction between a vision and an appearance of Jesus also implies that the resurrection appearances were physical.

b. The gospel accounts show the appearances were physical and bodily. Again, I want to make two points. First, every resurrection appearance related in the gospels is a physical, bodily appearance. The unanimous testimony of the gospels in this regard is quite impressive. If *none* of the appearances were originally bodily appearances, then it is very strange that we have a completely unanimous testimony in the gospels that *all* of them were physical, with no trace of the supposed original, non-physical appearances.

Second, the gospel accounts have been shown to be fundamentally historically reliable. As we have seen, there was insufficient time for legend to accumulate significantly. If all the appearances were originally non-physical visions, then one is at a complete loss to explain the rise of the gospel accounts. Since there was insufficient time for legend to accumulate, the gospel accounts must be basically reliable; and therefore, the appearances were physical and bodily.

Thus, on the basis of these three lines of evidence, we can conclude that the fact of Jesus' physical, bodily resurrection appearances is firmly established historically. But how do we explain these appearances? That leads me to my second major point:

Explaining the Resurrection Appearances

If one denies that Jesus actually rose from the dead, then he must try to explain away the resurrection appearances psychologically. It has been asserted that the appearances were merely hallucinations on the part of the disciples. But the hallucination theory faces formidable difficulties.

First, *the theory cannot account for the physicality of the appearances.* We have already seen that the gospel accounts of the resurrection appearances are fundamentally reliable and that the appearances were physical, bodily appearances. Therefore, the hallucination theory is ruled out of court from the beginning.

Second, *the theory cannot plausibly account for the number and various circumstances of the appearances.* Jesus did not appear to just one person but to many persons. He did not appear just one time but many times. He did not appear in just one place and circumstance, but in many places under varying circumstances. He did not appear just to individuals but to groups. And he did not appear just to believers but to unbelievers (James, Saul). Hallucinations cannot plausibly account for these facts.

Third, *the theory cannot account for the disciples' belief in Jesus' resurrection.* Hallucinations would not have led to the conclusion that Jesus had been raised from the dead. I'm going to develop this point below, but in passing, let me explain that since a hallucination is just a projection of the mind, it cannot contain anything that is not already in the mind. But the resurrection of Jesus was radically foreign to the disciples' minds in at least two respects, as we shall see.

Finally, *the theory fails to explain the full scope of the evidence.* The hallucination theory only seeks to explain the appearances, but it says nothing about the empty tomb. To explain the empty tomb one would have to conjoin another theory to the hallucination theory. But the resurrection of Jesus is a simpler explanation with greater explanatory power, since it accounts for all the facts, and therefore is to be preferred. Thus, for these four reasons, the hallucination theory fails to plausibly explain the resurrection appearances.

Conclusion

From the preceding we come to the conclusion that it is well-established that in multiple and varied circumstances, different individuals and groups saw Jesus physically and bodily alive from the dead. Furthermore, there is no way to explain this away psychologically. So once again, if we reject the resurrection of Jesus as the only reasonable explanation of the resurrection appearances, we are left with an inexplicable mystery.

THE ORIGIN OF THE CHRISTIAN FAITH

The third fact from which the resurrection of Jesus may be inferred is the very origin of the Christian faith.

The Fact of the Origin of the Christian Faith

Even the most skeptical NT scholars admit that the earliest disciples at least *believed* that Jesus had been raised from the dead. In fact, they pinned nearly everything on it. To take just one example: the belief that Jesus was the Messiah. The Jews had no conception of a dying, much less a rising, Messiah. The idea that the Messiah would be killed was utterly foreign to them. We find this attitude expressed in John 12:34: "The multitude therefore answered him, 'We have heard out of the Law that the Christ is to remain forever; and how can You say "The Son of man must be lifted up?" Who is this Son of Man?'"

Here Jesus predicts his crucifixion, and the people are utterly mystified. The Messiah would reign forever—so how could he be "lifted up"? It is difficult to overemphasize what a disaster the crucifixion was, therefore, for the disciples' faith. Jesus' death on the cross spelled the humiliating end for any hopes they had entertained that he was the Messiah.

But the belief in the resurrection of Jesus reversed the catastrophe of the crucifixion. Because God had raised Jesus from the dead, he was seen to be Messiah after all. Thus, Peter proclaims in Acts 2:23, 36: "This Man ... God raised ... again ... let all the house of Israel know for certain that God has made Him both Lord and Christ—this Jesus whom you crucified." It was on the basis of belief in the resurrection that the disciples could believe that Jesus was the Messiah.

Thus, without this belief in the resurrection, early Christianity could not have come into being. The origin of Christianity hinges on the belief of the early disciples that God had raised Jesus from the dead. But the question is: How does one explain the origin of that belief? As R. H. Fuller says, even the most skeptical critic must posit some mysterious X to get the movement going.[16] But what was that X?

Explaining the Origin of the Disciples' Belief in Jesus' Resurrection

If one denies that the resurrection itself was that X, then one must explain the disciples' belief in the resurrection as the result of either Christian influences, pagan influences, or Jewish influences. That is to say, one must hold that the disciples came to believe in Jesus' resurrection either because of the influence of early Christianity, the influence of pagan religions, or the influence of Jewish beliefs.

Not From Christian Influences

Now clearly their belief in Jesus' resurrection cannot be explained as a result of Christian influences, simply because there was no Christianity yet. Since the belief in the resurrection was itself the foundation for Christianity, it cannot be explained as the later product of Christianity.

Not From Pagan Influences

But neither can it be explained as the result of pagan influences on the disciples. Back around the turn of the century in the hey-day of the History of Religions school, scholars in comparative religion collected parallels to Jesus' resurrection in other religious movements, and some thought to explain Christian belief as the result of the influence of such myths. The movement soon collapsed, however, principally due to two factors: First, the parallels are dubious. The myths of dying and rising gods in pagan religions are merely seasonal symbols for the processes of nature and have no relation to historical individuals. As Grass points out, it would be "completely unthinkable" that the original disciples could have come to believe that Jesus of Nazareth was risen from the dead on the basis of pagan myths about dying and rising seasonal gods.[17] Secondly, there is in any case scarcely any trace at all of such pagan cults of dying and rising gods in first-century Palestine.[18] The causal connection is simply not there.

Not From Jewish Influences

The question then is: would the disciples have come up with the idea that Jesus had been raised from the dead because of Jewish influences? Again, the answer would seem to be, no. To understand this, we need to look at what the Jewish conception of the resurrection was. The belief in the resurrection of the dead is explicitly mentioned three times in the OT: Isaiah 26:19, Ezekiel 37, and Daniel 12:2. During the intertestamental period, the belief in the resurrection of the dead became a widespread hope. In Jesus' day this belief was held to by the party of the Pharisees, although it was denied by the party of the Sadducees. So the belief in resurrection was itself nothing new but rather was a prominent Jewish belief.

But the Jewish conception of the resurrection differed in two fundamental respects from the resurrection of Jesus. First, in Jewish thought the resurrection always occurred after the end of the world. The renowned NT scholar Joachim Jeremias explains:

> Ancient Judaism did not know of an anticipated resurrection as an event of history. Nowhere does one find in the literature anything comparable to the resurrection of Jesus. Certainly resurrections of the dead were known, but these always concerned resuscitations, the return to the earthly life. In no place in the late Judaic literature does it concern a resurrection to *doxa* [glory] as an event of history.[19]

For a Jew the resurrection always occurred after the end of history. He had no conception of a resurrection within history. We find this typical Jewish frame of mind in the gospels themselves. Look at John 11:23-24, for example. Here Jesus is about to raise Lazarus from the dead. He tells Martha, "Your brother shall rise again." What is her response? "Martha said to Him, 'I know that he will rise again in the resurrection on the last day.'"

She had no inkling of a resurrection within history; she thought Jesus was talking about the resurrection at the end of the world. I think that it's for this same reason that the disciples had so much trouble understanding Jesus' predictions of his own resurrection. They thought he was talking about the resurrection at the end of the world. Look at Mark 9:9-11, for example.

> And as they were coming down from the mountain, He gave them orders not to relate to anyone what they had seen, until the Son of Man should rise from the dead. And they seized upon that statement, discussing with one another what rising from the dead might mean. And they began questioning Him, saying, "Why is it that the scribes say that first Elijah must come?"

Here Jesus predicts his resurrection, and what do the disciples ask? "Why is it that the scribes say that first Elijah must come?" In the OT, it was predicted that the prophet Elijah would come again before the great and terrible Day of the Lord, the judgment day when the dead would be raised. The disciples could not understand the idea of a resurrection occurring within history prior to the end of the world. Hence, Jesus' predictions only confused them. Thus, given the Jewish conception of the resurrection, the disciples after Jesus' crucifixion would not have come up with the idea that he had been raised. They would have only looked forward to the resurrection at the last day and, in keeping with Jewish custom, perhaps preserved his tomb as a shrine where his bones could rest until the resurrection.

Second, in Jewish thought, the resurrection was always the resurrection of all the righteous or all the people. They had no conception of the resurrection of an isolated individual. Ulrich Wilckens, another prominent NT critic, explains:

> For nowhere do the Jewish texts speak of the resurrection of an individual which already occurs before the resurrection of the righteous in the end time and is differentiated and separate from it; nowhere does the participation of the righteous in the salvation at the end time depend on their belonging to the Messiah, who was raised in advance as "First of those raised by God" (1 Cor. 15:20).[20]

So once again we find that the resurrection of Jesus differed fundamentally from Jewish belief. The disciples had no idea of the resurrection of an isolated individual. Therefore, after Jesus' crucifixion, all they could do was wait with longing for the general resurrection of the dead to see their Master again.

For these two reasons, then, we cannot explain the disciples' belief in Jesus' resurrection as a result of Jewish influences. Left to themselves, the disciples would never have come to believe that Jesus' resurrection had already occurred. C. F. D. Moule of Cambridge University concludes:

> If the coming into existence of the Nazarenes, a phenomenon unde-niably attested by the New Testament, rips a great hole in history, a hole the size and shape of the Resurrection, what does the secular historian purpose to stop it up with? . . . the birth and rapid rise of the Christian Church . . . *remain an unsolved enigma for any histo-rian who refuses to take seriously the only explanation offered by the Church itself.*[21]

Translation Versus Resurrection

But let's push the argument one notch further. Suppose the disciples were not simply "left to themselves" after the crucifixion. Suppose that some-how Jesus' tomb was found empty and the shock of finding the empty tomb caused the disciples to see hallucinations of Jesus. The question is: Would they then have concluded that he had been raised from the dead!

Now you are probably thinking: "But those theories have already been refuted and shown to be false." That's true. But let's be generous and sup-pose for the sake of argument that this is what happened. Would the dis-ciples have concluded that Jesus had been raised from the dead?

The answer would seem to be, no. This brings us back to a point I men-tioned earlier. Hallucinations, as projections of the mind, can contain nothing new. Therefore, given the current Jewish beliefs about life after death, the disciples would have projected hallucinations of Jesus in heaven or in Abraham's bosom, where the souls of the righteous dead were believed to abide until the resurrection. And such visions would not have caused belief in Jesus' resurrection.

At the most, it would have only led the disciples to say Jesus had been *translated*, not *raised*. You see, the Jews had another belief besides resur-rection, called translation. In the OT, figures such as Enoch and Elijah did not die but were translated directly into heaven. In an extra-canonical Jewish writing called The Testament of Job, the story is told of the trans-lation of two children killed in the collapse of a house. The children are killed when the house collapses, but when the rescuers clear away the rub-ble their bodies are not to be found. Meanwhile, the mother sees a vision of the two children glorified in heaven, where they have been translated by God. It needs to be emphasized that for the Jew a translation is not the same as a resurrection. They are distinct categories. Translation is the bodily assumption of someone out of this world into heaven. Resurrection is the raising up of a dead man in the space-time universe.

Thus, given Jewish beliefs concerning translation and resurrection, the disciples would not have preached that Jesus had been raised from the dead. At the very most, the empty tomb and hallucinations of Jesus would have only caused them to believe in the translation of Jesus, for this fit in with their Jewish frame of thought. But they would not have come up with the idea that Jesus had been raised from the dead, for this contradicted the Jewish belief in at least two fundamental respects.

Conclusion

The origin of Christianity owes itself to the belief of the earliest disciples that God had raised Jesus from the dead. That belief cannot be accounted for in terms of either Christian, pagan, or Jewish influences. Even if we grant, for the sake of argument, that the tomb was somehow emptied and the disciples saw hallucinations—which we have seen to be false anyway—the origin of the belief in Jesus' resurrection still cannot be explained. Such events would only have led the disciples to say that Jesus had been translated, not resurrected. The origin of the Christian faith is therefore inexplicable unless Jesus really rose from the dead.

CONCLUSION

Now we are ready to summarize all three of our discussions: First, we saw that numerous lines of historical evidence prove that the tomb of Jesus was found empty by a group of his women followers. Furthermore, no natural explanation has been offered that can plausibly account for this fact. Second, we saw that several lines of historical evidence established that on numerous occasions and in different places Jesus appeared physically and bodily alive from the dead to various witnesses. Again, no natural explanation in terms of hallucinations can plausibly account for these appearances. And finally, we saw that the very origin of the Christian faith depends on belief in the resurrection. Moreover, this belief cannot be accounted for as the result of any natural influences.

As one reflects on this evidence, it is striking how successfully the historical facts undergirding the inference to the resurrection of Jesus pass the received tests of authenticity. Evans has recently argued that the same criteria used to establish the authenticity of the sayings of Jesus can also be used to establish the putatively miraculous deeds of Jesus.[22] What is intriguing is that a glance at our case on behalf of the historicity of Jesus' resurrection reveals that much of the evidence I have marshaled is based on an implicit application of precisely the same criteria employed by Evans. For example:

1. *Multiple Attestation.* The resurrection appearances enjoy multiple attestation from Pauline and gospel traditions, and the latter themselves multiply attest to appearances, in some cases the same ones. Moreover, the Johannine account of the empty tomb seems to be independent of that in the Synoptics. And, of course, the fact that the first disciples came to believe in Jesus' resurrection is attested throughout the NT.

2. *Dissimilarity.* The argument based on the origin of the Christian faith is a clear example of the application of this criterion, for the argument consists in showing that the origin of the disciples' belief in Jesus' resurrection cannot be explained as the result of either antecedent Jewish influences, because of its dissimilarity, nor as a retrojection of Christian theology.

3. *Embarrassment.* The force of the argument based on the discovery of the empty tomb by women derives in large part from this criterion, for their role in the story was useless, not to say counterproductive, for the early church and would have been much better served by men.

4. *Context and Expectation.* Again, the argument concerning the origin of the Christian way appeals to the absence of any expectation in Judaism of a dying, much less rising, Messiah in order to show that the disciples' belief in Jesus' resurrection cannot plausibly be explained as the outgrowth of Jewish beliefs and expectations.

5. *Effect.* According to this criterion, an adequate cause must be posited for some established effect. The conversion of James and Paul, the earliest Jewish polemic concerning the disciples' alleged theft of the body, and the disciples' transformation after the crucifixion all constitute effects which point to the resurrection appearances, the empty tomb, and the disciples' coming to believe that Jesus was risen as their sufficient causes.

6. *Principles of Embellishment.* It was on the basis of this criterion that I argued that the Markan account of the empty tomb, in contrast to the apologetically and theologically embellished account in the Gospel of Peter, was not a late legend.

7. *Coherence.* The very fact that we have three great, independently established facts pointing to the resurrection of Jesus—namely, the empty tomb, the resurrection appearances, and the origin of the Christian faith— is a powerful argument from coherence for the historicity of the resurrection. Moreover, these facts cohere interestingly with each other; for example, the coherence between Jesus' physical resurrection appearances, Paul's teaching on the nature of the resurrection body, and the empty tomb.

Thus, the complex of facts which we have examined in support of the historicity of Jesus' resurrection passes the same tests for authenticity that serve to establish the authentic core of Jesus' sayings and therefore deserves to be accorded no less degree of credibility than the genuineness of those utterances of Jesus.

But does the resurrection of Jesus adequately explain this body of evidence? Is it any better an explanation than the implausible naturalistic explanations proferred in the past? In order to answer these questions, let's recall McCullagh's seven criteria for the testing of a historical hypothesis and apply them to the hypothesis that God raised Jesus from the dead.

1. *The hypothesis, together with other true statements, must imply further statements describing present, observable data.* Dialectical theologians like Barth often spoke of the resurrection as a supra-historical event; but even though the cause of the resurrection is beyond history, that event nonetheless has a historical margin in the empty tomb and resurrection appearances. As J. A. T. Robinson nicely put it, there was not simply nothing to show for it; rather there was *nothing* to show for it (that is, an empty tomb)![123] Moreover, there is the Christian faith itself to show for it. The present, observable data is chiefly in the form of historical texts which form the basis of the historian's reconstruction of the events of Easter.

2. *The hypothesis must have greater explanatory scope than rival hypotheses.* The resurrection hypothesis, we have seen, exceeds counter-explanations like hallucinations or the wrong tomb theory precisely by explaining all three of the great facts at issue, whereas these rival hypotheses only explain one or two.

3. *The hypothesis must have greater explanatory power than rival hypotheses.* This is perhaps the greatest strength of the resurrection hypothesis. The conspiracy theory or the apparent death theory just do not convincingly account for the empty tomb, resurrection appearances, or origin of the Christian faith: on these theories the data (for example, the transformation in the disciples, the historical credibility of the narratives) become very improbable. By contrast, on the hypothesis of the resurrection it seems extremely probable that the observable data with respect to the empty tomb, the appearances, and the disciples' coming to believe in Jesus' resurrection should be just as it is.

4. *The hypothesis must be more plausible than rival hypotheses.* We have already seen that once one abandons the philosophical prejudice against the miraculous, the resurrection is no more implausible than its rivals, nor are they more plausible than the resurrection.

5. *The hypothesis must be less ad hoc than rival hypotheses.* It will be recalled that while McCullagh thought that the resurrection hypothesis possesses great explanatory scope and power, he nevertheless felt that it was *ad hoc*, which he defines in terms of the number of new suppositions made by a

hypothesis about the past which are not already implied by existing knowledge. So defined, however, it is difficult to see why the resurrection hypothesis is extraordinarily *ad hoc*. It seems to require only one new supposition: that God exists. Surely the rival hypotheses require many new suppositions. For example, the conspiracy theory requires us to suppose that the moral character of the disciples was defective, which is certainly not implied by already existing knowledge; the apparent death theory requires the supposition that the centurion's lance thrust into Jesus' side was just a superficial poke or is an unhistorical detail in the narrative, which again goes beyond existing knowledge; the hallucination theory requires us to suppose some sort of emotional preparation of the disciples which predisposed them to project visions of Jesus alive, which is not implied by our knowledge. Such examples could be multiplied. It should be noted, too, that scientific hypotheses regularly include the supposition of the existence of new entities, such as quarks, strings, gravitons, black holes, and the like, without those theories being characterized as *ad hoc*. Moreover, for the person who is already a theist, the resurrection hypothesis does not even introduce the new supposition of God's existence, since that is already implied by his existing knowledge. So the resurrection hypothesis cannot be said to be *ad hoc* simply in virtue of the number of new suppositions it introduces.

If our hypothesis is *ad hoc*, then, it must be for some other reasons. Philosophers of science have found it notoriously difficult to explain what it is exactly that makes a hypothesis *ad hoc*. There seems to be an ill-defined air of artificiality or contrivedness about a hypothesis deemed to be *ad hoc*, which can be sensed, if not explained, by those who are seasoned practitioners of the relevant science. Now I think that the sense of discomfiture which many, *even theists*, feel about appealing to God as part of an explanatory hypothesis for some phenomenon in the world is that so doing has this air of being contrived. It just seems too easy when confronted with some unexplained phenomenon to throw up one's hands and say, "God did it!" The universal disapprobation of the so-called "God of the gaps" and the impulse towards methodological naturalism in science and history spring from the sense of illegitimacy attending such appeals to God. Is the hypothesis that "God raised Jesus from the dead" *ad hoc* in this sense?

I think not. One of the most important contributions of the traditional defenders of miracles was their drawing attention to the religio-historical context in which a purported miracle occurs. A supernatural explanation of the facts of the empty tomb, the resurrection appearances, and the origin of the Christian faith is not *ad hoc* because those events took place, as we have seen, in the context of and as the climax to Jesus' own unparalleled life, ministry, and personal claims, in which a supernatural hypothesis readily fits. It is also precisely because of this historical context that the resurrection hypothesis does not seem *ad hoc* when compared to miraculous explanations of other sorts: for example, that a "psychological miracle" occurred, causing normal men and women to become conspirators and liars who would be willingly martyred for their subterfuge; or that a "biological miracle" occurred, which prevented Jesus' expiring on the cross (despite the spear-thrust through his chest, and so forth) or his dying of exposure in the tomb. It is these miraculous hypotheses which strike us as artificial and contrived, not the resurrection hypothesis, which makes abundantly good sense in the context of Jesus' ministry and radical personal claims. Thus, it seems to me that the resurrection hypothesis cannot be characterized as excessively *ad hoc*.

6. *The hypothesis must be disconfirmed by fewer accepted beliefs than rival hypotheses.* I can't think of any accepted beliefs which disconfirm the resurrection hypothesis—unless one thinks of, say, "Dead men do not rise" as disconfirmatory. But then we are just back to the problem of miracles again. I've argued that this inductive generalization does nothing to disconfirm the hypothesis that God raised Jesus from the dead. By contrast, rival theories are disconfirmed by accepted beliefs about, for example, the instability of conspiracies, the likelihood of death as a result of crucifixion, the psychological characteristics of hallucinatory experiences, and so forth, as we have seen.

7. *The hypothesis must so exceed its rivals in fulfilling conditions (2)-(6) that there is little chance of a rival hypothesis exceeding it in meeting these conditions.* There is certainly little chance of any of the rival hypotheses suggested to date ever exceeding the resurrection hypothesis in fulfilling the above conditions. The stupefaction of contemporary scholarship when confronted with the facts of the empty tomb, the resurrection appearances, and the origin of the Christian faith suggests that no better rival is anywhere on the horizon. Once one gives up the prejudice against miracles, it's hard to deny that the resurrection of Jesus is the best explanation of the facts.

In conclusion, therefore, three great, independently established facts—the empty tomb, the resurrection appearances, and the origin of the Christian faith—all point to the same marvelous conclusion: that God raised Jesus from the dead. Given that miracles are possible, this conclusion cannot be debarred to anyone seeking for the meaning to existence who sees therein the hope of eternal life.

Given the religio-historical context in which this event occurred, the significance of Jesus' resurrection is clear: it is the divine vindication of Jesus' radical personal claims. As Wolfhart Pannenberg explains,

The resurrection of Jesus acquires such decisive meaning, not merely because someone or anyone has been raised from the dead, but because it is Jesus of Nazareth, whose execution was instigated by the Jews because he had blasphemed against God. If this man was raised from the dead, then that plainly means that the God whom he had supposedly blasphemed has committed himself to him. . . . The resurrection can only be understood as the divine vindication of the man whom the Jews had rejected as a blasphemer.[24]

PRACTICAL APPLICATION

The material I've presented on the resurrection can be nicely summarized into an evangelistic message that can be used effectively on university campuses. It can even be used in personal evangelism, if you can arrange with the person with whom you're sharing to set up a time when you can lay out the evidence. It's more effective to thus lay out the case as a whole rather than present and discuss it piecemeal, for the impact of the cumulative case is greater.

For example, I was once discussing the gospel with a student who seemed open but was hesitant. I challenged him to consider the evidence for the resurrection of Jesus, and he told me, "If you can prove that Jesus rose from the dead, I'll become a Christian." So I made an appointment to see him the next week to lay out my case. When I met with him again, I submitted the evidence to him for an uninterrupted twenty minutes and then asked him what he thought. He was virtually speechless. I asked, "Are you now ready to become a Christian?" "Well, I don't know," he said indecisively. So I said that he should think about it some more and that I would come back again the following week to see what he had decided. By the third week, he was ready, and together in his dorm room we prayed to invite Christ into his life. It was one of the most thrilling experiences I have had in seeing God use apologetics to draw someone to himself!

Let me encourage you to work up a talk or a case of your own that you can use in evangelistic meetings or contacts. And then always be prepared to give this defense to anyone who calls you to account for the hope that is in you.

The Ultimate Apologetic

T HROUGHOUT THIS BOOK we've examined many arguments in support of the Christian faith. I've argued that we can know Christianity is true because of the self-authenticating witness of God's Holy Spirit, and that we can show it to be true by means of rational argument and evidence. We have seen the human predicament without God and immortality, and how this leads to futility and despair. But we have also examined the evidence for a Christian solution to this predicament: evidence that a personal Creator of the universe exists and that Jesus Christ's offer of eternal life to those who believe in him is genuine, being confirmed by his resurrection from the dead. But now I want to share with you what I believe to be the most effective and practical apologetic for the Christian faith that I know of. This apologetic will help you to win more persons to Christ than all the other arguments in your apologetic arsenal put together.

This ultimate apologetic involves two relationships: your relationship with God and your relationship with others. These two relationships are distinguished by Jesus in his teaching on the duty of man: "And one of them, a lawyer, asked him a question, to test him. 'Teacher, which is the great commandment in the law?' And he said to him, 'You shall love the Lord your God with all your heart, and with all your soul, and with all your mind. This is the great and first commandment. And a second is like it, You shall love your neighbor as yourself. On these two commandments depend all the law and the prophets'" (Matt 22:35-40). The first commandment governs our relationship to God; the second our relationship with our fellow man. Let's examine each of these relationships in turn.

First, our relationship with God. This is governed by the great commandment:

> Hear, O Israel; The Lord our God is one Lord; and you shall love the Lord your God with all your heart, and with all your soul, and with all your might. And these words which I command you this day shall be upon your heart; and you shall teach them diligently to your children, and shall talk of them when you sit in your house, and when you walk by the way, and when you lie down, and when you rise. And you shall bind them as a sign upon your hand, and they shall be as frontlets between your eyes. And you shall write them on the doorposts of your house and on your gates. (Deut 6:4-9)

Notice the importance given to this commandment—loving God is to be our preoccupation in life. Sometimes we get the idea that our main duty in life is to serve God, maybe by being a great apologist, and forget, as J. I. Packer reminds us, that our primary aim ought to be to learn to know God:

> We both can and must get our life's priorities straight. From current Christian publications you might think that the most vital issue for any . . . Christian in the world today is . . . social witness, or dialogue with other Christians and other faiths, or refuting this or that "-ism," or developing a Christian philosophy and culture, or what have you. But our line of study makes the present day concentration on these things look like a gigantic conspiracy of misdirection. Of course, it is not that; the issues themselves are real and must be dealt with in their place. But it is tragic that, in paying attention to them, so many in our day seem to have been distracted from what was, is, and always will be the true priority for every human being—that is, learning to know God in Christ.[1]

In our relationship with God we are to give him his legal right—namely, all that we have and are. The Christian is to be as a matter of course totally dedicated to God (Rom 12:1-2) and filled with the Holy Spirit (Eph 5:18). For his part God gives to us positionally, as we are in Christ, forgiveness of sins (Eph 1:7), eternal life (Rom 6:23), adoption as sons (Gal 4:5), and the availability of unlimited help and power (Eph 1:18-19). Think of how much that means! Moreover, he gives to us experientially, as we are Spirit-filled, the fruit of the Spirit: love, joy, peace, patience, kindness, goodness, faithfulness, gentleness, and self-control (Gal 5:22-23). When this relationship is intact, the product in our lives will be righteousness (Rom 6:16), and the by-product of righteousness is happiness. Happiness is an elusive thing and will never be found when pursued directly; but it springs into being as one pursues the knowledge of God and his righteousness is realized in us.

The other relationship is our relationship with our fellow men. This is governed by the second great commandment, as Paul explains: "The commandments, 'You shall not commit adultery, You shall not kill, You shall not steal, You shall not covet,' and any other commandment, are summed up in this sentence, 'You shall love your neighbor as yourself'" (Rom 13:9). Why is love the great commandment? Simply because all the other commandments are the outworking of love in practice (Rom 13:10). When we love others, we simply show that we have understood God's love for us, and it is being worked out in our lives toward others. As John says, "If God so loved us, we also ought to love one another" (1 John 4:11). What does love involve? To begin with, it means possessing the characteristics of love described in 1 Corinthians 13. Can we say, "I am patient and kind, I am not jealous or boastful, arrogant or rude; I am not selfish or irritable or resentful; I am not happy about wrong, but I rejoice in the right; I bear all things, believe all things, hope all things, endure all things"? Moreover, love will involve having a servant's heart, a willingness to count others better than yourself and to serve and look out for their interests as well as your own (Gal 5:13b-14; Phil 2:3). Certainly Jesus himself is our supreme model here: think of how he stooped to wash his disciples' dirty feet!

What will be the result when these two relationships are strong and close? There will be a unity and warmth among Christians. There will be a love that pervades the body of Christ; as Paul describes it, "speaking the truth in love, we are to grow up in every way into him who is the head, into Christ, from whom the whole body, joined and knit together by every joint with which it is supplied, when each part is working properly, makes bodily growth and upbuilds itself in love" (Eph 4:15-16). And what will be the result of this unity through love? Jesus himself gives us the answer in his prayer for the church: "that they may all be one; even as Thou, Father art in me, and I in Thee, that they also may be in Us; that the world may believe that Thou didst send Me . . . I in them, and Thou in Me, that they may be perfected in unity, that the world may know that Thou didst love Me and didst love them, even as Thou didst love Me" (John 17:21-23). According to Jesus, our love is a sign to all people that we are his disciples (John 13:35); but even more than that, our love and unity are living proof to the world that God the Father has sent his Son Jesus Christ and that the Father loves people even as he loves Jesus. When people see this—our love for one another and our unity through love—then they will in turn be drawn by this to Christ and will respond to the gospel's offer of salvation.

More often than not, it is what you *are* rather than what you *say* that will bring an unbeliever to Christ.

This, then, is the ultimate apologetic. For the ultimate apologetic is: your life.

LITERATURE
CITED OR RECOMMENDED

Chapter One:
FAITH AND REASON

HISTORICAL BACKGROUND

Augustine. *Against the Epistle of Manichaeus Called Fundamental*. Translated by Richard Stothert. In *The Nicene and Post-Nicene Fathers*. Vol. 4: *The Writings Against the Manichaeans and Against the Donatists*. Edited by Philip Schaff. Reprint. Grand Rapids: Eerdmans, 1956. Pp. 125-50.

———. *City of God*. 3 vols. Translated by D. B. Zema, *et al*. Introduction by Etienne Gilson. Fathers of the Church. New York: Fathers of the Church, 1950-4. See particularly 21.61; 22.5.

———. *Confessions*. Translated by V. J. Bourke. Fathers of the Church. New York: Fathers of the Church, 1953.

———. *Letters*. Vol. 1. Translated by Sister Wilfrid Parsons. Fathers of the Church. Washington: Catholic University of America, 1951-6. See particularly letters 22, 28, 82, 147.

———. *On True Religion*. Translated by J. H. Burleigh, Introduction by Louis O. Mink. Chicago: H. Regnery, 1959. See particularly 24; 25.

———. *The Teacher; The Free Choice of the Will; Grace and Free Will*. Translated by R. P. Russell. Fathers of the Church. Washington, D.C.: Catholic University of America, 1968.

Barth, Karl. *Dogmatics in Outline*. Translated by G. J. Thomson. New York: Philosophical Library, 1947.

———. *The Knowledge of God and the Service of God According to the Teaching of the Reformation*. Translated by J. L. M. Haire and I. Henderson. New York: Scribner's, 1939.

Bultmann, Rudolf. "The Case for Demythologizing: A Reply." In *Kerygma and Myth*. Edited by H.-W. Bartsch. Translated by R. H. Fuller. London: SPCK, 1953. 2: 181-94.

———. "Reply to the Theses of J. Schniewind." In *Kerygma and Myth*.

Edited by H.-W. Bartsch. Translated by R. H. Fuller. London: SPCK, 1953. 2: 102-33.

——. *Theologie des Neuen Testaments*. 7th ed. Edited by O. Merk. Tübingen: J. C. B. Mohr, 1961.

Cragg, Gerald R. *Reason and Authority in the Eighteenth Century*. Cambridge: Cambridge U., 1964.

Dodwell, Henry. *Christianity Not Founded on Argument*. 3d. ed. London: M. Cooper, 1743.

Gilson, Etienne. *Reason and Revelation in the Middle Ages*. New York: Scribner's, 1938.

Locke, John. *An Essay Concerning Human Understanding*. Edited with an Introduction by P. H. Nidditch. Oxford: Clarendon, 1975.

——. *The Works of John Locke*. 11th ed. Vol. 9: *A Discourse on Miracles*. London: W. Olridge & Son, 1812.

——. *The Works of John Locke*. 11th ed. Vol. 7: *The Reasonableness of Christianity*. London: W. Oldridge & Son, 1812.

Pannenberg, Wolfhart. *Jesus—God and Man*. Translated by L. L. Wilkins and D. A. Priebe. London: SCM, 1968.

——. "Redemptive Event and History." In *Basic Questions in Theology*. Translated by G. Kehm. Philadelphia: Fortress, 1970. 1: 15-80.

——. "Response to the Discussion." In *New Frontiers in Theology*. Vol. 3: *Theology as History*. Edited by J. M. Robinson and J. B. Cobb, Jr. New York: Harper & Row, 1967.

——. ed. *Revelation as History*. Translated by D. Granskou. London: Macmillan, 1968.

——. "The Revelation of God in Jesus of Nazareth." In *New Frontiers in Theology*. Vol. 3: *Theology as History*. Edited by J. M. Robinson and J. B. Cobb, Jr. New York: Harper & Row, 1967. Pp. 101-33.

Plantinga, Alvin. "Is Belief in God Rational?" In *Rationality and Religious Belief*. Edited by C. F. Delaney. Notre Dame, Ind: U. of Notre Dame, 1979. Pp. 7-27.

——. "Reason and Belief in God." In *Faith and Rationality*. Edited by Alvin Plantinga and Nicholas Wolterstorff. Notre Dame, Ind: U. of Notre Dame, 1983. Pp. 16-93.

——. "Self-Profile." In *Alvin Plantinga*. Edited by James E. Tomberlin and Peter Van Inwagen. Dordrecht, Holland: D. Reidel, 1985. Pp. 55-64.

——. "The Foundations of Theism: a Reply." *Faith and Philosophy* 3 (1986): 298-313.

——. "The Twin Pillars of Christian Scholarship." Grand Rapids: Calvin College and Seminary, 1990.

——. *Warrant: The Current Debate*. New York: Oxford University Press, 1993.

———. *Warrant and Proper Function.* New York: Oxford University Press, 1993.

Stephen, Leslie. *History of English Thought in the Eighteenth Century.* 3d ed. 2 vols. New York: Harcourt, Brace, & World; Harbinger, 1962.

Strauss, Gerhard. *Schriftgebrauch, Schriftauslegung, und Schriftbeweis bei Augustin.* Beiträge zur Geschichte der biblischen Hermeneutik 1. Tübingen: J. C. B. Mohr, 1959.

Thomas Aquinas. *On the Truth of the Catholic Faith [Summa contra gentiles].* 4 vols. Translated with Notes by A. C. Pegis *et al.* Notre Dame, Ind: U. of Notre Dame, 1975. See particularly 1.3, 5, 6, 9; 3.99-103, 154.

———. *Summa theologiae.* 60 vols. London: Eyre & Spottiswoode for Blackfriars, 1964. See particularly 1a.32.1; 1a. 105.8; 2a2ael.4; 3a43.1-4; 3a55.6.

ASSESSMENT

Alston, William P. *Perceiving God: the Epistemology of Religious Experience.* Ithaca, N.Y.: Cornell U. Press, 1991.

Caputo, John D. *Radical Hermeneutics.* Bloomington, Ind.: Indiana U. Press, 1979.

Carnell, Edward John. *An Introduction to Christian Apologetics.* Grand Rapids: Eerdmans, 1948.

Geivett, R. Douglas and Sweetman, Brendan, eds. *Contemporary Perspectives on Religious Epistemology.* New York: Oxford University Press, 1992. A thorough and balanced anthology of contemporary alternatives, with extensive bibliography.

Green, Michael. *Evangelism in the Early Church.* Grand Rapids. Eerdmans, 1970.

Hackett, Stuart. *Oriental Philosophy.* Madison, Wis.: Univ. of Wisconsin Press, 1979.

———. *The Resurrection of Theism.* 2d ed. Grand Rapids: Baker, 1982.

Hick, John. *Faith and Knowledge.* Ithaca, N.Y.: Cornell U., 1957.

Marsh, James L., Caputo, John D., and Westphal, Merold. *Modernity and Its Discontents.* New York: Fordham University Press, 1992.

Mavrodes, George. *Belief in God.* New York: Random House, 1970.

Chapter Two:

THE ABSURDITY OF LIFE WITHOUT GOD

HISTORICAL BACKGROUND

Dostoyevsky, Fyodor. *The Brothers Karamazov.* Translated by C. Garnett.

Foreword by M. Komroff. New York: New American Library, Signet Classics, 1957.

——. *Crime and Punishment*. Translated by C. Garnett. Introduction by E. Simmons. New York: Modern Library, 1950.

Kierkegaard, Soren. *Either/Or*. Translated by D. F. Swenson and L. M. Swenson. Princeton: Princeton U., 1944. Volume 1 describes the first stage of life and Volume 2 the second.

——. *Fear and Trembling*. Edited and translated with an Introduction and Notes by H. V. Hong and E. N. Hong. Princeton: Princeton U., 1983. This handles the religious stage.

Morris, Thomas V. *Making Sense of It All: Pascal and the Meaning of Life*. Grand Rapids: Eerdmans, 1992.

Pascal, Blaise. *Pensées*. Edited by Louis Lafuma. Translated by John Warrington. Everyman's Library. London: Dent, 1960.

Schaeffer, Francis. *Escape from Reason*. Downers Grove, Ill.: InterVarsity Press, 1968.

——. *The God Who Is There*. Chicago: InterVarsity Press, 1968.

——. *How Should We Then Live?* Wheaton, Ill.: Crossway, 1976.

ASSESSMENT

Beckett, Samuel. *Waiting for Godot*. New York: Grove, 1956.

Bloch, Ernst. *Das Prinzip Hoffnung*. 2d ed. 2 vols. Frankfurt am Main. Suhrkamp Verlag, 1959.

Camus, Albert. *The Myth of Sisyphus and Other Essays*. Translated by J. O'Brien. New York: Vintage, 1959.

——. *The Stranger*. Translated by S. Gilbert. New York: Vintage, 1958.

Crick, Francis. "Why I Study Biology." *Washington University Magazine*. Spring 1971, pp. 20-4.

Eliot, T. S. "The Hollow Men." In *The Complete Poems and Plays*. New York: Harcourt, Brace, 1934.

Encyclopaedia Britannica, 15th ed. *Propaedia*, s.v. "The Cosmic Orphan," by Loren Eiseley.

Hesse, Hermann. *Steppenwolf*. Translated by Basil Creighton. New York: Holt, Rinehart and Winston, 1961.

Hocking, W. E. *Types of Philosophy*. New York: Scribner's, 1959.

Hoyle, Fred. *From Stonehenge to Modern Cosmology*. San Francisco: W.H. Freeman, 1972.

Kaufmann, Walter. "Existentialism from Dostoyevsky to Sartre." In *Existentialism from Dostoyevsky to Sartre*. 2d ed. Edited by W. Kaufmann. New York: New American Library, Meridian, 1975. Pp. 11-51.

Kurtz, Paul. *Forbidden Fruit.* Buffalo, N.Y.: Prometheus, 1988.

Monod, Jacques. *Chance and Necessity.* Translated by A. Wainhouse. New York: Alfred A. Knopf, 1971.

Moreland, J.P. *Scaling the Secular City.* Grand Rapids: Baker, 1987. Chap. 4.

Moreland, J.P. and Nielsen, Kai. *Does God Exist?* Nashville: Thomas Nelson, 1990. Rep. ed.: Prometheus Books, 1993. Part II is an excellent debate over ethics without God.

Nielsen, Kai. "Why Should I Be Moral? Revisited." *American Philosophical Quarterly* 21 (1984): 81-91.

Nietzsche, Friedrich. "The Gay Science." In *The Portable Nietzsche.* Edited and translated by W. Kaufmann. New York: Viking, 1954. Pp. 93-102.

——. "The Will to Power." Translated by Walter Kaufmann. In *Existentialism from Dostoyevsky to Sartre.* 2d ed. Edited with an Introduction by W. Kaufmann. New York: New American Library, Meridian, 1975. Pp. 130-2.

Novikov, I.D., and Zeldovich, Ya. B. "Physical Processes Near Cosmological Singularities." *Annual Review of Astronomy and Astrophysics* 11(1973): 387-410.

Rue, Loyal D. "The Saving Grace of Noble Lies." Unpublished address to the American Academy for the Advancement of Science, February, 1991.

Russell, Bertrand. "A Free Man's Worship." In *Why I Am Not a Christian.* Edited by P. Edwards. New York: Simon & Schuster, 1957. Pp. 104-16.

——. Letter to the *Observer*, 6 October 1957.

Sagan, Carl. *Cosmos.* New York: Random House, 1980.

Sartre, Jean-Paul. *Being and Nothingness.* Translated with an Introduction by H. E. Barnes. New York. Washington Square, 1966.

——. "Existentialism Is a Humanism." Translated by P. Mairet. In *Existentialism from Dostoyevsky to Sartre.* 2d ed. Edited with an Introduction by W. Kaufmann. New York: New American Library, Meridian, 1975. Pp. 345-69.

——. *Nausea.* Translated by L. Alexander. London: H. Hamilton, 1962.

——. *No Exit.* Translated by S. Gilbert. New York: Alfred A. Knopf, 1963.

——. "Portrait of the Antisemite." Translated by M. Guggenheim. In *Existentialism from Dostoyevsky to Sartre.* 2d ed. Edited with an Introduction by W. Kaufmann. New York: New American Library, Meridian, 1975. Pp. 329-45.

——. "The Wall." Translated by L. Alexander. In *Existentialism from*

Dostoyevsky to Sartre. 2d ed. Edited with an Introduction by W. Kaufmann. New York: New American Library, Meridian, 1975. Pp. 281-99.

Taylor, Richard. *Ethics, Faith, and Reason.* Englewood Cliffs, N.J.: Prentice-Hall, 1985. An excellent illustration of the desperate lengths to which an ethicist is driven once a divine moral law giver is denied.

Wells, H. G. *The Time Machine.* New York: Berkeley, 1957.

Wurmbrand, Richard. *Tortured for Christ.* London: Hodder & Stoughton, 1967.

Chapter Three:
THE EXISTENCE OF GOD

HISTORICAL BACKGROUND

Al-Ghāzalī. *Kitab al-Iqtisad fi'l-I'tiqad.* Cited in Beaurecueil, S. de. "Gazzali et S. Thomas d'Aqin: Essai sur la preuve de l'existence de Dieu proposee dans l'Iqtisad et sa comparaison avec les `voies' Thomistes." *Bulletin de l'Institut Francais d'Archaeologie Orientale* 46 (1947): 199-238.

———. "The Jerusalem Tract." Translated and edited by A. L. Tibawi. *The Islamic Quarterly* 9 (1965): 95-122.

———. *Tahafut al-Falasifah [Incoherence of the Philosophers].* Translated by Sabih Ahmad Kamali. Lahore, Pakistan: Pakistan Philosophical Congress, 1958.

Anselm. *Proslogion.* In *Anselm of Canterbury.* 4 vols. Edited and translated by Jaspar Hopkins and Herbert Richardson. London: SCM, 1974. See particularly 2, 3.

Aquinas, Thomas. *On the Truth of the Catholic Faith.* Edited and translated by Anton C. Pegis, *et al.* Notre Dame, Ind.: U. of Notre Dame, 1975. See particularly 1.13.

———. *Summa theologiae.* 60 vols. London: Eyre & Spottiswoode for Blackfriars, 1964. See particularly 1a.2, 3.

Aristotle. *The Works of Aristotle.* 12 vols. Edited by W. D. Ross. Oxford: Clarendon, 1908-52.

Chroust, Anton-Hermann. "A Cosmological (Teleological) Proof for the Existence of God in Aristotle's *On Philosophy.*" In *Aristotle: New Light on His Lost Works.* London: Routledge & Kegan Paul, 1972. 2: 159-74.

Craig, William Lane. *The Cosmological Argument from Plato to Leibniz.* New York: Barnes & Noble, 1980.

Leibniz, G. W. F. von. "Monadology." In *Leibniz Selections.* Edited by P. Wiener. New York: Scribner's, 1951. Pp. 533-52.

———. "On the Ultimate Origin of Things." In *Leibniz Selections*. Edited by P. Wiener. New York: Scribner's, 1951. Pp. 345-55.

———. "The Principles of Nature and of Grace, Based on Reason." In *Leibniz Selections*. Edited by P. Wiener. New York: Scribner's, 1951. Pp. 522-33.

———. *Theodicy: Essays on the Goodness of God, the Freedom of Man, and the Origin of Evil*. Translated by E. M. Huggard. London: Routledge & Kegan Paul, 1951.

Paley, William. *Natural Theology: Selections*. Edited with an Introduction by F. Ferré. Indianapolis: Bobbs-Merrill, 1963.

Plato. *The Dialogues of Plato*. 4 vols. 4th ed., rev. Translated with Introductions and Analyses by B. Jowett. Oxford: Clarendon, 1953.

Stephen, Leslie. *History of English Thought in the Eighteenth Century*. 2 vols. 2d ed. London: Smith, Elder, 1881.

ASSESSMENT

Adams, Robert M. "Flavors, Colors, and God." In *The Virtue of Faith*. New York: Oxford University Press, 1987.

Barrow, John D. and Tipler, Frank J. *The Anthropic Cosmological Principle*. Oxford: Clarendon Press, 1986. A compendious update of Paley's catalogue.

Bore, Rick. "The Once and Future Universe." *National Geographic*, June 1983, pp. 704-49.

Brout, R. and Spindel, Ph. "Black Holes Dispute." *Nature* 337 (1989): 216-17.

Cowen, Ron. "Hubble: A Universe Without End." *Science News* 141 (1992): 79.

Craig, William Lane. *The Kalām Cosmological Argument*. New York: Barnes & Noble, 1979.

———. ed. "New Arguments for the Existence of God." *Truth* 3 & 4 (1991). Available from *Truth*, 13612 Midway Rd., Suite 500, Dallas, TX 75244.

———. "The Teleological Argument and the Anthropic Principle." In *The Logic of Rational Theism*. Ed. William L. Craig and M. McLeod. Lewiston, N.Y.: Edwin Mellen, 1990. Pp. 127-53.

Craig, William Lane and Smith, Quentin. *Theism, Atheism, and Big Bang Cosmology*. Oxford: Clarendon Press, 1993.

Davies, P. C. W. *The Physics of Time Asymmetry*. London: Surrey University Press, 1974.

———. "Spacetime Singularities in Cosmology." In *The Study of Time III*.

Edited by J.T. Fraser, N. Lawrence, D. Park. Berlin: Springer, 1978. Pp. 74-91.

Dicus, Duane, *et al.* "Effects of Proton Decay on the Cosmological Future." *Astrophysical Journal* 252 (1982): 1-9.

——. *et al.* "The Future of the Universe." *Scientific American*, March 1983, pp. 90-101.

Dingle, Herbert. *Science at the Crossroads.* London: Martin Brian and O'Keefe, 1972.

Dressler, A. "Cosmological Parameters of the Universe." In *Astronomy, Cosmology, and Fundamental Physics.* Ed. M. Caffo, *et al.* 3rd ESO/CERN Symposium. Dordrecht: Kluwer, 1989.

Eddington, Arthur. *Space, Time, and Gravitation.* 1920; rep. ed.: Cambridge: Cambridge University Press, 1987.

Frank, Carlos S., White, Simon D.M., and Davis, Marc. "Massive Neutrinos and Galaxy Formation." In *The Large Scale Structure of the Universe, Cosmology, and Fundamental Physics.* Ed. G. Setti and L. Van Hove. First ESO/CERN Symposium. Geneva, Switzerland: ESO and CERN, 1984.

Gamow, George. *One, Two, Three, . . . Infinity.* London: Macmillan, 1946.

Gott, J. Richard, *et al.* "Will the Universe Expand Forever?" *Scientific American.* March 1976, pp. 62-79.

Gribbin, John. "Oscillating Universe Bounces Back." *Nature* 259 (1976): 15-16.

Grünbaum, Adolf. "The Pseudo-Problem of Creation in Physical Cosmology." In *Physical Cosmology and Philosophy.* Ed. John Leslie. Philosophical Topics. New York: Macmillan Co., 1990. Pp. 92-112.

——. "Pseudo-Creation of the Big Bang." *Nature* 344 (1990): 821-2.

Hackett, Stuart. *The Resurrection of Theism.* 2d ed. Grand Rapids: Baker, 1982.

Hawking, Stephen. *A Brief History of Time.* New York: Bantam Books, 1988.

Hoyle, Fred. *Astronomy and Cosmology: A Modern Course.* San Francisco: W.H. Freeman, 1975.

Hume, David. *The Letters of David Hume.* 2 vols. Edited by J. Y. T. Greig. Oxford: Clarendon, 1932.

Isham, C.J. "Creation of the Universe as a Quantum Process." In *Physics, Philosophy, and Theology.* Ed. R.J. Russell, W. R. Stoeger, and G.V. Coyne. Vatican City State: Vatican Observatory, 1988.

——. "Quantum Theories of the Creation of the Universe." Unpublished paper, a preliminary version of which appears in *Interpreting the Universe as Creation.* Ed. V. Brummer. The Netherlands: Pharos, 1991.

———. "Space, Time, and Quantum Cosmology." Paper presented at the conference "God, Time, and Modern Physics." Science and Religion Forum, March 1990.

Jaki, Stanley L. *Science and Creation*. Edinburgh: Scottish Academic, 1974.

Jastrow, Robert. *God and the Astronomers*. New York: W.W. Norton, 1978.

King, Ivan. *The Universe Unfolding*. San Francisco: W. H. Freeman, 1976.

Leslie, John. *Universes*. London: Routledge, 1989.

Mackie, J. L. *The Miracle of Theism*. Oxford: Clarendon, 1982.

Novikov, I. D., and Zeldovich, Ya. B. "Physical Processes Near Cosmological Singularities." *Annual Review of Astronomy and Astrophysics* 11 (1973): 387-410.

Peebles, P.J.E. and Silk, Joseph. "A Cosmic Book of Phenomena." *Nature* 346 (1990): 233-9.

Plantinga, Alvin. *The Nature of Necessity*. Oxford: Clarendon, 1974. See particularly the section on the ontological argument.

———. "Two Dozen (or So) Theistic Arguments." Paper presented at the 33rd Annual Philosophy Conference, Wheaton College, October 23-25, 1986.

Physics Today. "Do Neutrinos Oscillate from One Variety to Another?" July 1980, pp. 17-19.

Russell, Bertrand. *Our Knowledge of the External World*. 2d ed. New York: W. W. Norton, 1929.

Sandage, Allan, and Tammann, G. A. "The Dynamical Parameters of the Universe." In *The Large Scale Structure of the Universe, Cosmology, and Fundamental Physics*. Ed. G. Setti and L. Van Hove. First ESO/CERN Symposium. Geneva, Switzerland: ESO and Cern, 1984.

———. "Steps Toward the Hubble Constant. I-IX." *Astrophysical Journal* 190 (1974): 525-38; 191 (1974): 603-21; 194 (1974): 223-43, 559-68; 196 (1975): 313-28; 197 (1975): 265-80; 210 (1976): 7-24; 256 (1982): 339-45; 365 (1990): 1-12.

Schlegel, Richard, "Time and Thermodynamics." In *The Voices of Time*. Ed. J.T. Fraser. London: Penguin, 1968.

Schlesinger, George. "The Similarities between Space and Time." *Mind* 84 (1975): 161-76.

Silk, Joseph. *The Big Bang*. 2d ed. San Francisco: W.H. Freeman, 1989.

———. "Cosmology Back to the Beginning." *Nature* 356 (1992): 742.

Tennant, F. R. *Philosophical Theology*. 2 vols. Cambridge: Cambridge University Press, 1930. His teleological argument is in volume 2.

Tinsley, Beatrice. "From Big Bang to Eternity?" *Natural History Magazine*. October 1975, pp. 102-5.

Trefil, James S. "How the Universe Began." *Smithsonian*. May 1983, pp. 132-51.

_____. "How the Universe Will End." *Smithsonian*. June 1983, pp. 72-83.

Vishniac, Ethan T. "Relativistic Collisionless Particles and the Evolution of Cosmological Perturbations." *Astrophysical Journal* 257 (1982): 456-72.

Wainright, William J. "Review of *The Kalām Cosmological Argument*, by William Lane Craig." *Noûs* 16 (1982): 328-34.

Chapter Four:
THE PROBLEM OF MIRACLES

HISTORICAL BACKGROUND

Brown, Colin. *Miracles and the Critical Mind*. Grand Rapids: Eerdmans, 1984.

Clarke, Samuel. *A Discourse concerning the Unchangeable Obligations of Natural Religion and the Truth and Certainty of the Christian Revelation*. London: W. Botham, 1706.

Diderot, Denis. "Philosophical Thoughts." In *Diderot's Early Philosophical Works*. Translated by M. Jourdain. Open Court Series of Classics of Science and Philosophy 4. Chicago: Open Court, 1916.

Houtteville, Abbé. *La religion chrétienne prouvée par les faits*. 3 vols. Paris: Mercier & Boudet, 1740.

Hume, David. *Enquiries Concerning Human Understanding and Concerning the Principles of Morals*. 3d ed. Edited by P. H. Nidditch. Oxford: Clarendon, 1975. Chapter 10 of the first enquiry constitutes his case against miracles.

Le Clerc, Jean. *Five Letters Concerning the Inspiration of the Holy Scriptures*. London: [n. p.], 1690.

Less, Gottfried. *Wahrheit der christlichen Religion*. 4th ed. Göttingen: Georg Ludewig Förster, 1776.

Paley, William. *A View of the Evidences of Christianity*. 2 vols. 5th ed. London: R. Faulder, 1796; rep. ed.: Westmead, England: Gregg International, 1970.

Sherlock, Thomas. *The Tryal of the Witnesses of the Resurrection of Jesus*. London: J. Roberts, 1729.

Spinoza, Baruch. *Tractatus theologico-politicus*. Trans. Samuel Shirley, with an Introduction by Brad S. Gregory. Leiden: E. J. Brill, 1989.

Stephen, Leslie. *History of English Thought in the Eighteenth Century*. 2 vols. 3d ed. New York: Harcourt, Brace, & World; Harbinger, 1962.

Turrettin, J. Alph. *Traité de la vérité de la religion chrétienne.* 2d ed. 7 vols. Translated by J. Vernet. Geneva: Henri-Albert Gosse, 1745-55.

Voltaire, Marie Francois. *A Philosophical Dictionary.* 2 vols. New York: Harcourt, Brace, & World; Harbinger, 1962. See particularly the article on miracles.

ASSESSMENT

Bilinskyj, Stephen S. "God, Nature, and the Concept of Miracle." Ph.D. dissertation. University of Notre Dame, 1982.

Dickens, Charles. "A Christmas Carol." In *Christmas Books*, by Charles Dickens. Introduced by E. Farejon. London: Oxford, 1954.

Encyclopedia of Philosophy. S.v. "Miracles," by Antony Flew.

Freddoso, Alfred J. "The Necessity of Nature." *Midwest Studies in Philosophy* 11 (1986): 215-42.

Hesse, Mary. "Miracles and the Laws of Nature." In *Miracles.* Edited by C.F.D. Moule. London: A.R. Mowbray, 1965.

Pannenberg, Wolfhart. "Jesu Geschichte und unsere Geschichte." In *Glaube und Wirklichkeit.* München: Chr. Kaiser, 1975.

——. *Jesus—God and Man.* Translated by L.L. Wilkins and D.A. Priebe. London: SCM, 1968.

Schweitzer, Albert. *The Quest of the Historical Jesus.* 3d ed. Translated by W. Montgomery. London: Adam & Charles Black, 1954.

Strauss, David Friedrich. *The Life of Jesus Critically Examined.* Translated by G. Eliot. Edited with an Introduction by P.C. Hodgson. Lives of Jesus Series. London: SCM, 1973.

Swinburne, Richard. *The Concept of Miracle.* New York: Macmillan, 1970.

——. ed. *Miracles.* Philosophical Topics. New York: Macmillan, 1989.

Chapter Five:

THE PROBLEM OF HISTORICAL KNOWLEDGE

HISTORICAL BACKGROUND

Anselm. *Cur Deus Homo.* In *Basic Writings.* 2d ed. Translated by S.N. Deane. Introduction by C. Hartshorne. Open Court Library of Philosophy. LaSalle, Ill.: Open Court, 1968. Pp. 171-288.

De la Chaise, Filleau. "Discours sur les livres de Moise." In *Discours sur les "Pensées" de M. Pascal.* Edited with an Introduction by V. Giraud. Collections des chefs-d'oeuvre méconnues. Paris: Editions Bossard, 1922.

Grotius, Hugo. *The Truth of the Christian Religion.* Notes by J. Le Clerc. Translated by J. Clarke. London: 1709.

Kümmel, Werner Georg. *The New Testament: The History of the Investigation of Its Problems.* Translated by S. McL. Gilmour and H. C. Kee. Nashville: Abingdon, 1972.

Ladd, George. "The Knowledge of God: The Saving Acts of God." In *Basic Christian Doctrines.* Edited by Carl F. H. Henry. New York: Holt, Rinehart, and Winston, 1962. Pp. 7-13.

Leslie, Charles. *A Short and Easie Method with the Deists.* 2d ed. London: C. Brome, E. Pode, & Geo. Strahan, 1699.

Mornay, Philippe de. *De la vérité de la religion chrétienne.* Anvers: Imprimerie de Christofle Plantin, 1581. Translated as *A Work Concerning the Trueness of the Christian Religion,* by P. Sidney and A. Goldring. London: 1617.

Thomas Aquinas. *Summa theologiae.* 60 vols. London: Eyre & Spottiswoode for Blackfriars, 1964.

Thompson, J. Westfall, and Holm, Bernard J. *A History of Historical Writing.* 2 vols. New York: Macmillan, 1942.

Vives, Juan Luis. *De veritate fidei christianae.* Reprint. London: Gregg International, 1964.

ASSESSMENT

Ankersmit, F.R. "The Dilemma of Contemporary Anglo-Saxon Philosophy of History." In "Knowing and Telling History: the Anglo-Saxon Debate." *History and Theory* Beiheft 25 (1986): 1-27.

Aron, Raymond. "Relativism in History." In *The Philosophy of History in Our Time.* Edited by H. Meyerhoff. Garden City, N.Y.: Doubleday, 1959. Pp. 153-62.

Beard, Charles. "That Noble Dream." In *The Varieties of History.* Edited by F. Stern. Cleveland: World, Meridian, 1956. Pp. 314-28.

Becker, Carl. "What Are Historical Facts?" In *The Philosophy of History in Our Time.* Edited by H. Meyerhoff. Garden City, N.Y.: Doubleday 1959. Pp. 120-39.

Berlin, Isaiah. "The Concept of Scientific History." In *Philosophical Analysis and History.* Edited by W. H. Dray. Sources in Contemporary Philosophy. New York: Harper & Row, 1966.

Bernstein, Richard J. *Beyond Objectivism and Relativism: Science, Hermeneutics, and Praxis.* Oxford: Basil Blackwell, 1983.

Blake, Christopher. "Can History Be Objective?" In *Theories of History.* Edited by P. Gardiner. Glencoe, Ill.: Free Press, 1959. Pp. 329-43.

Carr, E. H. *What Is History?* New York: Random House, Vintage, 1953.

Collingwood, R. G. "Are History and Science Different Kinds of Knowledge?" In *Essays in the Philosophy of History.* Edited by W. Debbins. Austin, Tex.: U. of Texas, 1965. Pp. 23-33.

——. *An Autobiography*. London: Oxford, 1939.

——. "Croce's Philosophy of History." In *Essays in the Philosophy of History*. Edited by William Debbins. Austin, Tex.: U. of Texas, 1965. Pp. 3-22.

——. *The Idea of History*. Edited by T. M. Know. Oxford: Oxford, Galaxy, 1956.

Copleston, Frederick. "Problems of Objectivity." In *On the History of Philosophy*. London: Search Press, 1979. Pp. 40-65.

"Creation/Evolution and Faith." *Christian Scholar's Review* 21/1 (1991).

Debbins, William. "Introduction." In *Essays in the Philosophy of History*, by R. G. Collingwood. Edited by W. Debbins. Austin, Tex.: U. of Texas, 1965.

Donagan, Alan. "Introduction." In *Philosophy of History*. Edited by A. Donagan and B. Donagan. Sources in Philosophy. New York: Macmillan, 1965. Pp. 1-22.

Dray, W.H. "Comment." In *Objectivity, Method and Point of View: Essays in the Philosophy of History*. Philosophy of History and Culture 6. Leiden: E.J. Brill, 1991. Pp. 170-90.

France, R.T. "The Gospels as Historical Sources for Jesus, the Founder of Christianity." *Truth* 1 (1985): 81-87.

Gardiner, Patrick. *The Nature of Historical Explanation*. London: Oxford, Galaxy, 1961.

Goldstein, Leon J. *Historical Knowing*. Austin, Tex.: University of Texas Press, 1976.

——. "History and the Primacy of Knowing." In "The Constitution of the Historical Past." *History and Theory* Beiheft 16 (1977): 29-52.

Harrison, R. K. *Introduction the Old Testament*. Grand Rapids: Eerdmans, 1969.

Lipton, Peter. *Inference to the Best Explanation*. London: Routledge, 1991.

McCullagh, C. Behan. *Justifying Historical Descriptions*. Cambridge: Cambridge University Press, 1984.

Mandelbaum, Maurice. *The Problem of Historical Knowledge*. New York: Harper & Row, Harper Torchbooks, 1967.

Nowell-Smith, P.H. "The Constructionist Theory of History." In "The Constitution of the Historical Past." *History and Theory* Beiheft 16 (1977): 1-28.

Orwell, George. *1984: A Novel*. London: Secker & Warburg, 1949.

Pirenne, Henri. "What Are Historians Trying to Do?" In *The Philosophy of History in Our Time*. Edited by H. Meyerhoff. Garden City, N.Y.: Doubleday, 1959. Pp. 87-100.

Plantinga, Alvin. "Methodological Naturalism." Paper presented at the symposium "Knowing God, Christ, and Nature in the Post-Positivistic Era." University of Notre Dame, April 14-17, 1993.

_____. *The Twin Pillars of Christian Scholarship*. Grand Rapids: Calvin College and Seminary, 1990.

Popper, Karl. "Has History Any Meaning?" In *The Philosophy of History in Our Time*. Edited by H. Meyerhoff. Garden City, N.Y.: Doubleday, 1959. Pp. 300-312.

_____. *The Poverty of Historicism*. London: Routledge & Kegan Paul, 1957. Reprint. New York: Harper & Row, Harper Torchbooks, 1964.

_____. *The Open Society and its Enemies*. London: Routledge & Kegan Paul, 1966.

Rubinoff, Lionel. "Historicity and Objectivity." In *Objectivity, Method and Point of View: Essays in the Philosophy of History*. Philosophy of History and Culture 6. Leiden: E.J. Brill, 1991. Pp. 133-53.

_____. "Introduction: W.H. Dray and the Critique of Historical Thinking." In *Objectivity, Method and Point of View: Essays in the Philosophy of History*. Philosophy of History and Culture 6. Leiden: E.J. Brill, 1991. Pp. 1-11.

Scheffler, Israel. *Science and Subjectivity*. 2d ed. Indianapolis: Hackett, 1982.

Suppe, Frederick, ed. *The Structure of Scientific Theories*. 2d ed. Urbana, Ill.: University of Illinois Press, 1977. See especially the Introduction and Afterword.

Van der Dussen, W.J. "The Historian and His Evidence." In *Objectivity, Method and Point of View: Essays in the Philosophy of History*. Philosophy of History and Culture 6. Leiden: E.J. Brill, 1991. Pp. 154-69.

Walsh, W. H. *Philosophy of History: An Introduction*. New York: Harper & Row, Harper Torchbooks, 1965.

White, Morton. "Can History Be Objective?" In *The Philosophy of History in Our Time*. Edited by H. Meyerhoff. Garden City, N.Y.: Doubleday, 1959. Pp. 188-202.

_____. *Foundations of Historical Knowledge*. New York: Harper & Row, Harper Torchbooks, 1965.

Yamauchi, Edwin. "Immanuel Velikovsky's Catastrophic History." *Journal of the American Scientific Affiliation* 25 (1973): 134-39.

Chapter Six:

THE HISTORICAL RELIABILITY OF THE NEW TESTAMENT

Aland, Kurt; and Aland, Barbara. *The Text of the New Testament*. 2nd ed. Grand Rapids: Eerdmans, 1989.

Alexander, Loveday. *The Preface to Luke's Gospel*. Cambridge: Cambridge University Press, 1993.

Archer, Gleason L. *Encyclopedia of Bible Difficulties*. Grand Rapids: Zondervan, 1982.

Aune, David E. *Prophecy in Early Christianity and the Ancient Mediterranean World*. Grand Rapids: Eerdmans, 1983.

———. *The New Testament in Its Literary Environment*. Philadelphia: Westminster, 1987.

Bailey, Kenneth E. "Informal Controlled Oral Tradition and the Synoptic Gospels." *Asia Journal of Theology* 5 (1991): 34-54.

Baird, J. Arthur. *A Comparative Analysis of the Gospel Genre: The Synoptic Mode and Its Uniqueness*. Lewiston, N.Y.: Mellen, 1991.

Barnett, Paul. *Is the New Testament History?* London: Hodder & Stoughton, 1986.

Beskow, Per. *Strange Tales about Jesus*. Philadelphia: Fortress, 1983.

Black, David A., and Dockery, David S., eds. *New Testament Criticism and Interpretation*. Grand Rapids: Zondervan, 1991.

Blaiklock, E. M. *The Archaeology of the New Testament*. Nashville: Thomas Nelson, 1984.

Blomberg, Craig L. *The Historical Reliability of the Gospels*. Leicester and Downers Grove, Ill.: InterVarsity, 1987.

Bruce, F. F. *The New Testament Documents: Are They Reliable?* Downers Grove, Ill.: InterVarsity Press, 1960.

Bultmann, Rudolf. *The History of the Synoptic Tradition*. Oxford: Blackwell, 1963.

Burridge, Richard A. *What Are the Gospels? A Comparison with Graeco-Roman Biography*. Cambridge: Cambridge University Press, 1992.

Callan, Terrence. "The Preface of Luke-Acts and Historiography." *New Testament Studies* 31 (1985): 576-81.

Carson, D. A., and Woodbridge, John D., eds. *Hermeneutics, Authority and Canon*. Grand Rapids: Zondervan, 1986.

Charlesworth, James H. *Jesus Within Judaism*. New York: Doubleday, 1988.

Crossan, John Dominic. *The Historical Jesus*. San Francisco: Harper Collins, 1991.

Dunn, James D. G. *The Evidence for Jesus*. Philadelphia: Westminster, 1985.

Evans, Craig A. "Authenticity Criteria in Life of Jesus Research." *Christian Scholar's Review* 19 (1989): 6-31.

———. "Life-of-Jesus Research and the Eclipse of Mythology." *Theological Studies* 54 (1993): 3-36.

France, R. T. *The Evidence for Jesus.* Downers Grove, Ill.: InterVarsity, 1986.

France, R. T., Wenham, David, and Blomberg, Craig, eds. *Gospel Perspectives.* 6 vols. Sheffield: *Journal for the Study of the New Testament,* 1980-86.

Funk, R. W.; and Hoover, R. *The Five Gospels: What Did Jesus Really Say?* New York: Macmillan, 1993.

Geisler, Norman L., and Nix, William E. *A General Introduction to the Bible.* rev. ed. Chicago: Moody, 1986.

Gerhardsson, Birger. *Memory and Manuscript.* Lund: C.W.K. Gleerup, 1961.

Goetz, Stewart C.; and Blomberg, Craig L. "The Burden of Proof." JSOT 11 (1981): 39-63.

Green, Joel B., McKnight, Scot, and Marshall, I. Howard, eds. *Dictionary of Jesus and the Gospels.* Downers Grove, Ill.: IVP, 1992.

Gruenler, Royce G. *New Approaches to Jesus and the Gospels.* Grand Rapids: Baker, 1982.

Guthrie, Donald. *New Testament Introduction.* rev. ed. Downers Grove, Ill.: IVP, 1990.

Habermas, Gary R. *Ancient Evidence for the Life of Jesus.* Nashville: Thomas Nelson, 1984.

Hemer, Colin. *The Book of Acts in the Setting of Hellenistic History.* Ed. Conrad H. Gempf. Tübingen: Mohr, 1989.

Hengel, Martin. *The Johannine Question.* Philadelphia: Trinity, 1990.

Hurtado, Larry W. "The Gospel of Mark: Evolutionary or Revolutionary Document?" JSOT 40 (1990): 15-32.

Kelber, Werner. *The Oral and Written Gospel.* Philadelphia: Fortress, 1983.

Kennedy, George A. *New Testament Interpretation Through Rhetorical Criticism.* Chapel Hill: University of North Carolina, 1984.

Klein, William W., Blomberg, Craig L., and Hubbard, Robert L., Jr. *Introduction to Biblical Interpretation.* Dallas: Word, 1993.

Latourelle, René. *Finding Jesus Through the Gospels.* New York: Alba, 1979.

Lemcio, Eugene E. *The Past of Jesus in the Gospels.* Cambridge: Cambridge University Press, 1991.

Lord, A. B. "The Gospels as Oral Traditional Literature." In *The Relationships among the Gospels.* Ed. William O. Walker, Jr. San Antonio: Trinity University Press, 1978. Pp. 33-91.

Mack, Burton L. *A Myth of Innocence.* Philadelphia: Fortress, 1988.

———. *The Lost Gospel: The Book of Q and Christian Origins.* San Francisco: Harper Collins, 1993.

Marshall, I. Howard. *I Believe in the Historical Jesus.* Grand Rapids: Eerdmans, 1977.

——. *Luke: Historian and Theologian.* 2nd ed. Grand Rapids: Zondervan, 1989.

Meier, John P. *A Marginal Jew.* 2 vols. Garden City, N.Y.: Doubleday, 1991.

Merkley, Paul. "The Gospels as Historical Testimony." *Evangelical Quarterly* 58 (1986): 328-36.

Neill, Stephen, and Wright, Tom. *The Interpretation of the New Testament, 1861-1986.* Oxford: Oxford University Press, 1988.

Noll, Mark A. *Between Faith and Criticism.* 2nd ed. Grand Rapids: Baker, 1991.

Powell, Mark A. *What Is Narrative Criticism?* Minneapolis: Fortress, 1990.

Riches, John K. *Jesus and the Transformation of Judaism.* London: Darton, Longman & Todd, 1980.

Riesner, Rainer. *Jesus als Lehrer.* Tübingen: Mohr, 1981.

Robinson, James M. *A New Quest of the Historical Jesus.* Naperville, Ill.: Allenson, 1959.

Robinson, John A. T. *Redating the New Testament.* Philadelphia: Westminster, 1976.

——. *The Priority of John.* Ed. J. F. Coakley. Oak Park, Ill.: Meyer-Stone, 1985.

Ryken, Leland, and Longman, Tremper, III, eds. *A Complete Literary Guide to the Bible.* Grand Rapids: Zondervan, 1993.

Sanders, E. P. *Jesus and Judaism.* Philadelphia: Fortress, 1985.

——. *The Tendencies of the Synoptic Tradition.* Cambridge: Cambridge University Press, 1969.

Schürrmann, Heinz. "Die vorösterlichen Anfänge der Logientradition." In *Der historische Jesus und der kerygmatische Christus.* Eds. Helmut Ristow and Karl Matthiae. Berlin: Evangelische Verlagsanstalt, 1960. Pp. 342-70.

Sherwin-White, A.N. *Roman Society and Roman Law in the New Testament.* Oxford: Clarendon, 1963.

Sloan, Robert B.; and Parsons, Mikeal C., eds. *Perspectives on John: Method and Interpretation in the Fourth Gospel.* Lewiston, N.Y.: Edwin Mellen, 1993.

Soulen, Richard. *Handbook of Biblical Criticism.* Richmond: John Knox, 1977.

Stanton, Graham N. *Jesus of Nazareth in New Testament Preaching.* Cambridge: Cambridge University Press, 1974.

——. *The Gospels and Jesus.* Oxford: Oxford University Press, 1989.

Stein, Robert H. *Difficult Passages in the Gospels*. Grand Rapids: Baker, 1984.

——. *The Synoptic Problem*. Grand Rapids: Baker, 1987.

Sterling, Gregory E. *Historiography and Self-Definition: Josephos, Luke-Acts and Apologetic Historiography*. Leiden: Brill, 1992.

Stuhlmacher, Peter, ed. *The Gospel and the Gospels*. Grand Rapids: Eerdmans, 1991.

Thompson, Michael B. *Clothed with Christ: The Example and Teaching of Jesus in Romans 12.1-15.13*. Sheffield: JSOT, 1991.

Tuckett, Christopher M. *Nag Hammadi and the Gospel Tradition*. Edinburgh: T & T Clark, 1986.

Wenham, John. *Christ and the Bible*. Downers Grove, Ill.: IVP, 1972.

——. *Redating Matthew, Mark and Luke*. Downers Grove, Ill.: IVP, 1992.

Winter, Bruce W., and Clarke, Andrew D., eds. *The Book of Acts in Its Ancient Literary Setting*. Grand Rapids: Eerdmans, 1993.

Chapter Seven:
THE SELF-UNDERSTANDING OF JESUS

HISTORICAL BACKGROUND

Bartsch, Hans-Werner, ed. *Kerygma and Myth*. 2 vols. Translated by R. H. Fuller. London: SPCK, 1953.

Kissinger, W.S. *The Lives of Jesus: A History and Bibliography*. New York: Garland Publishing, 1985.

Marshall, I. Howard. *I Believe in the Historical Jesus*. Grand Rapids: Eerdmans, 1977.

Paulus, Heinrich Eberh. Gottlob. *Das Leben Jesu, als Grundlage einer reinen Geschichte des Urchristentums*. 2 vols. Heidelberg: C. F. Winter, 1828.

Robinson, James. *A New Quest of the Historical Jesus*. Studies in Biblical Theology 25. London: SCM, 1959.

Schweitzer, Albert. *The Quest of the Historical Jesus*. 3d ed. Translated by W. Montgomery. London: Adam & Charles Black, 1954.

Strauss, David Friedrich. *The Life of Jesus Critically Examined*. Translated by G. Eliot. Edited with an Introduction by P. C. Hodgson. Lives of Jesus Series. London: SCM, 1973.

Wrede, Wilhelm. *The Messianic Secret*. Translated by J. O. G. Greig. Cambridge: James Clarke, 1971.

ASSESSMENT

Blackburn, Barry L. "Miracle Working in Hellenism and Hellenistic

Judaism." In *Gospel Perspectives VI.* Edited by David Wenham and Craig Blomberg. Sheffield, England: JSOT Press, 1986. Pp. 185-218.

Bultmann, Rudolph. *Jesus and the Word.* New York: Scribner's Sons, 1934.

Crossan, John Dominic. *The Historical Jesus: The Life of a Mediterranean Jewish Peasant.* Edinburgh: T.& T.Clark, 1991.

Denaux, Adelbert. "The Q-Logion Mt 11,27/Lk 10,22 and the Gospel of John." In *John and the Synoptics.* Edited by A. Denaux. Bibliotheca Ephemeridum Theologicarum Lovaniensium 101. Leuven, Belgium: Leuven University Press, 1992.

Dunn, James D. G. *Jesus and the Spirit.* London: SCM, 1975.

Ellis, E. E. "Dating the New Testament." *New Testament Studies* 26 (1980): 487-502.

Evans, Craig A. "Authenticity Criteria in Life of Jesus Research." *Christian Scholar's Review* 19 (1989): 6-31.

———. "Life-of-Jesus Research and the Eclipse of Mythology." *Theological Studies* 54 (1993): 3-36.

Funk, Robert W. and Hoover, Roy W., eds. *Five Gospels: What Did Jesus Really Say?* New York: Macmillan, 1993.

Green, Michael. "Jesus and Historical Skepticism." In *The Truth of God Incarnate.* Edited by M. Green. Grand Rapids: Eerdmans, 1977. Pp. 107-39.

———. "Jesus in the New Testament." In *The Truth of God Incarnate.* Edited by M. Green. Grand Rapids: Eerdmans, 1977. Pp. 17-57.

Gruenler, Royce Gordon. *New Approaches to Jesus and the Gospels.* Grand Rapids: Baker, 1982.

Guelich, Robert. *Sermon on the Mount.* Waco, Tex.: Word, 1982.

Gundry, Robert H. *Mark: A Commentary on His Apology for the Cross.* Grand Rapids: Eerdmans, 1993.

Hagner, Donald A. *The Jewish Reclamation of Jesus.* Grand Rapids: Zondervan, 1984.

Hemer, Colin. *The Book of Acts in the Setting of Hellenistic History.* Edited by Conrad H. Gempf. Wissenschaftliche Untersuchungen zum Neuen Testament 49. Tübingen: J.C.B. Mohr, 1989.

Hengel, Martin. *The Son of God: The Origin of Christology and the History of Jewish-Hellenistic Religion.* Translated by John Bowden. Philadelphia: Fortress, 1976.

Hick, John, ed. *The Myth of God Incarnate.* London: SCM, 1977.

Hooker, Morna. "On Using the Wrong Tool." *Theology* 75 (1972): 570-81.

Hutchinson, Robert J. "What the Rabbi Taught Me about Jesus." *Christianity Today,* 13 September 1993, pp. 27-29.

Jeremias, Joachim. *The Central Message of the New Testament*. London: SCM, 1965.

Kim, Seyon. *The Son of Man as the Son of God*. Grand Rapids: Eerdmans, 1985.

Marshall, I. Howard. *The Origins of New Testament Christology*. Downers Grove, Ill.: InterVarsity, 1976.

Meyer, Ben F. *The Aims of Jesus*. London: SCM, 1979.

Moule, C. F. D. *The Origins of Christology*. Cambridge: Cambridge Univ., 1977.

Pannenberg, Wolfhart. *Jesus—God and Man*. Translated by L.L. Wilkins and D.A. Priebe. London: SCM, 1968.

Pelikan, Jaroslav. *The Christian Tradition: A History of the Development of Doctrine*. Vol. 1: *The Emergence of the Catholic Tradition (100-600)*. Chicago: University of Chicago, 1971.

Pöhlmann, Horst Georg. *Abriss der Dogmatik*. 3d revised edition. Gütersloh: Gerd Mohn, 1980.

Riesner, Rainer. *Jesus als Lehrer*. Wissenschaftliche Untersuchungen zum Neuen Testament 2/7. Tübingen: J.C.B. Mohr, 1984.

Sherwin-White, A.N. *Roman Law and Roman Society in the New Testament*. Oxford: Clarendon Press, 1963.

Stein, Robert H. "The Criteria for Authenticity." In *Gospel Perspectives I*. Edited by R.T. France and David Wenham. Sheffield, England: JSOT Press, 1980. Pp. 225-63.

Trilling, Wolfgang. *Fragen zur Geschichtlichkeit Jesu*. Düsseldorf: Patmos Verlag, 1966.

Witherington, Ben III. *The Christology of Jesus*. Minneapolis: Fortress Press, 1990.

Yamauchi, Edwin. "Magic or Miracle? Diseases, Demons, and Exorcisms." In *Gospel Perspectives VI*. Edited by David Wenham and Craig Blomberg. Pp. 89-183.

Chapter Eight:
THE RESURRECTION OF JESUS

HISTORICAL BACKGROUND

Craig, William Lane. *The Historical Argument for the Resurrection of Jesus during the Deist Controversy*. Texts and Studies in Religion 23. Lewiston, N.Y.: Edwin Mellen, 1985.

Ditton, Humphrey. *A Discourse Concerning the Resurrection of Jesus Christ*. London: J. Darby, 1712.

Fuller, Daniel P. *Easter Faith and History*. London: Tyndale, 1968.

Houttevile, Abbé. *La religion chrétienne prouvée par les faits*. 3 vols. Paris: Mercier & Boudet, 1740.

Less, Gottfried. *Wahrheit der christlichen Religion*. Göttingen: G. L. Förster, 1776.

Paley, William. *A View of the Evidences of Christianity*. 2 vols. 5th ed. London: R. Faulder, 1796. Reprint. Westmead, England: Gregg, 1970.

Reimarus, Hermann Samuel. *Fragments*. Translated by R. S. Fraser. Edited by C. H. Talbert. Lives of Jesus Series. London: SCM, 1971.

Semler, Johann Salomo. *Abhandlung von freier Untersuchung des Canon*. Texte zur Kirchen- und Theologiegeschichte 5. Gütersloh: G. Mohn, 1967.

———. *Beantwortung der Fragmente eines Ungennanten insbesondere vom Zweck Jesu and seiner Jünger*. 2d ed. Halle: Verlag des Erziehungsinstituts, 1780.

Sherlock, Thomas. *The Tryal of the Witnesses of the Resurrection of Jesus*. London: J. Roberts, 1729.

Strauss, David Friedrich. "Hermann Samuel Reimarus and His 'Apology.'" In *Fragments*, by H. S. Reimarus. Translated by R. S. Fraser. Edited by C. H. Talbert. Lives of Jesus Series. London: SCM Press, 1971. Pp. 44-57.

———. *The Life of Jesus Critically Examined*. Translated by G. Eliot. Edited with an Introduction by P. C. Hodgson. Lives of Jesus Series. London: SCM, 1973.

Tholuck, Friedrich August. "Abriss einer Geschichte der Umwälzung, welche seit 1750 auf dem Gebiete der Theologie in Deutschland statt gefunden." In *Vermischte Schriften grösstentheils Apologetischen Inhalts*. 2 vols. Hamburg: Friedrich Perthes, 1859.

Turrettin, J. Alph. *Traité de la vérité de la religion chrétienne*. Translated by J. Vernet. 2d ed. 7 vols. Geneva: Henri Albert Gosse, 1745-55.

ASSESSMENT

Alsup, John. *The Post-Resurrection Appearances of the Gospel Tradition*. Stuttgart: Calwer Verlag, 1975. This is the most important work on the post-resurrection appearances.

Blinzler, Josef. "Die Grablegung Jesu in historischer Sicht." In *Resurrexit*. Edited by Edouard Dhanis. Rome: Editrice Libreria Vaticana, 1974. The best piece on the burial.

Bode, Edward Lynn. *The First Easter Morning*. Analecta Biblica 45. Rome: Biblical Institute Press, 1970. The best work on the empty tomb.

Craig, William Lane. *Assessing the New Testament Evidence for the*

Historicity of the Resurrection of Jesus. Studies in the Bible and Early Christianity 16. Lewiston, N.Y.: Edwin Mellen, 1989.

Dodd, C. H. "The Appearances of the Risen Christ: A Study in the Form Criticism of the Gospels." In *More New Testament Studies.* Manchester: U. of Manchester, 1968. Pp. 102-33.

Ellis, E. Earle, ed. *The Gospel of Luke.* New Century Bible: London: Nelson, 1966.

Evans, Craig A. "Life-of-Jesus Research and the Eclipse of Mythology." *Theological Studies* 54 (1993): 3-36.

Fuller, R. H. *The Formation of the Resurrection Narratives.* London: SPCK, 1972.

Grass, Hans. *Ostergeschehen und Osterberichte.* 4th ed. Göttingen: Vandenhoeck & Ruprecht, 1974. This influential work is the most important overall treatment of the historicity of the resurrection.

Gundry, Robert. *Sōma in Biblical Theology.* Cambridge: Cambridge Univ., 1976. The best work on the second part of 1 Corinthians 15.

Jeremias, Joachim. "Die älteste Schicht der Osterüberlieferung." In *Resurrexit.* Edited by Edouard Dhanis. Rome: Editrice Libreria Vaticana, 1974.

Klappert, Berthold. "Einleitung." In *Diskussion um Kreuz und Auferstehung.* Edited by B. Klappert. Wuppertal: Aussaat Verlag, 1971. Pp. 9-52.

Kremer, Jacob. *Die Osterevangelien—Geschichten um Geschichte.* Stuttgart: Katholisches Bibelwerk, 1977.

Lehmann, Karl. *Auferweckt am dritten Tag nach der Schrift.* Quaestiones disputatae 38. Freiburg: Herder, 1968. The most important work on the first part of 1 Corinthians 15.

Moule, C. F. D. *The Phenomenon of the New Testament.* Studies in Biblical Theology 2/1. London: SCM, 1967.

Müller, Julius. *The Theory of Myths, in Its Application to the Gospel History Examined and Confuted.* London: John Chapman, 1844.

Perrin, Norman. *The Resurrection according to Matthew, Mark, and Luke.* Philadelphia: Fortress, 1977.

Robinson, John A.T. *The Human Face of God.* London: SCM, 1973.

Sherwin-White, A. N. *Roman Society and Roman Law in the New Testament.* Oxford: Clarendon, 1963.

Van Daalen, D. H. *The Real Resurrection.* London: Collins, 1972.

Von Campenhausen, Hans Freiherr. *Der Ablauf der Osterereignisse und das leere Grab.* 3d rev ed. Sitzungsberichte der Heidelberger Akademie der Wissenschaften. Heidelberg: Carl Winter, 1966.

Wilckens, Ulrich. *Auferstehung.* Themen der Theologie 4. Stuttgart: Kreuz Verlag, 1970.

NOTES

INTRODUCTION

1. Charles Malik, "The Other Side of Evangelism," *Christianity Today* (November 7, 1980), p. 40.
2. *Ibid.*
3. J. Gresham Machen, "Christianity and Culture," *Princeton Theological Review* 11 (1913): 7.
4. *Ibid.*
5. Critical Notice of Ian G. Barbour, *Religion in an Age of Science*, reviewed by John K. La Shell, *Journal of the Evangelical Theological Society* 36 (1993): 261.
6. Machen, "Christianity and Culture," p. 13.

CHAPTER ONE: Faith and Reason: How Do I Know Christianity Is True?

1. Augustine, *Against the Epistle of Manichaeus Called Fundamental* 5.6.
2. Augustine, *Letters* 82.3; idem *City of God* 21.6.1.
3. Augustine, *On Free Will* 2.1.6.
4. Augustine, *City of God* 22.5.
5. Thomas Aquinas, *Summa theologiae* 1a.32.1; cf. idem, *Summa contra gentiles* 1.9.
6. Thomas Aquinas, *Summa theologiae* 2a2ae.1.4 *ad* 2.
7. Thomas Aquinas, *Summa contra gentiles* 3.154; 1.6.
8. *Ibid.*, 1.9.
9. *Ibid.* 1.9.
10. John Locke, *An Essay Concerning Human Understanding*, 4.10.1.
11. *Ibid.*, 4.18.5.
12. *Ibid.*, 4.19.4.
13. Karl Barth, *The Knowledge of God and the Science of God According to the Teaching of the Reformation*, trans. J.L.M. Haire and I. Henderson (New York: Scribner's, 1939), p. 27.
14. Karl Barth, *Dogmatics in Outline*, trans. G.J. Thomson (New York: Philosophical Library, 1947), p. 24.
15. Barth, *Knowledge*, p. 109.
16. Rudolf Bultmann, *Theologie des Neuen Testaments*, 7th ed., ed. O. Merk (Tübingen: J.C.B. Mohr, 1961), p. 295.
17. Rudolf Bultmann, "Reply to the Theses of J. Schniewind," in *Kerygma and Myth*, ed. H.-W. Bartsch, trans. R.H. Fuller (London: SPCK, 1953), 1: 112.
18. Rudolf Bultmann, "The Case for Demythologizing: A Reply," in *Kerygma and Myth*, 2: 191.
19. Wolfhart Pannenberg, ed. *Revelation as History*, trans. D. Granskou (London: Macmillan, 1968), p. 9.

20. Wolfhart Pannenberg, "The Revelation of God in Jesus of Nazareth," in *New Frontiers in Theology*, vol. 3: *Theology as History*, ed. J.M. Robinson and J.B. Cobb, Jr. (New York: Harper & Row, 1967), p. 131.

21. Wolfhart Pannenberg, "Redemptive Event and History," in *Basic Questions in Theology*, trans. G. Kehm (Philadelphia: Fortress, 1970), 1: 78.

22. Wolfhart Pannenberg, *Jesus—God and Man*, trans. L. L. Wilkins and D.A. Priebe (London: SCM, 1968), pp. 27-8.

23. See Alvin Plantinga, *The Twin Pillars of Christian Scholarship* (Grand Rapids: Calvin College and Seminary, 1990), pp. 53-5.

24. Edward John Carnell, having borrowed this notion from Edgar Sheffield Brightman, popularized it among evangelical apologists (Edward John Carnell, *An Introduction to Christian Apologetics* [Grand Rapids, MI: Wm. B. Eerdmans, 1948], pp. 56-64). My explication of this notion is, however, different than Carnell's.

25. I'm reminded of a delightful anecdote related by a Christian professor about the day he told his philosophy class (including the Dean, who was sitting in that day) as seriously as he could that "This piece of chalk is not a piece of chalk," and thereafter asked them what they had learned. The students, and the hapless Dean as well, tried vainly to extract some knowledge from this self-contradictory nonsense, until finally an inner-city black pastor in the class exclaimed in frustration, "Man, I ain't learned nothin' at all!" The professor said he was relieved that at least one person in his class could still think rationally. Somebody needs similarly to tell the post-modernist (see below) that the emperor is wearing no clothes.

26. For a good discussion, see Stuart C. Hackett, *Oriental Philosophy* (Madison: University of Wisconsin Press, 1979).

27. John D. Caputo, *Radical Hermeneutics* (Bloomington: Indiana University Press, 1987), p. 156.

28. For a trenchant critique of post-modern (ir)rationality, as well as attempted responses, see the discussion in James L. Marsh, John D. Caputo, and Merold Westphal, *Modernity and Its Discontents* (New York: Fordham University Press, 1992), pp. 18-19, 89-92, 168-74, 199-201. See also the entertaining discussion in Plantinga, *Twin Pillars*, pp. 17-23.

CHAPTER TWO: *The Absurdity of Life Without God*

1. The definitive ordering and numbering of these notes is that of Louis Lafuma, and the *Pensées* are cited in reference to the number of each fragment.

2. Blaise Pascal, *Pensées* 29.

3. *Ibid.*, 11.

4. *Ibid.*, 217, 246.

5. *Ibid.*, 343.

6. *Ibid.*

7. Kai Nielsen, "Why Should I Be Moral?" *American Philosophical Quarterly* 21 (1984): 90.

8. Paul Kurtz, *Forbidden Fruit* (Buffalo, N.Y.: Prometheus, 1988), p. 73.

9. Richard Taylor, *Ethics, Faith, and Reason* (Englewood Cliffs, N.J.: Prentice Hall, 1985), pp. 90, 84.

10. H. G. Wells, *The Time Machine* (New York: Berkeley, 1957), chap. 11.

11. T.S. Eliot, "The Hollow Men," in *Collected Poems 1909-1962* (New York: Harcourt, Brace, Jovanovich, Inc., 1934). Reprinted by permission of the publisher.

12. W. E. Hocking, *Types of Philosophy* (New York: Scribner's, 1959), p. 27.
13. Friedrich Nietzsche, "The Gay Science," in *The Portable Nietzsche*, ed. and trans. W. Kaufmann (New York: Viking, 1954), p. 95.
14. Friedrich Nietzsche, "The Will to Power," trans. W. Kaufmann, in *Existentialism from Dostoyevsky to Sartre* , 2d. ed., ed. with an Introduction by W. Kaufmann (New York: New American Library, Meridian, 1975), pp. 130-1.
15. Bertrand Russell, "A Free Man's Worship," in *Why I Am Not a Christian*, ed. P. Edwards (New York: Simon & Schuster, 1957), p. 107.
16. Bertrand Russell, Letter to the *Observer,* 6 October 1957.
17. Jean Paul Sartre, "Portrait of the Antisemite," trans. M. Guiggenheim, in *Existentialism*, p. 330.
18. Richard Wurmbrand, *Tortured for Christ* (London: Hodder & Stoughton, 1967), p. 34.
19. Ernst Bloch, *Das Prinzip Hoffnung*, 2d. ed., 2 vols. (Frankfurt am Main: Suhrkamp Verlag, 1959), 2: 360-1.
20. Loyal D. Rue, "The Saving Grace of Noble Lies," address to the American Academy for the Advancement of Science, February 1991.

CHAPTER THREE: The Existence of God

1. J. Gresham Machen, "Christianity and Culture," *Princeton Theological Review* 11 (1913): 7.
2. "Modernizing the Case for God," *Time* (April 7, 1980), pp. 65-6. See also *Truth*, vols. 3 and 4, "New Arguments for the Existence of God," ed. William Lane Craig (1990).
3. Anselm, *Proslogion* 2,3.
4. Al-Ghāzalī, *Kitab al-Iqtisad fi'l-I'tiqad*, cited in S. de Beaurecueil, "Gazzali et S. Thomas d'Aquin: Essai sur la preuve de l'exitence de Dieu proposée dans l'Iqtisad et sa comparaison avec les 'voies' Thomiste," *Bulletin de l'Institut Francais d'Archaeologie Orientale* 46 (1947): 203.
5. Thomas Aquinas, *Summa theologiae* 1 a.2, 3 cf. idem *Summa contra gentiles* 1.13.
6. G. W. F. von Leibniz, "On the Ultimate Origin of Things," in *Leibniz Selections*, ed. P. Wiener (New York: Scribner's, 1951), pp. 527-9; idem, "Monadology," in *Selections*, p. 540; idem, *Theodicy*, trans. E.M. Huggard (London: Routledge & Kegan Paul, 1951), p. 127.
7. Leibniz, "Nature and Grace," in *Selections*, p. 527.
8. Plato, Laws 12.966e.
9. Plato, Laws 10.893b-899c; idem *Timaeus*.
10. Aristotle, *Metaphysica* 1.982610-15.
11. Aristotle, *On Philosophy*
12. Leslie Stephen, *History of English Thought in the Eighteenth Century*, 2 vols., 2d ed. (London: Smith, Elder, 1881), 1: 408.
13. Frederick Ferré, Introduction to *Natural Theology: Selections*, by William Paley, (Indianapolis: Bobbs-Merrill, 1963), pp. xi-xxxii.
14. Paley, *Natural Theology*, pp. 3-4.
15. *Ibid.*, p. 13.
16. *Theism, Atheism, and Big Bang Cosmology* (Oxford: Clarendon Press, 1993), p. 135.
17. J. L. Mackie, *The Miracle of Theism* (Oxford: Clarendon, 1982), p. 94.
18. *Ibid.*, p. 89.
19. David Hume, *The Letters of David Hume*, 2 vols., ed. J.Y.T. Greig (Oxford: Clarendon, 1932), 1: 187.
20. Mackie, *Theism*, p. 89.

21. The story of Hilberts Hotel is related in George Gamow, *One, Two, Three, Infinity* (London: Macmillan, 1946), p. 17.
22. William J. Wainwright, review of *The Kalām Cosmological Argument*, *Nous* 16 (1982): 328-34.
23. Mackie, *Theism*, p. 93.
24. Students frequently ask if God, therefore, cannot be infinite. The question is based on a misunderstanding. When we speak of the infinity of God, we are not using the word in a mathematical sense to refer to an aggregate of an infinite number of finite parts. God's infinity is, if you will, qualitative, not quantitative. It means that God is metaphysically necessary, morally perfect, omnipotent, omniscient, eternal, etc.
25. Bertrand Russell, *Our Knowledge of the External World*, 2d ed. (New York: W.W. Norton, 1929), p. 170.
26. Mackie, *Theism*, p. 93.
27. J. Richard Gott, *et al.*, "Will the Universe Expand Forever?" *Scientific American* (March 1976): 65.
28. P.C.W. Davies, "Spacetime Singularities in Cosmology," in *The Study of Time III*, eds. J.T. Fraser, N. Lawrence, and D. Park (Berlin: Springer, 1978), pp. 78-79.
29. John Barrow and Frank Tipler, *The Anthropic Cosmological Principle* (Oxford: Oxford University Press, 1986), p. 442.
30. Fred Hoyle, *Astronomy and Cosmology* (San Francisco: W.H. Freeman, 1975), p. 658.
31. See Robert Jastrow, *God and the Astronomers* (New York: W.W. Norton, 1978), pp. 28, 112-13.
32. Stanley L. Jaki, *Science and Creation* (Edinburgh: Scottish Academic Press, 1974), p. 347.
33. Ivan R. King, *The Universe Unfolding* (San Francisco: W.H. Freeman, 1976), p. 462.
34. John Gribbin, "Oscillating Universe Bounces Back," *Nature* 59 (1976): 15.
35. Astrophysicist C.J. Isham's comment seems particularly apt with respect to Sagan: "Perhaps the best argument in favour of the thesis that the Big Bang supports theism is the obvious unease with which it is greeted by some atheist physicists. At times this has led to scientific ideas, such as continuous creation [steady state] or an oscillating universe, being advanced with a tenacity which so exceeds their intrinsic worth that one can only suspect the operation of psychological forces lying very much deeper than the usual academic desire of a theorist to support his/her theory" (C.J. Isham, "Creation of the Universe as a Quantum Process," in *Physics, Philosophy, and Theology*, eds. R.J. Russell, W.R. Stoeger, and G.V. Coyne [Vatican City State: Vatican Observatory, 1988], p. 378).
36. Beatrice Tinsley, personal letter.
37. Duane Dicus, *et al.*, "The Future of the Universe," *Scientific American* (March 1983): 101; idem, "Effects of Proton Decay on the Cosmological Future," *Astrophysical Journal* 252 (1982): 1- 9.
38. Dicus, "Cosmological Future," p. 8.
39. Ethan T. Vishniac, "Relativistic Collisionless Particles and the Evolution of Cosmological Perturbations," *Astrophysical Journal* 257 (1982): 472.
40. See Allan Sandage and G.A. Tammann, "The Dynamical Parameters of the Universe," in *The Large Scale Structure of the Universe, Cosmology, and Fundamental Physics*, ed. G. Setti and L. Van Hove, First ESO/CERN Symposium (Geneva, Switzerland: ESO and CERN, 1984), p. 137; A. Dressler, "Cosmological Parameters of the Universe," in *Astronomy, Cosmology, and Fundamental Physics*, ed. M. Caffo, et. al., Third ESO/CERN Symposium (Dordrecht: Kluwer, 1989),

p. 23; Ron Cowen, "Hubble: A Universe without End," *Science News* 141 (1992): 79.

41. Sandage and Tammann, "Dynamical Parameters," p. 137.
42. P.J.E. Peebles and Joseph Silk, "A Cosmic Book of Phenomena," *Nature* 346 (1990): 23-239; Carlos S. Frenk, Simon D.M. White, and Marc Davis, "Massive Neutrinos and Galaxy Formation," in *Large Scale Structure of the Universe*, pp. 257-65.
43. Joseph Silk, "Cosmology Back to the Beginning," *Nature* 356 (1992): 742; Peebles and Silk, "Book of Phenomena," pp. 233-9.
44. Joseph Silk, *The Big Bang*, 2d ed. (San Francisco: W.H. Freeman, 1989), p. 388.
45. Allan Sandage and G.A. Tammann, "Steps Toward the Hubble Constant. VII," p. 23.
46. Sandage and Tammann, "Dynamical Parameters," p. 144.
47. R. Brout and Ph. Spindel, "Black Holes Dispute," *Nature* 337 (1989): 216. Brout admitted to me with a smile that such models were "crazy" and said that F. Englert has also discarded this approach.
48. See Isham, "Creation of the Universe as a Quantum Process," pp. 385-7.
49. Christopher Isham, "Space, Time, and Quantum Cosmology," paper presented at the conference "God, Time, and Modern Physics," of the Science and Religion Forum, March 1990.
50. Brout and Spindel, "Black Holes Dispute," p. 216.
51. Stephen Hawking, *A Brief History of Time* (New York: Bantam Books, 1988), p. 9.
52. *Ibid.*, p. 46.
53. *Ibid.*, p. 136.
54. *Ibid.*, p. 134.
55. *Ibid.*, p. 136.
56. *Ibid.*, pp. 140-1.
57. Isham, "Creation of the Universe as a Quantum Process," p. 402.
58. Hawking, *Brief History of Time*, p. 134.
59. Herbert Dingle, *Science at the Crossroads* (London: Martin, Brian and O'Keefe, 1972), pp. 31-2. My emphasis.
60. Arthur Eddington, *Space, Time and Gravitation* (1920; rep. ed.: Cambridge: Cambridge University Press, 1987), p. 48
61. *Ibid.*, p. 181.
62. Hawking, *Brief History of Time*, pp. 134-5.
63. *Ibid.*, pp. 138-9.
64. George Schlesinger, "The Similarities between Space and Time," *Mind* 84 (1975): 171.
65. Hawking, *Brief History of Time*, p. 139.
66. Quentin Smith, "The Wave Function of a Godless Universe," in Craig and Smith, *Theism, Atheism, and Big Bang Cosmology*, p. 319. Smith's own position is to interpret the imaginary space-time stage instrumentally and to maintain that the universe came into being uncaused out of nothing at the first moment of real time—a position which the truth of the first premiss of the *kalām* cosmological argument rules out.
67. See Christopher Isham, "Quantum Theories of the Creation of the Universe," unpublished paper, a preliminary version of which appears in *Interpreting the Universe as Creation*, ed. V. Brummer (The Netherlands: Pharos, 1991).
68. Beatrice Tinsley, "From Big Bang to Eternity?" *Natural History Magazine*, October 1975, p. 103.
69. Dicus, "Future of the Universe," p. 99.
70. Tinsley, "Big Bang," p. 105.

71. Richard Schlegel, "Time and Thermodynamics," in *The Voices of Time*, ed. J.T. Fraser (London: Penguin, 1948), p. 511.
72. Dicus, "Cosmological Future," pp. 1, 8.
73. I.D. Novikov and Ya. B. Zeldovich, "Physical Processes Near Cosmological Singularities," *Annual Review of Astronomy and Astrophysics* 11 (1973): 401-2.
74. Silk, *Big Bang*, pp. 311-12.
75. P.C.W. Davies, *The Physics of Time Asymmetry* (London: Surrey University Press, 1974), p. 104.
76. For discussion see William Lane Craig, "The Teleological Argument and the Anthropic Principle," in *The Logic of Rational Theism*, ed. Wm. L. Craig and M. McLeod (Lewiston, N.Y.: Edwin Mellen, 1990), pp. 127-53.
77. Barrow and Tipler, *Anthropic Cosmological Principle*, p. 565.
78. *Ibid.*, p. 3.
79. Jastrow, *God and the Astronomers*, p. 116.
80. Adolf Grünbaum, "The Pseudo-Problem of Creation in Physical Cosmology," in *Physical Cosmology and Philosophy*, ed. John Leslie, Philosophical Topics (New York: Macmillan, 1990), pp. 92-112.
81. Adolf Grünbaum, "Pseudo-Creation of the Big Bang," *Nature* 344 (1990): 821-2.
82. In fact, I am not at all opposed to creation science, broadly conceived. I see no justification for the methodological naturalism in science or history to which even many evangelical as well as Catholic scholars seem strangely attracted. But my strategy of evangelism is that we should make the non-Christian jump through as few hoops as possible in order to become a Christian. Therefore, I take the more modest line of not propounding a theistic science in arguing for God's existence.
83. This illustrates the methodological principle of apologetical modesty, or evidential overkill. There is a temptation, out of a desire to convince others, to make very bold claims on behalf of the evidence for the Christian world view. But those who make extravagant claims like "There is more historical evidence for the resurrection of Jesus than that Julius Caesar existed" or "The evidence for God's existence is overwhelming" are setting themselves up for a fall. By unrealistically raising the expectations of their listeners so high, it becomes almost impossible for them to meet such expectations, and, as a result, their arguments, which may be quite good, are dismissed because they are not literally compelling. A far more effective strategy is to make a modest claim, like "It is rational to believe that God exists" or "Theism is more plausible than atheism" and then to support this modest claim with evidence that is as overpowering as possible. In this way, one has more than succeeded in supporting his modest claim, and the psychological effect on the listener is that your case comes across as much more convincing. Thus, for strategic reasons, we ought to make modest claims even when we are personally convinced that the evidence warrants a much stronger claim, and then to establish those modest claims superlatively well.

CHAPTER FOUR: The Problem of Miracles

1. Denis Diderot, "Philosophical Thoughts," in *Diderot's Philosophical Works*, trans. M. Jourdain (Chicago: Open Court, 1916), p. 18.
2. *A Philosophical Dictionary* (New York: Harcourt, Brace, & World, 1962), s.v. "Miracles," by Marie Francois Arouet de Voltaire.
3. David Hume, *Enquiry Concerning Human Understanding*, 10.1.90.
4. *Ibid.*, 10.2.101.
5. Jean Le Clerc, *Five Letters Concerning the Inspiration of the Holy Scriptures* (London: [n.p.], 1690), pp. 235-6.

6. Samuel Clarke, *A Discourse Concerning the Unchangeable Obligations of Natural Religion and the Truth and Certainty of the Christian Revelation* (London: W. Batham, 1706), pp. 367-8.

7. J. Alph. Turrettin, *Traité de la vérité de la religion chrétienne*, 2d ed., 7 vols., trans. J. Vernet (Geneva: Henri-Albert Gosse, 1745-55), 5: 2-3.

8. *Ibid.*, 5: 240.

9. Abbé Houtteville, *La religion chretienne prouvee par les faits*, 3 vols. (Paris: Mercier & Boudet, 1740), 1: 33.

10. David Friedrich Strauss, *The Life of Jesus Critically Examined*, trans. G. Eliot (London: SCM, 1973), p. 737.

11. *Ibid.*, p. 75.

12. Albert Schweitzer, *The Quest of the Historical Jesus*, 3d ed., trans. W. Montgomery (London: Adam & Charles Black, 1954), p. 111.

13. Mary Hesse, "Miracles and the Laws of Nature," in *Miracles*, ed. C. F. D. Moule (London: A.R. Mowbray, 1965), p. 38.

14. For discussion see Stephen S. Bilinskyj, "God, Nature, and the Concept of Miracle" (Ph.D. dissertation, University of Notre Dame, 1982); Alfred J. Freddoso, "The Necessity of Nature," *Midwest Studies in Philosophy* 11 (1986): 215-42.

15. *Encyclopedia of Philosophy*, s.v. "Miracles," by Antony Flew.

16. Wolfhart Pannenberg, *Jesus—God and Man*, trans. L.L. Wilkins and D.A. Priebe (London: SCM, 1968), p. 67.

17. Charles Dickens, "A Christmas Carol," in *Christmas Books*, by Charles Dickens (London: Oxford, 1954), pp. 18-19.

18. *Encyclopedia of Philosophy*, s.v. "Miracles."

CHAPTER FIVE: *The Problem of Historical Knowledge*

1. Anselm, *Cur Deus homo* 2.22.

2. Thomas Aquinas, *Summa theologiae* 3a.43.3.

3. J. Westfall Thompson and Bernard J. Holm, *A History of Historical Writing*, 2 vols. (New York: Macmillan, 1942), 2: 94.

4. Philippe de Mornay, *De la vérité de la religion chrestienne* (Anvers: Imprimerie de Christofle Plantin, 1581), Preface.

5. *Ibid.*, p. 835.

6. Filleau de la Chaise, "Discours sur les livres de Moise," in *Discours sure les "Pensées" de M. Pascal*, ed. with an Introduction by V. Gitaud (Paris: Ediotions Bossard, 1922), pp. 104-5.

7. Richard J. Bernstein, *Beyond Objectivism and Relativism* (Oxford: Basil Blackwell, 1983), pp. 7, 13.

8. *Ibid.*, p. 1.

9. F.R. Ankersmit, "The Dilemma of Contemporary Anglo-Saxon Philosophy of History," in "Knowing and Telling History: the Anglo-Saxon debate," *History and Theory* Beiheft 25 (1986): 1-27.

10. Leon J. Goldstein, "History and the Primacy of Knowing," in "The Constitution of the Historical Past," *History and Theory* Beiheit 16 (1977): 29-52. See also his *Historical Knowing* (Austin, Tex.: University of Texas Press, 1976).

11. Patrick Gardiner, *The Nature of Historical Explanation* (London: Oxford, 1961), p. 35.

12. Goldstein, "History and Primacy of Knowing," pp. 30-1.

13. Carl Becker, "What Are Historical Facts?" in *The Philosophy of History in Our Time*, ed. H. Meyerhoff (Garden City, N.Y.: Doubleday, 1959), pp. 130-1.

14. Gardiner, *Historical Explanation*, p. 35.
15. Henri Pirenne, "What Are Historians Trying to Do?" in *Philosophy of History*, p. 97.
16. Karl Popper, "Has History Any Meaning?" in *Philosophy of History*, p. 303.
17. P.H. Nowell-Smith, "The Constructionist Theory of History," in "The Constitution of the Historical Past," *History and Theory* Beiheft 16 (1977): 1-2.
18. Alvin Plantinga, *The Twin Pillars of Christian Scholarship* (Grand Rapids: Calvin College and Seminary, 1990), pp. 21-2.
19. Lionel Rubinoff, "Introduction," in *Objectivity, Method and Point of View* (Leiden: E.J. Brill), p. 3.
20. See discussion in Frederick Suppe, "Afterword," in *The Structure of Scientific Theories*, 2d ed. (Urbana, Ill.: University of Illinois Press, 1977), pp. 717-27.
21. W.H. Dray, "Comment," in *Objectivity, Method and Point of View*, p. 183.
22. Nowell-Smith, "Constructionist Theory of History," p. 4.
23. R. G. Collingwood, *An Autobiography* (London: Oxford, 1939), p. 135.
24. W.J. Van der Dussen, "The Historian and His Evidence," in *Objectivity, Method, and Point of View*, p. 157; cf. Gardiner, *Historical Explanation*, p. 39.
25. R. K. Harrison, *Introduction to the Old Testament* (Grand Rapids: Eerdmans, 1969), p. 292.
26. R. G. Collingwood, "Croce's Philosophy of History," in *Essays in the Philosophy of History*, ed. W. Debbins (Austin, Tex.: University of Texas, 1965), p. 19.
27. See Suppe, "Afterword, " pp. 633-49.
28. Israel Scheffler, *Science and Subjectivity*, 2d ed. (Indianapolis: Hackett, 1982), p. 19.
29. Lionel Rubinoff, "Historicity and Objectivity," in *Objectivity, Method, and Point of View*, p. 137.
30. Frederick Copleston, "Problems of Objectivity," in *On the History of Philosophy* (London: Search Press, 1979), p. 54.
31. *Ibid.*, p. 55.
32. *Ibid.*, pp. 53-54.
33. *Ibid.*, p. 57.
34. Frederick Suppe, "The Search for Philosophic Understanding of Scientific Theories," in *Structure of Scientific Theories*, pp. 218-20.
35. See *ibid.*, pp. 199-208.
36. See discussion in *ibid.*, pp. 208-17.
37. Suppe, "Afterword," pp. 633-4.
38. R. G. Collingwood, *The Idea of History*, ed. T.M. Know (Oxford: Oxford, 1956), p. 246.
39. William Debbins, "Introduction," in *Essays in the Philosophy of History*, p. xiv. See also Dray, "Comment," p. 182.
40. C. Behan McCullagh, *Justifying Historical Descriptions* (Cambridge: Cambridge University Press, 1984), p. 19.
41. R. G. Collingwood, "Are History and Science Different Kinds of Knowledge?" in *Essays in the Philosophy of History*, p. 32.
42. Maurice Mandelbaum, *The Problem of Historical Knowledge* (New York: Harper & Row, 1967), p. 184.
43. Morton White, "Can History Be Objective?" in *Philosophy of History* (London: Routledge & Kegan Paul), 1957), p. 199.
44. E. H. Carr, *What Is History?* (New York: Random House, 1953), p. 8.
45. Becker, "Historical Facts," p. 132.
46. Isaiah Berlin, "The Concept of Scientific History," in *Philosophical Analysis and History*, ed. W.H. Dray (New York: Harper & Row, 1966), p. 11.

47. Christopher Blake, "Can History Be Objective?" in *Theories of History*, ed. P. Gardiner (Glencoe, Ill.: Free Press, 1959), p. 331.

48. W. H. Walsh, *Philosophy of History: An Introduction* (New York: Harper & Row, 1965), p. 111.

49. Morton White, *Foundations of Historical Knowledge* (New York: Harper & Row, 1965), p. 268; see also Karl Popper, *The Open Society and Its Enemies*, 5th rev. ed. (London: Routledge & Kegan Paul, 1966).

50. George Orwell, *1984: A Novel* (London: Secker & Warburg, 1949), pt. 3, chap. 2.

51. Edwin Yamauchi, "Immanuel Velikovsky's Catastrophic History," *Journal of the American Scientific Affiliation* 25 (1973): 138, 134.

52. Karl Popper, *The Poverty of Historicism* (London: Routledge & Kegan Paul, 1957), p. 152.

53. Raymond Aron, "Relativism in History," in *Philosophy of History*, p. 160.

54. Mandelbaum, *Problem of Historical Knowledge*, pp. 298-304.

55. R.T. France, "The Gospels as Historical Sources for Jesus, the Founder of Christianity," *Truth* 1 (1985): 86.

56. See Peter Lipton, *Inference to the Best Explanation* (London: Routledge, 1991), p. 122.

57. McCullagh, *Justifying Historical Descriptions*, p. 21.

58. See the special issue "Creation/Evolution and Faith," of *Christian Scholar's Review* 21/1 (1991); Alvin Plantinga, "Methodological Naturalism," paper presented at the symposium "Knowing God, Christ, and Nature in the Post-Positivistic Era," University of Notre Dame, April 14-17, 1993.

CHAPTER SIX: The Historical Reliability of the New Testament

1. The standard introduction is Kurt Aland and Barbara Aland, *The Text of the New Testament*, 2nd ed. (Grand Rapids: Eerdmans, 1989). For a briefer survey, see J. Harold Greenlee, *Introduction to New Testament Textual Criticism* (Grand Rapids: Eerdmans, 1964).

2. See, e.g., Gary M. Burge, "A Specific Problem in the New Testament Text and Canon: The Woman Caught in Adultery (John 7: 53-8: 11)," *Journal of the Evangelical Theological Society* 27 (1984): 141-8.

3. Cf. further Norman L. Geisler and William E. Nix, *A General Introduction to the Bible*, rev. ed. (Chicago: Moody, 1986), pp. 385-489.

4. These statistics come from F. F. Bruce, *The New Testament Documents: Are They Reliable?* (Downers Grove, Ill.: IVP, 1960), p. 16.

5. Nestle-Aland, *Novum Testamentum Graece*; and the United Bible Societies' *Greek New Testament*.

6. Putting it another way, the authors of this book are firm believers in biblical inerrancy. I came to that conviction largely *through* my historical study of Scripture, not in spite of it. But some parts are easier to defend than others. The person who rejects my explanations of certain apparent historical discrepancies does not have to feel that the only alternative to belief in inerrancy is the rejection of the Christian faith. Many kinds of genuine Christians have not believed in inerrancy, while still accepting all of the tenets of the ancient, orthodox creeds. I believe they are *wrong* to reject inerrancy, but this scarcely disqualifies them from being *Christian*.

7. Graham N. Stanton, *Jesus of Nazareth in New Testament Preaching* (Cambridge: Cambridge University Press, 1974), p. 189.

8. See esp. John D. Woodbridge, *Biblical Authority: A Critique of the Rogers/McKim Proposal* (Grand Rapids: Zondervan, 1982).

9. Origen, *Commentary on John* X, 16.
10. See, e.g., Heinz Schürmann, *Das Lukasevangelium* (Freiburg: Herder, 1969), 1: 320.
11. Augustine, *Harmony of the Gospels*, II. 21.
12. John Calvin, *A Harmony of the Gospels Matthew, Mark and Luke*, trans. A. W. Morrison, David W. Torrance, and Thomas F. Torrance (Edinburgh: St. Andrew, 1972), 1: 204-5.
13. See, e.g., George A. Kennedy, *New Testament Interpretation Through Rhetorical Criticism* (Chapel Hill: University of North Carolina, 1984), pp. 67-9.
14. See Robert H. Stein, *Difficult Passages in the Gospels* (Grand Rapids: Baker, 1984), p. 12.
15. Trans. John Marsh, *The History of the Synoptic Tradition* (Oxford: Blackwell, 1963). Cf. also Martin Dibelius, *From Tradition to Gospel* (Cambridge: James Clarke, 1934 [Germ. orig. 1919]).
16. Vincent Taylor, *The Formation of the Gospel Tradition* (London: Macmillan, 1933); C.H. Dodd, *The Apostolic Preaching and Its Developments* (London: Hodder & Stoughton, 1936).
17. For more detailed surveys, see Craig L. Blomberg, "Form Criticism," in *Dictionary of Jesus and the Gospels*, eds. Joel B. Green, Scot McKnight, and I. Howard Marshall (Downers Grove, Ill.: IVP, 1992), pp. 243-50; and Darrell L. Bock, "Form Criticism," in *New Testament Criticism and Interpretation*, eds. David A. Black and David S. Dockery (Grand Rapids: Zondervan, 1991), pp. 175-96.
18. None of the English translations appeared until the 1960s. See G. Bornkamm, G. Barth, and H. J. Held, *Tradition and Interpretation in Matthew* (Philadelphia: Westminster, 1963); Willi Marxsen, *Mark the Evangelist* (Nashville: Abingdon, 1969); and Hans Conzelmann, *The Theology of St. Luke* (New York: Harper & Row, 1960).
19. Richard Soulen, *Handbook of Biblical Criticism* (Richmond: John Knox, 1977), pp. 142-3.
20. See, e.g., James M. Robinson, *A New Quest of the Historical Jesus* (Naperville, Ill.: Allenson, 1959). For a more detailed survey of the method, see Grant R. Osborne, "Redaction Criticism," in *New Testament Criticism and Interpretation*, eds. Black and Dockery, pp. 199-224.
21. For a good survey of literary methods, see Mark A. Powell, *What Is Narrative Criticism?* (Minneapolis: Fortress, 1990).
22. Cf. R. Alan Culpepper, *The Anatomy of the Fourth Gospel* (Philadelphia: Fortress, 1983), with E. Ruckstuhl, *Die literarische Einheit des Johannesevangeliums* (Göttingen: Vandenhoeck & Ruprecht, 1987).
23. See further, Richard A. Horsley, *The Liberation of Christmas* (New York: Crossroad, 1989), pp. 39-49. For a detailed introduction to liberationist hermeneutics, see Christopher Rowland and Mark Corner, *Liberating Exegesis: The Challenge of Liberation Theology to Biblical Studies* (Louisville: Westminster/Knox, 1989).
24. The ovular work of non-evangelical feminist criticism, which traces the history of Christian origins, separating "acceptable" egalitarian traditions from "unacceptable" patriarchal ones, is Elisabeth Schussler Fiorenza, *In Memory of Her* (New York: Crossroad, 1983). See also Letty M. Russell, *Feminist Interpretation of the Bible* (Philadelphia: Westminster, 1985).
25. See Stephen Neill and Tom Wright, *The Interpretation of the New Testament 1861- 1986* (Oxford: Oxford University Press, 1988), pp. 379-403.
26. E. P. Sanders, *Jesus and Judaism* (Philadelphia: Fortress, 1985), p. 2; cited and endorsed by James H. Charlesworth, *Jesus Within Judaism* (New York: Doubleday,

1988), p. 205. For an excellent introduction to gospel criticism and a survey of what we can know about Jesus according to recent, more positive scholarship see Graham N. Stanton, *The Gospels and Jesus* (Oxford: Oxford University Press, 1989).

27. (San Francisco: Harper Collins, 1991).
28. Robert W. Funk and Roy W. Hoover, eds., *The Five Gospels: What Did Jesus Really Say?* (New York: Macmillan, 1993).
29. *Ibid.*, p. 36.
30. The story is well-chronicled in Mark A. Noll, *Between Faith and Criticism*, 2nd ed. (Grand Rapids: Baker, 1991), pp. 11-61.
31. R. T. France, David Wenham, and Craig Blomberg, eds., *Gospel Perspectives*, 6 vols. (Sheffield: JSOT, 1980-86); popularized and elaborated in Craig L. Blomberg, *The Historical Reliability of the Gospels* (Leicester and Downers Grove, Ill.: IVP, 1987). Though more wide-ranging than the issue of historicity, cf. esp. *Dictionary of Jesus and the Gospels*.
32. Colin J. Hemer, *The Book of Acts in the Setting of Hellenistic History*, ed. Conrad H. Gempf (Tübingen: Mohr, 1989). See also Bruce W. Winter and Andrew D. Clarke, *The Book of Acts in Its Ancient Literary Setting* (Grand Rapids: Eerdmans, 1993), vol. 1 of a projected six-volume series entitled *The Book of Acts in Its First-Century Setting*.
33. See, respectively, Eta Linnemann, *Historical Criticism of the Bible: Methodology or Ideology?* (Grand Rapids: Baker, 1990) (esp. p. 20); and idem, *Is There a Synoptic Problem?* (Grand Rapids: Baker, 1992).
34. See the unusually critical review of my *Historical Reliability* by J. W. Scott, *Westminster Theological Journal* 50 (1988): 357-59, criticism one might expect from a very liberal reviewer but not from a fellow evangelical.
35. The logic is classically unpacked in B. B. Warfield, *The Inspiration and Authority of Scripture* (Philadelphia: Presbyterian & Reformed, 1948). See also John W. Wenham, *Christ and the Bible* (Downers Grove, Ill.: IVP, 1972).
36. Martin Hengel (*Studies in the Gospel of Mark* [Philadelphia: Fortress, 1985], pp. 64-84) even makes a plausible case for dating the titles to the last third of the first century.
37. The standard collections which include these and other works are Wilhelm Schneemelcher, ed., *New Testament Apocrypha*, 2 vols. (Philadelphia: Westminster, 1991-93); and James M. Robinson, ed., *The Nag Hammadi Library in English* (Leiden: Brill, 1977).
38. See the lengthy discussion in Martin Hengel, *The Johannine Question* (Philadelphia: Trinity, 1990).
39. This is the most common solution to what is called the Synoptic Problem—the question of the literary interrelationships among Matthew, Mark, and Luke. For an excellent introduction, see Robert H. Stein, *The Synoptic Problem* (Grand Rapids: Baker, 1987).
40. For a vigorous defense of the reliability of Papias's testimony regarding Mark, see Robert H. Gundry, *Mark: A Commentary on His Apology for the Cross* (Grand Rapids: Eerdmans, 1993), pp. 1026-45.
41. See Craig L. Blomberg, *Matthew* (Nashville: Broadman, 1992), pp. 37-41, and the literature there cited. Cf. Donald A. Hagner, *Matthew 1-13* (Dallas: Word, 1993), pp. xliii-xlvi.
42. See the robust defense of this interpretation in Hemer, *Acts*, pp. 308-64, particularly against those who propose that the author is merely relying on Luke's diaries as a source or utilizing an entirely fictitious device.

43. Again, see esp. *ibid.*, pp. 244-76. See also F. F. Bruce, *Paul: Apostle of the Heart Set Free* (Grand Rapids: Eerdmans, 1977).

44. B. F. Westcott, *The Gospel according to St. John* (London: John Murray, 1908), pp. x-lii. For an updating of Westcott's arguments, see Leon Morris, *Studies in the Fourth Gospel* (Grand Rapids: Eerdmans, 1969), pp. 45-92.

45. For details, see Hemer, *Acts*, pp. 365-410.

46. See I. Howard Marshall, "Acts and the 'Former Treatise,'" in *Acts*, eds. Winter and Clarke, pp. 163-82.

47. Or even the very early sixties. If Luke was with Paul in Rome from A.D. 60-62, we do not have to assume much of a time lag at all after Mark completed his gospel in that same city before Luke could have utilized it.

48. See John A. T. Robinson, *Redating the New Testament* (Philadelphia: Westminster, 1976), pp. 19-21. For details on the tradition-history of these chapters, see esp. David Wenham, *The Rediscovery of Jesus' Eschatological Discourse* (Sheffield: JSOT, 1984).

49. For a detailed presentation of the evidence for and against these dates, with similar conclusions to ours, see Donald Guthrie, *New Testament Introduction*, rev. ed. (Downers Grove, Ill.: IVP, 1990); and D. A. Carson, Douglas J. Moo, and Leon Morris, *An Introduction to the New Testament* (Grand Rapids: Zondervan, 1992). John Wenham, *Redating Matthew, Mark and Luke* (Downers Grove, Ill.: IVP, 1992) has made an intriguing case for even earlier dates—Luke in the mid-50s, Mark around 45, and Matthew near 40. But there are several unproven assumptions behind his arguments which make these dates somewhat improbable (e.g., that Luke was the unnamed famous "brother" of 2 Corinthians 8: 18, and that the "service of the gospel" for which he is praised is his writing of the work we know as the Gospel of Luke).

50. See further Robin L. Fox, *The Search for Alexander* (Boston: Little, 1980).

51. See Craig L. Blomberg, "The Legitimacy and Limits of Harmonization," in *Hermeneutics, Authority and Canon*, eds. D. A. Carson and John D. Woodbridge (Grand Rapids: Zondervan, 1986), pp. 169-73.

52. See, e.g., Conrad Gempf, "Published Speaking and Public Accounts," in *Acts*, eds. Winter and Clarke, pp. 259-303.

53. Blomberg, *Historical Reliability*, pp. 113-89, and literature there cited.

54. Hemer, *Acts*, pp. 244-307, 63-100. For similar harmonizations, cf.David Wenham, "Acts and the Pauline Corpus II: The Evidence of Parallels," in *Acts*, eds. Winter and Clarke, pp. 215-58.

55. For a more selective list of problems and possible solutions, but one which covers the whole Bible, see Gleason L. Archer, *Encyclopedia of Bible Difficulties* (Grand Rapids: Zondervan, 1982).

56. For a much more detailed survey of the current range of hermeneutical issues facing the would-be interpreter of Scripture and for guidance in using the various tools, see William W. Klein, Craig L. Blomberg, and Robert L. Hubbard, Jr., *Introduction to Biblical Interpretation* (Dallas: Word, 1993).

57. See esp. Harald Riesenfeld, "The Gospel Tradition and Its Beginnings," *Texte und Untersuchungen* 73 (1959): 43-65; Birger Gerhardsson, *Memory and Manuscript* (Lund: Gleerup, 1961); Rainer Riesner, *Jesus als Lehrer* (Tübingen: Mohr, 1981); idem, "Jesus as Preacher and Teacher," in *Jesus and the Oral Gospel Tradition*, ed. Henry Wansbrough (Sheffield: JSOT, 1991), pp. 185-210.

58. See esp. Heinz Schürmann, "Die vorösterlichen Anfänge der Logientradition," in *Der historische Jesus und der kerygmatische Christus*, eds. H. Ristow and K. Matthiae (Berlin: Evangelische Verlagsanstalt, 1960), pp. 342-70. See also Robert H. Stein,

"An Early Recension of the Gospel Traditions?" *Journal of the Evangelical Theological Society* 30 (1987): 167-83.

59. J. Arthur Baird, *A Comparative Analysis of the Gospel Genre: The Synoptic Mode and Its Uniqueness* (Lewiston, N.Y.: Mellen, 1991). Some of the details of Baird's genre analysis are idiosyncratic, but these particular conclusions at least seem sound. Cf. also idem, "The Holy Word: The History and Function of the Teachings of Jesus in the Theology and Praxis of the Early Church," *New Testament Studies* 33 (1987): 585-99.

60. See esp. A. B. Lord, *The Singer of Tales* (Cambridge, Mass.: Harvard University Press, 1960); idem, "The Gospels as Oral Traditional Literature," in *The Relationships among the Gospels*, ed. William O. Walker, Jr. (San Antonio: Trinity University Press, 1978), pp. 33-91.

61. Kenneth E. Bailey, "Informal Controlled Oral Tradition and the Synoptic Gospels," *Asia Journal of Theology* 5 (1991): 34-54.

62. See E. P. Sanders, *The Tendencies of the Synoptic Tradition* (Cambridge: Cambridge University Press, 1969). In Thomas, parables are consistently abbreviated; see Craig L. Blomberg, "Tradition and Redaction in the Parables of the Gospel of Thomas," in *Gospel Perspectives*, vol. 5, ed. David Wenham (Sheffield: JSOT, 1985), pp. 177-205.

63. Leslie R. Keylock, "Bultmann's Law of Increasing Distinctness," in *Current Issues in Biblical and Patristic Interpretation*, ed. Gerald F. Hawthorne (Grand Rapids: Eerdmans, 1975), pp. 193-210.

64. See esp. David E. Aune, *Prophecy in Early Christianity and the Ancient Mediterranean World* (Grand Rapids: Eerdmans, 1983).

65. Richard Bauckham, "The Delay of the Parousia," *Tyndale Bulletin* 31 (1980): 3-36.

66. See Paul Merkley, "The Gospels as Historical Testimony," *Evangelical Quarterly* 58 (1986): 328-36.

67. *Ibid.*, pp. 319-27.

68. A. N. Sherwin-White, *Roman Society and Roman Law in the New Testament* (Oxford: Clarendon, 1963), pp. 187 (italics mine).

69. For excellent evangelical introductions to the distinctive theologies of the four Evangelists, see R. T. France, *Matthew: Evangelist and Teacher* (Grand Rapids: Zondervan, 1989); Ralph P. Martin, *Mark: Evangelist and Theologian* (Grand Rapids: Zondervan, 1972); I. Howard Marshall, *Luke: Historian and Theologian*, rev. ed. (Grand Rapids: Zondervan, 1989); and Stephen S. Smalley, *John: Evangelist and Interpreter* (Exeter: Paternoster, 1978).

70. For additional examples, see Blomberg, "Harmonization," pp. 158-60.

71. Eugene E. Lemcio, *The Past of Jesus in the Gospels* (Cambridge: Cambridge University Press, 1991).

72. An excellent evangelical anthology of applications of literary criticism is Leland Ryken and Tremper Longman, III, eds., *A Complete Literary Guide to the Bible* (Grand Rapids: Zondervan, 1993).

73. For an overview, see Craig L. Blomberg, "The Diversity of Literary Genres in the New Testament, in *New Testament Criticism and Interpretation*, eds. Black and Dockery, pp. 507-32.

74. The letters to the seven churches (Rev 2—3) make particularly good sense once one understands the historical background of each of the cities to which they are written. See esp. Colin J. Hemer, *The Letters to the Seven Churches of Asia in Their Local Setting* (Sheffield: JSOT, 1986).

75. Norman Perrin, *The New Testament: An Introduction* (New York: Harcourt, Brace, Jovanovich, 1974), pp. 287-8.

76. In addition to Josephus, discussed below, there are brief references to Jesus in the later rabbis and in Roman historians Thallus, Pliny, Tacitus and Suetonius. But they do not allow us to say any more about Jesus than Perrin has. For a brief overview, see Blomberg, *Historical Reliability*, pp. 196-201. For a detailed presentation, see John P. Meier, *A Marginal Jew*, 2 vols. (Garden City: Doubleday, 1991), pp. 89-111.

77. See esp. *ibid.*, pp. 56-88.

78. See the chart in Paul Barnett, *Is the New Testament History?* (London: Hodder & Stoughton, 1986), pp. 159-63.

79. See esp. Richard A. Burridge, *What Are the Gospels? A Comparison with Graeco-Roman Biography* (Cambridge: Cambridge University Press, 1992).

80. See Craig L. Blomberg, "Quirinius," in *International Standard Bible Encyclopedia*, ed. Geoffrey W. Bromiley (Grand Rapids: Eerdmans, 1988), 4: 12-3.

81. For surveys of this material, see Rainer Riesner, "Archeology and Geography," in *Dictionary of Jesus and the Gospels*, pp. 33-46; E. M. Blaiklock, *The Archaeology of the New Testament* (Nashville: Thomas Nelson, 1984).

82. Loveday Alexander, *The Preface to Luke's Gospel* (Cambridge: Cambridge University Press, 1993).

83. Terrence Callan, "The Preface of Luke-Acts and Historiography," *New Testament Studies* 31 (1985): 576-81. Cf. David E. Aune, *The New Testament in Its Literary Environment* (Philadelphia: Westminster, 1987), pp. 17-157; Burridge, *What Are the Gospels?*

84. Gregory E. Sterling, *Historiography and Self-Definition: Josephos, Luke-Acts and Apologetic Historiography* (Leiden: Brill, 1992).

85. Robert Guelich, "The Gospel Genre," in *The Gospel and the Gospels*, ed. Peter Stuhlmacher (Grand Rapids: Eerdmans, 1991), p. 206.

86. Published respectively by Eerdmans, Word, Zondervan, IVP/Eerdmans, Eerdmans, and Broadman.

87. Blomberg, *Historical Reliability*, pp. 156-9. On historical problems with the Gospel of John more generally, see the entire chapter in which this section is embedded (pp. 153-89).

88. James D. G. Dunn, "Let John Be John: A Gospel for Its Time," in *The Gospel and the Gospels*, p. 322.

89. Burridge, *What Are the Gospels?*, pp. 220-39.

90. See further my "To What Extent is John Historically Reliable?" in *Perspectives on John: Method and Interpretation in the Fourth Gospel*, eds. Robert B. Sloan and Mikeal C. Parsons (Lewiston, N.Y.: Mellen, 1993), pp. 27-56.

91. See the literature cited in n. 81 above.

92. Reversing the trend of much modern scholarship, John A. T. Robinson, *The Priority of John*, ed. J. F. Coakley (Oak Park, Ill.: Meyer-Stone, 1985), finds John *more* historically reliable than the Synoptics!

93. E. Stauffer, "Historische Elemente im vierten Evangelium," in *Bekenntnis zur Kirche*, ed. Ernst-Heinz Amberg and Ulrich Kuhn (Berlin: Evangelische Verlagsanstalt, 1960), pp. 33-51. For a parallel catalogue of hints of eyewitness testimony in Mark, see Barnett, *History?*, pp. 91-8.

94. Darryl W. Palmer, "Acts and the Historical Monograph," *Tyndale Bulletin* 43 (1992): 373-88.

95. *Contra* esp. Richard I. Pervo, *Profit with Delight* (Philadelphia: Fortress, 1987), who links Acts with largely fictitious romances and adventure novels of antiquity.

96. See the comprehensive compilation of these and similar details in Hemer, *Acts*, pp. 101-243.

97. Among his many works, of particular note are *St. Paul the Traveller and the Roman*

Citizen (London: Hodder & Stoughton, 1895); and *The Bearing of Recent Discovery on the Trustworthiness of the New Testament* (London: Hodder & Stoughton, 1915).

98. Michael B. Thompson, *Clothed with Christ: The Example and Teaching of Jesus in Romans 12.1-15.13* (Sheffield: JSOT, 1991), builds on these data to argue for allusions and echoes of the Jesus tradition throughout virtually every section of this portion of Paul's exhortation.

99. See the list in Peter H. Davids, *The Epistle of James* (Grand Rapids: Eerdmans, 1982), pp. 47-8.

100. See esp. Gregory K. Beale, "The Use of Daniel in the Synoptic Eschatological Discourse and in the Book of Revelation," in *Gospel Perspectives*, vol. 5, pp. 129-53.

101. In fact, a variety of studies suggest that even the second-century Apostolic Fathers quoted Gospel traditions in forms which suggest that they received them from the persistent oral tradition rather than directly from the written texts. And in many cases, these forms show signs of an earlier stage of the tradition than our canonical forms. See my survey in *Historical Reliability*, pp. 202-8.

102. This is the weakness of the seemingly commendable approach that requires the burden of proof to be on any given scholar to demonstrate his or her case for or against historical trustworthiness, as, e.g., Sanders, *Jesus and Judaism*, p. 13.

103. For the whole line of logic concerning the burden of proof and historiographic procedure more generally, see Stewart C. Goetz and Craig L. Blomberg, "The Burden of Proof," *Journal for the Study of the New Testament* 11 (1981): 39-63. Cf. E. Earle Ellis, "Reading the Gospels as History," *Criswell Theological Review* 3 (1988): 3-15.

104. The terminology can be confusing, because we may also speak of the science of textual criticism (see above) as determining the authenticity of various documents. There, "authenticity" means careful preservation of the text; here it means the truthfulness or accuracy of purportedly historical reporting. In still other contexts, the term may mean that a document is genuinely written by the author to whom it is commonly attributed.

105. See, e.g., Robert H. Stein, "The 'Criteria' for Authenticity," in *Gospel Perspectives*, vol. 1, eds. R. T. France and David Wenham (Sheffield: JSOT, 1980), pp. 225-63; Craig A. Evans, "Authenticity Criteria in Life of Jesus Research," *Christian Scholars' Review* 19 (1989): 6-31.

106. See further Craig L. Blomberg, *Interpreting the Parables* (Downers Grove, Ill.; IVP, 1990); George R. Beasley-Murray, *Jesus and the Kingdom of God* (Grand Rapids: Eerdmans, 1986).

107. For an important treatment of the similarities and differences between Jesus and the Judaism of his day, see John K. Riches, *Jesus and the Transformation of Judaism* (London: Darton, Longman & Todd, 1980).

108. See Craig L. Blomberg, "The Miracles as Parables," in *Gospel Perspectives*, vol. 6, eds. David Wenham and Craig Blomberg (Sheffield: JSOT, 1986), pp. 327-59. For a good introduction to the application of the criteria to historical Jesus research more generally, see I. Howard Marshall, *I Believe in the Historical Jesus* (Grand Rapids: Eerdmans, 1977).

109. Recall the mention of Perrin in n. 75 above. A striking recent example is Crossan, *Historical Jesus*.

110. As in the "third quest." In addition to the works cited in n. 26 above and elsewhere, one may consult Ben F. Meyer, *The Aims of Jesus* (London: SCM, 1979); A. E. Harvey, *Jesus and the Constraints of History* (Philadelphia:

Westminster, 1982); Ben Witherington III, *The Christology of Jesus* (Minneapolis: Fortress, 1990); and Ben Wiebe, *Messianic Ethics* (Scottdale: Herald, 1992).

111. René Latourelle, *Finding Jesus through the Gospels* (New York: Alba, 1979), pp. 238-9.

112. Royce G. Gruenler, *New Approaches to Jesus and the Gospels* (Grand Rapids: Baker, 1982), pp. 19-131.

113. See esp. Craig A. Evans, "Life-of-Jesus Research and the Eclipse of Mythology," *Theological Studies* 54 (1993): 3-36. Cf. René Latourelle, *The Miracles of Jesus and the Theology of Miracles* (New York: Paulist, 1988).

114. Burton L. Mack, *A Myth of Innocence* (Philadelphia: Fortress, 1988); idem, *The Lost Gospel: The Book of Q and Christian Origins* (San Francisco: Harper Collins, 1993).

115. See esp. Werner Kelber, *The Oral and the Written Gospel* (Philadelphia: Fortress, 1983).

116. Meier, *A Marginal Jew*, p. 177, declares, "A tweedy poetaster who spent his time spinning out parables and Japanese koans, a literary aesthete who toyed with 1st-century deconstructionism, or a bland Jesus who simply told people to look at the lilies of the field—such a Jesus would threaten no one, just as the university professors who create him threaten no one."

117. Despite frequent claims to the contrary, the substantial dependence of Thomas on the Synoptics still remains the most probable hypothesis. See esp. Christopher M. Tuckett, "Thomas and the Synoptics," *Novum Testamentum* 30 (1988): 132-57; and Meier, *A Marginal Jew*, pp. 123-39.

118. For example, the docetic crucifixion account in the Gospel of Peter or the fragmentary evidence of Clement of Alexandria alluding to a Secret Gospel of Mark. For an appropriate assessment of the Gnostic documents, see esp. Christopher M. Tuckett, *Nag Hammadi and the Gospel Tradition* (Edinburgh: T & T Clark, 1986).

119. For these last several points, see esp. Larry W. Hurtado, "The Gospel of Mark: Evolutionary or Revolutionary Document?" *Journal for the Study of the New Testament* 40 (1990): 15-32. Cf. Paul J. Achtemeier, "*Omne Verbum Sonat*: The New Testament and the Oral Environment of Late Western Antiquity," *Journal of Biblical Literature* 109 (1990): 3-27; and Loveday Alexander, "The Living Voice: Skepticism towards the Written Word in Early Christian and in Graeco-Roman Texts," in *The Bible in Three Dimensions*, eds. David J. A. Clines, Stephen E. Fowl, and Stanley E. Porter (Sheffield: JSOT, 1990), pp. 221-47.

120. (Grand Rapids: Zondervan, 1970; 2nd ed., 1989).

121. Dec. 10, 1990; cf. Harold Bloom with David Rosenberg, *The Book of J* (New York: Grove Weidenfeld, 1990).

122. Richard N. Ostling, "Handmaid or Feminist?" *Time* (December 30, 1991), pp. 62-6.

123. John Lee, "A Holy Furor," *Time* (August 15, 1988), pp. 34- 36; Richard N. Ostling, "Who Was Jesus?" *ibid.*, pp. 37-42. The garbled reference occurs on p. 41: "'It is fair to say that all the alleged inconsistencies among the Gospels have received at least plausible resolutions,' concludes an international panel of 34 Evangelical scholars in the 1987 report *The Historical Reliability of the Gospels*." The title and date of the "report" are actually those of my book, not that of the "panel" (i.e., the *Gospel Perspectives* series of 1980-86); the quotation is actually a paraphrase of an oral telephone conversation with an associate of the project in Cambridge, England, and the number 34 is inaccurate, but otherwise the substance of the "quotation" fairly represents what our project was trying to affirm!

124. A few scholars debate whether or not one tiny piece of a scroll contains fragmentary portions of a few verses of the Gospel of Mark, but it was clear that this was not what the news reporter was speaking about! For accurate, up-to-date information on the state of the discoveries, see Joseph A. Fitzmyer, *Responses to 101 Questions on the Dead Sea Scrolls* (New York: Paulist, 1992).

125. For a good survey of the most famous of these, see Per Beskow, *Strange Tales about Jesus* (Philadelphia: Fortress, 1983). See also Douglas Groothuis, *Revealing the New Age Jesus* (Downers Grove, Ill.: IVP, 1990).

126. James W. Deardorff, *Celestial Teachings: The Emergence of the True Testament of Jmmanuel (Jesus)* (Tigard, Or.: Wild Flower Press, 1990). (The J is not a typographical error; he spells it that way.) Astonishingly, Deardorff's work, stripped of its most objectionable speculation, has been published by an allegedly reputable academic publishing house as *The Problem of New Testament Gospel Origins* (San Francisco: Mellen Research University Press, 1992).

127. See esp. Meier, *A Marginal Jew*, pp. 112-66.

128. Jeffery L. Sheler, "Who Was Jesus?" *U.S. News and World Report* (December 20, 1993), pp. 58-66.

CHAPTER SEVEN: The Self-Understanding of Jesus

1. As Bultmann finely put it, "In my opinion, of the life and personality of Jesus we can now know as good as nothing" (Rudolph Bultmann, *Jesus* [Tübingen: J.C.B. Mohr, 1951], p. 11).

2. See Morna Hooker, "On Using the Wrong Tool," *Theology* 75 (1972): 570-81.

3. See Robert W. Funk and Roy W. Hoover, eds., *Five Gospels: What Did Jesus Really Say?* (New York: Macmillan, 1993).

4. For helpful discussions, see Robert H. Stein, "The Criteria for Authenticity," in *Gospel Perspectives I*, ed. R.T. France and David Wenham (Sheffield, England: JSOT Press, 1980), pp. 225-63; Craig A. Evans, "Authenticity Criteria in Life of Jesus Research," *Christian Scholar's Review* 19 (1989): 6-31.

5. John Dominic Crossan, *The Historical Jesus: The Life of a Mediterranean Jewish Peasant* (Edinburgh: T. & T. Clark, 1991), p. xxxii.

6. A.N. Sherwin-White, *Roman Law and Roman Society in the New Testament* (Oxford: Clarendon Press, 1963), pp. 186-9.

7. Sherwin-White's contention has been powerfully driven home by the epochal study by Colin Hemer, *The Book of Acts in the Setting of Hellenistic History*, ed. Conrad H. Gempf, Wissenschaftliche Untersuchungen zum Neuen Testament 49 (Tübingen: J.C.B. Mohr, 1989). Through a painstaking analysis of papyrological, epigraphical, and other evidence Hemer demonstrates convincingly the wealth of historical material contained in the book of Acts and thus, by implication, Luke's care as a historian.

8. Donald A. Hagner, *The Jewish Reclamation of Jesus* (Grand Rapids: Zondervan, 1984).

9. S. Ben-Chorin, *Jesus in Judenthum* (Wuppetal: R. Brockhaus, 1970), p. 41, cited in Hagner, *Reclamation*, p. 105.

10. Craig A. Evans, "Life-of-Jesus Research and the Eclipse of Mythology," *Theological Studies* 54 (1993): 3-36.

11. For a critique, see Barry L. Blackburn, "'Miracle Working' in Hellenism (and Hellenistic Judaism)," in *Gospel Perspectives VI*, ed. David Wenham and Craig Blomberg (Sheffield, England: JSOT Press, 1986), pp. 185-218; see also Edwin Yamauchi, "Magic or Miracle? Diseases, Demons, and Exorcisms," in *Gospel Perspectives VI*, pp. 89-183.

12. Jaroslav Pelikan, *The Christian Tradition: A History of the Development of Doctrine*, vol. 1: *The Emergence of the Catholic Tradition* (100-600), p. 173.

13. See Ben Witherington, III, *The Christology of Jesus* (Minneapolis: Fortress Press, 1990), pp. 233-62; see also Robert Gundry, *Mark: A Commentary on His Apology for the Cross* (Grand Rapids: Eerdmans, 1993), pp. 118-9, 587, and the therein cited literature, as well as Seyon Kim, *The Son of Man as the Son of God* (Grand Rapids: Eerdmans, 1985).

14. Joachim Jeremias, *The Central Message of the New Testament* (London: SCM Press, 1965), pp. 16, 19.

15. Adelbert Denaux, "The Q-Logion Mt 11, 27/Lk 10, 22 and the Gospel of John," in *John and the Synoptics*, ed. A. Denaux, Bibliotheca Ephemeridum Theologicarum Lovaniensium 101 (Leuven, Belgium: Leuven University Press, 1992).

16. Witherington, *Christology of Jesus*, p. 65.

17. Jacob Neusner, *A Rabbi Talks with Jesus* (New York: Doubleday, 1993), pp. xii, 5.

18. Robert J. Hutchinson, "What the Rabbi Taught Me about Jesus," *Christianity Today*, September 13, 1993, p. 28.

19. Neusner, *Rabbi Talks with Jesus*, p. 14.

20. Robert Guelich, *Sermon on the Mount* (Waco, Tex.: Word, 1982), p. 185.

21. Witherington, *Christology of Jesus*, p. 188.

22. Ahad ha' Am, "Judaism and the Gospels," in *Nationalism and the Jewish Ethic*, ed. H. Kohn (New York: Schocken Books, 1962), p. 298.

23. According to Witherington, that Jesus was an exorcist is "one of the most incontestable facts about his ministry," being attested in nearly all layers of tradition and by allusions in sayings, narratives, and summaries (Witherington, *Christology of Jesus*, p. 201).

24. Ben F. Meyer, *The Aims of Jesus* (London: SCM Press, 1979), pp. 155-6.

25. *Ibid.*, p. 136.

26. Royce Gordon Gruenler, *New Approaches to Jesus and the Gospels* (Grand Rapids: Baker, 1982), pp. 46, 59, 49. This claim comes to explicit expression in Mark 2: 1-12, whose authenticity is defended by Gundry, *Mark*, pp. 110-22.

27. As Meyer explains, through table fellowship the Jewish ritual distinction of clean and unclean and the Jewish moral distinction of righteous and unrighteous, which shaped and permeated the self-understanding of Judaism, came to concrete expression. With respect to Jesus' ignoring such distinctions, Meyer comments, "Nothing . . . could have dramatized the gratuity and the present realization of God's saving act more effectively than this unheard of initiative toward sinners" (Meyer, *Aims*, p. 161). Jesus' iconoclasm in this regard lends credibility to Mark's comment that Jesus consciously overturned OT food laws (Mark 7: 19), which underscores the point above concerning his authority to correct the Torah, as is pointed out by Gundry, *Mark*, pp. 356, 367-71.

28. James D. G. Dunn, *Jesus and the Spirit* (London: SCM Press, 1975), p. 60. On the authenticity of the passage, see Witherington, *Christology of Jesus*, p. 165.

29. Witherington points out: "The emphasis here is on the present fulfillment of Old Testament hopes for the messianic or eschatological age" (Witherington, *Christology of Jesus*, p. 44; cf. p. 172).

30. Comments made in discussion of Kee's paper at the conference "Christianity Challenges the University," Dallas, Texas, February, 1985.

31. A multiply attested Q-saying, the authenticity of 12: 8 is defended by Wolfhart Pannenberg, *Jesus—God and Man*, trans. L.L. Wilkins and D.A. Priebe (London: SCM Press, 1968), pp. 58-60.

32. Witherington, *Christology of Jesus*, p. 268.

33. Gruenler, *New Approaches to Jesus and the Gospels*, p. 74.
34. Dunn, *Jesus*, p. 86.
35. Horst Georg Pöhlmann, *Abriss der Dogmatik*, 3rd rev. ed. (Düsseldorf: Patmos Verlag, 1966), p. 230.
36. *Ibid.*

CHAPTER EIGHT: *The Resurrection of Jesus*

1. William Paley, *A View of the Evidences of Christianity*, 2 vols., 5th ed. (London: R. Faulder, 1796; rep. ed.: Westmead, England: Gregg, 1970), 1: 327-8.
2. Hermann Samuel Reimarus, *Fragments*, trans. R.S. Fraser, ed. C.H. Talbert, Lives of Jesus Series (London: SCM, 1971), p. 104.
3. Johann Salomo Semler, *Beantwortung der Fragmente eines Ungennanten insbesondere vom Zweck Jesu und seiner Jünger*, 2d ed. (Halle: Verlag des Erziehungsinstitut, 1780), p. 266.
4. David Friedrich Strauss, "Herrmann Samuel Reimarus and His 'Apology,'" in *Fragments*, pp. 280-1.
5. David Friedrich Strauss, *The Life of Jesus Critically Examined*, trans. G. Eliot, ed. with an Intro. P.C. Hodgson, Lives of Jesus Series (London: SCM, 1973), p. 70.
6. *Ibid.*, p. 736.
7. E. Earle Ellis, ed., *The Gospel of Luke*, New Century Bible (London: Nelson, 1966), p. 273.
8. D. H. Van Daalen, *The Real Resurrection* (London: Collins, 1972), p. 41.
9. Jacob Kremer, *Die Osterevangelien—Geschichten um Geschichte* (Stuttgart: Katholisches Bibelwerk, 1977), pp. 49-50.
10. C. H. Dodd, "The Appearances of the Risen Christ: A study in the form criticism of the Gospels," in *More New Testament Studies* (Manchester: University of Manchester, 1968), p. 128.
11. Josephus, *Antiquities of the Jews* 20.200.
12. Hans Grass, *Ostergeschehen und Osterberichte*, 4th ed. (Göttingen: Vandenhoeck & Ruprecht, 1974), p. 80.
13. Norman Perrin, *The Resurrection According to Matthew, Mark, and Luke* (Philadelphia: Fortress, 1974), p. 80.
14. Julius Müller, *The Theory of Myths, in Its Application to the Gospel History Examined and Confuted* (London: John Chapman, 1844), p. 26.
15. A. N. Sherwin-White, *Roman Society and Roman Law in the New Testament* (Oxford: Clarendon, 1963), pp. 188-91.
16. R. H. Fuller, *The Formation of the Resurrection Narratives* (London: SPCK, 1972), p. 2.
17. Grass, *Ostergeschehen*, p. 133.
18. Gerhard Kittel, "Die Auferstehung Jesu," *Deutsche Theologie* 4 (1937): 159. Not until the time of Hadrian in the second century is there evidence of an Adonis cult at Bethlehem.
19. Joachim Jeremias, "Die älteste Schicht der Osteruberlieferung," in *Resurrexit*, ed. Edouard Dhanis (Rome: Editrice Libreria Vaticana, 1974), p. 194.
20. Ulrich Wilckens, *Auferstehung*, Themen der Theologie 4 (Stuttgart: Kreuz Verlag, 1970), p. 131.
21. C. F. D. Moule, *The Phenomenon of the New Testament*, Studies in Biblical Theology 2/1 (London: SCM, 1967), pp. 3, 13.
22. Craig A. Evans, "Life-of-Jesus Research and the Eclipse of Mythology," *Theological Studies* 54 (1993): 21-33.

23. John A. T. Robinson, *The Human Face of God* (London: SCM Press, 1973), p. 136.

24. Wolfhart Pannenberg, "Jesu Geschichte und unsere Geschichte," in *Glaube und Wirklichkeit* (München: Chr. Kaiser, 1975), pp. 92-4.

CONCLUSION: The Ultimate Apologetic

1. J. I. Packer, *Knowing God* (London: Hodder & Stoughton, 1973), p. 314.

INDEX

Abbadie, Jacques, 164
Abrahams, Israel, 240
Adams, Robert, 91
Alexander, Loveday, 216
al-Ghazali, 79-80
Ankersmit, F.R., 167
Analogy of being vs. analogy of faith, 24-26
Anselm, 36, 79, 159
Anthropic Principle, 91, 118-119
Anti-intellectualism, danger of, xii-xv
Anti-realism, 167-168, 171, 175-177
Apologetics, apostolic use of, 47-48
   cultural, 51
   defensive, xv-xvi
   defined, xi
   historical, 19, 161-169, 253, 265-271
   offensive, xv-xvi
   theoretical vs. practical, xi-xii, 299-302
Aristotle, 79-80, 84-85
Aron, Raymond, 187
Arrian, 207, 217
Artemon, 257
Astronomy and astrophysics, 100-116, 123
Athanasius, 258
Atheism, practical impossibility of, 64-72
Athenagoras, 163
Augustine, 17-21, 159, 196
Authoritarianism, 18-21, 26
Authority, medieval concept of, 18-20, 158
   of Scripture, 18, 19, 20, 21, 163
   of the church, 18, 19
   of the Holy Spirit, 24

Bahrdt, Karl, 234
Bailey, Kenneth, 210

Baird, J. A., 209
Barrow, John, 118
Barth, Karl, 24-26, 236, 295
Bauer, Bruno, 168
Basic beliefs, 28-31, 36
Baumgarten, S. J., 267
Bayle, Pierre, 164
Beard, Charles, 166
Becker, Carl, 166, 171, 181, 185
Beckett, Samuel, 60
Ben-Chorin, Schalom, 240
ben Dosa, Hanina, 241, 250
Berkeley, George, 79
Berlin, Isaiah, 185
Bernstein, Richard, 167
Biblical criticism, 196-218, 265-272
   Form criticism, 197-199, 209-211
   Genre criticism, 214-218
   Literary criticism, 199-200, 209, 213-214
   Redaction criticism, 198-199, 209, 211-213
Big Bang (see *Universe*)
Blake, Christopher, 185
Blomberg, Craig, x
Bloom, Harold, 228
Bode, E.L., 275
Bornkamm, Günther, 198
Bossuet, J. B., 164
Braun, Herbert, 128
Brout, Robert, 107
Bultmann, Rudolph, 24-26, 127, 197-198, 209-210, 236, 241, 271
Burden of proof, 221-222, 226, 237, 239-240
Burridge, Richard, 218

Caesar, Julius, 194
Cage, John, 56

Caius, 258
Calvin, John, 29, 197
Camus, Albert, 60, 65, 66
Caputo, John, 43
Causal principle, 80, 92-93
Celsus, 163, 258
Charlesworth, James, 200
Christological titles, 243-244
Christology, implicit, 244-251
Church, a sign of credibility, 19, 21, 160
Cicero, 220
Clarke, Samuel, 132-133, 138-139, 142, 146
Clement of Alexandria, 163, 206, 258, 262
Collingwood, R. G., 158, 176-177, 182-183
Conzelmann, Hans, 198
Copleston, Frederick, 178-179
Cosmological argument, 22, 79, 91-122, 163
Creatio ex nihilo, 93-94, 102
Crick, Francis, 63, 69-70
Criteria of authenticity, 221-226, 237-238, 240, 253, 293-294
Crossan, John Dominic, 201, 225, 238
Cyprian, 257
Cyril, 258

Davies, P.C.W., 101, 116
Deconstructionism, 43-44
Deductive reasoning, 38-39
Deism, 23, 128-140, 145, 154-155, 164, 255, 265-266
de la Chaise, Filleau, 164-165
Delitzsch, F., 201
Descartes, René, 79
Dialectical theology 24-27, 168-169, 236, 295
Dickens, Charles, 149
Diderot, Denis, 129
Dingle, Herbert, 110
Dio Cassius, 217
Dionysius, 257
Dissimilarity criterion (see *Criteria of authenticity*)
Ditton, Humphrey, 260, 263-265
Dodd, C. H., 198, 282
Dodwell, Henry, 23-24
Dostoyevsky, Fyodor, 54-55, 61, 66
Dray, W.H., 175
Dulles, Avery, ix

Dunn, James D. G., 250, 252

Eddington, Arthur, 102, 111
Einstein, Albert, 102
Eiseley, Loren, 57
Eliot, T.S., 62
Ellis, E.E., 274
Enlightenment, the, 22-24, 43, 57, 128, 197
Epictetus, 262
Erasmus, 161-162
Eusebius, 206, 257
Evans, Craig A., 293
Evidentialism, 26-28
Existentialism, 51, 60
Existential theology, 24-27, 168-169, 236
Explanation, models of, hypothetico-deductive, 39, 182, 203
  inference to best explanation, 39, 188, 189

Faith, 20-21, 24
Ferré, Frederick, 86
Feyerabend, Paul, 170
Fideism, 25-26, 29, 49, 78
Flew, Antony, 148, 152-153
Flusser, David, 240
Form criticism (see *Biblical criticism*)
Foundationalism, 22, 28
France, R.T., 188
Freud, Sigmund, 63
Fuller, R. H., 289

Gardiner, Patrick, 169, 171
Gerhardsson, Birger, 209, 240
God, and time, 94, 119
  arguments for, 79-122
  death of, 57, 63-64
  existence of, 20, 22, 28, 52, 54, 79-122, 133, 146-147
  necessary condition for meaningful life, 60-70
Gospels, apocryphal, 225, 228, 230, 258
  authenticity of, 214, 222-225, 240, 256-259ff.
  authorship of, 203-206, 226, 256-258
  date of, 203, 206-207, 226, 256
  reliability of, 165, 203, 207, 222, 226-227, 239, 259-264, 285
  textual purity of, 259
Grass, Hans, 283, 290
Green, Michael, 48

Gribbin, John, 103, 116
Grotius, Hugo, 161, 163
Goldstein, Leon, 167, 170, 174-175
Grünbaum, Adolf, 120-121
Guelich, Robert, 217, 247
Gundry, Robert, 244
Gunkel, Herman, 197

ha'Am, Ahad, 248
Harrison, R. K., 177
Hartshorne, Charles, 79
Hawking, Stephen, 108-113, 124
Hegel, G. W., 56, 237
Heidegger, Martin, 127, 237
Hemer, Colin, 202, 208
Hengel, Martin, 243
Hengstenberg, E., 201
Herodotus, 217, 285
Hermas, 262
Herrmann, Wilhelm, 235
Hesse, Hermann, 60
Hick, John, 242
Hilbert, David, 95, 97
Hippolitus, 257
Historical facts, nature of, 181-182
Historical method, 21, 160, 165
Historical relativism, 157, 166-191
Historicism, 166-168, 190
Hodge, A.A., 201
Hodge, C., 201
Holy Spirit, the, 31-38, 46-48, 299
  use of argumentation by, 46, 47
  witness of, 31-36
Honi the Circle Drawer, 241, 250
Houtteville, Claude François, 134-135,
  138, 142, 145, 148, 259, 263-264
Hoyle, Fred, 69, 102
Hubble, Edwin, 100
Huet, Daniel, 164
Hume, David, 86, 91, 93, 128, 130-132,
  134-139, 147, 149-154
Hutchinson, Robert, 247

ibn Rushd, 79
ibn Sina, 79
Ignatius, 257, 262
Imaginary time, 108, 110-113
Immortality, 59-60, 255
Inductive reasoning, 38-39, 45
Infinite, actual vs. potential, 95
  density, 101

impossibility of forming by successive
  addition, 98-100
number of things, 94-97
past, 82, 97-99
regress of simultaneous causes, 80-81
temporal regress, 80, 97-98, 100
Irenaeus, 163, 206, 257, 262
Isham, Christopher, 107, 109
Isidore, 158
Isocrates, 218

Jaki, S.L., 102
Jastrow, Robert, 119
Jeremias, Joachim, 244, 249, 290
Jesus, a mythological product, 235, 237,
  242, 269-270
  burial of, 272-273
  claim to divine authority, 246-250,
  252
  early Christian worship of, 243
  liberal portrait of, 234-239
  radical self-understanding of, 233-254
Jesus Seminar, xiv, 201, 225-226, 230,
  237-238, 242, 244, 247, 253
Josephus, 215, 217, 257, 262, 270
Julian, 163, 258
Justin Martyr, 257, 262
Juvenal, 262

Kähler, Martin, 168
Kalam (see *Cosmological argument*)
Kant, Immanuel, 90
Käsemann, Ernst, 237
Kee, Howard, 250
Keil, C.F., 201
Kierkegaard, Soren, 55-56
King, Ivan, 103
Klausner, Joseph, 240
Kremer, Jacob, 277
Kuhn, Thomas, 170, 177

Ladd, George, 157
Lake, Kirsopp, 279
Langer, W., 185
Lapide, Pinchas, 240
Laplace, Pierre Simon de, 128
La Shell, John, xiv
Latourelle, René, 224
Law of Contradiction, 41
Law of Excluded Middle, 41
Laws of nature, 128-154
Le Clerc, Jean, 132, 148

Leibniz, Gottfried, 79, 82-83
Lemcio, E. E., 213
Leslie, Charles, 165
Leslie, John, 91
Less, Gottfried, 135-140, 145, 151, 256-257, 259, 264
Lessing, Gottfried, 266
Lewis, Gordon, ix
Life of Jesus movement, 140, 168, 233-236
Linnemann, Eta, 202
literary criticism (see *Biblical criticism*)
Livy, 194
Loci communes, ix-x
Locke, John, 22-23, 79, 165
Logic, defense of classical, 41-44
Lord, A. B., 210
Lucian, 218
Luther, Martin, x, 36

Machen, J. Gresham, xiii, xv, 78, 202
Mack, Burton, 225
Mackie, J. L., 93, 97, 99-100
Maimonides, 79
Malcolm, Norman, 79
Malebranche, Nicolas, 164
Malik, Charles, xii, xv
Mandelbaum, Maurice, 184, 187
Marcus Aurelius, 262
Marshall, I. H., 228
Martial, 262
Marxsen, Willi, 198
McCullagh, C. Behan, 183, 188-189, 295
Melanchthon, Philip, x
Messiah, the, 235, 266, 288-289, 291
Meyer, Ben, 248-249
Miracle(s), 127-155, 163, 165, 250-251, 297
    apostolic use of, 47
    identification of, 128, 130-131, 136, 140, 148-149
    of the church, 19, 21
    possibility of, 128-131, 138, 140, 143, 146, 148, 151-153
    sign of credibility, 18, 21-23, 52, 54, 159-160
"Missing mass", 105-106
Monod, Jacques, 60
Montaigne, Michel de, 52
Moral argument, 88-90
Mornay, Philippe de, 161-163
Morrison, Phillip, 102

Moule, C. F. D., 243-244, 292
Müller, Julius, 284-285

Natural law, causal dispositions theory of, 143-144
    nomic necessity theory of, 143
    regularity theory of, 143
Natural theology, xv, 28
Nepos, 218
Nernst, Walter, 102
Newman, Cardinal John, 68
Newton, Isaac, 128-129, 140
Newtonian world machine, 128-129, 140
Nielsen, Kai, 61
Nietzsche, Friedrich, 63-64, 153
Noble Lie, 71-72
Novikov, I. D., 69

Ogden, Schubert, 128
O'Hair, Madeleine Murray, 78
Ontological argument, xv, 79, 90
Origen, 163, 196, 257-258
Orwell, George, 70, 186
Oscillating model (see *Universe*)
Osiander, Andreas, 197

Packer, J. I., 300
Paley, William, 85-88, 137-140, 146, 151
Pannenberg, Wolfhart, 26-28, 149, 153-154, 297
Papias, 204, 270
Parmenides, 44
Pascal, Blaise, 51-54, 72, 150, 164
Paradigm, (see *Weltanschauung analysis of science*)
past, infinite (see *Infinite past*)
    lack of direct access to, 169-181, 190
    lack of neutrality in investigating, 184-190
Peacocke, Arthur, 155
Pelikan, Jaroslav, 243
Penzias, A. A., 103
Perrin, Norman, 214-215, 225, 284
Pesch, Rudolf, 274-275
Philo, 218, 257
Philostratus, 218
Pirenne, Henri, 172
Plantinga, Alvin, 28-31, 44-45, 79, 90-91, 173
Plato, 78, 79, 84, 88
Pliny the Younger, 262
Plotinus, 41

Plutarch, 207, 218
Pöhlmann, Horst Georg, 252
Polycarp, 163, 257, 262
Popper, Karl, 172, 187
Porphyry, 258
Post-modernism, 43-44, 70, 167, 170, 173, 177, 179, 207
Principle of analogy, 153
Principle of Bivalence, 41, 42
Principle of Sufficient Reason, 83
Prophecy, apostolic use of, 47
    as sign of credibility, 18, 21-23, 52, 54, 159, 165
Quadratus, 257, 262
Quantum gravitation models, 108-113
Quantum physics, 106-113, 140-141
Quest for the historical Jesus, 168, 199-200, 236, 241
    new quest, 200-201, 237, 240
    third quest, 200-201, 225, 240-241

Ramsay, William M., 220
Rand, Ayn, 61
Ranke, Leopold von, 166-169
Rationalism, biblical, 265-266, 268
    philosophical, 22
    theological, 22, 28, 43, 49
    reason, magisterial vs. ministerial use of, 36-38
    Index:Redaction criticism (see *Biblical criticism*)
Reformation, the, 25, 161
Reimarus, Herrmann Samuel, 266-271
Renan, Ernst, 168
resurrection of Jesus, apostles neither deceivers nor deceived, 164, 260-264, 269, 278
    apparent death theory, 268, 279, 295
    appearances, 266-267, 280—288, 295, 297
    conspiracy theory, 260-261, 263-264, 266, 278, 295-296
    empty tomb, 272-280, 293, 295, 297
    hallucination theory, 287-288, 296
    mythological explanation of, 269-271
    origin of disciples' belief in, 288-293
    OT concept of, 290-292
    physicality of, 281, 285, 287
    spiritual body, 286
    Semler's treatment of, 267-268
    translation vs., 292-293
    wrong tomb theory, 279-280

Revelation, 23, 24, 165
Riesenfeld, Harald, 209
Riesner, Rainer, 209, 240
Ritschl, Albrecht, 168, 235
Robinson, James, 237-239, 295
Rorty, Richard, 173
Rousseau, Jean Jacques, 271
Rubinoff, Lionel, 174
Russell, Bertrand, 64, 66, 67, 99
Rue, L.D., 71

Sagan, Carl, 69, 103
Sallust, 217, 220
Sandage, Allan, 101, 105-106
Sanders, E. P., 200, 240
Sandmel, Samuel, 240
Sartre, Jean-Paul, 58, 60-61, 65, 67-68
Satyrus, 218
Schaeffer, Francis, xi, 51, 56-57, 65
Scheffler, Israel, 177
Schlatter, Adolf, 201
Schleiermacher, F. D. E., 268, 279
Schlesinger, George, 112
Schweitzer, Albert, 140, 236, 241
Scotus, Duns, 79
Semler, Johann Salomo, 267-269
Sherlock, Thomas, 134-135, 139, 142, 148, 151, 260
Sherwin-White, A. N., 212, 239, 285
Silk, Joseph, 105, 116
Signs of credibility (see also *Church, Miracle, Prophecy*), 18, 19, 21, 77, 159, 162, 165—166
Skinner, B. F. 63, 70
Smith, Quentin, 92, 113
Son of Man, 221, 243-244, 251, 289
Sorley, William, 88-90
Spindel, Ph., 107
Spinoza, Benedict de, 79, 129-130, 132, 134, 138-140, 145-150, 154
Stanton, Graham, 195
Stauffer, E., 219
Steady state model (see *Universe*)
Stephen, Leslie, 85
Stewart, John, 93
Strauss, David F., 140, 168, 234-236, 241, 268-271
Strauss, Gerhard, 18
Suetonius, 218, 262
Suppe, Frederick, 179-180

Tacitus, 194, 217-218, 262

Tammann, G. A., 101, 106
Tatian, 196, 258
Taylor, Vincent, 198
Teleological argument, 83-88, 91
Tennant, F. R., 91
Tertullian, 163, 257
Theophilus, 257
Thermodynamics, second law of, 113-116
Thomas Aquinas, 17, 20-22, 79, 80-82, 85, 88, 159-160
Thompson, J. Westfall, 161
Tillich, Paul, 57
Tinsley, Beatrice, 103, 114
Tipler, Frank, 118
Trilling, Wolfgang, 250
Troeltsch, Ernst, 153
Truths of reason vs. truths of faith, 20, 21, 159-160, 166
Turrettin, J. Alphonse, 133
Two-story universe (see *Universe*)

Universe, beginning of, 80, 92, 94-122
    Big Bang model of, 100, 179
    contraction of, 103-104, 114-115
    density of, 104-106
    expanding, 100-101, 104-106, 114
    heat death of, 114-116
    oscillating model of, 103-106, 115-116
    open vs. closed, 104
    personal creator of, 108-109, 116-122, 299
    quantum models of, 106-113
    steady state model of, 103-104, 179
    two-story, 65

Vacuum fluctuation, 106-107
Valla, Lorenzo, 160
Van Daalen, D.H., 277
Van der Dussen, W. J., 177

van Til, Cornelius, 202
Velikovsky, Immanuel, 186-187
Venturini, Karl, 234
Vermes, Geza, 240
Vernet, Jacob, 133-134, 139, 148, 256-257, 263
Vives, Juan Luis, 161-163
Voltaire, François, 129

Wager, Pascal's, 54
Wagner, Richard, 67
Wainwright, William J., 97
Walsh, W. H., 186
Warfield, B. B., 202
Watch-maker argument (see *Teleological argument*)
Wellhausen, Julius, 197
Wells, H. G., 62
Weltanschauung analysis of science, 170-171, 177, 179-180
Wesley, Charles, 24
Wesley, John, 24
Westcott, B. F., 205
White, Morton, 184, 186
Whitefield, George, 24
Wilson, R. D., 202
Wilson, R. W., 103
Witherington, Ben, 247-248, 251
Wittgenstein, Ludwig, 167
Woolston, Thomas, 134
Word of God, 18, 25-26, 267-268
Wrede, Wilhelm, 235-236
Wurmbrand, Richard, 67

Xenophon, 218

Yamauchi, Edwin, 187

Zeldovich, Ya.B., 69

A World Religions Reader

B

To my Father